ABOUT PHILOSOPHY

ABOUT PHILOSOPHY

FOURTH EDITION

Robert Paul Wolff
University of Massachusetts

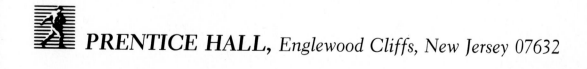
PRENTICE HALL, *Englewood Cliffs, New Jersey 07632*

LIBRARY OF CONGRESS
Library of Congress Cataloging-in-Publication Data

Wolff, Robert Paul.
    About philosophy / Robert Paul Wolff. -- 4th ed.
        p.   cm.
    Includes bibliographies and index.
    ISBN 0-13-000431-6
    1. Philosophy--Introductions.   I. Title.
BD21.W64 1989
    100--dc19   88-15681
                                                         CIP

Editorial/production supervision: *Edith Riker*
Interior design: *Berta Lewis/Peggy Kenselaar*
Cover design: *Peggy Kenselaar*
Cover photo: *Character House/Photo Researchers*
Manufacturing buyer: *Peter Havens*
Photo editor: *Page Poore*
Photo research: *Terri Stratford*

 © 1989, 1986, 1981, 1976 by Prentice-Hall, Inc.
A Division of Simon & Schuster
Englewood Cliffs, New Jersey 07632

Printed in the United States of America
10 9 8 7 6 5 4 3

ISBN   0-13-000431-6

Prentice-Hall International (UK) Limited, *London*
Prentice-Hall of Australia Pty. Limited, *Sydney*
Prentice-Hall Canada Inc., *Toronto*
Prentice-Hall Hispanoamericana, S.A., *Mexico*
Prentice-Hall of India Private Limited, *New Delhi*
Prentice-Hall of Japan, Inc., *Tokyo*
Simon & Schuster Asia Pte. Ltd., *Singapore*
Editora Prentice-Hall do Brasil, Ltda., *Rio de Janeiro*

CONTENTS

PREFACE

This book is the outgrowth of three decades of teaching. I faced my first philosophy class in the fall of 1955, when I was a graduate student not much older than my students. Because I was young, it was easier then for me to put myself in their place and try to see philosophy through their eyes, as an entirely new experience. As the years have passed, I have grown older, but my students remain the same age. So the gap between us widens, and I must work harder each year to recapture their perspective. Long familiarity with the problems and methods of philosophy has led me to take them too much for granted. Again and again, I must remind myself that philosophy is a special way of looking at life, a way that is *natural*, but not therefore obvious. And should I forget this fact, my students will very quickly remind me!

In this introduction to philosophical problems, theories, and personalities, I have tried always to keep the student's point of view central. I imagine my reader to be intelligent, naturally curious, but skeptical. He or she is willing to listen to new ideas, but not to accept them merely on the authority of an author or teacher. My job is to present philosophy as an activity that sensible, intelligent people would *want* to engage in. It is not enough for me to explain in a clear, uncluttered way what the great philosophers said. I must also help my reader to understand *why* they said it, why they felt compelled to think about their moral, scientific, religious, or logical problems as they did.

In writing this book, I have had the help of a great many men and women, and it is a pleasure to have the opportunity to acknowledge my debt to them. My first thanks must go to the several thousand students who have listened to me, argued with me, learned from me, and taught me over the past twenty years. Some of them have become teachers of philosophy themselves; others are craftsmen, lawyers, clerks, doctors, politicians, policemen, and I know not what else. But all have helped me to become a better teacher. I hope their voices echo in these pages.

Several of my colleagues at the University of Massachusetts answered my questions and corrected some of my misconceptions in one or another of the branches of philosophy touched on in this book. First among them is Professor Robert J. Ackermann, an extraordinarily gifted and widely learned man whom I am fortunate to count as my friend. Professor Mary Sirridge guided me through some of the complexities of the philosophy of art, a field in which she is an expert and I am a novice.

The single most important source of assistance was Dr. Karen Warren, who devoted several months to invaluable research and background work on every chapter of the book. To say that Dr. Warren was my "research assistant" entirely fails to do justice to the nature and magnitude of her contribution. Dr. Warren was, by the common agreement of my colleagues, far and away the most successful teacher among all the graduate students who have come through the Philosophy Department of the University of Massachusetts. Her research for me included beautifully clear analyses of key issues in each field of philosophy, as well as the more conventional mustering of sources and biographical details. Her own teaching skill enabled her to lay out the material for me so that I in turn could present it in what I hope is a coherent and comprehensible manner. I quite literally could not have written this book without her aid.

This is now the fourth edition of the original book, and the text has gone through a number of transformations and revisions over the years. Here again, I have benefitted from the flow of comments, reactions, criticisms, and suggestions from teachers who have used earlier editions. The present edition, for example, introduces a number of teaching aids that users of the book expressed a desire for, as well as a number of new readings at the ends of chapters.

The central message of the book remains unaltered, however: Philosophy is an *activity* whose guiding principle is reason and whose goal is a critical self-understanding. If this book can prod, guide, assist, or provoke you into entering into that activity of self-examination, then I will be happy indeed.

Robert Paul Wolff
Pelham, Massachusetts

Acknowledgments

Reviewers of the fourth edition manuscript are as follows. I appreciate their thoughtful comments.

J.R. Frisch, Morton College
R.O. Long, Wittenberg University
D.T. Hohlt, Blinn College
D. Smith, Lakeland Community College
M. Vengrin, Radford University

T. Franks, Eastern Michigan University
Z. Edelson, Community College of
  Allegheny County
A.E. Keaton, New Mexico State University
T. Messenger, University of North Dakota

Alexis De Tocqueville, *The Old Regime and the French Revolution*, trans. by S. Gilbert. © 1955 Doubleday & Co. Reprinted by permission of Doubleday & Co.

Erik H. Erikson, *Childhood and Society*, 2nd ed. By permission of W.W. Norton & Co., Inc. Copyright 1950, © 1963 by W.W. Norton & Co., Inc.

Sigmund Freud, *The Future of an Illusion*, trans. by James Strachey. Reprinted with permission of W.W. Norton & Co., Inc. Copyright © 1961 by James Strachey.

Paul Goodman, selections from "Pornography, Art, and Censorship," from *Commentary* (March 1961). Copyright © 1961 by Paul Goodman. Reprinted from *Utopian Essays and Practical Proposals*, by Paul Goodman, by permission of Random House, Inc.

Douglas R. Hofstadter, *Metamagical Themas: Questing for the Essence of Mind and Pattern*. © 1985 by Basic Books, Inc., Publishers. Reprinted by permission of the publisher.

Immanuel Kant, *Groundwork of the Metaphysic of Morals*, trans. by H.J. Paton (New York: Harper & Row, 1964). Reprinted by permission of the publisher.

Immanuel Kant, *Immanuel Kant's Critique of Pure Reason*, trans. by Norman Kemp Smith. Reprinted by permission of St. Martin's Press, Inc., and Macmillan, London and Basingstoke.

Søren Kierkegaard, excerpts from *Concluding Unscientific Postscript*, trans. by David F. Swenson and Walter Lowrie. Copyright 1941 © 1969 by Princeton University Press. Reprinted by permission of Princeton University Press and the American Scandinavian Foundation.

Herbert Marcuse, *One-dimensional Man*. Copyright © 1964 by Herbert Marcuse. Reprinted by permission of Beacon Press.

Photo Credits

ABOUT
PHILOSOPHY

1

WHAT IS PHILOSOPHY?

SOCRATES (469?–399 B.C). was tried by the Athenians on charges of "impiety" and "corrupting the young of Athens," but it seems clear that his real offense was opposition to, or even lack of sufficient support for, the leaders of the newly restored democratic regime.

Socrates had associated with the aristocratic families which overthrew the first democracy, and his disciple, Plato, was a member of one of the powerful families that ruled Athens for a while before the restoration. Since an amnesty had been declared, it was legally impossible for the rulers to prosecute Socrates for political offenses, so they trumped up the religious accusations and enlisted a religious fanatic, Meletus, to bring charges against the seventy-year-old philosopher.

Socrates could have fled from Athens before the trial, conviction in which could carry a death sentence. Even after his conviction, he could have proposed banishment as an alternative to death, and the Athenian jury of 501 citizens would almost certainly have accepted such a compromise. But Socrates was convinced that he had done Athens no harm by his philosophical questioning. Indeed, he insisted that he had, by his activities, been a benefactor of his native city, and so, as an alternative to the death penalty demanded by the prosecution, he proposed that Athens pension him off as a respected citizen.

The Athenian rulers, trapped by Socrates' uncompromising integrity, were forced to carry out the sentence of death, though they would probably have been all too happy to allow their prisoner to escape before the execution. One month after the trial, following a long night of philosophical discussion with his friends, Socrates drank the poison hemlock prepared for him by his jailers and died.

I *What Do Philosophers Do? The Study of Human Nature*

When I was a student, one of my professors told us about the conversations he would strike up in the club car on the train from Boston to New York. A group of men would gather around the bar, and each in turn would introduce himself, saying a few words about the line of work he was in. One would announce himself as a lawyer, a second as a traveler in ladies' apparel, a third as an engineer. When it was my professor's turn, he would say, "I am a philosopher." That, he told us, would always bring the conversation to a dead halt. No one knew quite what to say to a man who described himself as a philosopher. The others were too polite to ask, "What does a philosopher do?" But the announcement always cast a pall over the gathering. Eventually, he took to saying, "I am a teacher." That went over all right, and so long as no one asked what he taught, they could get on to more congenial topics, such as the prospects for the Red Sox, or the weather.

What *do* philosophers do? Oddly enough, that is a question philosophers have been asking for as long as there has been a discipline called philosophy. Indeed, "What do philosophers do?" is probably the most common philosophical question! But all this sounds like double talk, which is just what makes people nervous about philosophy in the first

3

place. You all know what a doctor does; you know what physicists, historians, composers, and sanitation engineers do. Most of you probably even have some sort of idea of what microbiologists do. But philosophers are something else again. Philosophers ask questions—odd questions, like "Could my whole life be a dream?" and dangerous questions, like "What right does the government—any government—have to tell me what to do?"

The best way to find out what philosophers do is to take a look at one of them, and on anybody's list, the natural first choice must be the most famous philosopher of all times, *Socrates*. Socrates was born in 469 B.C. to a stonemason and a midwife in the Greek city-state of Athens. As far as we know, he spent his entire life in and about Athens, serving his time in the army at one point, taking his turn in the government at another. He was a rather homely man in a society that prized manly beauty, and though he was hardly poor, he seems to have managed on much less money than his friends and disciples had. Athens itself was a city of 130,000, busy and prosperous by the standards of the time but small enough so that everyone who was anyone knew everyone else. In his youth, Socrates studied the scientific theories a number of original thinkers had developed in the preceding several centuries, but he soon became convinced that the most important and puzzling subject was the human condition itself. He developed the practice of going into the public squares and meeting places of Athens to cajole, goad, or draw his fellow townsmen into discussions about how men ought to live their lives. (In the Athens of Socrates' day, it was taken for granted that women would play no role in these discussions, or indeed in any other public business.) Socrates was quick-witted, clever, and tenacious. He had a knack for asking hard or embarrassing questions that forced others to think a good deal more than they really wanted to. Because some of the people he quizzed were important politicians and famous teachers, it was fun to watch him trip them up—as long as you weren't one of those made to look foolish. So a number of wealthy young men gathered around Socrates as a band of disciples and as a sort of permanent audience. Sometimes he talked with them, quizzing them in the same way and forcing them to examine their own lives; sometimes they watched as he took on a local bigwig or visiting personage.

If this practice of asking questions were all there was to Socrates' life, we would have never have heard of him 2400 years later, and we certainly wouldn't think of him as the first and greatest of all philosophers. But three things transformed Socrates from a local curiosity and general pain in the neck into the patron saint of philosophy and one of the great figures of Western civilization.

The first thing was an accident. Among those who followed Socrates was a brilliantly gifted, wealthy young man named Plato. Plato was only twenty-eight when his teacher died, but he was deeply, permanently affected by his relationship with the aging Socrates, and many years later he began to write his Dialogues, playlets in which the style and personality of Socrates were captured, transformed, and elevated into works of great art. Most of what we believe about Socrates comes to us from these Dialogues, including most importantly our conception of Socrates' techniques of questioning. Scholars still debate how much in the Dialogues is Plato's artistic invention and how much is accurate historical portrayal. But there can be no question that the essential style belonged to Socrates himself.

The second thing that happened was not really an accident, though it may seem so at first glance. The rulers of Athens decided that Socrates was more than an annoyance; he was becoming a threat to their political security. So they trumped up some charges against him and put him on trial. Socrates could have plea-bargained, in effect, and gotten off with a

Ruins of the Acropolis in Athens, dating from the fifth century before Christ. (D.A. Harissiadis, Athens)

> **Philosophy**   Literally, love of wisdom. Philosophy is the systematic,
> critical examination of the way in which we judge, evaluate, and act,
> with the aim of making ourselves wiser, more self-reflective, and
> therefore better men and women.

punishment of exile, which would have put him safely out of Athens
without making him a martyr. But he chose instead to defend himself
and his life without excuses or apologies. He had done nothing wrong,
he insisted, and now that he was seventy, Athens should be thinking of
giving him a pension rather than threatening to put him to death. In the
end, Socrates forced the government's hand, and a sentence of death
was handed down. Even then, he probably could have escaped from jail
with the help of his friends, but he stayed and took the poison his jailers
gave him. And so he became the first martyr to philosophy. It is easy to
second-guess the Athenian rulers and conclude that they could have
spared themselves a lot of trouble by handling the case a bit more skillfully. But Socrates' persistent questioning of established doctrines and
received opinions really was a threat, not only to the government but also
to the lifestyle of the families who ruled Athens. In a way, the accident is
not that Socrates was put to death at the age of seventy, but rather that
he had been permitted to go on for so long before those in power landed
on him.

The third and most important reason for Socrates' immortality is no
accident at all, but the very essence of his life and calling. Witty though
he was, irreverent though he could be, annoying though he certainly
became, Socrates was deadly serious about his questioning. His death
only confirmed what his life had already proved—that for him, the relentless examination of every human action and belief was more important
than survival itself. As Socrates said at his trial, "The unexamined life is
not worth living," and by drinking the poison, he showed that he would
rather die honorably in the cause of that principle than flee in dishonor
to some foreign refuge.

Each of us makes countless decisions which affect our lives and the
lives of those around us to some degree. Many of the decisions are of
very little importance, such as whether or not to go to the movies, where
to have dinner, or what to wear. A few of the decisions are truly momen-
tous—whom to marry, what career to pursue; and for some of us, caught
up in a war or facing a personal tragedy, our decisions may literally deter-

mine life and death. Socrates believed in his own time (and I think he would still believe if he were alive today) that these decisions must be questioned, examined, and criticized if we are to live truly good and happy lives. Most of us make even the most important decisions without really asking ourselves what principles we are basing our choices on, and whether those principles are worthy of our respect and commitment. When war comes, young men go off to fight and die with hardly more than a passing thought about whether it is morally right to kill another person. A student spends ten years of his or her life working to become a doctor, simply because Mom and Dad always wanted it. A man and a woman drift into marriage, have children, buy a house and settle down, and only twenty years later does one of them ask, "What am I doing here?"

Socrates had a theory about how each of us ought to examine his or her life, subjecting it to critical analysis and questioning. He never set this theory down anywhere, of course (he never set *anything* down, actually), but from what Plato has reported, we can reconstruct what Socrates had in mind. This theory, on which he based the special style of teaching and philosophizing that has come to bear his name, rested on four basic principles:

1. The unexamined life is not worth living. In other words, it is undignified, not really honorable, simply to live from day to day without ever asking oneself, What am I doing here? Why am I living as I am? To be truly and completely human, Socrates thought, each man and woman must subject his or her life and convictions to the test of critical self-examination. What is more, by means of this process of self-examination, one can achieve genuine happiness.

2. There really are valid principles of thought and action which must be followed if we are to live good lives—if we are to be, at the same time, genuinely happy and genuinely good. These principles are objective—they are true for all men and women, whenever and wherever they may live. Some people are unjust, self-indulgent, obsessed with worthless goals, estranged from their fellow men and women, confused and blind about what is truly important. These people do not know that certain things are beneath notice, unimportant. They are terrified of shadows, incapable of living or of dying with grace. Such people need to find the truth and live in accordance with it.

3. The truth lies within each of us, not in the stars, or in tradition, or in religious books, or in the opinions of the masses. Each of us has

within, however hidden, the true principles of right thinking and acting. In the end, therefore, no one can teach anyone else the truth about life. If that truth isn't within you, you will never find it; if it is within you, then only relentless critical self-examination will reveal it.

4. But though no one can teach anyone else about the fundamental principles of right action and clear thinking, some people—call them teachers, philosophers, gadflies—can ask questions that prod men and women to begin the task of self-examination. These teachers may also be able to guide the process, at least in its early stages, because they have been over the same ground themselves and know where the pitfalls are.

From these four principles, it follows that philosophy consists of a process of question and answer, and **dialogue** between two people, one of whom is seeking rational insight and understanding, the other of whom has already achieved some measure of self-knowledge and wishes to help the novice. The dialogue begins with whatever beliefs the student brings to the quest. If she thoughtlessly repeats the traditional moral sayings of her society, then the philosopher will try to force her to question those sayings; if she takes up the position that everything is relative, that nothing is true or valid for all persons (a stance many students adopt at about the time they leave home or cut loose from their parents), then the philosopher will try a different line of questioning. The end point of the journey is always the same: wisdom, rational insight into the principles of thought and action, and thus a happier, more integrated, more worthwhile life. But the starting points are as many as the students who make the journey.

Socrates discovered that each journey to wisdom has an enormous obstacle blocking the road. Modern psychoanalysts call the roadblock "resistance," but a simpler way of putting it is that no one wants to admit that he or she needs to learn. Certainly the politicians and public figures with whom Socrates talked didn't think of themselves as in need of further wisdom. They were quite convinced they already knew how to run the state and how to order their own lives. Socrates had to discover a trick for getting inside their defenses so that he could make them see— really see—that they were not yet truly wise. What he did was to invent a verbal form of judo. The basic trick of judo is to let your opponent's force and momentum work for you. Instead of launching a frontal attack, you let him swing or grab, and then you roll with his motion so that, in

In judo, as in Socratic argument, the trick is to use your opponent's momentum against him or her. (Bonnie Freer/Photo Researchers)

effect, he throws himself on the mat. Socrates achieved the same effect in his debates by means of a literary device called "irony." Although this is a book about philosophy, not literature, it might be worth taking a few moments to explain how irony works, so that we can see what Socrates was trying to accomplish.

Irony is a kind of speech or communication that assumes a *double audience*. When a speaker makes an ironic statement, she seems to be directing it at one group of people. This group is called the first, or superficial, audience. But in reality, she is directing her remarks at a second audience, called the real audience. Her statement has a double meaning, and the trick of the irony is that while the first audience understands only the superficial or apparent meaning, the second audience understands *both* meanings. This second audience knows that the first audience has misunderstood, so the irony becomes a private joke between the speaker and the second audience—a joke at the expense of the first audience, which never suspects a thing.

For example, suppose a stranger drives up to the general store in a small town to ask directions. "You there!" he says to a farmer seated on

The farmer is speaking ironically.

the front porch of the store. "Can you tell me the fastest way to get to the state capital? Be quick about it! I have a very important meeting with the governor." "Yes," replies the farmer, with just the slightest wink to his friends on the porch. "I *can* tell you the fastest way." He then proceeds to give the stranger totally wrong directions that will take him hours out of his way.

The farmer is speaking ironically. The stranger is the superficial audience, and the other people on the porch are the real audience. The apparent meaning, as understood by the stranger, is that this country bumpkin, who has been properly impressed with the stranger's importance, can tell him the fastest way and has done so. The real, secret, ironic meaning is of course that the farmer can tell this pompous ass the fastest way, but has no intention of doing so because he has been so rude. The reply is a private joke between the farmer and his friends at the stranger's expense.

When Socrates strikes up a conversation with a self-important, self-confident, but really rather ignorant man, he does not try a frontal attack, arguing directly against his opponent's false beliefs. That would simply lead to an impasse, in which each participant would be asserting his own convictions and neither would engage in critical self-examination. Instead, Socrates says, with a deceptively modest air, "Of course, I don't know anything at all, and you seem to be very wise indeed, so perhaps you would be so good as to enlighten me." His opponent, thinking Socrates means literally what he says, gets all puffed up with his own importance and pontificates on goodness or justice or truth or beauty or piety. Then Socrates goes to work on him, pretending to be puzzled, asking politely for clarification, poking away at just those places in his opponent's position that are most vulnerable. After a while, the poor man is thoroughly deflated. Embarrassed by his inability to give coherent, defensible answers to Socrates' apparently humble questions, he finally reaches the rather painful conclusion that he doesn't know what he thought he knew. Now, and only now, can Socrates help him to set out on the path to wisdom, for as Socrates so often insists, the first act of true wisdom is to admit that you are ignorant.

When Socrates says that he himself is ignorant, he is speaking ironically. In fact, he is uttering what students of literature call a "double irony." In the first place, he is having a private joke with his followers, at the expense of the man with whom he is debating. His opponent thinks Socrates is really being deferential, that Socrates actually wants to sit at the great man's feet and learn great truths. But of course Socrates means that he is "ignorant" of those great "truths" just because they are false, confused, and not worth knowing. We have all met someone who thinks he is an expert on some subject when in fact he doesn't know beans

Dialectical Method   A technique of probing questions, developed by Socrates, for the purpose of prodding, pushing, and provoking unreflective persons into realizing their lack of rational understanding of their own principles of thought and action, so that they can set out on the path to philosophical wisdom. As used by Socrates, the dialectical method was a powerful weapon for deflating inflated egos.

about it. "Tell me more!" we say, and sure enough he does, not realizing that we are kidding him.

At a deeper level, which Socrates' own followers sometimes don't really understand, Socrates genuinely means that he is ignorant, in the sense that *he* doesn't have a truth to teach any more than his puffed-up opponent does. The disciples think that Socrates knows what truth, beauty, justice, goodness, and wisdom really are, and they expect that just as soon as he has deflated his opponent, he will teach them. But Socrates believes that every man must find the truth for himself, and so his followers cannot shortcut their journey by learning the truth from Socrates any more than they could by observing the mistakes and confusions of Socrates' opponents. In this deeper double irony, we, the readers of Plato's dialogue, are the real audience, and both Socrates' opponent *and* his disciples are superficial or apparent audiences.

The process of questions and answers, by which we gradually, step by step, reach a deeper and deeper insight into the principles of truth and goodness, is called the **dialectical method**. It is a very powerful technique of argument, of course, and Socrates clearly used it because it gave him an edge on those with whom he argued. But it also serves an independent theoretical purpose—a philosophical purpose, we might say. This next point is a bit tricky, but it is worth paying attention to, because it gives us a real insight into what Plato (or Socrates) is doing.

According to Socrates, things are not always what they seem. We all know that there may be a difference between the way things look on the surface, or at first, and how they really are. A stick half in water and half out looks bent, even though it is straight. The sun looks larger when it is low in the horizon than when it is high in the sky, although it hasn't changed its shape. The magician looks as though she is pulling that coin out of your ear, but really it is coming out of her hand, and so forth.

Socrates took this old, familiar distinction between the way things seem to be and the way they really are and ran with it. He extended the distinction into areas where we might not be so used to encountering it. He pointed out that sometimes an experience *seems* bad for us, but is really good (the dentist is a familiar example). Frequently, the opinions of our friends, our family, or our society *seem* correct, but are really wrong. And so forth.

Socrates thought that in every part of our lives, we must try as hard as we can to get behind the misleading surface appearances and grasp the true, underlying reality. Indeed, a large part of Socrates' wisdom consisted precisely in being able to tell appearance from reality, whether in politics, in ethics, or in daily life.

Now, the superficial meaning of an ironic statement is like the surface appearance, behind which the reality lies. Just as the world of the senses is merely an appearance of the true reality grasped, Socrates thought, by reason, so too the superficial meaning of an ironic statement is the apparent meaning that hides the deeper, real meaning intended for the real audience. Thus, the structure of language mirrors the structure of reality.

This idea—that there is a parallel between language and the world—comes up again and again in philosophy. It is a very important notion, and for two thousand years, philosophers have been turning it this way and that, extracting interesting conclusions from it. Socrates is the philosopher who first developed the idea and used it in his own philosophy.

We have talked enough about Socrates and his debating tricks. It is time to see him in action. The following passage comes from the most famous of Plato's Dialogues, the *Republic.* Socrates and some friends have been having a discussion about the nature of *justice,* by which they mean the fundamental principles of right and wrong. Several suggestions have been made, which Socrates has disposed of without much trouble, and now a young, very excitable, and very bright member of the party named Thrasymachus jumps into the debate. He has been listening to the others impatiently, barely able to control himself.

> What is the matter with you two, Socrates? Why do you go on in this imbecile way, politely deferring to each other's nonsense? If you really want to know what justice means, stop asking questions and scoring off the answers you get. You know very well it is easier to ask questions than to answer them. Answer yourself, and tell us what you think justice means. I won't have you telling us it is the same as what is obligatory or useful or advantageous or profitable or expedient; I want a clear and precise statement; I won't put up with that sort of verbiage.

This is a shrewd attack on Thrasymachus' part, for if he can get Socrates to advance a definition, then perhaps he can turn the tables on the master. But his own uncontrolled impetuosity gets the better of him. When Socrates turns aside the attack with a few mock-humble words, Thrasymachus cannot resist the temptation to teach the teacher. And that, as we shall see, is his downfall. Thrasymachus is no pushover for

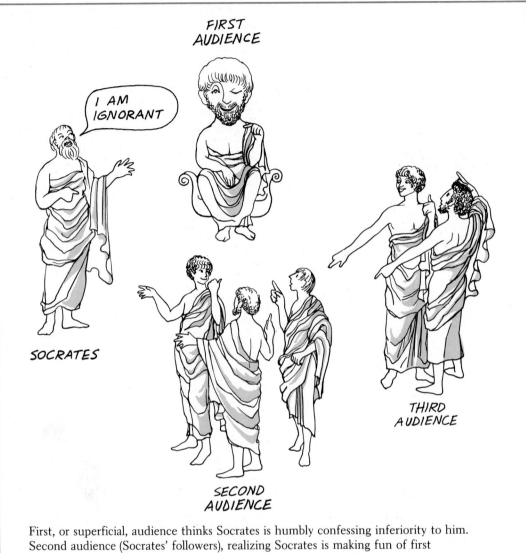

First, or superficial, audience thinks Socrates is humbly confessing inferiority to him. Second audience (Socrates' followers), realizing Socrates is making fun of first audience, laughs at first audience. Third audience (the reader) laughs at first audience, smiles at second. Third audience realizes *both* that Socrates is making fun of first audience *and* that Socrates' own followers don't realize the true meaning of his statement.

Socrates, and in a sense their debate ends in a deadlock. In this passage, however, we can see how Socrates uses Thrasymachus' own self-confidence to trip him up, just like a judo master who allows his opponent to rush at him headlong, and then with a flip of the hip tosses him on his back. Notice the ironic modesty with which Socrates turns aside Thrasymachus' blunt attacks, each time gently showing him that he has not yet thought clearly or deeply enough. The contrast between Socrates' inner quiet and Thrasymachus's tempestuousness is also intended by Plato to teach us a lesson, for he, like Socrates, believed that the truly wise possess a tranquility which the ignorant cannot achieve.

Listen then, Thrasymachus began. What I say is that "just" or "right" means nothing but what is to the interest of the stronger party. Well, where is your applause? You don't mean to give it me.

I will, as soon as I understand, I said. [This is Socrates talking] I don't see yet what you mean by right being the interest of the stronger party. For instance, Polydamas, the athlete, is stronger than we are, and it is to his interest to eat beef for the sake of his muscles; but surely you don't mean that the same diet would be good for weaker men and therefore be right for us?

You are trying to be funny, Socrates. It's a low trick to take my words in the sense you think will be most damaging.

No, no, I protested; but you must explain.

Don't you know, then, that a state may be ruled by a despot, or a democracy, or an aristocracy?

Of course.

And that the ruling element is always the strongest?

Yes.

Well then, in every case the laws are made by the ruling party in its own interest; a democracy makes democratic laws, a despot autocratic ones, and so on. By making these laws they define as "right" for their subjects whatever is for their own interest, and they call anyone who breaks them a "wrongdoer" and punish him accordingly. That is what I mean: in all states alike "right" has the same meaning, namely what is for the interest of the party established in power, and that is the strongest. So the sound conclusion is that what is "right" is the same everywhere: the interest of the stronger party.

Now I see what you mean, said I; whether it is true or not, I must try to make out. When you define right in terms of interest, you are yourself giving one of those answers you forbade to me; though, to be sure, you add "to the stronger party."

An insignificant addition, perhaps!

Its importance is not clear yet; what is clear is that we must find out whether your definition is true. I agree myself that right is in a sense a matter of interest; but when you add "to the stronger party," I don't know about that. I must consider.

Go ahead, then.

I will. Tell me this. No doubt you also think it is right to obey the men in power?

I do.

Are they infallible in every type of state, or can they sometimes make a mistake?

Of course they can make a mistake.

In framing laws, then, they may do their work well or badly?

No doubt.

Well, that is to say, when the laws they make are to their own interest; badly, when they are not?

Yes.

But the subjects are to obey any law they lay down, and they will then be doing right?

Of course.

If so, by your account, it will be right to do what is not to the interest of the stronger party, as well as what is so.

What's that you are saying?

Just what you said, I believe; but let us look again. Haven't you admitted that the rulers, when they enjoin certain acts on their subjects, sometimes mistake their own best interest, and at the same time that it is right for the subjects to obey, whatever they may enjoin?

Yes, I suppose so.

Well, that amounts to admitting that it is right to do what is not to the interest of the rulers or the stronger party. They may unwittingly enjoin what is to their own disadvantage; and you say it is right for the others to do as they are told. In that case, their duty must be the opposite of what you said, because the weaker will have been ordered to do what is against the interest of the stronger. You with your intelligence must see how that follows. . . .

Now, Thrasymachus, tell me, was that what you intended to say—that right means what the stronger thinks is to his interest, whether it really is so or not?

Most certainly not, he replied. Do you suppose I should speak of a man as "stronger" or "superior" at the very moment when he is making a mistake?

I did think you said as much when you admitted that rulers are not always infallible.

That is because you are a quibbler, Socrates. Would you say a man deserves to be called a physician at the moment when he makes a mistake in treating his patient and just in respect of that mistake; or a mathematician, when he does a sum wrong and just in so far as he gets a wrong result? Of course we do commonly speak of a physician or a mathematician or a scholar having made a mistake; but really none of these, I should say, is ever mistaken, in so far as he is worthy of the name we give him. So strictly speaking—and you are all for being precise—no one who practises a craft makes mistakes. A man is mistaken when his knowledge fails him; and at the moment he is no craftsman. And what is true of craftsmanship or any sort of skill is true of the ruler: he is never mistaken so long as he is acting as a ruler; though anyone might speak of a ruler making a mistake, just as he might of a physician. You must understand that I was talking in that loose way when I answered your question just now; but the precise statement is this. The ruler, in so far as he is acting as a ruler, makes no mistakes and consequently enjoins what is best for himself; and that is what the subject is to do. So, as I said at first, "right" means doing what is to the interest of the stronger.

Very well, Thrasymachus, said I. So you think I am quibbling?

I am sure you are.

You believe my questions were maliciously designed to damage your position?

I know it. But you will gain nothing by that. You cannot outwit me by cunning, and you are not the man to crush me in the open.

Bless your soul, I answered, I should not think of trying. But, to prevent any more misunderstanding, when you speak of that ruler or stronger party whose interest the weaker ought to serve, please make it clear whether you are using the words in the ordinary way or in that strict sense you have just defined.

I mean a ruler in the strictest possible sense. Now quibble away and be as malicious as you can. I want no mercy. But you are no match for me.

Do you think me mad enough to beard a lion or try to outwit a Thrasymachus?

You did try just now, he retorted, but it wasn't a success.

—PLATO, *Republic*

Although it may not be obvious on first reading, the crucial turning point in this exchange is the point at which Socrates gets Thrasymachus to admit that the people should obey their superior rulers *only* when the rulers are issuing commands that really are in their own interest. If the strong, through ignorance or error, accidentally issue commands that work to the benefit of the weak, then the weak are not to obey!

This may not look like much of an admission, but it is actually fatal to Thrasymachus' position. The reason is that it introduces into the discussion the idea that rulers have a right to be obeyed only when they are, in some way or other, using their intellectual abilities to rule well. At this point, of course, "ruling well" simply means "ruling in such a way as to advance their own interests," but once Thrasymachus has agreed that standards are to be applied to the performance of the rulers, he has started down a slippery slope. Now Socrates has an opening in which to start talking about good and bad rulers, and that permits him to raise all sorts of issues that Thrasymachus has no desire at all to let into the debate.

Needless to say, Socrates foresees all of this when he asks the first innocent-looking question, just as a chess master foresees the next ten moves when he makes his first simple move. That is part of the skill of philosophical argument.

II What Do Philosophers Do? The Study of the Universe

I told you that Socrates spent some time when he was young studying the theories about the nature of the universe which had been developed by other Greek thinkers during the 200 years before his own time. The Greek word for world or universe is *kosmos*, so we call the study of the nature of the world **cosmology**. The study of the human condition and the study of the cosmos are the two great branches of philosophy, and there is no division more fundamental in philosophy than that between the philosophers who study the human experience and the philosophers who speculate about the order of the entire universe. (Later on, we shall see that some philosophers have tried to unite the two in a single theoretical framework, but that is getting ahead of our story.)

The Greeks, like all peoples, had their religious myths about the creation of the world and the origins of their civilization, but some time roughly 600 years before the birth of Christ, a number of men began to search for a more rational, more factually well-grounded theory of the composition, order, and origin of the world. Some of these early scientists—for that is what they were—flourished in a city-state named Miletus on the coast of what is now Turkey, in the eastern Mediterranean. They are known as Milesians, after their hometown, and they appear to

A schematic representation of the universe as it was pictured by the great Egyptian astronomer, Ptolemy. The earth is at the center, and there are seven heavenly bodies orbiting about it: the sun, the moon, Mercury, Venus, Mars, Jupiter, and Saturn. Note that the representation on the earth of Africa and the Orient is pretty accurate. (The Bettmann Archive)

have been the very first philosophers in what we are calling the cosmological tradition. For various reasons, only bits and pieces of what they wrote still survive, and most of what we know about them must be learned indirectly from what other ancient writers say about them. They are little more than names to us today, but perhaps it is worth telling you their names, for we owe them an intellectual debt almost too great to calculate. There was *Thales,* usually spoken of as the very first philosopher of all. Thales was what we today would call an astronomer; the story is told that while walking one evening with his eyes turned to the stars, he fell into a well, and thereby created the myth of the absentminded professor. But it is also said of him that by using his superior knowledge of the weather, acquired by his astronomical studies, he managed to corner the market in olive oil and make a fortune. Following Thales were the Milesians *Anaximander* and *Anaximenes*, who expanded and developed speculative theories about the basic components of nature and their order. Their names are strange, and we have long since lost almost all of what they wrote and said, but as you study your physics, chemistry, or astronomy, or watch a rocket lift off for yet another space probe, you might just give them a thought, for they started Western civilization on its scientific journey.

The theories of the ancient cosmologists seem odd to modern readers. When we look behind the surface detail, however, we can see some surprisingly modern ideas. The fundamental problem of the Milesians was to determine the basic stuff or component matter from which all the variety of things in the world were composed. The four categories into

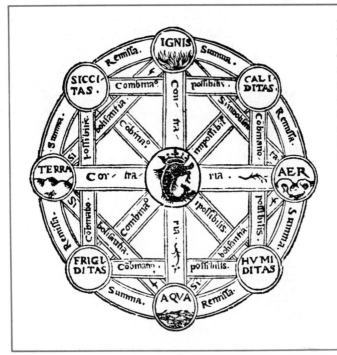

In this schematic representation of the elements, fire is at the top, air on the right, water at the bottom, and earth to the left. The fifth substance, or "quintessence," is in the center. Fire is a mixture of dryness and heat, air is a mixture of heat and humidity, water is a mixture of humidity and coldness, and earth is a mixture of coldness and dryness.

New York Public Library Picture Collection

which they divided all things were earth, water, air, and fire. Thales claimed that at base everything in the universe was water; earth, air, and fire were simply forms of water, or water in other guises. Anaximenes, by contrast, said that everything was air. Now all of this sounds quaint and very peculiar, but suppose that we say solid instead of earth, liquid instead of water, gas instead of air, and energy instead of fire. Then we have the theory that everything in the universe is solid, liquid, gaseous, or some form of energy, and that isn't a bad guess at all! What is more, the search for some underlying element that simply *appears* in one or another of these forms has a distinctly modern ring to it. The nineteenth-century theory of the atom, for example, told us that ninety and more elements found in nature could really be reduced to differing arrangements of three basic building blocks: neutrons, protons, and electrons. The theory of subatomic particles has become much more complicated since that simple model of the atom was proposed, but the Milesian search goes on today for the building blocks of the universe.

The second great theme of the Milesians and their successors was that natural events were to be understood by appeal to natural forces, not by appeal to the actions of the gods or the interventions of some non-natural forces. The keynote of these early philosopher-scientists was that nature is natural, and in their speculations and observations, they showed remarkable shrewdness and good sense. For example, water seems to turn into ice (a solid) when it is very cold, and into steam (a gas) when it is very hot. Solid things (such as iron) which are very solid indeed actually melt when made hot enough. All of this suggests that there is some underlying stuff which takes on different forms under different conditions.

Here is a short passage from a philosopher who lived very much later in the ancient world, but whose attention to the evidence of his senses is typical of the cosmological frame of mind. Lucretius was a Roman philosopher and poet who lived in the first century before Christ, nearly five centuries after the Milesians. He defended a cosmological theory

Cosmology   Literally, the study of the order of the world. Now used to refer to the branch of astronomy that investigates the organization and structure of the entire physical universe, including its origins. In philosophy, cosmology is a part of the subfield called metaphysics, or the study of first principles.

called atomism, according to which everything in the universe, including even the human soul, is composed of little bits of matter called atoms, which are so small that they cannot be seen by the naked eye (another surprisingly modern doctrine!). As you can see, Lucretius uses a variety of familiar observations to prove that despite appearances to the contrary, all things are composed of tiny, indestructible atoms which themselves have no parts and are absolutely solid.

> Now mark me: since I have taught that things cannot be born from nothing, cannot when begotten be brought back to nothing, that you may not haply yet begin in any shape to mistrust my words, because the first-beginnings of things cannot be seen by the eyes, take moreover this list of bodies which you must yourself admit are in the number of things and cannot be seen. First of all the force of the wind when aroused beats on the harbours and whelms huge ships and scatters clouds; sometimes in swift whirling eddy it scours the plains and strews them with large trees and scourges the mountain summits with forest-rending blasts: so fiercely does the wind rave with a shrill howling and rage with threatening roar. Winds therefore sure enough are unseen bodies which sweep the seas, the lands, ay and the clouds of heaven, tormenting them and catching them up in sudden whirls. . . . Then again we perceive the different smells of things, yet never see them coming to our nostrils; nor do we behold heats nor can we observe cold with the eyes nor are we used to see voices. Yet all these things must consist of a bodily nature, since they are able to move the senses; for nothing but body can touch and be touched. Again clothes hung up on a shore which waves break upon become moist, and then get dry if spread out in the sun. Yet it has not been seen in what way the moisture of water has sunk into them nor again in what way this has been dispelled by heat. The moisture therefore is dispersed into small particles which the eyes are quite unable to see. Again after the revolution of many of the sun's years a ring on the finger is thinned on the under side by wearing, the dripping from the eaves hollows a stone, the bent ploughshare of iron imperceptibly decreases in the fields, and we behold the stone-paved streets worn down by the feet of the multitude; the brass statues too at the gates show their right hands to be wasted by the touch of the numerous passers by who greet them. These things then we see are lessened, since they have been thus worn down; but what bodies depart at any given time the nature of vision has jealously shut out our seeing. . . . Nature therefore works by unseen bodies.
>
> —LUCRETIUS, *On the Nature of Things*

Cosmological speculation goes on today, as it did 2500 years ago. From the earliest times, philosophers have been actively involved in the experimental and theoretical advances of what today we call science. Indeed, it is difficult to say just where hard science leaves off and speculative, philosophical cosmology begins. Thales himself, for example, was said to have discovered a method for measuring the height of the Egyptian pyramids, by waiting until the precise hour of the day when a body's shadow was equal to its height. Anaximander devised an instrument known as a gnomon, a rod whose shadow permits us to calculate the direction and height of the sun. The great fourth-century B.C. philosopher Aristotle, pupil and follower of Plato, virtually invented the science of formal logic, and made significant contributions to what we would today call taxonomy. Plato's school of followers, the Academy, did important work in the branch of mathematics known as solid geometry. Two thousand years later, René Descartes, the French philosopher and scientist, invented analytic geometry (which we still study in school today) as a tool for analyzing and giving expression to his theory of the nature of the material universe. His successor, Gottfried Leibniz, invented a version of the differential calculus as part of his dispute with Descartes about the nature of matter. In our own century, the logicians and philosophers Bertrand Russell and Alfred North Whitehead established the modern discipline of mathematical logic with their monumental *Principia Mathematica*. Throughout the entire course of Western civilization, philosophical speculation, scientific experiment, and pure logical and mathematical theorizing have advanced together, often in the writings of the same thinkers, sometimes in the very same works. The philosophical enterprise begun by the ancient Milesians has borne splendid fruit, both in an expanded scientific understanding of nature and in a refined conceptual sophistication about those original questions of the nature and order of the cosmos. Before leaving our discussion of this great tradition of philosophical thought, let us read a few selections of modern cosmology. The first deals with the microcosm—the unimaginably tiny bits of stuff from which all else in the universe is compounded. These speculations, we may imagine, are the lineal descendants of the ancient atomistic theories of Democritus, Epicurus, and the Roman Lucretius. The second deals with the macrocosm, the universe as a whole, and specifically with its origins. It traces its lineage to the inspired guesses of the Milesians and their followers.

In this century it has been possible to describe the atom as a hard core surrounded by orbiting electrons; and then the atomic nucleus appeared as a composite of neutrons and protons held together by a short-range force much stronger than the electric force which would tend to push them apart. Both these concepts are easy to visualize.

But with the elementary particles, including neutrons, and protons, physicists just don't know what the underlying causes of behavior are.

On the other hand, they have discovered more than a hundred particles, many of them created in high-energy accelerators and existing for only a fraction of an instant. They have catalogued them and classified them according to their mass, their electric charge, the way they spin, and various other qualities.

They have found that some of the particles can be organized in groups of eight or ten with similar properties. But understanding, as well as explanations of inconsistencies in the groupings, remain elusive.

One promising concept, which however hasn't yielded very good numerical results, is that the particles that are subject to the strong force binding nucleus are made up out of each other, so that none of them is fundamental.

The basis for this theory, called the bootstrap hypothesis, comes from the way forces are applied between particles. Physicists found they could describe electromagnetic forces by saying that charged particles exchanged another particle, called a photon, and by this means exerted electromagnetic force on each other.

The strong forces are also exerted by exchanging particles other than photons. What the bootstrap theory suggests is that any strongly interacting particle can serve as the means of exerting strong forces between two others. When two particles exert a strong force, they create another, producing a bound system; and that system, according to the theory, is the created particle.

Another theory, easier to visualize but extremely unlikely to be more than a mathematical tool, is the . . . quark model, which holds that the particles are made up of combinations of two or three different kinds of subparticles.

Developed by Dr. [Murray] Gell-Mann, the quark hypothesis predicts the groupings of particles into already observed sets of eight and ten.

—*Science News*

Cosmology attempts to deduce the history of the universe from astronomical observation. Its great difficulty is that the events concerned take millions or billions of years to work themselves out, and it is therefore hard to observe the history in progress and be exactly sure what one is seeing.

An electron microscope photograph of diatoms, tiny one-celled algae. With modern techniques, scientists can actually see the molecular structures that the ancient atomists merely speculated about. (Manfred Kage/ Peter Arnold)

Modern cosmologists are left with two general classes of theory: the so-called big-bang or cosmic fireball and the steady-state or continuous creation theories.

In the middle 1960s radio astronomical observations provided evidence that was taken as very dramatic support for the big-bang theory, and the buildup of data became so convincing to many cosmologists that they were ready to bury the rival steady-state theory. Recent observations in infrared light, which have been possible only in the last few years, give proponents of the steady-state ammunition to strike back.

The difference between the two theories rests on the density of the universe. If the universe has been expanding for any length of time, everyone agrees that there must have been a time when it was very small, and the question is: Did it then have the same amount of matter as it has now?

If it did, then the pressure temperature and density were beyond anything imaginable today. This is the cosmic fireball and its physical conditions suggest that it must have exploded and thus given the impetus for the expansion now seen.

The other side says that this did not happen. The matter in the universe was always as dense as it is now, and therefore there was never a hot high-density state. This requires that matter be added as the universe expands. It can be continually created out of nothing or pumped in from some realm beneath the universe, possibly through galaxy centers. . . .

The source of matter for galactic expansion . . . could be some kind of continuous creation or pumping-in process at the centers. Some of the matter is annihilated at or near the source; some survives to build up the galaxy.

Acceptance of this idea immediately raises the problem of antimatter. Accordingly to currently accepted laws of particle physics, when matter is created, so is an equal amount of antimatter.

There is no observational evidence for any large amounts of antimatter in the visible universe. On the other hand, there is no observational evidence against its presence. An antistar would look precisely like a star, so there is no way to tell. . . .

Meanwhile the evidence on which the proponents of the big-bang theory based their jubilation a few years ago remains, though its interpretation is more and more questioned. Radio astronomers had found a background of radio waves whose spectrum corresponded to a perfect thermal radiator or blackbody at a temperature of three degrees above absolute zero (SN: 7/5, p. 9). Existence of such a blackbody background is a prediction of the big-bang theory, and the discovery seemed to be evidence for it.

There are other possible interpretations of this radio spectrum, although the blackbody is the simplest. Extension of the observations into the infrared was eagerly awaited since it was in this range that the background's blackbody character should show up unmistakably.

The infrared observations so far have not been happy for the blackbody enthusiasts. The first of them showed background infrared fluxes, which, if they were thermal, were hotter than three degrees. These could be explained away as the background plus something else . . .

The battle between the rival cosmologies is far from over, but with the advent of infrared observations it is becoming clear that the steady-state theory, over which some cosmologists were reading funeral orations a few years ago, is very much alive again.

—*Science News*

One final point before we move on. Thales, Anaximander, and the rest are called "philosophers" in dictionaries of biography or histories of Western thought. But if you look up Murray Gell-Mann in *Who's Who*, you will find him listed as a physicist. Why is it that cosmological questions are investigated by scientists today, although they were investigated by the philosophers 2000 years ago? Is this just what labor unions call a "jurisdictional dispute" or has some important theoretical change taken place here?

The most common answer to this question is that "philosophy" used to include just about everything that men and women did by way of systematic, reasoned investigation of the heavens, the earth, or the human condition. In the writings of Plato, Aristotle, and the other ancients, we find discussions which today would be labeled physics, mathematics, astronomy, biology, psychology, economics, political science, sociology, anthropology, theology, and even engineering. Over the past two millennia, one after another of these branches of human knowledge has pulled itself together, broken off from "philosophy," and established itself as an independent discipline with its own rules of inquiry, objects of investigation, and theoretical framework. Philosophy today, according to this way of looking at things, is what remains after all the intellectual children have left home. Roughly speaking, that reduces philosophy to conceptual analysis plus some armchair speculation on whatever the other sciences haven't laid claim to yet.

There is another view, however, which seems to me to be a good deal closer to the truth. Philosophy, it holds, is the systematic reflection of the mind upon the criteria of right thought and right action which it employs in all of its activities. On this view, there is a "philosophical" component to virtually everything we do. Political scientists (and politicians too), scientists, artists, economists, and astronomers all need to reflect on the nature of their enterprises, and the people officially called philosophers are simply those among us who concentrate their attention on this self-critical or reflective side of our intellectual undertakings.

III *What Do Philosophers Do? Human Nature and the Universe*

Although the study of the human condition and the study of the cosmos are the two great themes of Western philosophy, it must not be supposed that they developed in an unconnected way. Philosophers are, above all else, seekers after unity. Where human experience presents a manyness, they seek the underlying oneness. In the long history of Western thought, philosophers have tried two basically different strategies for bringing the two branches of philosophy into some interconnected whole.

The first strategy was tried by some of the earliest philosophers, among whom were a group known as **Stoics**. The Stoics claimed that the natural world exhibited a rational order which could be explained by appeal to the existence and operations of a power of reason, which they called *logos*. (We get our word **logic** from this term, and also the word ending -ology, meaning "study of.") In the cosmos, this logos was often

identified with what we today would call God, but it could also be identified with the power of reason in each human being. Therein lies the
principle that bridged the gap between the study of human nature and
the study of physical nature, for the very same fundamental logos or
rational order which made itself known in the order of the planets, the
succession of the seasons, and the regular behavior of natural bodies in
space and time also exhibited itself in our capacity for logical reasoning,
in our ability to control our passions by the power of our understanding,
and in the proper order and arrangement of men and women in a stable,
just, and rationally ordered society. Our power of reason was said to be
a "spark" or fragment of the divine Logos which informed and governed
the universe. Eventually, this ancient Greek doctrine was taken up into
the theology of the Christian, Jewish, and Muslim religions, and became the basis for much of the religious theology that flourished in the
Middle Ages.

After studying cosmology as a youth, Socrates turned away from it,
convinced that the proper study for us is our own nature. But if the
Stoics were correct, then a philosopher could study human nature and
physical nature together, for the same principles that explained the arrangements of the heavenly bodies would, properly understood, also explain how we should live our lives within a well-ordered set of social arrangements.

The unifying doctrine of the Stoics gave rise to one of the most important philosophical ideas in Western thought—the idea of **natural law**.
God, or the power of Reason, created the universe in accordance with a
rational idea of the proper form and order of its organization. On the
cosmic level, this conception determined the existence, nature, and relative positions of the stars, the sun, the moon, and the earth. At the social
level, this same idea determined the appropriate hierarchy of classes and
statuses from the king or emperor down to the lowliest serf. Within each
individual human being, the same idea determined the relative order and
importance of the rational, passional, and appetitive elements of the soul.
Human beings were unique in the natural order by virtue of their possession of a spark of that logos or reason, for it permitted them at one and
the same time to understand the grand plan and also to live their own
lives freely and responsibly in conformity with it.

Among the greatest of the ancient Stoics was a Roman emperor who
ruled from A.D. 161 to 180. Marcus Aurelius combined great skill as a
general and ruler with a contemplative nature. His reflections on the
universe and our brief stay in it have come down to us in the form of a

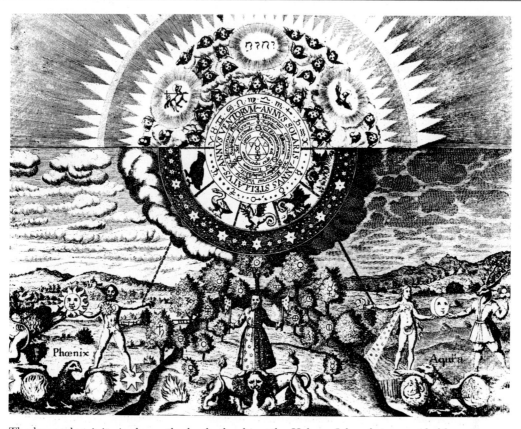

The heavenly trinity is above, the lamb, the dove, the Hebrew Jehovah, surrounded by angels. Below is the world of matter. The starry heaven encircles the hermetic work. The philosophic stone in the center is a triangle with the double sign of mercury and gold; flanked by the three signs of alchemistic procedure, air, water, mercury. The seven circles include fire, mercury, sulphur, salt, time of the solar year, year of stars and year of the winds.

New York Public Library Picture Collection

series of meditations. Following are a few selections which convey the themes and something of the flavor of his thought.

> Constantly regard the universe as one living being, having one substance and one soul; and observe how all things have reference to one perception, the perception of this one living being; and how all things act with one movement; and how all things are the co-operating causes of all things which

MARCUS AURELIUS (A.D. 121–180) was one of the most remarkable men to hold the exalted position of Roman emperor. For almost five centuries, Rome ruled a vast empire stretching from Great Britain through what is now Western Europe, entirely around the shores of the Mediterranean Sea, and deep into northern Africa and the Middle East. Marcus was both a gifted and successful general, winning many battles against the barbarian tribes who repeatedly attacked Rome's border provinces; and also a wise and thoughtful philosopher, learned in the writings of the Greeks and his Roman predecessors, and without illusions about the fleetingness of the power and glory which were his as emperor. During the second century after the birth of Christ, the empire persecuted the followers of that Eastern prophet, and Marcus, despite (or perhaps even because of) his commitment to Stoicism, carried forward these persecutions. It was not until more than a century later, with the con-

version of the Emperor Constantine, that Christianity ceased to be the object of official attack, and became instead the established religion of the Roman Empire.

exist; observe too the continuous spinning of the thread and the contexture of the web.

The intelligence of the universe is social. Accordingly it has made the inferior things for the sake of the superior, and it has fitted the superior to one another. Thou seest how it has subordinated, co-ordinated and assigned to everything its proper portion, and has brought together into concord with one another the things which are the best.

All things are implicated with one another, and the bond is holy; and there is hardly anything unconnected with any other thing. For things have been co-ordinated, and they combine to form the same universe (order). For there is one universe made up of all things, and one God who pervades all things, and one substance, and one law, one common reason in all intelligent animals, and one truth; if indeed there is also one perfection for all animals which are the same stock and participate in the same reason.

To the rational animal the same act is according to nature and according to reason.

—MARCUS AURELIUS, *Meditations.*

So, the first strategy devised by philosophers for uniting the study of human nature with the study of physical nature was the Stoic doctrine of natural law. The second strategy was worked out 2000 years later by a brilliant group of seventeenth- and eighteenth-century philosophers in the British Isles and on the continent of Europe. We shall be taking a close look at some of their theories in Chapter Seven when we talk about the branch of philosophy known as the "theory of knowledge." In this introductory look at the nature of philosophy in general, we ought nevertheless to try to form some preliminary idea of what they were doing, for their ideas and their writings have been among the most influential in the entire literature of Western thought.

The key to the new strategy was a very simple, very powerful idea: The universe is vast, and ten thousand generations would be too short a time to say everything that can be learned about it; but every single fact, every theory, every insight, guess, hypothesis, or deduction is *an idea in the human mind.* So instead of turning our eyes outward to the universe, let us turn our eyes inward to the nature of the human mind itself. Let us study *the way in which* we know, rather than *what* we know. The universe may be infinite, but the mind is finite. What is more (these philosophers thought), though the universe is infinitely varied, the human mind is everywhere and always exactly the same. (They hadn't yet heard of evolution, or the variation in conceptual frameworks from culture to culture.) Instead of writing many books on cosmology, physics, psychology, politics, morals, and religion we need to write just one book on the powers, capacities, forms, and limits of the human mind. So during the seven-

Epistemology Literally, the study of knowledge. Epistemology is the study of how we come to know things, what the limits are of our knowledge, and what sort of certainty or uncertainty attaches to our knowledge. Psychology also studies how we come to know, but epistemology is concerned less with the mechanics of knowing than with the possibility of defending, proving, or justifying what we think we know. Since the early seventeenth century, epistemology has been the most important branch of philosophy.

teenth and eighteenth centuries, we find titles like the following crop-
ping up in the philosophical literature: *An Essay Concerning Human
Understanding*, by the Englishman John Locke; *Principles of Human
Knowledge*, by the Irishman George Berkeley; A *Treatise of Human Nature*, by the Scotsman David Hume; and the greatest of them all, A *Critique of Pure Reason*, by the Prussian Immanuel Kant.

Now, it might look at first glance as though these philosophers had
simply taken Socrates' advice to forget about the study of physical nature
and seek instead a knowledge of human nature. But that would be a
mistake, for the British empiricists (as Locke, Berkeley, Hume, and their
lesser compatriots are called) and the continental rationalists (Descartes,
Leibniz, Kant, and their fellow philosophers) had got their hands on a
wholly different way of doing philosophy. Socrates never imagined that
we could learn something about the natural sciences by studying ourselves. He simply thought that the search for the just and happy life was
more important than speculation about the elements of the universe or
the origin of the order of the heavenly bodies. The British empiricists
and Continental rationalists, by contrast, thought they had found a device for combining the study of human nature and the study of the universe in one single philosophical enterprise. If they could learn *how* we
know—whether it is by looking with our eyes, touching with our hands,
and listening with our ears, or whether it is by reasoning with our minds
and ignoring the evidence of our senses, or perhaps whether it is by some
combining of what the senses tell us with what reason tells us—if philosophy could study the process of knowledge rather than getting all tangled
up in the details of particular bits of knowledge of this and that, then
maybe philosophy could give us some very general answers to such questions as, Can we know anything at all? How much can we know? Can
we know about things that happened before we were born, or somewhere else in space? Can we know that things *must* happen the way they
do, or must we simply say, "This happens, and then this . . . " and let it
go at that? Can we know about things we can't see or feel, like atoms, or
the unconscious, or even God? Can one person know for sure that there
are other persons in the world, and not just bodies that look like persons?
Can I, myself, be sure that the whole world isn't simply my dream? All
these questions, and many more besides, might be answered by a systematic study of the human mind itself. In this way, the study of physical
nature would be combined with the study of human nature, not through
a theory of universal logos or intelligence, as the Stoics thought, but
through a theory of how we know.

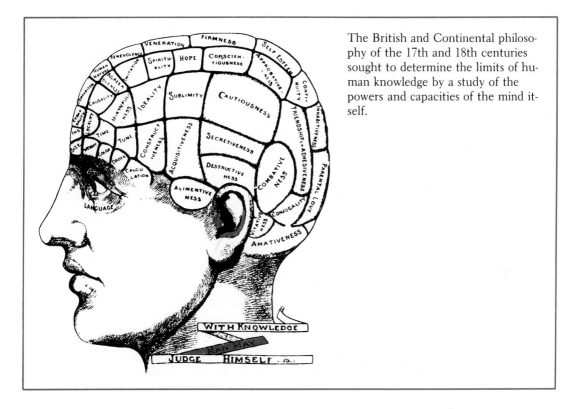

The British and Continental philosophy of the 17th and 18th centuries sought to determine the limits of human knowledge by a study of the powers and capacities of the mind itself.

One of the best statements of the new strategy is to be found in the introduction to David Hume's great work, *A Treatise of Human Nature*. Hume was a Scotsman, born in 1711. The *Treatise*, in three volumes, was published in 1739 and 1740, when Hume was not yet thirty years old! There are three important points to notice in the following passage from Hume's *Treatise*. First, as we have already remarked, the basic idea of Hume's strategy is to turn the multiplicity of sciences and fields of study into a unified examination of human nature and the mind's power of knowing. Second, Hume thinks that he shall have to study "the nature of the ideas we employ," for it is from those ideas that we form whatever judgments we wish to make in physics, religion, politics, or morals. And finally, Hume says, he shall have to examine "the operations we perform in our reasonings." In Chapter Seven, we shall see that this distinction between the nature of our ideas, on the one hand, and the nature of our reasonings with our ideas, on the other, is an important weapon in the strategy of the new theorists of knowledge.

Reading selections from the works of the great philosophers is a bit like watching videotape replays of great football stars. Since we know who made it to stardom, it is easy for us to spot their greatness from the very first. But let us have a little pity for the poor book reviewer who was handed an anonymous work entitled *A Treatise of Human Nature* and told to write a brief review of it in a few weeks. Here is what one nameless unfortunate had to say about Hume's *Treatise*, in a literary journal rather imposingly called *A History of the Works of the Learned.*

> . . . A Man, who has never had the pleasure of reading Mr. Locke's incomparable Essay, will peruse our author with much less Disgust, than those can who have been used to the irresistible Reasoning and wonderful Perspicuity of that admirable Writer.

Poor Hume was so upset by the negative reviews of the *Treatise* that later in life he disowned it, saying it was merely a first effort of his youth. How many of us, I wonder, would recognize the greatness of a new book of philosophy within months of its publication?

> It is evident, that all the sciences have a relation, greater or less, to human nature; and that, however wide any of them may seem to run from it, they still return back by one passage or another. Even *Mathematics, Natural Philosophy,* and *Natural Religion,* are in some measure dependent on the science of MAN; since they lie under the cognisance of men, and are judged of by their powers and faculties. It is impossible to tell what changes and improvements we might make in these sciences were we thoroughly acquainted with the extent and force of human understanding, and could explain the nature of the ideas we employ, and of the operations we perform in our reasonings. And these improvements are the more to be hoped for in natural religion, as it is not content with instructing us in the nature of superior powers, but carries its views further, to their disposition towards us, and our duties towards them; and consequently, we ourselves are not only the beings that reason, but also one of the objects concerning which we reason.
>
> If, therefore, the sciences of mathematics, natural philosophy, and natural religion, have such a dependence on the knowledge of man, what may be expected in the other sciences, whose connection with human nature is more close and intimate? The sole end of logic is to explain the principles and operations of our reasoning faculty, and the nature of our ideas; morals and criticism regard our tastes and sentiments; and politics consider men as united in society, and dependent on each other. In these four sciences of

DAVID HUME (1711–1776) was one of those precocious philosophers whose greatest work was done early in life. Born and reared near Edinburgh in Scotland, Hume attended Edinburgh University, where he studied the new physics of Isaac Newton and the new philosophy of John Locke. When still a teenager, Hume conceived the idea of developing a full-scale theory of human nature along the lines of Newton's revolutionary theory of physical nature. After what seems to have been some sort of mental breakdown, Hume went to France to rest and recover, and while there he wrote his first and greatest book, the monumental *Treatise of Human Nature*.

Hume went on to become an extremely popular and successful essayist and man of letters. His six-volume *History of England* established his reputation as the first major modern historian. Nevertheless, his sceptical doubts about religion and his attacks on the metaphysical doctrines of his continental and British predecessors earned him many enemies. One of his most brilliant works, twelve *Dialogues Concerning Natural Religion*, was only published after his death. His friends, including the economist Adam Smith, persuaded him that the book was too controversial and might permanently damage his reputation.

As you can see from the portrait of Hume, the lightness and quickness of his mind was entirely hidden by the lumpishness of his appearance. Nature often plays such tricks on us!

Empiricism/Rationalism   Empiricism and rationalism are the two leading epistemological theories of the past four centuries. *Empiricism* is the theory that all human knowledge comes from the evidence of our five senses, and therefore that we can never know more, or know with greater certainty, than our sense will allow. *Rationalism* is the theory that at least some human knowledge comes from reason, unaided by the senses, and therefore that we can know about things that the senses do not reveal to us, and can know with greater certainty than the senses alone will allow.

Logic, Morals, Criticism, and *Politics,* is comprehended almost everything which it can anyway import us to be acquainted with, or which can tend either to the improvement or ornament of the human mind.

Here then is the only expedient, from which we can hope for success in our philosophical researches, to leave the tedious lingering method, which we have hitherto followed, and, instead of taking now and then a castle or village on the frontier, to march up directly to the capital or centre of these sciences, to human nature itself; which being once masters of, we may everywhere else hope for an easy victory. From this station we may extend our conquests over all those sciences, which more intimately concern human life, and may afterwards proceed at leisure, to discover more fully those which are the objects of pure curiosity. There is no question of importance, whose decision is not comprised in the science of man; and there is none, which can be decided with any certainty, before we become acquainted with that science. In pretending, therefore, to explain the principles of human nature, we in effect propose a complete system of the sciences, built on a foundation almost entirely new, and the only one upon which they can stand with any security.

—DAVID HUME, *A Treatise of Human Nature*

The new study of the mind's capacity for knowing came to be called **epistemology,** from the Greek for the study or science (-ology) of knowledge (*episteme*). It was not to be merely descriptive, like psychology, however. Its purpose was to settle some ancient philosophical disputes by finding out what we can legitimately claim to know, and what we can not claim to know because our claims carry us beyond the limits of the powers of the mind. This *critical* dimension of the new strategy extended across the entire spectrum of philosophical investigations, as the passage from Hume's *Treatise* indicates. In a brief excerpt from Immanuel Kant's

Critique of Pure Reason, you can get some sense of what a dramatic challenge the new critical epistemology was to established ways of thinking.

> We often hear complaints of shallowness of thought in our age and of the consequent decline of sound science. But I do not see that the sciences which rest upon a secure foundation, such as mathematics, physics, etc., in the least deserve this reproach. On the contrary, they merit their old reputation for solidity, and, in the case of physics, even surpass it. The same spirit would have become active in other kinds of knowledge, if only attention had first been directed to the determination of their principles. Till this is done, indifference, doubt, and, in the final issue, severe criticism, are themselves proof of a profound habit of thought. Our age is, in especial degree, the age of criticism, and to criticism everything must submit. Religion through its sanctity, and law-giving through its majesty, may seek to exempt themselves from it. But they then awaken just suspicion, and cannot claim the sincere respect which reason accords only to that which has been able to sustain the test of free and open examination.
>
> —IMMANUEL KANT, A *Critique of Pure Reason*

IV *Philosophers Attack Philosophy*

From the very beginning, philosophers have been objects of suspicion and even ridicule. Socrates was satirized in a play by the brilliant comic poet Aristophanes as a man with his head in the clouds who talked in a crazy fashion about nonsensical matters. We have already seen that the very first philosopher, Thales, acquired the reputation of being absent-minded. Usually, philosophers are accused of quibbling about questions so divorced from any genuine human concern that only someone unfit for real life would make his living worrying about them.

Needless to say, I don't think this caricature of philosophy has much truth in it; otherwise, I would hardly have spent my own life thinking about philosophical questions. But it is not hard to see how the notion has gained popularity. Suppose that I say to you, Four is two plus two. Four is also three plus one. Therefore two plus two is three plus one. All right, you would answer. Perfectly reasonable. If A is B and A is C then B must be C. Right? Fine, I go on. Socrates is wise, and Socrates is ugly. Therefore Wisdom must be Ugliness! Now right there, you know you have been had. Something has gone badly wrong.

Here's another one. Yesterday, I remembered seeing a friend of mine, but after thinking about it for a moment, I realized that I must have been remembering a dream, because my friend has been in Europe for two years. Last night I dreamed that I was the king of Persia, and at the time it was so real I could fairly smell the incense and hear the court musicians! It would seem that sometimes, when we think we are awake, we are really dreaming; and some of the things we think we actually remember doing are just recollections of dreams. So maybe everything I see, touch, smell, and hear is a dream. Maybe my whole life is a dream, and I have never been awake. Well, there you are again! I start out with some perfectly reasonable premise and end with a conclusion so wild that only a philosopher would take it seriously.

Peculiar puzzles and strange counterintuitive conclusions have been popping up in philosophical books ever since the days of the ancient Milesians, but somehow the arguments of the British empiricists and the continental rationalists in the seventeenth and eighteenth centuries contained more really puzzling statements than was usual even for philosophers. Somewhat in reaction to their way of doing philosophy, a gifted Austrian mathematician and philosopher named Ludwig Wittgenstein developed a new and extremely controversial theory of what philosophical problems are and what we ought to do about them.

Wittgenstein (1889–1951) suggested that a philosophical problem is a sort of cross between a logical confusion, a grammatical mistake, and a mental illness. Philosophers start off using language in a perfectly proper way to talk about the world, and then they formulate a question or propose a thesis which *sounds* all right but is really odd in some way. Instead of realizing that they have gone wrong, however, they press right on, drawing more and more bizarre conclusions, obsessed with the seeming plausibility of their own words.

For example, it makes perfectly good sense to ask, How high is the Empire State Building? How high is the moon? But it makes no sense to ask, How high is up? That is just a child's joke. Well, it also makes perfectly good sense to ask, Was that a dream or did I really see my friend? Am I dreaming now, or am I really the king of Persia? But perhaps it *doesn't* make sense to ask, Is my whole life a dream? That question *looks* sensible enough, but then, so does, How high is up?

Wittgenstein proposed that philosophers treat their problems as symptoms of a conceptual disorder rather than as subjects for investigation and debate. Whenever we come upon someone who is really mes-

LUDWIG WITTGENSTEIN (1889–1951) was born in Vienna, and spent his formative years in Austria. He wrote virtually all his philosophical works in German, but his principal influence has been on English and American philosophy, where he is probably the single most important philosophical thinker of the twentieth century. After early training in engineering, Wittgenstein turned to mathematical logic, under the influence of the work of the Englishman Bertrand Russell. Eventually Wittgenstein came to Cambridge, England, where he spent much of his adult life.

Highly original research in logic led Wittgenstein to a theory of language, truth, and meaning, which he set forth, in a laconic and distinctive style, in his *Tractatus Logico—Philosophicus*. This was the only philosophical book published by Wittgenstein during his lifetime, but he wrote great quantities of philosophy which appeared posthumously. Later in life, he thoroughly reversed his own earlier theories, and set forth a new account of language and meaning in his *Philosophical Investigations*. Wittgenstein was an intense, brooding man who made so deep an impression on his students and colleagues that even now, over a quarter of a century after his death, there are many distinguished English and American philosophers who still consider themselves his disciples.

merized by a philosophical problem, we ought to try to relieve her of her distress by dissolving the problem, by showing her where she went wrong and how she can get back onto the path of talking ordinary common sense. These two statements from Wittgenstein's book, *Philosophical Investigations*, capture the spirit of his approach:

> My aim is: to teach you to pass from a piece of disguised nonsense to something that is patent nonsense.

> The philosopher's treatment of a question is like the treatment of an illness.

The second statement suggests that philosophers ought really to be in the business of putting themselves out of business! If philosophical puzzles are like illnesses, then the sooner we cure the people who have come down with a bad case of philosophy, the sooner there will be no philosophy left to cure. Odd as it may seem, Wittgenstein is not the only great philosopher to claim that his philosophy would put philosophy out of business. Immanuel Kant thought roughly the same thing.

V Philosophy Is Just Talk

Philosophy is a reflective self-examination of the principles of the just and happy life, says Socrates. Philosophy is a study of the universe, its origins, elements, and laws, say the ancient cosmologists and their modern descendants. Philosophy is a search for the rational principles that bind the universe and human life together into a single, logical whole, say the Stoics and many others. Philosophy is a critique and dissection of the mind's power to know, say the epistemologists of the seventeenth and eighteenth centuries. Philosophy is a conceptual disease of which we should be cured, says Wittgenstein. It would seem that there couldn't be five more dissimilar conceptions of philosophy imaginable. On second look, however, we see that they all have something in common. They all say philosophy is something you *think about*, not something you *do* something about. Philosophers are dreamers, popular opinion has it, even if they don't think that all of life is a dream. Philosophers sit in their cozy studies, or in their ivory towers.

Strange as it may seem, the most devastating criticism of philosophy as mere do-nothing talk that anyone has ever made was written by, of all people, Plato! You will remember that Plato came from a wealthy and powerful Athenian family, and the normal thing for the son of such a family to do was to go into politics, to participate in the public life of Athens. Roughly in middle life, Plato was faced with a hard choice: whether to go on with his philosophical studies, gathering around him the group of followers and fellow thinkers with whom he had been spending his time; or to give up philosophy and take his natural place in the affairs of his city-state. Plato had already begun to write the Dialogues for which he is famous, and so in one of them, *Gorgias*, he talked about the problem indirectly. The Dialogue is really three arguments between Socrates and a series of opponents (a bit like an elimination

"How much would you pay for all the secrets of the universe? Wait, don't answer yet. You also get this six-quart covered combination spaghetti pot and clam steamer. *Now* how much would you pay?"

match). A famous teacher and lecturer, Gorgias, has come to town, bragging that he can give a public speech on any subject his audience wants to hear about. Socrates takes him on, and suggests that Gorgias explain to them what *rhetoric* is. The discussion becomes a more general examination of the nature of the good life, and as we might expect, Gorgias is no match for Socrates. Very quickly, he gets tangled up in his own definitions, and Socrates has little trouble throwing him verbally to the mat. Then one of Gorgias' disciples, a young man named Polus, steps in. He isn't really any brighter than Gorgias, but he is full of self-confident enthusiasm, and he manages a few tussles with Socrates before he too is thrown. Now the real antagonist steps forward. He is a gifted young man named Callicles, with a quick wit, a sharp mind, and much of the same

impatience that we saw at the beginning of this chapter in Thrasymachus. The remainder of the Dialogue is a knock-down, drag-out match
between Callicles and Socrates, and Plato puts so many good arguments
into Callicles' mouth that we cannot really say either man is the final
winner. During one of his several long speeches (Callicles tends to talk
too long, not answering Socrates' questions), Callicles ridicules Socrates
for spending his time philosophizing instead of engaging in grown-up
and manly pursuits, such as politics. Dramatically, this passage is an attack by Callicles on Socrates, but because Plato wrote both sides, he is
really arguing with himself about what he ought to do in his own life. As
you know, Plato decided to continue talking and writing philosophy, but
it is a part of his greatness that he can give such witty expression to the
opposing point of view.

> Here, then, you have the truth of the matter. You will become convinced
> of it if you only let philosophy alone and pass on to more important consider-
> ations. Of course, Socrates, philosophy does have a certain charm if one
> engages with it in one's youth and in moderation; but if one dallies overlong,
> it's the ruin of a fellow. If a man, however well endowed, goes on philoso-
> phizing throughout his life, he will never come to taste the experiences
> which a man must have if he's going to be a gentleman and have the world
> look up to him. You know perfectly well that philosophers know nothing
> about state laws and regulations. They are equally ignorant of the conversa-
> tional standards that we have to adopt in dealing with our fellow men at
> home and abroad. Why, they are inexperienced even in human pleasures
> and desires! In a word, they are totally innocent of all human character. So,
> when they come to take part in either a private or a public affair, they make
> themselves ridiculous—just as ridiculous, I dare say, as men of affairs may
> be when they get involved in your quibbles, your 'debates.' . . .
>
> But the best course, no doubt, is to be a participant in both. It's an
> excellent thing to grasp as much philosophy as one needs for an education,
> and it's no disgrace to play the philosopher while you're young; but if one
> grows up and becomes a man and still continues in the subject, why, the
> whole thing becomes ridiculous, Socrates. My own feeling toward its prac-
> titioners is very much the same as the way I feel toward men who lisp and
> prattle like a child. When I see a child, who ought to be talking that way,
> lisping and prattling, I'm pleased, it strikes me as a pleasant sign of good
> breeding and suitable to the child's age; and when I hear a little lad speaking
> distinctly, it seems to me disagreeable and offends my ears as a mark of
> servile origin. So, too, when I hear a grown man prattling and lisping, it
> seems ridiculous and unmanly; one would like to strike him hard! And this
> is exactly the feeling I have about students of philosophy. When I perceive

philosophical activity in a young lad, I am pleased; it suits him, I think, and shows that he has good breeding. A boy who doesn't play with philosophy I regard as illiberal, a chap who will never raise himself to any fine or noble action. Whereas when I see an older man still at his philosophy and showing no sign of giving it up, that one seems to me, Socrates, to be asking for some hard knocks! For, as I said just now, such a man, even if he's well endowed by nature, must necessarily become unmanly by avoiding the center of the city and the assemblies where as the Poet says, "men win distinction." Such a fellow must spend the rest of his life skulking in corners, whispering with two or three little lads, never pronouncing any large, liberal, or meaningful utterance.

—PLATO, *Gorgias*

Now that you are launched into the study of philosophy, it might help you to know what is coming up in the chapters ahead. Chapters Two, Three, Four, and Five are devoted to philosophical investigations of various aspects of the human condition, including ethics, social philosophy, political philosophy, and the philosophy of art. Chapter Six combines an examination of the nature and existence of God with an analysis of the personal nature of religious experience. Chapter Seven explores the efforts by the great philosophers of human knowledge to study the nature of the universe through an analysis of the cognitive powers of the human mind.

Finally, Chapter Eight introduces you to one of the most controversial topics in the branch of philosophy called "metaphysics," namely, the relation of the human mind to the human body.

At the end of each chapter, a special section contains a modern discussion of some immediate practical problem to which the philosophy of the chapter can contribute. In this way, you will learn how today's thinkers—both philosophers and nonphilosophers—try to bring the wisdom of philosophy to bear on our current concerns. Perhaps by the time you have finished reading this book, you will find new ways to make philosophy relevant to modern life.

The Main Points in Chapter One

1. The first great philosopher, Socrates, thought of philosophy as a process of critical self-examination, the purpose of which is to arrive at correct principles of judging, choosing, and acting.

2. The Socratic Method of question-and-answer uses *irony* to penetrate the defenses of those who do not wish to face the fact that they are ignorant or confused.

3. The two major traditions of philosophy are (a) the study of human nature and (b) the study of nature. The ancient philosophers who studied nature came up with very modern-sounding theories of atoms and their combinations.

4. In the seventeenth and eighteenth centuries, philosophers combined the two traditions of philosophy of studying human nature *in order* to discover the limits of our knowledge of nature. This new technique began with Descartes and was brought to its height by Kant.

5. There have always been philosophers who attacked philosophy, either for being concerned with unimportant subjects, or for raising pseudo-questions, or for serving as a justification of the existing political order. One of the most severe critics of philosophy in this century is the Austrian philosopher Wittgenstein.

Study Questions

1. These days, astronomers study the stars, physicists study subatomic particles, psychiatrists study the nature of the healthy personality, and neurophysiological psychologists study the relation between the physical and psychological aspects of personality. What is left for philosophers to do? Is philosophy an activity that has, over the past several centuries, put itself out of business?

2. The first great philosopher to make a living as a professor of philosophy was Immanuel Kant in the eighteenth century. These days, it seems, everyone who is considered a philosopher earns a living as a professor. Is there something odd, or inappropriate, about a philosopher being paid money to teach philosophy? If Socrates is right that no one can teach anyone else wisdom, what is it that philosophers teach?

3. The great seventeenth- and eighteen-century philosophers all thought that a study of human nature could reveal the limits and foundation of our knowledge of nature. How would they have responded to the possibility that there are rational, nonhuman forms

of life in the universe that have knowledge, but do not have a human nature?

4. It is pretty clear what you hope to get out of studying French, or physics, or history, or business administration. What can you hope to get out of studying philosophy? How can you tell whether you are getting out of philosophy what you hope to get? Is your grade in this course a good indicator? Why? Why not?

2

*ETHICS

IMMANUEL KANT (1724–1804) was born, lived out his life, and died in the provincial city of Königsberg in Prussia. Kant's early studies were concentrated in the areas of natural science, mathematics, and philosophy. At the University of Königsberg, he learned the philosophical theories of Leibniz, as they had been interpreted by a widely read German philosopher, Christian Wolff. After graduating from the university, Kant took a number of jobs as a tutor to children in the houses of Prussian aristocrats. Finally, he returned to the university to become what was called a *privatdozent*. This meant that he was licensed by the university to offer lectures, which the students could attend. But he was not paid by the university; instead, he had to collect fees from the students. The more popular he was, the more money he made! For more than a dozen years, Kant lectured as much as twenty-one hours a week on virtually every subject imaginable, from mathematics and logic to geography and history. Finally, in 1770, he was appointed to the position of Professor of Logic and Metaphysics.

Kant was already well known throughout Germany for his writings on physics, astronomy, and metaphysics, but his important work was still far in the future. For eleven years, from 1770 until 1781, he published virtually nothing. All that time, he was struggling with fundamental problems of human knowledge. Finally, in 1781, there appeared the book that was to revolutionize all philosophy: *The Critique of Pure Reason*. During the next ten years, book after book flowed from his pen. After the *Critique*, Kant published *Prolegomena to any Future Metaphysics* (1783), *The Groundwork of the Metaphysic of Morals* (1785), *Metaphysical Foundations of Natural Science* (1786), *Critique of Practical Reason* (1788), and the *Critique of Judgment* (1790).

Kant continued writing and revising his theories until finally, at the age of eighty, shortly after the start of the new century, he died. Though he had never left his native Königsberg, his mind had spanned all time and all space, and he had left an indelible mark on the thought of his civilization.

I   *Kant and the Commands of Duty*

Irwin Edman, a well-known early-twentieth-century Columbia University professor of philosophy, is said to have stopped a student on the street one day. "Excuse me," Edman said. "Can you tell me whether I am walking north or south?" The startled student replied, "You are walking south, Professor." "Ah, good," Edman replied. "Then I have already eaten lunch."

Well, it isn't much of a joke, and it has been told of half the professors in America, but it does capture the popular impression of philosophy professors as rather unworldly characters, out of touch with the real world—people, as American businesspeople are fond of saying, who have "never met a payroll."

Immanuel Kant is the greatest philosopher to live and write since the ancient times of Plato and Aristotle; he is the first great philosopher in modern times (after the end of the Middle Ages) to make his living as what we would call a professor of philosophy; and he is also about as close as any great philosopher has ever come to the standard caricature of the professor. Kant is said to have lived so regular and retiring a life that the townspeople of Königsberg, his lifelong home, could set their clocks by him as he went on his daily walk. One would expect a professorial type like Kant to make contributions to such abstruse technical fields as cosmology, metaphysics, or the theory of knowledge, and so he did. But it is rather surprising to discover that Kant also wrote profound, powerful, and deeply moving books on the problems of morality. Despite the uneventful regularity of his own private life, Kant was able to confront and grapple with the great issues of duty, right, justice, and virtue which have troubled the human soul since the ancient times recorded in the Old Testament. The contrast between Kant's outer life and his inner thoughts serves as a reminder to us that the greatness of a philosopher's insights cannot readily be measured by the external excitements of his or her life or times.

Kant was born on April 22, 1724 to a north Prussian family of modest means in the port city of Königsberg on the North Sea. Two centuries earlier, Luther had turned Central Europe upside down with his Reformation of the Catholic Church, and out of Luther's challenge to the institution of the papacy and to the rituals of medieval Christianity had sprung a number of Protestant sects. Kant's family belonged to the sect known as Pietism, an extremely individualistic form of Protestant Christianity which rejected the mystery, ritual, and ceremony that the Catholic Church had interposed between the ordinary Christian and his God. Pietism emphasized the direct, inner relationship of the individual worshipper to God. It placed a strong inner conscience and a stern self-control at the center of its religious doctrine. Kant's mother was particularly devout, and it was universally said of him that he owed both his religious faith and his overpowering sense of moral duty to her influence.

Although he was a believing Christian, Kant rejected the notion that religious doctrine could provide a foundation for morality. Quite to the contrary, he insisted that our moral principles must be established on purely rational grounds, open to criticism and capable of a defense as solid as that which philosophers offered for the principles of pure logic itself.

For Kant, the central question of morality was not, What should I do? This he firmly believed was perfectly well-known to every decent man and woman, whether a peasant or a professor. As he remarked at one point in his moral writings, the truths of **ethics** had been known for thousands of years, so that a moral philosopher could hardly expect to discover something *new* in ethics. Rather, Kant saw the real moral problem in the way that most Puritans and other individualistic Protestants did, as the constant struggle to do what we know is right in the face of temptations and distractions. The soldier who knows that his duty requires him to stand fast even as his fear tempts him to run; the merchant

An open-air market on Manhattan's West 14th Street. Every day, the fruit vendor must decide whether to cheat his customers or give fair measure from his scale. (Ellis Herwig/Taurus Photos)

who knows that she should give honest measure for honest measure in the marketplace, but nevertheless secretly wishes to tilt the scales in her own favor; the good husband who knows that his marriage vow is absolutely binding but feels the temptation of adultery—these and others like them are the men and women Kant has in mind when he writes on moral questions.

Kant was a student of the new science of Newton as well as a deeply committed Pietist. He saw a fundamental conflict between the scientific explanation of natural events, which emphasized their subordination to causal laws, and the moral assumption that we are free to choose our actions and hence are morally responsible for what we do. How can we demand that a person resist temptation and hold to the moral law if every action is merely another causally determined event in the universal natural order? How can we conceive of persons as free, responsible beings and yet also acknowledge their place in the system of events and objects studied by science?

Equally important to Kant, how can we prove, absolutely and without the slightest room for doubt or uncertainty, that the fundamental moral beliefs shared by all right-thinking persons are true, and not merely public opinion? As we saw in the first chapter, Kant insisted that even religion and morality submit to the spirit of *criticism*. The simple peasants and proud professors of north Prussia might believe that they knew the truth about ethics, but until they could produce a valid proof of their

> **Ethics**   In philosophy, the systematic study of how we ought to act, both toward ourselves and to others, and also the study of what things, character traits, or types of persons are good, estimable, admirable, and what kinds are bad, reprehensible, worthy of being condemned. Ethics deals both with general rules or principles, and also with particular cases.

beliefs, they would have no argument to offer against the skeptic, the relativist, the doubter who said that all opinions were equally good or even that there was no truth about ethics to be known at all.

Kant had some ideas about how to handle these two problems. He thought that he could work out a philosophical truce between ethics and science that would give each its rightful place in the totality of human knowledge; at the same time, he hoped to provide a proof of the fundamental principles of ethics. In this way, he would bring all the parts of his own life and work into harmony with one another. In his philosophical system, there would be a place for the devout faith imparted to him by his mother, a proof of the moral maxims he had grown up with and which to his death he never doubted, and a conceptual framework for the great new achievements of science and mathematics which so dominated the intellectual world of his day and to which he devoted so much of his own life and work. Kant's struggle to achieve a harmonious accommodation among his scientific interests, his moral convictions, and his religious faith was a model for many later struggles by other philosophers.

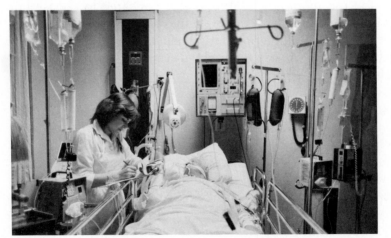

Modern medical technology enables doctors to prolong the lives of terminally ill patients. This poses difficult moral dilemmas for the doctors, the families of patients, and society. (Ken Karp)

Today more than ever, science seems to encroach upon religion and morality. New developments in behavioral psychology threaten our age-old belief in moral freedom. Though many philosophers have challenged Kant's solution, few would deny that he saw deeply into the problem and forced the rest of us to confront it as philosophers.

II Three Reasons to Think About Ethics

Having read this far into a chapter on ethics, some of you may have the feeling that you don't quite recognize the subject as one that you can relate yourself to. Perhaps Kant knew perfectly well what was right, but many of *us* are filled with doubts. Furthermore, you may want to say, his singleminded emphasis on duty, on conscience, on doing the *right* thing, misses the real flavor of much of our thinking about how to live our lives. The fact is that although this book contains only one chapter called Ethics, there are many quite different sorts of problems that have been discussed under that name since the time of the ancient Greeks. There is hardly enough room in a single chapter, let alone in one book, to talk about them all, but at least *three* are important enough to demand some extended examination.

Kant has already introduced us to the first reason that people worry about what is called Ethics, namely, a desire to discover an absolutely certain, irrefutable proof of the moral principles which we are already convinced are true. This proof serves two purposes: first, it answers the skeptic, who denies that there are any moral truths at all; and, second, it answers the relativist, who says, in effect, "Everyone's opinions are as good as everyone else's."

A second reason why people worry about ethics is that sometimes we get into situations in which we want to do the right thing but really don't know what it is. For example, a woman may find that she is pregnant and feel that to have a baby will simply turn her life inside out. Perhaps she wants to continue her studies in order to prepare for a career; perhaps the pregnancy is the result of a casual affair with a man whom she does not love; perhaps she and her husband already have as many children as they want and feel they can care for. Should she have an abortion? Part of her says that abortion is morally wrong; another part tells her that to have the baby would be wrong. She wants to do what is right, but she just doesn't know what *is* right in the situation.

Or a young man wants to leave home and start a life of his own, despite his parents' pleas that he remain with them and care for them. On the one hand, he feels love for his parents and a debt of gratitude and loyalty for all the years they have given to him. On the other hand, he knows that this is his only life, and that it is wrong for him to sacrifice it to the needs or demands of his parents. Again, he wants to do what is right, but he does not know whether he really has an obligation to stay at home, and if he does, for how long.

In philosophy, cases such as these are sometimes called "hard cases." They are real-life moral dilemmas in which ordinary moral opinions are either hopelessly contradictory or else just confused. Many philosophers have sought some method or rule by which we could decide hard cases, either by a process of moral reasoning or even by a sort of calculation. Genuine confusion rather than temptation is the motivation here, and frequently the emphasis is less on an absolutely rock-solid *proof* of things we already believe than it is on some genuinely new insight into an otherwise unsolvable dilemma.

But the oldest tradition of ethical reflection in Western thought has nothing to do with rights and duties, temptations and their denial, hard cases and tortured choices. For Plato, for Epicurus, for the ancient Stoics, and for countless philosophers since their time, Ethics has been concerned with the definition, analysis, search for, and achievement of the Good Life. Our stay on this earth is brief, the years pass faster and faster as we grow older, and all too soon we are forever dead. As we grow up and grow old, how shall we live our lives? What set of precepts, what style of inner feelings and outer relationships, what set of commitments will make us truly happy during the short passage of our lives? Should we strive to pile wealth upon wealth? fulfill our talents? aim for power and fame? retire to quiet contemplation? taste every experience, pleasurable or not, before death comes? Can reason and philosophy even help us in this choice? Or is the life of the mind itself just one path among many, and not the happiest at that?

Sometimes, when we say that someone lived a "good life" we mean that he or she experienced a great deal of pleasure—ate, drank, made merry. As it is said in Italian, such a person lived *la dolce vita*, the "sweet life." But just as often, we mean that the life was one of virtue, of service, of honor and dignity, that it was a life in which there was goodness. Many philosophers deliberately preserve this ambiguity because they believe that a truly happy life must also be a virtuous life, a life of goodness. Plato is perhaps the philosopher most often associated with this claim,

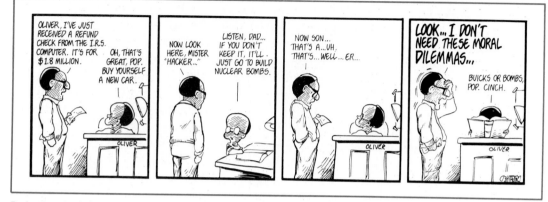

Berke Breathed, *Bloom County; Babylon, Five Years of Basic Naughtiness.* Copyright © 1986 by the Washington Post Company.

and we shall read something by him on the subject later on in this chapter. But many other philosophers have, in one way or another, made the same claim, among whom are such unlikely bedfellows as Confucius and Karl Marx.

Here, then, are three reasons for thinking about ethics—or better, three searches which are usually grouped under the heading "Ethics": the search for absolutely certain, universally valid first principles of conduct that can stand against the challenges of the skeptic and the relativist; the search for a method or process of reasoning to help us in deciding hard cases and other real-world moral choices; and the search for the good life, the life that combines virtue and happiness in true human fulfillment. Most of the remainder of this chapter will be devoted to a deeper examination of these three approaches to the subject of ethics.

III *Ethical Disagreement and the Categorical Imperative*

When we are very little, our parents stop us from doing things we shouldn't—hitting baby brother, eating paint, touching a wall plug—by physically pulling us away and saying "No!" in a loud, firm voice. You can't have a philosophical discussion with a two-year-old, as I was forced very quickly to recognize with my own two sons. As we grow older, we internalize those "No's" in the form of some set of rules, or norms, some conception of what is right and wrong. For a very long time, we simply accept these rules as given, a part of the world just as trees and tables, our parents and friends are a part of the world. Pretty early on, of course, we discover that not everyone abides all the time by the rules that our parents have taught us, but we can handle that fact, conceptually, by means of the category "bad." "Why can't I hit my brother? Tommy does." "Because it is wrong. Tommy is a bad boy, and I don't want you to be a bad boy like him."

So we grow older, with a more or less coherent moral code as part of our mental equipment. There are bad guys, naughty children, villains, criminals, but they are the "others," the ones who aren't nice, the sort of people *we* don't want to be like.

Then, one day, somewhere, there comes the great shock. It may be when we are still children, or when we go away to college, or when we move from a tight little homogeneous neighborhood to a big, heterogeneous city. It may simply be something we see on television. But all of a sudden, we encounter a whole group of people who seem to be good, decent, respectable, law-abiding, and upright, except that they call good what we call bad! We think it is good to fight for our country, and they think it is wicked. We think homosexuality is evil, and they think it is a perfectly acceptable lifestyle. They think abortion is a sensible technique for rational family planning and population control, and we call it murder.

This discovery, in whatever form it comes, is a genuine shock. The problem doesn't lie in the realization that some people do bad things. Ever since we saw Tommy hit his brother, we have known that. The real problem is that these people doing "bad" things and living by the "wrong" rules are *good* people. They are responsible; they are respected by their friends and neighbors. They may even be held up to children as models of virtue. And yet they do bad things! A man comes home from a war in which he gunned down two hundred defenseless women and children in a village, and he is paraded along Main Street as a hero. A mother and father refuse to allow their baby to receive medical treatment, the baby dies, and they are praised in their church as pillars of rectitude. A governor calls out the National Guard to shoot striking prison inmates, and he is immortalized in marble in front of the state capital.

If it is unsettling to encounter men and women within our own society whose moral codes differ markedly from our own, think how much more unsettling it is to discover whole cultures or civilizations in which

In big cosmopolitan cities, many peoples, cultures, and religions meet, sometimes in harmony, sometimes in conflict. (Clockwise from top: Eugene Gordon, United Nations, Eugene Gordon)

what we call virtue is despised as vice and what we condemn as wicked is celebrated as noble! Even a study of the history of the literate civilizations of the East and West provides countless examples of this sort of variation in moral beliefs. When the anthropologists' experiences with nonliterate cultures are added to our stock of information, it begins to appear that there isn't a single rule, precept, or moral belief that has been accepted by decent men and women everywhere. War? Torture? Child murder? Adultery? Suicide? Theft? Lying? Every single one has been condemned by some cultures and accepted, approved, or even praised by others.

There are basically three ways in which a philosopher can deal with the troublesome problem of the variation in moral codes from person to person, group to group, and culture to culture. The first way is to deny that the variation exists, despite appearances to the contrary. The second way is to admit that the variation exists and conclude that there are therefore no universally valid moral norms applicable to all persons in all places at all times. The third way is to acknowledge the variation but insist nonetheless that some moral principles are true and other supposed principles are false, no matter how many people believe them. Those who take this last route then do their best to provide some sort of proof for the principles they believe to be valid.

How can philosophers possibly maintain that there is no real disagreement about norms and moral principles, when the evidence of personal and cultural variation is all around them? Essentially, their tactic is to argue that when two people or two cultures seem to disagree about what is right or good, they are *really* only disagreeing about some of the facts of the case. If they could settle that disagreement, then it would turn out that they actually make the same moral judgments. For example, the Christian Scientist, like the nonbeliever, wants what is best for his sick child. But he firmly believes that the body is not real and that salvation depends upon holding firm to that belief. So for him to consent to an operation for his child would be as irresponsible (on his assessment of the facts) as for another parent to give a diabetic child all the candy she wants. To take another example, the culture that condemns abortion may believe that the fetus is already a person; the culture that approves abortion does not think the fetus is a person until after it is born. Both condemn murder, defined as the willful killing of a person, but they disagree on the factual question of whether abortion is murder.

A number of philosophers have taken this line, including the Scotsman David Hume whom you encountered in Chapter One. Anthropologists have actually carried out cross-country surveys of norms in an effort to discover any constants. Although it does appear that the ban or taboo on incest is widespread, the effort has essentially been a failure. There aren't any broad moral principles of justice, charity, equity, or benevolence which can be discovered in the moral systems of all cultures. (There is a much deeper question which we have not touched on yet. Even if there *were* universally accepted norms, what would that fact prove? Does everybody believing something make it right? Don't we need some justification for our moral convictions which goes beyond saying, "Everybody agrees with me?" This problem troubled Kant a great deal, and a bit later in this chapter, we shall see how he tried to deal with it.)

The second response to moral disagreement—the denial of objective, universal moral norms—has actually been relatively rare in the history of Western ethical theory, but it has had its defenders from the time of the ancient Greeks to the present day. Strictly speaking, there are two different forms of this position; the first, which can be called *ethical skepticism*, denies that we can have the slightest certainty about questions of the right and the good. Sometimes the ethical skeptic says that words like "right," "good," "ought", and "duty" just don't have any meaning; sentences containing them are a bit like incantations or cheers of approval or perhaps just plain gibberish. Because the very words we use to make moral judgments have no meaning, our moral judgments can hardly be called true or false, valid or invalid. At other times, the ethical skeptic merely points out that no valid argument can be found for any particular moral principle. If I doubt that murder is wrong, you cannot find an argument that will prove to me that it is. If I can't see why I should help another person in distress, there is no way it can be demonstrated to me that I should. Philosophers who take either of these lines frequently think that science and scientific language are the models on which we should base all of our knowledge. They point to the nondescriptive character of moral statements (they don't tell us how things are; they claim to tell us how things ought to be). They contrast the orderly experimentation and examination of data in the sciences with the haphazard, intuitive, unfactual character of moral disputes. Sometimes they suggest that moral arguments really come down to disagreements over matters of taste, and as the old saying has it, *de gustibus non disputandem est* (there is no disputing in matters of taste).

The *ethical skeptic* is sometimes joined in the fight against objective moral principles by the **ethical relativist**. How often, in a bull session, have we heard someone say, "Oh well, it's all relative!" Sometimes that means "Everyone *has* her own opinion." Sometimes it means "Everyone *is entitled* to her own opinion." But sometimes it means "Everyone's opinion is true to her, even though it may not be true for someone else." As a student said to me once in class when I asked whether he thought that Hitler had been wrong to kill millions of people in death camps, "Well, it wouldn't be right for me, but I guess it was right for him."

In the following passage, the American anthropologist Ruth Benedict draws on her wide knowledge of the varieties of human culture to argue for the fundamental relativity of moral judgments. There is something very unsettling about the fact that a scientist who has seen so much of human culture and society in all its forms should come to a relativist position.

> No one civilization can possibly utilize in its mores the whole potential range of human behavior. . . .
>
> Every society, beginning with some inclination in one direction or another, carries its preference farther and farther, integrating itself more and more completely upon its chosen basis, and discarding those types of behavior that are uncongenial. Most of those organizations of personality that seem to us more incontrovertibly abnormal have been used by different civilizations in the very foundations of their institutional life. Conversely the most valued traits of our normal individuals have been looked on in differently organized cultures as aberrant. Normality, in short, within a very wide range, is culturally defined. . . . The very eyes with which we see the problem are conditioned by the long traditional habits of our own society.
>
> It is a point that has been made more often in relation to ethics than in relation to psychiatry. We do not any longer make the mistake of deriving the morality of our own locality and decade directly from the inevitable constitution of human nature. We do not elevate it to the dignity of a first

Ethical Relativism   The theory that whether an act is right or wrong depends on—is relative to—the society in which one lives. Sometimes ethical relativists merely claim that we must take social contexts and rules into account, but sometimes they assert that one and the same act is right for men and women in one society and wrong for men and women in another. Frequently confused with *Ethical Skepticism*, which doubts that any acts are right or wrong, and *Ethical Nihilism*, which denies that any acts are either right or wrong.

principle. We recognize that morality differs in every society, and is a convenient term for socially approved habits. Mankind has always preferred to say, "It is morally good," rather than "It is habitual," and the fact of this preference is matter enough for a critical science of ethics. But historically the two phrases are synonymous.

—RUTH BENEDICT, *Anthropology and the Abnormal*

Immanuel Kant is the strongest opponent of the ethical relativist position. A major aim of Kant's philosophical efforts was to provide an absolutely solid, totally universal proof of the validity of that moral principle which he considered the foundation of all ethics, the principle which he called the **Categorical Imperative**. Kant was well aware that there were serious ethical disagreements among philosophers on particular questions of moral judgment, though he was not so impressed as Hume had been by the systematic cultural differences which appeared to divide "cultivated" peoples. But Kant was extremely concerned about the lack of solid foundations for even those ethical beliefs which were more or less broadly agreed upon. In a number of profound and very difficult treatises on ethics, Kant undertook to lay those foundations.

Saying just a few words about Kant's philosophy is like saying just a few words about quantum mechanics or the theory of relativity! Nevertheless, some of the key notions of Kant's moral philosophy can be understood pretty well without plunging into the depths of his argument, and in the remainder of this section, I shall introduce you to those notions through a combination of my exposition and Kant's own words.

Kant first set out his moral philosophy in a little book called *Groundwork of the Metaphysic of Morals* (a rather imposing title). He intended the book to be just an introduction to his theory, and shortly thereafter he published another, longer work called *Critique of Practical Reason*. But as often happens, the short "introductory" book took on a life of its own, and today it is widely viewed as the finest statement of Kant's position.

The aim of the *Groundwork* is to discover, analyze, and defend the fundamental principle of morality. As you know, Kant didn't think he had discovered a *new* principle, and he liked to say that his categorical imperative was nothing more than a philosophically more precise statement of the old Golden Rule: Do unto others as you would have others do unto you. Here is the way in which Kant revised and restated that rule:

Moses bringing the Ten Commandments to the Hebrews. Kant believed that the Golden Rule, "Do unto others as you would have others do unto you," is a summary statement of the Ten Commandments, and that his Categorical Imperative is simply a philosophical restatement of the Golden Rule. (The Bettman Archive)

THE CATEGORICAL IMPERATIVE

Act only on that maxim through which you can at the same time will that it should become a universal law.

That doesn't *look* much like the Golden Rule, but Kant thought it contained the same basic notion, which is that we ought to put aside our own private interests and act instead on the basis of rules that would be equally reasonable for all moral agents to adopt as their own. "Do unto others as you would have others do unto you" doesn't mean "Go ahead and steal from your neighbor so long as you don't squawk when he steals from you." It means something more like "Treat other people with the same respect and dignity that you expect to be treated with." As we shall see, the idea of human dignity plays a central role in Kant's moral philosophy.

There are three ideas that lie at the heart of Kant's ethics. If we can understand something about each of them, we can form at least a preliminary notion of his theory. The ideas are, first, that persons are rational creatures, capable of thinking about the choices they face and selecting among them on the basis of reasons; second, that persons have an infinite worth or dignity which sets them above all merely condition-

> **Categorical Imperative**   A term invented by Immanuel Kant to refer to a command that orders us to do something unconditionally—that is, regardless of what we want or what our aims and purposes are. According to Kant, we experience the principles of morality as Categorical Imperatives. The term is also used, by Kant and those following him, to refer to one particular moral principle, which Kant calls The Highest Moral Law.

ally valuable things in this world, that they are what Kant calls ends-in-themselves; and, third, that persons, as rational ends-in-themselves, are the *authors* of the moral law, so that their obedience to duty is not an act of slavish submission but an act of dignified *autonomy*. Persons as rational agents, persons as ends-in-themselves, and persons as autonomous—these are the basic building blocks out of which Kant constructs his proof of the Categorical Imperative.

When Kant asserts that persons are rational agents, he means more than merely that they are capable of making judgments about the nature of the world, or inferences from one set of propositions to another. A rational agent is a person who is capable of *moving himself or herself to act* by reason. David Hume, like many other philosophers, had thought that reason was incapable of moving us to action. Hume argued that *desire* moved us to act; reason could merely point out the most efficient path to the goal that desire chose. So Hume said, in a much-quoted passage, that "reason is, and ought only to be the slave of the passions, and can never pretend to any other office than to serve and obey them" (*Treatise of Human Nature*, Book III). Kant replied that if we are to make any sense at all out of our condition as creatures capable of choice and deliberation, we must acknowledge that we can be moved by *reasons*, not merely by *desires*.

If Kant is right that we can be moved by reason, then it makes sense to ask whether we have acted wisely or foolishly, whether we have reasoned consistently in our choice of ends and means. It makes sense, also, to ask whether in our reasoning we have taken special account of our own particular wishes and interests, or instead have limited ourselves only to reasons which would be compelling reasons for any person in the same circumstances. In short, it makes sense to ask whether we have acted *rationally*.

This notion of "reasons good for all rational agents" is a difficult one

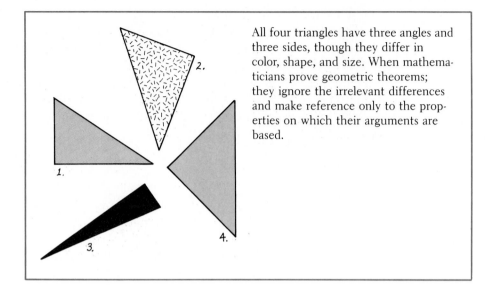

All four triangles have three angles and three sides, though they differ in color, shape, and size. When mathematicians prove geometric theorems; they ignore the irrelevant differences and make reference only to the properties on which their arguments are based.

to grasp. Perhaps one way to get some idea of Kant's meaning is to compare a moral agent to a mathematician doing a geometry problem. Suppose the mathematician is trying to show that the square of the hypotenuse of a right triangle is equal to the sum of the squares of the other two sides (the so-called Pythagorean theorem that some of you studied in high school). Now, the first thing she does in developing the proof is to draw a triangle, and because every triangle has to be some size and shape or other, the particular triangle the mathematician draws will be some particular size (maybe 4½ inches by 6 inches by 7½ inches), and it will also be some particular color (depending upon the color of the paper she draws it on), and so forth. But of course she isn't supposed to pay any attention to the actual size and color of the triangle. They are there, all right, but she is supposed to ignore them. The only thing she is allowed to count in her proof is the fact that the triangle has a right angle in it. If our imaginary mathematician constructs her proof by using only the fact that her triangle is a right triangle, then her conclusions, when she gets them, will apply to *all* right triangles, not just to the one she actually drew.

In the same way, Kant claims that moral agents, when they reason about what they ought to do, should ignore all the particular facts about their own interests, special desires, individual circumstances, and so on, and concentrate just on those facts which hold for *all* rational agents as such. If they do that, he says, then the conclusions they come to will be valid for all rational agents, not just for themselves. In short, their conclusions will be universal laws, not just personal rules. Kant uses the word "maxim" to mean a personal rule on which we actually base our decisions. (In the following selection, he also uses the term "subjective principle" with this meaning.) So he is telling us that when we make our decisions, we, like the mathematician, should restrict ourselves to rules, or maxims, that could just as well serve any rational agent. In other words, he tells us to restrict ourselves to maxims that could serve as universal laws. That is what he is trying to say in the Categorical Imperative: Act only on that maxim through which you can at the same time will that it should become a universal law.

If we do succeed in acting in a genuinely rational way, Kant says, we show ourselves to possess a dignity that sets us above everything else in the world. Indeed, the statement that moral agents, as persons, have an infinite worth or dignity, is, according to Kant, just another way of saying what has already been said in the Categorical Imperative. Here is the famous passage in which Kant develops the notion that persons are ends-in-themselves. Difficult as Kant's argument is, I think you will be able to see in it something of the grandeur and profundity which made Kant so great a moral philosopher:

> Now I say that man, and in general every rational being, *exists* as an end in himself, *not merely as a means* for arbitrary use by this or that will: he must in all his actions, whether they are directed to himself or to other rational beings, always be viewed *at the same time as an end.* All the objects of inclination have only a conditioned value; for if there were not these inclinations and the needs grounded on them, their object would be valueless. Inclinations themselves, as sources of needs, are so far from having an absolute value to make them desirable for their own sake that it must rather be the universal wish of every rational being to be wholly free from them. Thus the value of all objects that can *be produced* by our action is always conditioned. Beings whose existence depends, not on our will, but on nature, have none the less, if they are non-rational beings, only a relative value as means and are consequently called *things.* Rational beings, on the other hand, are called *persons* because their nature already marks them out as ends in themselves and consequently imposes to that extent a limit on all arbitrary treatment of them (and is an object of reverence). Persons, therefore, are not merely subjective ends whose existence as an object of our actions has a value *for us*: they are *objective ends*—that is, things whose existence is in itself an end, and indeed an end such that in its place we can put no other end to which they should serve *simply* as means; for unless this is so, nothing at all of *absolute* value would be found anywhere. But if all value

were conditioned then no supreme principle could be found for reason at all.

If then there is to be a supreme practical principle and a categorical imperative, it must be such that from the idea of something which is necessarily an end for every one because it is an *end in itself* it forms an *objective* principle of the will and consequently can serve as a practical law. The ground of this principle is: *Rational nature exists as an end in itself.* This is the way in which a man necessarily conceives his own existence: it is therefore so far a *subjective* principle of human actions. But it is also the way in which every other rational being conceives his existence on the same rational ground which is valid also for me; hence it is at the same time an *objective* principle, from which, as a supreme practical ground, it must be possible to derive all laws for the will. The practical imperative will therefore be as follows: *Act in such a way that you always treat humanity, whether in your own person or in the person of any other, never simply as a means, but always at the same time as an end.*

—IMMANUEL KANT, *Groundwork of the Metaphysic of Morals*

Hume had described reason as the "slave" of the passions, subservient to their direction. Kant is the sworn foe of such slavery, as he was of slavery in the political realm. If my reason is the slave of my passions, then I forfeit the dignity that I possess in virtue of being an end-in-myself. There is no honor in subservience to passion, any more than in subservience to a king or emperor. In the inner life of each man and woman, as in the public life of the State, honor is to be found only in submission to self-made laws. The citizen of a republic, who makes the laws to which he bows his head, loses no dignity by his obedience, for he is obeying only himself when he abides by the law. His obedience is an act of responsibility rather than of servitude.

The same principle, Kant thought, holds true within the individual soul. When reason bows to passion, it forfeits its claim to honor and dignity. But if reason can itself legislate the laws to which it submits, if reason can itself write the Categorical Imperative that binds it, then it will preserve its freedom in the very act of submission. To give laws to oneself is, following the Greek, to be *auto-nomos*—giver of law to oneself—in short: autonomous. The principle of the autonomy of reason is, Kant says, yet another version of the Categorical Imperative.

Having set forth three key principles—(1) the rationality of the will, (2) the infinite worth of persons as ends-in-themselves, and (3) the self-legislating, or autonomous, character of reason—Kant now pulls them all together in the notion of a society of moral agents, all of whom govern their actions by reason, all of whom are ends-in-themselves, and all of whom are autonomous. He calls this society a *kingdom of ends*, and we can imagine it as an ideal community of upright, responsible, rational men and women who base their actions on universally valid laws which they autonomously lay down for themselves. It is a community that lives according to the Categorical Imperative. In our last passage from Kant, we see all of these themes united:

> In the kingdom of ends everything has either a *price* or a *dignity*. If it has a price, something else can be put in its place as an equivalent; if it is exalted above all price and so admits of no equivalent, then it has a dignity.
>
> What is relative to universal human inclinations and needs has a *market price*; what, even without presupposing a need, accords with a certain taste has a *fancy price* (*Affektionspreis*); but that which constitutes the sole condition under which anything can be an end in itself has not merely a relative value but has an intrinsic value—that is, *dignity*.
>
> Now morality is the only condition under which a rational being can be an end in himself; for only through this is it possible to be a lawmaking member in a kingdom of ends. Therefore morality, and humanity so far as it is capable of morality, is the only thing which has dignity. Skill and diligence in work have a market price; wit, lively imagination, and humour have a fancy price; but fidelity to promises and kindness based on principle (not on instinct) have an intrinsic worth. In default of these, nature and art alike contain nothing to put in their place; for their worth consists, not in the effects which result from them, not in the advantage or profit they produce, but in the attitudes of mind which are ready in this way to manifest themselves in action even if they are not favoured by success. Such actions too need no recommendation from any subjective disposition or taste in order to meet with immediate favour and approval; they need no immediate propensity or feeling for themselves; they exhibit the will which performs them as an object of immediate reverence; nor is anything other than reason required to *impose* them upon the will, nor to *coax* them from the will—which last would anyhow be a contradiction in the case of duties. This assessment reveals as dignity the value of such a mental attitude and puts it infinitely above all price, with which it cannot be brought into reckoning or comparison without, as it were, a profanation of its sanctity.
>
> What is it then that entitles a morally good attitude of mind to make claims so high? It is nothing less than the *share* which it affords to a rational being *in the making of universal law*, and which therefore fits him to be a member in a possible kingdom of ends. For this he was already marked out in virtue of his own proper nature as an end in himself and consequently as a maker of laws in the kingdom of ends—as free in respect of all laws of nature, obeying only those laws which he makes himself and in virtue of

which his maxims can have their part in the making of universal law (to which he at the same time subjects himself). For nothing can have a value other than that determined for it by the law. But the law-making which determines all value must for this reason have a dignity for the appreciation of which, as necessarily given by a rational being, the word *'reverence'* is the only becoming expression. *Autonomy* is therefore the ground of the dignity of human nature and of every rational nature.

—IMMANUEL KANT, *Groundwork of the Metaphysic of Morals*

IV   *Utilitarianism and the Calculation of Pleasures and Pains*

How shall we deal with those terrible situations in which we want very much to do the right thing but simply cannot figure out what it is? Sometimes, there are two different and conflicting things, both of which seem right in the situation. Sometimes the situation is such a tangle that we are just at a loss. The source of our uncertainty is not temptation, or skepticism, or relativism, but the genuine moral difficulty of the case itself. One of the most ancient attempts to deal with such hard cases, and also to lay down a rule for action which will always tell us what we ought to do, is the moral philosophy which these days goes under the name of **utilitarianism**. In this section, we are going to take a look at several varieties of utilitarianism, see what the theory says and how it works, and also consider some serious objections to it.

Utilitarianism is simply the rule that we should always try to make as many people as happy as possible. Indeed, it is sometimes called The Greatest Happiness Principle for this reason. The cosmologist Lucretius was a utilitarian, and so was the man whose teachings he followed, Epicurus. In the modern world, the most famous utilitarian, generally credited with establishing the doctrine as a serious contender in moral philosophy, was the eighteenth-century Englishman Jeremy Bentham.

Bentham argues that however people may appear to use the words "good" and "evil," they really just mean "pleasant" or "pleasurable" when they say "good" and "painful" when they say "evil." More good is better than less, which is to say that more pleasure is better than less. And, of course, less pain is better than more. The only good reason for doing anything is to increase the amount of pleasure that human beings experience, or at least reduce the amount of pain. What is more, plea-sures and pains can, in a manner of speaking, be added to and subtracted from one another. I can ask myself, Which gave me more pleasure: the good movie I saw last week or the mediocre movie I saw last night plus the really good pizza I had afterward? I can also ask myself, which will be more painful: three dentist's visits now, complete with drillings, or a toothache followed by an extraction followed by the annoyance of a miss-ing tooth later? If the mediocre movie plus the pizza gave me more plea-sure, then the next time I have to choose between a good movie and no pizza or a mediocre movie and pizza, I ought to take the mediocre movie plus pizza. And, more seriously, if the dentist's visits, bad as they are, add up to less pain than the rotting of my tooth, then I ought to go to the dentist even though I don't want to, because the only rational thing to do is to minimize the total amount of pain in my life.

Bentham announced the doctrine now known as utilitarianism in a book entitled *Introduction to the Principles of Morals and Legislation*, first printed in 1780 and formally published in 1789. Here is a selection from the opening chapter. Notice the complete identification of pleasure with good and pain with evil. This is the heart and soul of Bentham's utilitar-ian doctrine.

Nature has placed mankind under the governance of two sovereign masters, *pain* and *pleasure*. It is for them alone to point out what we ought to do, as well as to determine what we shall do. On the one hand the standard of right and wrong, on the other the chain of causes and effects, are fastened to their throne. They govern us in all we do, in all we say, in all we think: every effort we can make to throw off our subjection, will serve but to dem-onstrate and confirm it. In words a man may pretend to abjure their empire: but in reality he will remain subject to it all the while. The *principle of utility* recognizes this subjection, and assumes it for the foundation of that system, the object of which is to rear the fabric of felicity by the hands of reason and law. Systems which attempt to question it, deal in sounds instead of sense, in caprice instead of reason, in darkness instead of light.

But enough of metaphor and declamation: it is not by such means that moral science is to be improved.

The principle of utility is the foundation of the present work: it will be proper therefore at the outset to give an explicit and determinate account of what is meant by it. By the principle of utility is meant that principle which approves or disapproves of every action whatsoever, according to the tendency which it appears to have to augment or diminish the happiness of the party whose interest is in question: or, what is the same thing in other

words, to promote or to oppose that happiness. I say of every action whatsoever; and therefore not only of every action of a private individual, but of
every measure of government.

By utility is meant that property in any object, whereby it tends to produce benefit, advantage, pleasure, good, or happiness (all this in the present
case comes to the same thing) or (what comes again to the same thing) to
prevent the happening of mischief, pain, evil, or unhappiness to the party
whose interest is considered: if that party be the community in general,
then the happiness of the community; if a particular individual, then the
happiness of that individual.

The interest of the community is one of the most general expressions
that can occur in the phraseology of morals: no wonder that the meaning
of it is often lost. When it has a meaning, it is this. The community is a
fictitious *body*, composed of the individual persons who are considered as
constituting as it were its *members*. The interest of the community then is,
what?—the sum of the interests of the several members who compose it.

It is in vain to talk of the interest of the community, without understanding what is the interest of the individual. A thing is said to promote
the interest, or to be *for* the interest, of an individual, when it tends to add
to the sum total of his pleasures: or what comes to the same thing, to diminish the sum total of his pains.

An action then may be said to be conformable to the principle of utility,
or, for shortness sake, to utility, (meaning with respect to the community at
large) when the tendency it has to augment the happiness of the community
is greater than any it has to diminish it.

A measure of government (which is but a particular kind of action, performed by a particular person or persons) may be said to be conformable to
or dictated by the principle of utility, when in like manner the tendency
which it has to augment the happiness of the community is greater than
any which it has to diminish it.

—JEREMY BENTHAM,
An Introduction to the Principles of Morals and Legislation

The crucial step in Bentham's argument is his move from the total
pleasure and pain experienced by one person to the total pleasure or
pain experienced by all the members of the community taken together.
This is the device which permits Bentham to extract a moral principle
from his theory. The point is that whenever I do anything at all, my
action has effects which impinge on the lives of other people. Sometimes
I cause them pleasure, sometimes I cause them pain, and sometimes of
course I cause some of them pleasure and others pain. For example, if
the young man we mentioned earlier decides to stay at home with his

JEREMY BENTHAM (1748–1832) was the founder of the ethical doctrine now known as utilitarianism. He began his long life during the reign of King George II, and died in the year of the Reform Bill that extended the franchise to virtually all of middle-class England. He lived through the American Revolution, the French Revolution, the Napoleonic wars, and the rise of parliamentary government in England, and he nearly survived into the reign of Queen Victoria. He was the godfather of John Stuart Mill, son of his friend and colleague James Mill. John Stuart was, in his own turn, the godfather of Bertrand Russell, the great English philosopher who near the end of his own long and distinguished life led the British campaign for nuclear disarmament in the 1960s. So in three generations of great English philosophers, we move from the mid-eighteenth-century world of wigs, carriages, and kings, to the mid-twentieth-century world of jets, nuclear weapons, and popular democracy.

Bentham's primary concern as a philosopher was with legal and social reform. The law in the eighteenth century was a crazy quilt of precedents, quibbles, hanging offenses, and rank injustices. Several of Bentham's books were devoted to the attempt to sort things out and find some rational system of principles to put in place of the tangle that had grown up over so many centuries. He hoped that his simple, intuitively appealing principle of utility—the Greatest Happiness of the Greatest Number—would serve as the basis for a thoroughgoing reform of the law.

To Leave Home or Not to Leave Home: A Utilitarian Calculation

If I Leave	Units of Pleasure	If I Don't Leave	Units of Pleasure
1. Independence	+ 1000	1. Lack of independence	− 1000
2. Loneliness	− 200	2. Parents' happiness	+ 2000
3. Parents' unhappiness	− 1000	3. No personal growth	− 600
4. New experiences	+ 350	4. Family wrangling	− 250
5. Setting a good example for younger sister	+ 400	5. Financial burden on parents	− 400
The utility of leaving	+ 550	The utility of staying	− 250

+550 IS GREATER THAN −250. THEREFORE, I LEAVE

According to Bentham, the rational person will choose the alternative that offers the greatest total of pleasure. Does anyone ever make an important decision this way? Would you?

parents rather than leave and set out on his own, he will probably cause himself pain and his mother and father pleasure. That is just why he doesn't know what to do! If his staying at home caused his parents pain too (they, after all, might want to live their own lives), then the decision would be an easy one for him.

Whenever we face hard choices, Bentham tells us, we can translate an impossible moral dilemma into a problem of addition and subtraction. For the young man, the choice is between staying home with his parents and leaving. He adds up all the pleasure and pain (negative values for pain, of course) that anybody in the situation will experience as the result of his staying and compares it with the total pleasure and pain that everyone will experience as a result of his leaving home. He then chooses the alternative with the highest positive total (or, if it is one of those "least of evils" situations, the alternative with the smallest negative total). For example, suppose that the young man desperately wants to leave home. Then we can assume that he will suffer great pain if he must stay, and he will gain great pleasure if he goes. Let us also assume that his parents would like him to stay at home, but they are not dead set on it. They will manage all right if he leaves. Now we have great pain plus moderate pleasure on the side of staying, and great pleasure plus moderate pain on the side of going. Obviously, this adds up to a decision to go.

A great many objections can be raised to utilitarianism, and I am about to raise several of the more serious ones. But before we start chopping this theory down, it is worth taking a few moments to look at its very considerable strengths. In the first place, utilitarianism assumes that everyone wants to be happy, and it is hard to argue with that. But even more important, utilitarianism explains happiness in terms that everyone can understand. It doesn't say that happiness is oneness with the infinite, or self-fulfillment, or the integration of adult roles with childhood ego formations, or what have you. It says that happiness is pleasure, unhappiness is pain, and the more pleasure or the less pain the better.

Nor does utilitarianism demand strange, painful sacrifices from its believers. Kant believed, for example, that we should keep our promises and tell the truth no matter who gets hurt. That is a dark saying, fraught with potentiality for terrible choices where lives are lost or hideous pain inflicted simply because someone will not violate an absolute moral rule. But Bentham says nothing of that sort. By all means lie, he says, if the total pain produced by the truth is greater than that produced by the lie. Make sure to add in the side effects of the lie, such as the likelihood that the next time you tell the truth it won't be believed. But when all those long-term, short-term, direct, and indirect effects have been calculated, then just choose the course promising the greatest happiness for the greatest number of people.

The most impressive strength of utilitarianism is its ability to trans-

The ancient Egyptians were forced to re-survey their fields each year after the Nile River overflowed its banks. This practical problem led them to make important advances in mathematics. (The Bettmann Archive)

Act Utilitarianism/Rule Utilitarianism   Utilitarianism is the moral theory that holds that everyone—private individuals or lawmaking governments—should always seek to produce the greatest happiness for the greatest number of people. *Act Utilitarianism* asserts that each of us should use this rule in choosing every single act that we perform, regardless of whether we are private citizens or legislators making general laws for a whole society. *Rule Utilitarianism* says that governments should use this rule in choosing the general laws they enact, but then should simply treat individuals fairly according to the existing rules, with like cases handled in a like manner.

form seemingly impossible problems of moral deliberation into manageable empirical problems of investigation and addition. To see what that means, imagine that we lived a long time ago in an agricultural society which had not yet discovered geometry. Each year, as the flood waters from the river receded, it would become necessary to divide up the land again for the spring planting. The plots all must be triangular (owing to some religious belief, we may suppose). The high priest would stake out each family's land, and then the arguing would begin over whose plot was bigger, and who had been slighted in the dividing up. The wise men would gather, great deliberations would ensue, with much prayer and meditation, and in the end no one would really be satisfied with the high priest's decisions. Now just think what it would mean, in such a society, for someone to discover the simple geometric theorem that the area of a triangle is equal to one-half the base times the height! All those moral and religious disputes would be dissolved in an instant into a process of calculation. The royal surveyor would just measure the bases of the family plots, multiply by their heights (the plots' not the families'), and then make adjustments until each family had the same area. It would put the royal moral philosopher and the royal priest out of business!

Well, Bentham had hopes that his Great Happiness Principle would do the same for the modern wizards who in his own society did the job of the ancient priests and moral philosophers—namely, the judges and lawyers. He believed that rational legislators, with the principle of utility to guide them, could replace the hideous tangle of laws and punishments of the English common law with a single reasonable schedule of punishments designed to produce the greatest happiness for the greatest number. Where the legislators lacked enough facts to make a sensible deci-

A satirical drawing of a trial in eighteenth century England. Bentham hoped to correct the abuses of the English legal system. (The Bettmann Archive)

sion, instead of digging around in their law books for precedents and corollary cases, they could go out and collect some facts to settle the matter. Here is another selection from Bentham's *Principles* which shows how he hoped to use the Greatest Happiness Principle in practice:

1. The general object which all laws have, or ought to have, in common, is to augment the total happiness of the community; and therefore, in the first place, to exclude, as far as may be, every thing that tends to subtract from that happiness: in other words, to exclude mischief.

2. But all punishment is mischief: all punishment in itself is evil. Upon the principle of utility, if it ought at all to be admitted, it ought only to be admitted in as far as it promises to exclude some greater evil.

3. It is plain, therefore, that in the following cases punishment ought not to be inflicted.

1. Where it is *groundless*; where there is no mischief for it to prevent: the act not being mischievous upon the whole.

2. Where it must be *inefficacious*: where it cannot act so as to prevent the mischief.

3. Where it is *unprofitable,* or too *expensive*: where the mischief it would produce would be greater than what it prevented.

4. Where it is *needless*: where the mischief may be prevented, or cease of itself, without it: that is, at a cheaper rate. . . .

CASES WHERE PUNISHMENT IS UNPROFITABLE

These are,

1. Where, on the one hand, the nature of the offence, on the other hand, that of the punishment, are, *in the ordinary state of things,* such, that when compared together, the evil of the latter will turn out to be greater than that of the former.

Now the evil of the punishment divides itself into four branches, by which so many different sets of persons are affected. 1. The evil of *coercion* or *restraint*: or the pain which it gives a man not to be able to do the act, whatever it be, which by the apprehension of the punishment he is deterred from doing. This is felt by those by whom the law is *observed*. 2. The evil of *apprehension*: or the pain which a man, who has exposed himself to punishment, feels at the thoughts of undergoing it. This is felt by those by whom the law has been *broken*, and who feel themselves in *danger* of its being executed upon them. 3. The evil of *sufferance*: or the pain which a man feels, in virtue of the punishment itself, from the time when he begins to undergo it. This is felt by those by whom the law is broken, and upon whom it comes actually to be executed. 4. The pain of sympathy, and the other *derivative* evils resulting to the persons who are in *connection* with the several classes of original sufferers just mentioned. Now of these four lots of evil, the first will be greater or less, according to the nature of the act from which the party is restrained: the second and third according to the nature of the punishment which stands annexed to that offence.

On the other hand, as to the evil of the offence, this will also, of course, be greater or less, according to the nature of the offence. The proportion between the one evil and the other will therefore be different in the case of each particular offence. The cases, therefore, where punishment is unprofitable on this ground, can by no other means be discovered, than by an examination of each particular offence; which is what will be the business of the body of the work.

2. Where, although in the *ordinary state* of things, the evil resulting from the punishment is not greater than the benefit which is likely to result from the force with which it operates, during the same space of time, towards the excluding the evil of the offence, yet it may have been rendered

so by the influence of some *occasional circumstances*. In the number of these circumstances may be, 1. The multitude of delinquents at a particular juncture; being such as would increase, beyond the ordinary measure, the *quantum* of the second and third lots, and thereby also of a part of the fourth lot, in the evil of the punishment. 2. The extraordinary value of the services of some one delinquent; in the case where the effect of the punishment would be to deprive the community of the benefit of those services. 3. The displeasure of the *people*; that is, of an indefinite number of the members of the *same* community, in cases where (owing to the influence of some occasional incident) they happen to conceive, that the offence or the offender ought not to be punished at all, or at least ought not to be punished in the way in question. 4. The displeasure of *foreign powers*; that is, of the governing body, or a considerable number of the members of some *foreign* community or communities, with which the community in question, is connected.

—JEREMY BENTHAM,
An Introduction to the Principles of Morals and Legislation

Utilitarianism has probably had more words written about it than all the other moral theories put together. It is a clear, simple, natural-sounding moral philosophy, and it has a thousand things wrong with it as a theory! That is a perfect formula for a philosophical argument. Two sorts of objections turn up over and over again in philosophical discussions. First, critics say that although utilitarianism looks clear and simple, it is actually so confused that we can't tell exactly what it says. And, second, these same critics argue that, even after we have decided what utilitarianism says, we find that it tells us to do things that most of us would consider deeply immoral. Let us take a look at both of these objections.

What does utilitarianism say? Very simple: maximize happiness. But what exactly does that mean? The most natural answer is, add up all the pleasure experienced by all the people in the world, subtract all the pain they suffer, and that is the total. Then anything that increases the total is good, anything that decreases it is bad, and if two actions promise to increase the total, the one that offers a bigger increase is just that much better. What could be clearer?

Ah well. A little philosophy teaches us that a trap very often lurks in even the simplest-looking statement. If *total* happiness is all that counts, then a world with a *billion* slightly happy people will be morally better than a world with a *million* extremely happy people. The point is that if the very happy people are only five hundred times happier than the marginally happy people, then one billion times the small happiness in the first world will be a bigger total than one million times the tremendous happiness in the second world. Something is obviously wrong with that conclusion. In an already overcrowded world, it makes no sense to go on increasing the population as long as each additional person can be said to experience a slight balance of pleasure over pain. Surely Bentham wasn't merely arguing for a population explosion.

So maybe what he really meant was to maximize the *average* happiness experienced by the people already on this earth. That makes a good deal more sense. A world of a million very happy people is obviously preferable to a world of a billion marginally happy people, because in the first world, the *level* of happiness—in other words, the average—is higher. And it is the level of happiness we are really interested in.

But once again, serious problems arise. Suppose we can make some people very happy indeed by making other people miserable. That isn't an implausible hypothesis at all. Slavery is a social system which lays the burden of work and suffering on one group—the slaves—so that another group—the masters—can lead easy, comfortable lives. (So is capitalism, but we shall get to that in the next chapter.) Is Bentham really in favor of slavery?

Bentham has an answer, of sorts. His principle, he claims, calls for "the greatest happiness of all those whose interest is in question." Because everyone (even a slave) is someone whose interest is in question, it follows that utilitarianism calls for the greatest possible happiness for everyone, not just the greatest happiness for the slave-owners, or the capitalists, or the rulers. Now the trouble with this interpretation of the Principle of Utility is that on closer examination, it turns out not to be any sort of rule at all.

Sometimes, life offers me a way to make everybody happier at the same time, and obviously when a chance like that comes along, I take it. Too often, life offers me a way to make everybody unhappier at the same time, and if I have any sense at all, I stay away from chances like that. But most of the time, what I do will make some people happier and other people unhappier. Remember the young man trying to decide whether to leave his parents? His first choice, to stay home, makes his parents happier and him unhappier. His second choice, to leave, makes him happier and his parents unhappier. There just isn't any way to make all of them happier at the same time. That is precisely why it is a hard case. Now, we don't need Bentham to tell us what to do on those rare occasions when we can make everyone happier simultaneously. But utilitarianism is supposed to give us a rule, a method, for handling just the hard-to-decide cases in which one person's happiness has to be balanced off against another person's unhappiness. Plausible as "the greatest happiness for the greatest number" sounds, it doesn't work out in practice to be a rule that is going to settle any hard cases for us.

Suppose we go back therefore to the notion of the greatest average happiness. (Notice, by the way, that if you keep the population stable, greatest average happiness is exactly equal to greatest total happiness, so that is probably what Bentham has in mind.) How does that stand up as a rule for deciding what to do? At least it is unambiguous; if we have enough information to predict the outcomes of our actions, then we can add up the pleasures, subtract the pains, divide by the total population, and get some sort of average. But now we run into the second sort of objection to utilitarianism—namely, that it tells us to do things that seem immoral.

Once again, the problem is making some people suffer so that others may be happy. Let me sketch out a bizarre example that will help to make this point. Suppose that Americans, like the ancient Romans, positively enjoyed watching people being tortured. (Naturally, such an assumption is totally contrary to the real facts, because American taste in movies, television shows, and novels shows that we are all kindly, peace-loving, sympathetic creatures who hate the sight of violence!) Now Bentham will obviously believe that torture is an evil to the person who suffers it, for torture is painful, and pain is evil. But the pleasure that a group of sadists gets from watching the torture is good, for pleasure, says Bentham, is good. So for a utilitarian, torture can be justified when the total pleasure produced outweighs the total pain produced, including side effects, long-run effects, and so forth. What is more, if torture produces, in total and on balance, greater happiness than any other alternative open to us, then it is the positively right thing to do, according to utilitarianism.

We shall therefore institute a new TV show called "Torture of the Week." This is a live show in which real victims really do get tortured. (Sadists get little or no pleasure from watching simulated torture.) The victims are simply snatched off the street by force (no one except a masochist is going to offer himself as a victim, and real sadists don't enjoy watching masochists undergo torture). According to utilitarianism, if there are enough viewers who are ecstatic at the sight of this torture, then their pleasure must outweigh the pain suffered by the victim. And if no other show on television has anything resembling its high ratings, then we can assume that putting on the torture show is not only justified, but positively morally obligatory!

Just to handle an obvious objection, let us also assume that a board of social psychologists concludes that the torture show does not increase the probability of violent crime in the society. Indeed, it may even decrease such crime, by offering an outlet for sadistic desires. In short, assume that from any point of view, this torture show meets the criterion of the Principle of Utility.

What is wrong with this proposal? Don't tell me that there aren't enough people around who would enjoy the show. The point of the example was to show that according to utilitarianism the show *would* be right if there *were* such people in America. Besides, we could always increase the pleasure product by beaming the show overseas so that sadists all over the world could watch it. And don't tell me that the pain of the victim's suffering outweighs the pleasure of millions of sadistic viewers. That is implausible, and what is more, I can always adjust the torture inflicted on the victim downward until the pleasure of the viewers outweighs it.

No, what really convinces me that my proposal is immoral (and I suspect many of you feel the same way) is that society has *no right* to make one man or woman suffer for the mere amusement of others. This is one of those cases, something inside me says, where adding up pleasures and pains is the wrong way to find out what we ought to do. If America's sadists have to suffer the pain and frustration of losing their favorite show, then so much the worse for them!

We have opened up a very large and complicated subject with this appeal to the notion of *rights*, and a few words can only begin to indicate some of its ins and outs. Nevertheless, let's explore it for a bit, just to see what makes Bentham's pleasure-pain calculus seem such an inadequate expression of our moral convictions. To begin with, we must not go overboard and say that society *never* has the right to derive benefits from the suffering of one of its members. Leaving aside obvious but controversial cases like wars, we can simply recall that every time a major bridge or tunnel is built, several workers lose their lives. It may seem callous when we put it into words, but all of us employ a rough utilitarian calculation in judging the social desirability of large-scale public works. We try hard to minimize the loss of life in heavy construction, but we refuse to bring it to a dead halt simply because we know that men and women lose their lives on the job. If a project is going to cost hundreds of lives, we will

Workers painting high up on a bridge. The construction and maintenance of great structures like this regularly cost the lives of many workers. Are they worth the price? Why? Who is to say? (M.E. Warren/Photo Researchers)

probably veto it. If only a few are likely to be killed, we will give it the go-ahead. Aren't we weighing one person's life against the convenience of the motorists who will use the bridge? How does that differ from weighing the pain of the victim against the pleasure of the sadistic viewers?

Well, one answer is that the construction workers choose voluntarily to work on the bridge, knowing that it is a risky job, whereas the torture victim is forced into his or her role. That certainly is part of the difference, for I imagine we would take a *somewhat* different view of the show if we knew that the victims were volunteers.

But there still seem to be other differences. The motorist benefits from the suffering of the construction worker, to be sure. But that suffering isn't the *object* of his or her pleasure. The sadist, on the other hand, takes pleasure in the victim's pain. Now, it seems to me that there are some pleasures that are evil in and of themselves. They are bad pleasures, pleasures which people should not have; and pleasure taken in the pain of another person is one of those evil pleasures. So the torture example suggests, at least to me, that Bentham's original assumption was wrong. Not all pleasures are equal, save for quantity or intensity. And "good" does not simply mean "pleasant." So when we perform Bentham's social arithmetic, adding up pleasures and pains in order to evaluate a social policy, we most certainly ought not to put the sadist's pleasure on the plus side. He or she doesn't have a right to that pleasure, and if it is to be weighed at all, it ought to be put on the negative side with the pains. (Needless to say, there may be some pains which ought to go on the positive side! As you can see, this subject gets more and more complicated the deeper into it you go.)

It may even be, as Immanuel Kant thought, that there are some considerations more important than pleasure and pain—considerations of justice and freedom. Kant would argue that the torture show degrades both the victim and the viewers, that it treats them—in his famous phrase—as means merely and not as ends-in-themselves.

But when all is said and done, when examples like the torture show have been brought forward to refute utilitarianism, when the unclarities in the very meaning of the principle have been exposed to view, there still remains a natural appeal of Bentham's theory that will not go away. In the next chapter, when we meet John Stuart Mill, Bentham's most famous follower, we shall try once again to discover the kernel of truth that seems to lie inside the moral philosophy of utilitarianism.

V *The Theory of the Healthy Personality*

The Greeks spoke of the search for the principles of the good life. The Romans had a phrase, *mens sana in corpore sano*—a sound mind in a sound body. Psychoanalysts today talk about an integrated ego. Karl Marx wrote of "alienation" and a future of "unalienated labor." The idea is essentially the same in each case, even though the emphasis, the underlying theory, or the viewpoint differs. For ages, men and women have been seeking a style of life and spirit that achieves a wholeness, an integration, an authenticity of mind and body, of reason, passion, and desire. These days, the search is left to psychologists and the religious—at least in England and America—but in the tradition of Western thought, it is philosophers who have given the most sustained and thoughtful attention to the search for the good life.

Everyone who has reflected for even a short while on the problem of achieving an integrated, fulfilled, virtuous life agrees that the key to a solution lies in the discovery of the proper internal order of the self itself (what the Greeks call the "soul" or *psyche*). And, needless to say, there are almost as many theories about the precise nature of that desirable inner order as there are writers on the subject. But on one fundamental issue, the philosophers of the good life divide into two distinct camps. One group, which includes Stoics like Marcus Aurelius, claims that inner peace and harmony can be achieved regardless of the character of the society in which we live, regardless of the external circumstances of peace or war, tyranny or justice, health or disease. The other group emphasizes the interplay between the individual personality and the larger society, claiming that not even a wise man or woman can be truly happy save in a truly just and virtuous society. In this latter category we find Plato, Aristotle, Karl Marx, and such modern psychological theorists as Eric Fromm and Erik Erikson. You have already had an opportunity to read a bit of what Marcus Aurelius wrote about the good life. In this last section, we shall explore the view of Plato and others that the inner harmony of the self must be integrated with a proper order of society before a truly good life can be achieved.

In philosophy, we return to the same great books again and again. In Chapter One, you read a selection from an early section of Plato's immortal dialogue, the *Republic*. Now we shall jump ahead more than a hundred pages to the point at which Plato pulls together the long argument he has been developing. The official subject of the *Republic* is a search for a definition of "justice," a word to which Plato gives a broader meaning than we do today. Plato suggests two analogies or comparisons as aids in discovering the nature of justice, or true morality. The first analogy is between the soul (that is, the personality) and the body. He argues that we can speak of a healthy body and also of a healthy soul, of a diseased body and also of a diseased soul. Health of the body rests on a proper harmony or order of the bodily elements, and health of the soul in like manner consists of the correct ordering of the psychic elements. In this Dialogue, Plato distinguishes three functional parts of the soul. (I say "in this Dialogue" because Plato didn't have a fully worked out theory of psychology, and in other Dialogues he divided the human personality up in other ways. Don't just memorize "the parts of the soul in Plato"—try to see what he is driving at, and put his thought into your own words if you can.) The three elements are (1) reason, or the power to deliberate, compare alternatives, suppress unwise impulses, and make sensible choices; (2) the "spirited element," or the aggressive, warlike,

In Plato's ideal state, the wisest men and women would rule, the most warlike would serve as guardians of the state, and the rest of the population would labor in the fields. (Top, Bibliotheque Nationale, Paris: bottom, Cliche des Musees Nationaux, Paris)

willful part of one's personality; and (3) appetite or desire. Each of these elements has a role to play in the healthy, virtuous soul, but each must learn its proper function and perform it willingly and in harmony with the other elements. Reason must rule, governing the spirited element and directing its aggression in wise, nondestructive ways. The healthy, necessary appetites must be regulated by reason and satisfied in the proper proportion and to the appropriate degree. Too much indulgence of one or many desires may produce superficial and short-lived pleasure, but in the end causes inner conflict and unhappiness. A well-integrated soul is a smoothly functioning whole in which each element performs its proper function and all together maintain balance, health, and true happiness.

The second of Plato's analogies is between the individual soul and the society as a whole. Just as there are several elements in the soul with special functions and a just order of subordination to one another, so there are several classes of citizens in the society with special functions and a proper social relationship to one another. The wisest citizens must rule in society, as reason does in the soul, for they possess at one and the same time the knowledge of what is truly good for the society and the rational self-control to resist the temptation of harmful desires.

In this passage from the *Republic*, Socrates is summarizing his argument. Thrasymachus and most of the others have dropped out of the conversation, and there remain only two young men, Glaucon and Adeimantus (in real life, Plato's older brothers). Socrates speaks first:

And so, after a stormy passage, we have reached the land. We are fairly agreed that the same three elements exist alike in the state and in the individual soul.

That is so.

Does it not follow at once that state and individual will be wise or brave by virtue of the same element in each and in the same way? Both will possess in the same manner any quality that makes for excellence.

That must be true.

Then it applies to justice: we shall conclude that a man is just in the same way that a state was just. And we have surely not forgotten that justice in the state meant that each of the three orders in it was doing its own proper work. So we may henceforth bear in mind that each one of us likewise will be a just person, fulfilling his proper function, only if the several parts of our nature fulfil theirs.

Certainly.

And it will be the business of reason to rule with wisdom and forethought on behalf of the entire soul; while the spirited element ought to act as its subordinate and ally. The two will be brought into accord, as we said earlier, by that combination of mental and bodily training which will tune up one string of the instrument and relax the other, nourishing the reasoning part on the study of noble literature and allaying the other's wildness by harmony and rhythm. When both have been thus nurtured and trained to know their own functions, they must be set in command over the appetites, which form the greater part of each man's soul and are by nature insatiably covetous. They must keep watch lest his part, by battening on the pleasures that are called bodily, should grow so great and powerful that it will no longer keep to its own work, but will try to enslave the others and usurp a dominion to which it has no right, thus turning the whole of life upside down. At the same time, those two together will be the best of guardians for the entire soul and for the body against all enemies from without: the one will take counsel, while the other will do battle, following its ruler's commands and by its own bravery giving effect to the ruler's designs.

Yes, that is all true.

And so we call an individual brave in virtue of this spirited part of his nature, when, in spite of pain or pleasure, it holds fast to the injunctions of reason about what he ought or ought not to be afraid of.

True.

And wise in virtue of that small part which rules and issues these injunctions, possessing as it does the knowledge of what is good for each of the three elements and for all of them in common.

Certainly.

And, again, temperate by reason of the unanimity and concord of all three, when there is no internal conflict between the ruling element and its two subjects, but all are agreed that reason should be ruler.

Yes, that is an exact account of temperance, whether in the state or in the individual.

Finally, a man will be just by observing the principle we have so often stated.

Necessarily.

Now is there any indistinctness in our vision of justice, that might make it seem somehow different from what we found it to be in the state?

I don't think so.

Because, if we have any lingering doubt, we might make sure by comparing it with some commonplace notions. Suppose, for instance, that a sum of money were entrusted to our state or to an individual of corresponding character and training, would anyone imagine that such a person would be specially likely to embezzle it?

No.

And would he not be incapable of sacrilege and theft, or of treachery

to friend or country; never false to an oath or any other compact; the last
to be guilty of adultery or of neglecting parents or the due service of the
gods?

Yes.

And the reason for all this is that each part of his nature is exercising
its proper function, of ruling or of being ruled.

Yes, exactly.

Are you satisfied, then, that justice is the power which produces states
or individuals of whom that is true, or must we look further?

There is no need; I am quite satisfied.

And so our dream has come true—I mean the inkling we had that, by
some happy chance, we had lighted upon a rudimentary form of justice
from the very moment when we set about founding our commonwealth.
Our principle that the born shoemaker or carpenter had better stick to his
trade turns out to have been an adumbration of justice; and that is why it
has helped us. But in reality justice, though evidently analogous to this principle, is not a matter of external behaviour, but of the inward self and of
attending to all that is, in the fullest sense, a man's proper concern. The just
man does not allow the several elements in his soul to usurp one another's
functions; he is indeed one who sets his house in order, by self-mastery and
discipline coming to be at peace with himself, and bringing into tune those
three parts, like the terms in proportion of a musical scale, the highest and
lowest notes and the mean between them, with all the intermediate inter-
vals. Only when he has linked these parts together in well-tempered harmony and has made himself one man instead of many, will he be ready to
go about whatever he may have to do, whether it be making money and
satisfying bodily wants, or business transactions, or the affairs of state. In all
these fields when he speaks of just and honourable conduct, he will mean
the behaviour that helps to produce and to preserve this habit of mind; and
by wisdom he will mean the knowledge which presides over such conduct.
Any action which tends to break down this habit will be for him unjust; and
the notions governing it he will call ignorance and folly.

That is perfectly true, Socrates.

Good, said I. I believe we should not be thought altogether mistaken, if
we claimed to have discovered the just man and the just state, and wherein
their justice consists.

Indeed we should not.

Shall we make that claim, then?

Yes, we will.

So be it, said I. Next, I suppose, we have to consider injustice.
Evidently.

This must surely be a sort of civil strife among the three elements,
whereby they usurp and encroach upon one another's functions and some

part of the soul rises up in rebellion against the whole, claiming a supremacy to which it has no right because its nature fits it only to be the servant of the ruling principle. Such turmoil and aberration we shall, I think, identify with injustice, intemperance, cowardice, ignorance, and in a word with all wickedness.

Exactly.

And now that we know the nature of justice and injustice, we can be equally clear about what is meant by acting justly and again by unjust action and wrongdoing.

How do you mean?

Plainly, they are exactly analogous to those wholesome and unwhole-some activities which respectively produce a healthy or unhealthy condition in the body; in the same way just and unjust conduct produce a just or unjust character. Justice is produced in the soul, like health in the body, by establishing the elements concerned in their natural relations of control and subordination, whereas injustice is like disease and means that this natural order is inverted.

Quite so.

It appears, then, that virtue is as it were the health and comeliness and well-being of the soul, as wickedness is disease, deformity, and weakness.

True.

And also that virtue and wickedness are brought about by one's way of life, honourable or disgraceful.

That follows.

So now it only remains to consider which is the more profitable course: to do right and live honourably and be just, whether or not anyone knows what manner of man you are, or to do wrong and be unjust, provided that you can escape the chastisement which might make you a better man.

But really, Socrates, it seems to me ridiculous to ask that question now that the nature of justice and injustice has been brought to light. People think that all the luxury and wealth and power in the world cannot make life worth living when the bodily constitution is going to rack and ruin; and are we to believe that, when the very principle whereby we live is deranged and corrupted, life will be worth living so long as a man can do as he will, and wills to do anything rather than to free himself from vice and wrong-doing and to win justice and virtue?

Yes, I replied, it is a ridiculous question.

—PLATO, *Republic*

For the first two millennia of Western philosophy, the wise under-standing of the human condition was the province of philosophers and poets. In the past three quarters of a century, however, their intuitive insight has been supplemented, though not supplanted, by the systematic scientific investigations of countless theorists of human personality. Plato's brilliant recognition of the analogy between the health of the body and the health of the mind has been embodied in a branch of medicine called psychiatry, whose practitioners study the forms, causes, symptoms, and cures for what we now routinely call "mental illness." With psychiatrists, as with philosophers, there is a fundamental split between those who examine the individual psyche in separation from its social setting and those who study the connections between individual mental health or illness and the network of social and institutional relationships which surround the patient.

Sigmund Freud (1856–1939), the founder of modern psychoanalytic theory and practice, tended toward the first method of investigation. Although he wrote several provocative essays on the psychic roots of social phenomena, his primary interest was in the inner dynamics of the psyche itself. Among all those who have followed Freud's lead in developing a science of psychiatry, perhaps no figure comes closer to Plato both in spirit and fineness of sensibility than the contemporary analyst, historian, author, and philosopher Erik H. Erikson (1902–   ). Erikson has sought to build on Freud's investigation of the infantile stages of personality development by analyzing the later stages through which each of us passes in coming either well or badly to maturity and old age. It was Erikson who actually coined the now familiar phrase "identity crisis" in an essay on the emotional upheaval that so many young men and women go through in late adolescence and early adulthood. But Erikson was also interested in the continuing development of personality later in life. He discovered from his clinical practice with patients of all ages that as an individual grew through infancy, childhood, adolescence, young adulthood, mature adulthood, and old age, he or she faced a series of turning points, or crises. At each stage, the individual might resolve the crisis successfully and grow into a stronger, more fulfilled person, or fail to

Identity Crisis   A term invented by the psychoanalyst Erik Erikson to refer to the period of instability, uncertainty, and personality formation through which teen-agers pass in societies like ours. Erikson intended to suggest, by the term, that the period is one of genuine flux and indeterminacy, with the outcome—a healthy, coherent adult personality—hanging in the balance.

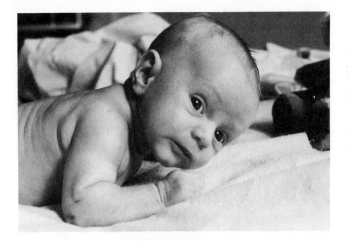

Erik Erikson's theory of the healthy development of personality is based on the natural cycle of infancy, childhood, young adulthood, maturity, and old age. Men and women at each stage need those at other stages to help them grow in a healthy way. (Clockwise from top: Teri Stratford, Ken Karp, RSVP/Action/Vetter, Laimute Druskis, Ken Karp.)

handle the crisis well and bear ever after the scars of that failure. In old age, those who have lived the cycle of childhood, adulthood, and maturity well achieve thereby an inner harmony which Erikson calls "ego integrity." It is very much like what Plato calls wisdom. This ego integrity gives meaning to the life that has been lived and permits the individual to face impending death with acceptance, dignity, and pride. Here is Erikson's description of this final stage of the life cycle.

> Only in him who in some way has taken care of things and people and has adapted himself to the triumphs and disappointments adherent to being the originator of others or the generator of products and ideas—only in him may gradually ripen the fruit of these seven stages. I know no better word for it than ego integrity. Lacking a clear definition, I shall point to a few constituents of this state of mind. It is the ego's accrued assurance of its proclivity for order and meaning. It is a postnarcissistic love of the human ego—not of the self—as an experience which conveys some world order and spiritual sense, no matter how dearly paid for. It is the acceptance of one's one and only life cycle as something that had to be and that, by necessity, permitted of no substitutions: it thus means a new, a different love of one's parents. It is a comradeship with the ordering ways of distant times and different pursuits, as expressed in the simple products and sayings of such times and pursuits. Although aware of the relativity of all the various life styles which have given meaning to human striving, the possessor of integrity is ready to defend the dignity of his own life style against all physical and economic threats. For he knows that an individual life is the accidental coincidence of but one life cycle with but one segment of history; and that for him all human integrity stands or falls with the one style of integrity of which he partakes. The style of integrity developed by his culture or civilization thus becomes the "patrimony of his soul," the seal of his moral paternity of himself. . . . In such final consolidation, death loses its sting.
>
> The lack or loss of this accrued ego integration is signified by fear of death: the one and only life cycle is not accepted as the ultimate of life. Despair expresses the feeling that the time is now short, too short for the attempt to start another life and to try out alternate roads to integrity. Disgust hides despair, if often only in the form of "a thousand little disgusts" which do not add up to one big remorse . . .
>
> Each individual, to become a mature adult, must to a sufficient degree develop all the ego qualities mentioned, so that a wise Indian, a true gentlemen, and a mature peasant share and recognize in one another the final stage of integrity. But each cultural entity, to develop the particular style of integrity suggested by its historical place, utilizes a particular combination of these conflicts, along with specific provocations and prohibitions of infantile

sexuality. Infantile conflicts become creative only if sustained by the firm support of cultural institutions and of the special leader classes representing them. In order to approach or experience integrity, the individual must know how to be a follower of image bearers in religion and in politics, in the economic order and in technology, in aristocratic living and in the arts and sciences. Ego integrity, therefore, implies an emotional integration which permits participation by followership as well as acceptance of the responsibility of leadership.

Webster's Dictionary is kind enough to help us complete this outline in a circular fashion. Trust (the first of our ego values) is here defined as "the assured reliance on another's integrity," the last of our values. I suspect that Webster had business in mind rather than babies, credit rather than faith. But the formulation stands. And it seems possible to further paraphrase the relation of adult integrity and infantile trust by saying that healthy children will not fear life if their elders have integrity enough not to fear death.

—ERIK H. ERIKSON, *Childhood and Society*

The Main Points in Chapter Two

1. The eighteenth-century Prussian philosopher Immanuel Kant tried to find a way to make the science of Newton compatible with the strict moral beliefs of his Protestant upbringing, and also to provide a rigorous logical proof of the fundamental principles of morality.

2. When philosophers talk about ethics, there are really three very different questions they ask, namely:
   a. How can I be certain that my moral beliefs are correct?
   b. How can I decide moral hard cases?
   c. How can I live a good life?

3. Kant put forward a moral principle called the Categorical Imperative as the absolutely right principle for all persons in any situation. Ethical Relativists *and* Ethical Skeptics deny that there is any such universally valid principle.

4. To decide hard cases, defenders of Utilitarianism, such as Jeremy Bentham and John Stuart Mill, offer the Principle of the Greatest Happiness for the Greatest Number. Utilitarianism is the most widely-debated moral theory of modern-day philosophy.

5. Philosophers from Plato to Karl Marx have put forward theories of

the health of the self or personality as the basis for a conception of the good life. The central idea of these philosophers is that the way to have a genuinely good life is to develop an inwardly well-ordered or healthy psyche. Today, these same ideas are explored by psychoanalysts as well as philosophers.

Abortion—A Civilized Exchange

No issue of personal morality and public policy has so deeply divided Americans in recent years as *abortion*. Both the proponents of legal abortion (who argue for a woman's right to control her body), and the opponents of legal abortion (who consider abortion to be murder), consider themselves to be defending inalienable human rights.

A host of profound philosophical questions come together in the practical issue of the rights or wrongs of abortion. In addition to the ethical issues, there are disputes about what a human being is, disagreements about when life begins, debates about the relation of mind to body, and, of course, bitter arguments about the conflict between the rights of the individual and the authority of the state. In this case, surprisingly, it is the anti-abortionists, usually considered politically conservative, who have adopted extralegal tactics, blockading and even bombing abortion clinics, while the defenders of abortion have appealed to the American Constitution to support their position.

The central issue is ethical: What is the proper extent or limit of the rights of the pregnant woman in relation to the rights of the unborn fetus? Does anyone have the right to require a woman to continue a pregnancy which she does not wish to bring to term? Are there any conditions under which the mother, or anyone else, has the right to terminate the life of the fetus, for *any* reason, at *any* stage in the pregnancy?

The brief selection included here is a debate by two well-known commentators on matters of public policy and morality: Ernest van den Haag, a psychiatrist who has written extensively on the relation between psychiatry and the law, and John Noonan, Jr., a widely read Catholic legal philosopher. Notice how intertwined are questions of medical fact, morality, public policy, and metaphysics in their discussion.

Humanity: The Central Question

ERNEST VAN DEN HAAG

The central issue in the abortion debate is the humanity of the fetus. No other consideration is decisive. Indeed the opponents of abortion rest their entire case on a single argument:

If the fetus is a human being, then abortion is murder.

The fetus is a human being.

Abortion is murder.

The difficulty is with the second premise. How can one demonstrate that the fetus is a human being? To define it as a human being is not sufficient. After all, during the first few weeks of gestation it little resembles a human being. That it will become one does not demonstrate that it already is one.

Proponents of legal abortion contend that the fetus is not a human being but rather a part of the mother's body, wherefore abortion is not murder and indeed is no more than the exercise of a right of the mother to dispose of her own body. Yet, biologically, the fetus has the potential for independence from the beginning. In *Roe* v. *Wade* the Supreme Court sided with the proponents and declared abortion to be a constitutional right of the mother. Although *Roe* qualified the

right to abortion, so that in the last few months it is granted only if the mother's health requires it, the Court also (in *Doe* v. *Bolton*) defined maternal health so as to allow, in effect, unlimited discretion to the mother and her physician.

The controversy about whether the fetus is actually a human being from conception, or if not, then about when the fetus does become human or even independently alive, cannot be resolved empirically. It depends exclusively on how one defines "human" and "being."

Certainly neither a sperm nor an ovum is a human being. It seems unpersuasive to regard the combination as human *ab initio*. The combination, the fertilized ovum, is a *potential* human being: A fetus will normally develop into a human being. But a seed, a potential tree, is not an actual tree unless one chooses to so define it; one can do so only by neglecting to distinguish between what is and what will be. On the other hand, long before birth the embryo shares essential physical characteristics of human beings.

Although we cannot decide empirically whether or when a fetus ought to be defined as a human being, we can decide whether the fetus is sentient or, rather, when it is not. Sentience is a criterion that is at once more stringent and more empirical than humanity, neither a mat-

National Review September 6, 1985. Mr. van den Haag is John M. Olin Professor of Jurisprudence and Public Policy at Fordham University in New York City.

ter of definition, nor of metaphysics. Not all sentient beings are human, but certainly all human beings normally are sentient. Sentient beings can be killed, though they are murdered only if human as well. (Cows are killed, not murdered.)

If the fetus is sentient, abortion kills, regardless of whether the killing is murder. It kills at least a potential human being, for nobody denies that the fetus is that.

When does the fetus become sentient? I do not presume to know. For that matter, nobody knows for certain. Nonetheless we do know when the fetus can *not* be sentient, i.e. feel pain or pleasure. Sperm is not sentient; nor is an ovum. There is no reason to believe that the fertilized ovum is sentient from the moment of conception, since there is, as yet, no neural system. Although we do not know for certain whether and when sentience begins in intrauterine existence, we do know that there can be no sentience without an elementary nervous system and brain. Without a functioning brain even fully grown human beings do not feel pain; and if the appropriate nerve is cut, they do not feel pain even with a brain. Hence, embryos cannot feel pain until they have an active brain with a functioning cortex and functioning nerves. Embryos get something like a neural system and a brain—using these terms quite liberally—only toward the end of the first trimester. It follows that they cannot feel anything before then. (Nobody is quite sure about after. Movements of the embryo may be reflex movements, in response to various stimuli, and

may, but need not, indicate pain or pleasure.) Abortion undertaken in the first twelve weeks does not kill a sentient being.

Thus, to oppose abortion because it may be painful to the fetus, or may kill a sentient, potentially human, being, should mean opposing it only after the first trimester. Furthermore, although potentially human all along, the fetus is much more actually human after the first twelve weeks of gestation. Hence, it seems plausible to extend legal protection to it after twelve weeks.

One may still oppose abortion, even in the first 12 weeks, for philosophical reasons. The current position of the Roman Catholic Church on this matter, if not practical, is consistent. The Church opposes the prevention of human life by any artificial (positive) means; therefore it opposes abortion at any time and contraception as well. The case against abortion in the first trimester must rest entirely on metaphysics and philosophy. However, there are empirical reasons for opposing abortion after three months of gestation, which require anyone morally opposed to infanticide to oppose such abortions.

Consider now some related matters.

Viability seems irrelevant. Suppose we could make a fertilized ovum viable outside the uterus. That would make it neither human nor sentient in the first 12 weeks of development. So the issue of viability seems irrelevant. Nonviability, however, if clear, is an acceptable reason for abortion.

That the pregnancy is *inconvenient* or unwanted is irrelevant after the first three months. Maternal preferences cannot justify abortion thereafter unless they are allowed to justify infanticide as well: The difference between a fetus and an infant rapidly decreases after three months.

Rape makes the rapist guilty of a crime and the victim's pregnancy unwanted. The fetus is not guilty and is entitled to be treated like any other: We cannot, once the fetus is sentient, kill him because the father committed a crime and the mother does not want him.

On the other hand, to keep the fetus alive the mother must, as it were, extend him hospitality. He is an uninvited and perhaps a despised guest. We would not legally compel a woman to keep another person in her house for nine months, and certainly not linked to her body, even if the other person would die unless so kept.

Thus we are faced with a dilemma. We do not want the innocent fetus to perish, merely because he has been conceived without the consent of the woman he inhabits. But we do not want to compel a woman to lend her body—and suffer all the inconveniences and dangers of doing so—to somebody whose arrival she had not wished even to risk.

The rape victim, then, should have the right that any woman should have to abort the fetus during the clearly non-sentient first 12 weeks. Rape is simply an additional reason for granting this right. If she fails to abort, however, she must be understood to have consented to bring the fetus to term. She should not later be allowed to kill a possibly sentient, poten-

tially human, and certainly innocent being. Still, we should not compel the mother to raise a baby conceived by her without her having consented to the act that risked conception. Rather, if she so wishes, we should make it easy for her to turn the child over to foster or adoptive parents. So far as possible, the burden should fall on the society that did not protect her from rape.

In the case of *disabling defects*, the fetus should, once sentient, be treated exactly as a disabled infant. Only if we allowed parents to let such infants die, or to kill them, should we allow parents to eliminate a fetus after the first trimester.

The principle is clear. However, some practical considerations might modify its application. Up until now, at least, deformities and defects have been ascertainable only after the first 12 weeks. Moreover, though we can make abortion unlawful we cannot prevent it. Making it illegal would diminish the number of abortions just as making burglary illegal diminishes the number of burglaries. Abortion, however, would not be diminished as much, since it is harder to detect (often there is no complainant), and since it was more widely accepted even when unlawful. Pregnant women who learn after the first trimester that their babies will be severely defective are much more likely to obtain an abortion, however unlawful, than women who expect normal babies. Should we let them do legally, within appropriate limits, what they would otherwise do illegally without any limits?

There might be a case for abortion if it

is certain that the baby could not survive infancy; or would be so severely handicapped, mentally and physically, as to be unable to have other than a vegetative existence. (There may be a case for not helping adults to survive in these conditions either.)

The decision about abortion, however, must be based on the best interests of the fetus, not on the interests of the parents. The decision should be based on the answer to the question: If the fetus knew everything we know, and were competent to decide rationally, would it prefer to be aborted? Except for gross abuses, the decision should be left to parents informed by medical advisors.

Traditionally we have qualified rights and duties. For instance, we believe that a man has a duty to render military service, including the killing of enemies, when drafted to do so. We know, however, that some persons have strong conscientious objections to performing such a duty. Rather than compelling or punishing them, we permit them, as a privilege, not to do their duty, because of their special difficulties. We might make a similar exception for women pregnant with highly defective babies. To be sure, there are differences. Conscientious objection does not kill anyone (although, if the objector does not serve, and you go in his place, you may be killed in his place); legal abortion of a defective fetus after the first trimester would kill the fetus. But I see no practical way of protecting him from a mother strongly motivated to kill him; and it may be in his interest to be killed.

A new scientific procedure based on chorionic-villi sampling, done painlessly, and apparently with little risk, may ease this dilemma a bit. It promises to make available in the eighth to 12th week of gestation all the information amniocentesis makes available in the 16th week. If chorionic-villi sampling (currently being investigated by the National Institutes of Health) keeps its promise, pregnant women could know within the first trimester whether a fetus is defective. The desire to abort defective fetuses after sentience would occur much less often, although, in the interest of the fetus, such abortion still may be permitted.

A calm review of the central issues yields, then, three conclusions:

Abortion before sentience should be generally permitted.

Abortion after sentience should be generally prohibited.

Abortion of highly defective fetuses might be permitted even after sentience when in the interest of the fetus.

Sentience Is Not the Issue

John T. Noonan, Jr.

Opponents of abortion contend that:

1. The fetus is a human being.
2. To kill a human being in the womb is abortion (*not* murder).
3. Abortion is morally evil.

Opponents of abortion do not confuse what is potential with what is actual. A fertilized ovum already has some actuality. If it were pure potential, it would not be observable. The actuality the fertilized ovum has is actuality as a human being.

Why? Because its progenitors are human beings. It is not mineral or vegetable or animal. Its chromosomes are the number that make a human being human. It has the DNA that contains the genetic signals governing its future development as a human being. Very soon it can be identified as he or she. These five reasons require us to recognize the new humanity that exists after fertilization.

Sentience is not a criterion for deciding whether a human being can be killed. If it were, we could anaesthetize intended victims and painlessly kill them. We cannot kill innocent human beings, sentient or not.

The pain experienced by the victims of abortion does serve to remind us that we are taking life. We know as much (or as little, if you like) about the pain experienced by the unborn as we do about the pain experienced by animals. In neither case do they say: "Ouch! It hurts"; or "I'm in pain." But we do not need those verbal formulae. For the most part we rely on the knowledge that if pressure is brought to bear on the skin or on the vital organs of a living creature, that creature's natural movement will show aversion as a reaction to pain. All that is necessary is that a neural system and sense receptors be in place, as Mr. van den Haag seems to admit.

The hard cases will always be hard cases. They were very deliberately exploited by the proponents of abortion in the 1960s. They were the effective edge of the wedge. They deserve relatively little attention now when we are trying to deal with abortion on the massive scale of 1.5 million per year. They distract from the real horror.

Yet, for completeness, let me say that in this age of candor about sex, any victim of rape should be told that just as soon as possible steps should be taken to destroy the semen. The case is a classic case of double effect. It is entirely legitimate to destroy the seed; the effect on

National Review, September 6, 1985. Mr. Noonan is a professor of law at the University of California at Berkeley. His most recent book is *Bribes*.

a possible fertilized ovum is not one for which there is moral liability. As to deformed children, the most common case is that of Down's syndrome. I do not believe that Down's-syndrome babies should be killed after birth or before birth. General rules governing the circumstances in which it is not mandatory to prolong dying life apply, of course, to human beings in the womb as well as outside it.

A Brief Rejoinder

Some of Professor Noonan's points puzzle me. They are:

1. How can it be "*not* murder" to intentionally and with premeditation "kill a human being in the womb," even if it legally be called abortion?

2. Why is there no "moral liability" for killing a "human being in the womb" if the father was guilty of rape and the mother a victim thereof? Does that make the fetus guilty too?

3. Although it is "*not* murder," Professor Noonan contends that "we cannot kill innocent human beings, sentient or not." Right. The question Professor Noonan begs here is whether or not the pre-sentient fetus is an actual rather than a potential human being.

4. He begs this question by contending that if the fetus "were pure potential it would not be observable." Who said "*pure* potential"? We all, including fetuses, are actually what we are and potentially what we will become. I presume Professor Noonan actually is a middleaged man and potentially an old and ultimately a dead man. The former can, but the latter two cannot, be observed as yet. This would not lead me to contend that Professor Noonan is actually dead, or to confuse a potential human being with an actual one.

5. Professor Noonan offers five reasons explaining why "the actuality the fertilized ovum has is actuality as a human being." His reasons range from progenitors to chromosomes and DNA. They apply not only to fetuses but also, *mutatis mutandis*, to fertilized hens' eggs. Yet I do not call an egg a chicken, despite its potential to become one. Does Professor Noonan? If not, why does he identify the potential with the actual when it comes to fetuses?

—ERNEST VAN DEN HAAG

Study Questions

1. Think back over your life, and pick the hardest choice you ever had to make. Was it a *moral* choice? Did it involve a decision about what is right and wrong? If the answer is yes, ask yourself whether it would have helped you to carry out a utilitarian-style calculation of pleasures and pains to yourself and others. Would Kant's rule—the Categorical Imperative—have helped you at all? How *did* you actually make the decision?

2. The example in the text of a torture show is intended partly as a joke (although it isn't very funny!), but there really are many situations in which we seem to trade off one person's extreme misery for minor increases in the happiness of many others. For example: long experience shows that whenever we undertake a major construction project—a large bridge, a subway system, a tunnel—at least one construction worker is killed accidentally during the duration of the project. Knowing this, we must ask ourselves, when we are considering, say, a new bridge to speed rush hour traffic, how many human lives is it worth to enable commuters to get home ten minutes earlier each evening? Suppose we could accomplish the greater speed not by building a bridge, but just by choosing one of the construction workers by lot and killing him or her. Should we do it?

3. The central thesis of the theory of the healthy personality is that people with coherent, healthy, harmonious personalities will not act cruelly and unjustly. Certainly it is true that *some* immoral acts flow from disordered personalities, but is it reasonable to suppose that all do? Can there be a happy, well-adjusted mass murderer?

4. What do you think Kant's ethical theory tells us about the morality or immorality of abortion? Is it clear what utilitarianism tells us? Is it reasonable to pick your moral theory on the basis of what it tells you about issues, like abortion, on which you already have fixed views? Why? Why not? If you leave out any religious considerations, where do you think the truth lies on the question of the morality of abortion?

3

SOCIAL PHILOSOPHY

JOHN STUART MILL (1806–1873) was the most important English philosopher during the 125 years between the death of David Hume in 1776 and the turn of the twentieth century. Trained from his youth by his father, James Mill, to be a defender of the utilitarian doctrine of Jeremy Bentham and the Philosophical Radicals, Mill devoted his early years to an unquestioning support of his father's principles. After undergoing a severe emotional crisis in his twenties, Mill gave up the narrow doctrine of Bentham and became instead an eclectic synthesizer of the views of such diverse schools as the French utopian socialists and the German romantics.

Mill was active in the public life of England, first as an officer (and eventually head) of the great East India Company, a principal instrument of English economic expansion during the nineteenth century, and later as a member of parliament. In addition to the books on moral and political topics which have established him as one of the leading advocates of liberalism, Mill also wrote a number of highly influential works on logic and the theory of knowledge, including *A System of Logic* and *An Examination of Sir William Hamilton's Philosophy*.

As a young man, Mill befriended Mrs. Harriet Taylor, with whom he maintained a close relationship until, after her husband's death, they were married in 1851. Mill believed Mrs. Taylor to be an enormously gifted thinker and he was convinced that she would have made her mark on English letters had it not been for the powerful prejudice against women that operated then, as it does now. His relationship with Mrs. Taylor made Mill sensitive to the discrimination against women, with the result that he became one of the few philosophers to speak out on the matter. His discussion of the problem appears in a late work, *The Subjection of Women*, published four years before his death.

I Mill and Classical Laissez-Faire Liberalism

Some, it is said, are born great; some achieve greatness; and some have greatness thrust upon them. To that saying we might add, and some are trained from birth for greatness. Of all the philosophers who have won for themselves a place in the ranks of the great, none was more carefully groomed, schooled, prodded, and pushed into greatness than the English empiricist and utilitarian thinker of the nineteenth century, John Stuart Mill. Never has a child been given less chance to "do his own thing," and never has a man defended with greater eloquence the right of every man and woman to be left free from the intrusions of well-meaning parents, friends, and governments. Though it would be wrong to reduce Mill's mature philosophical views to the level of mere psychological reflections on his childhood experiences, the temptation is irresistible to see in his adult career a reaction to the pressures of his youth.

Mill was born in 1806, at a time when a strong movement was developing to reform the political life of England. The intellectual leader of the movement was the same Jeremy Bentham whose utilitarian doctrines you encountered in Chapter Two. We took our first look at utilitarianism in its guise as a moral philosophy designed to lay down a principle for calculating what actions are right for an individual facing a decision. But as your reading on the reform of the penal code makes clear, Bentham's primary interest was in social issues, not in private morality. He conceived the Principle of Utility as a weapon in the attack on the traditions, privileges, laws, and perquisites of the English upper classes. So long as courts and governments could hide behind precedent, or immemorial custom, it was extremely hard to force them to admit the injustices and irrationalities of the social system. But once those ancient customs were put to the test of the Principle of Utility, it was immediately clear how badly they failed to produce the greatest happiness for the greatest number.

> James Mill (1773–1836) was a close friend and colleague of Jeremy Bentham, the founder of the doctrine known as utilitarianism. Mill led a group of English political reformers who believed that social justice and wise government required a broadening of the franchise to include the industrial middle classes in England, and a thoroughgoing overhaul of the antiquated laws and governmental machinery which, in Mill's day, strongly favored the landed interests in England. Mill and the Philosophical Radicals, as his circle of supporters were called, succeeded in generating enough support to carry through a number of major reforms, culminating in the sweeping Reform Bill of 1832. Mill's son, the great John Stuart Mill, had this to say about his father's position in *The Autobiography of John Stuart Mill*:

>> So complete was my father's reliance on the influence of reason over the minds of mankind, whenever it is allowed to reach them, that he felt as if all would be gained if the whole population were taught to read, if all sorts of opinions were allowed to be addressed to them by word and by writing, and if by means of the suffrage they could nominate a legislature to give effect to the opinions they adopted.

One of Bentham's close friends and associates in the reform movement was a philosopher named James Mill; Mill was a thinker of considerable distinction, although he has long since been eclipsed by his more famous son. His writings on economics and moral philosophy erected a system, on Benthamite foundations, which served as a fortress from which the Philosophical Radicals, as they were called, sallied forth to do battle with the last remnants of the aristocratic hosts. Shortly after the birth of his son John Stuart, James Mill met Bentham and joined forces with him. Mill decided to train his son up as a soldier in the reform movement, and no medieval squire ever had a more rigorous preparation for combat. Little John Stuart began studying Greek at the age of three. His father surrounded him with Latin-speaking servants so that by the age of eight he could dig into that other ancient tongue. Logic was young

John Stuart's fare at twelve, to be followed shortly by the study of the new science of political economy. Formal religion was deliberately omitted from the curriculum, but the poor lad may be forgiven for having somewhat formed the notion that he was being raised an orthodox utilitarian.

By the time he reached adulthood, John Stuart Mill was a brilliant, finely honed logical weapon in the armory of his father's political battles. He wrote attacks on the antiquated legal and political institutions of England, defending his points with straight utilitarian dogma.

Not surprisingly, Mill finally broke under the strain of this rigid doctrinaire discipline. At the age of twenty, he suffered an internal emotional crisis, and began what was to be a lifelong reevaluation of the Benthamism of his father and his father's allies. Though it is always a mistake to sum up a great philosopher's work in a single phrase, we can get some general overview of Mill's subsequent intellectual development by saying that he spent his life struggling to broaden, deepen, and complicate the extremely simple philosophical theory into which he was initiated as a boy.

The doctrine of the reformers was clear, coherent, and attractively free from the mystifications which clouded the writings of the conservative defenders of the old order. As Bentham had laid it down, the only good in this world is pleasure, the only evil pain. Human actions are goal-oriented, purposeful actions. Our desires determine what objects or experiences we choose as our goals, and reason aids us in discovering the most efficient path to those goals. The question, What ought I to do? is either a question of goals—What should I desire?—or else it is a question of means—How can I reach my goal most easily? But there is no point in disputing about desires. We either want something or we don't, and whatever pleasure we experience comes to us as the result of satisfying a desire. So the only questions worth debating are factual questions of means: Is this the best way to satisfy my desire, or would that way be quicker, cheaper, easier?

If abstruse questions of natural rights and absolute goodness are to be disputed, then common men and women will be hard put to keep up with trained philosophers, lawyers, or theologians. But if Bentham is right, then the fundamental moral question is simply, Does it feel good? Is this experience pleasurable? Now each one of us is the best judge of whether he or she is feeling pleasure or pain, so utilitarianism has the effect of eliminating expertise and putting all men and women on an equal footing in moral debates. What is more, Bentham insisted, the only

"I keep my life well ordered so I can be outrageous in my private thoughts."

morally relevant distinction between pleasures and pains is a quantitative distinction of more and less. As Bentham put it, pushpin (a child's game) is as good as poetry, so long as it gives you an equal amount of pleasure. This doctrine too had the effect of leveling the social distinctions between the high- and low-born, for it had been easy for the cultivated upper classes to insist that they were privy to joys and sorrows too refined for the lower classes even to imagine. In these ways—by making each person the judge of his or her own happiness and by making quantity the only significant variable—utilitarianism provided a philosophical justification for a democratic social program.

All persons are basically prudent, rationally self-interested actors. That is to say, we seek to satisfy our desires in the most extensive and pleasurable way, and we use the resources available to us—money, talent, power—in the most efficient manner possible. But there are two great obstacles to fully rational self-interested action. The first of these, the target of the eighteenth-century enlightenment, is superstition. So long as people falsely believe that they have no right to satisfy their desires; so long as religion, or ancient custom, or class distinctions inhibit common men and women from using the resources they have for the achievement of their own happiness; so long, in short, as the reasoning power of the mind is clouded by fear, awe, and false belief, then just so long will the injustices and inequalities of society continue. The second obstacle is the ignorance which even enlightened men and women suffer of the facts of science and public affairs, ignorance of the most efficient means for pursuing legitimate satisfactions.

Education was the weapon utilitarians aimed at these twin enemies, superstition and ignorance. Education was to perform two tasks: first, to liberate enslaved minds from the superstitious religious and political dogmas of the past and, second, to introduce the liberated minds to the facts of science and society. An educated population could then be counted on to support wise public policy, for such policy would aim at the greatest happiness of the greatest number, and that simply meant their own happiness as private citizens. Thus utilitarianism combined a psychological theory of individual motivation with a moral theory of the good and an educational theory of enlightenment to produce what we today call a political theory of liberal democracy.

It remains to mention one last element of the utilitarian system, an element which may well have been the most important of all, namely the laissez-faire economic theory created by Adam Smith and David Ricardo and deployed by James Mill and his son in the great debates over public policy. This is not an economics textbook, and philosophy is hard enough all by itself, but at least a few words must be said about the laissez-faire theory in order to fill out Mill's position and set the stage for the powerful attacks which Karl Marx launched against it a very few years later.

The major fact of the end of the eighteenth century and the beginning of the nineteenth was, of course, the growth of mercantile and industrial capitalism. The key to the new capitalism was the systematic investment of accumulated wealth, or "capital," for the purpose of producing goods which could be sold at a profit in the marketplace. The individual who set the economic activity in motion was called an "entrepreneur," which is French for "undertaker" and means someone who undertakes to do something, not someone who buries someone (although critics of capitalism might have argued that there was indeed a connection between the two meanings). The capitalist undertook to rent the land, hire the labor, buy the raw materials, and bring together these factors of production in a process which resulted in finished goods. The

Laissez-faire   Literally to allow to do. Laissez-faire is the system of free market exchanges, with an absolute minimum of government control, which nineteenth-century liberals believed would result in the most efficient use of resources, and the greatest material well-being for a society. *Laissez-faire capitalism* refers to the early stage in the development of capitalism, when firms were small, owner-run, and controlled both in their purchases and in their sales by market pressures.

goods were put on sale in a market where no law fixed the prices that must be paid or the profits that could be made. Adam Smith, in his famous treatise *The Wealth of Nations*, argued that if everyone were permitted to do the best he could for himself—worker, capitalist, merchant, and consumer—then the net result would be the most efficient use of the resources of the nation for the production of goods designed to satisfy human desires. The consumers would spend their money in the marketplace in such a way as to get the greatest pleasure for value. If one sort of product rose too high in price, they would shift to another, for paying all your money for a single piece of meat would be foolish when the same money could buy you fish, eggs, shoes, and a coat. The capitalists would pull their capital out of areas where too much was being produced, because as supply exceeded demand, they would be forced to drop their prices in order to unload their inventory, and profits would tumble. In the same way, if there were customers clamoring for a commodity that wasn't being produced, they would bid up the price in the

ADAM SMITH (1723–1790) was born in Scotland at a time when that small country was one of the liveliest intellectual centers in Europe. Like his countryman, David Hume, Smith wrote on a wide variety of problems in what we would now call the social sciences. His masterwork was a long, difficult, revolutionary study of the foundations of economic activity in a free market capitalist economy, entitled *Inquiry into the Nature and Causes of the Wealth of Nations*. With this book, Smith created the field of economics, and laid the theoretical basis for the doctrine of laissez-faire which still has wide support two centuries later. *The Wealth of Nations* was published in 1776, just at the time when the American colonies were declaring their independence of the English crown, and it is fitting that history should have linked these two events, for the Founding Fathers were deeply imbued with the laissez-faire spirit of individual freedom, minimal government, and the pursuit of rational self-interest.

market, drive up profits in that branch of business, and attract profit-seeking capitalists who would open new factories to "capitalize" on the unsatisfied demand.

Since happiness is pleasure, and pleasure results from the satisfaction of desire, and consumers buy goods to satisfy desires, it follows that the capitalists trying to make a profit are at the same time actually working to make the consumers happy. They aren't *trying* to make them happy, of course! The capitalists, like all men and women, are rationally *self-interested* pleasure maximizers. But the genius of the new capitalist free market system was precisely that each person, seeking only his or her own good, automatically advanced the good of others. Thus selfishness could be counted on to do rationally and efficiently what altruism never quite managed—namely, to produce the greatest happiness possible for the greatest number of people. Here is how Adam Smith puts it in a passage that is much quoted and copied. Smith is actually in the midst of a discussion of restrictions on imports, but the thesis he enunciates has a quite general application:

> But the annual revenue of every society is always precisely equal to the exchangeable value of the whole annual produce of its industry, or rather is precisely the same thing with that exchangeable value. As every individual, therefore, endeavours as much as he can both to employ his capital in the support of domestic industry, and so to direct that industry that its produce may be of the greatest value; every individual necessarily labours to render the annual revenue of the society as great as he can. He generally, indeed, neither intends to promote the public interest, nor knows how much he is promoting it. By preferring the support of domestic to that of foreign industry, he intends only his own security; and by directing that industry in such a manner as its produce may be of the greatest value, he intends only his own gain, and he is in this, as in many other cases, led by an invisible hand to promote an end which was no part of his intention. Nor is it always the worse for the society that it was no part of it. By pursuing his own interest he frequently promotes that of the society more effectually than when he really intends to promote it. I have never known much good done by those who affected to trade for the public good. It is an affectation, indeed, not very common among merchants, and very few words need be employed in dissuading them from it.
>
> —ADAM SMITH, *The Wealth of Nations*

Mill read widely in authors whose views were far removed from those of Bentham and his father. He learned from the Romantic critics of the reform movement even as he sought to counter their arguments. He studied the writings of such acute conservative observers as Alexis de Tocqueville, and even absorbed the lessons of the French socialists, though he seems not to have read or appreciated the more powerful theoretical assault mounted by the great German socialist Karl Marx. The breadth of his learning and his personal dissatisfaction with the narrow dogma of his father led Mill to doubt or even to deny some of the central tenets of utilitarian philosophy and social policy. Nevertheless, to the end of his life, his mind remained trapped within the confines of the principles he had been taught as a youth.

In at least *three* important ways, Mill questioned the theses of the orthodox reform doctrine. First, he denied Bentham's egalitarian insistence that any pleasure, in and of itself, was as good as any other (which, as we have seen, was a roundabout way of saying that any person was as good as any other). As far back as Plato, philosophers had argued that some pleasures were simply finer, higher, morally better than other pleasures. Usually, as we might expect, they claimed that the pleasures of the mind were superior to the pleasures of the body. Bentham was prepared to admit that some pleasures were more intense, or more long-lasting, or had more pleasant aftereffects than others. A quart of bad wine might give less pleasure than a sip of fine brandy. A night of drinking might be followed by such a horrendous morning after that the total experience would add up to a minus rather than a plus. Some pleasures, like some foods, might be acquired tastes, requiring knowledge and long practice before they could be properly appreciated. But after all this had been taken into account—and Bentham carefully did take it into account—utilitarianism still insisted that only quantity and not quality of pleasure mattered. Mill could not accept this teaching, fundamental though it was to the philosophy he had been trained to defend. He was stung by the critics of utilitarianism who made it out to be a brutish or degraded philosophy, a philosophy of the base appetites. In replying to their charge, he drew a distinction between higher and lower pleasures which fundamentally altered the significance and logical force of utilitarianism. Here is the passage, taken from an essay called "Utilitarianism" which Mill first published in a magazine and later as a short book.

> Now such a theory of life excites in many minds, and among them in some of the most estimable in feeling and purpose, inveterate dislike. To suppose that life has (as they express it) no higher end than pleasure—no better and nobler object of desire and pursuit—they designate as utterly mean and

Hogarth's famous engraving, Gin Lane, illustrating rather forcefully the negative consequences of a night of drinking! (The Metropolitan Museum of Art, Harris Brisbane Dick Fund, 1932)

groveling, as a doctrine worthy only of swine, to whom the followers of Epicurus were, at a very early period, contemptuously likened; and modern holders of the doctrine are occasionally made the subject of equally polite comparisons by its German, French, and English assailants.

When thus attacked, the Epicureans have always answered that it is not they, but their accusers, who represent human nature in a degrading light, since the accusation supposes human beings to be capable of no pleasures except those of which swine are capable. If this supposition were true, the charge could not be gainsaid, but would then be no longer an imputation; for if the sources of pleasure were precisely the same to human beings and to swine, the rule of life which is good enough for the one would be good enough for the other. The comparison of the Epicurean life to that of beasts is felt as degrading, precisely because a beast's pleasures do not satisfy a human being's conceptions of happiness. Human beings have faculties more elevated than the animal appetites and, when once made conscious of them, do not regard anything as happiness which does not include their gratification. . . .

. . . It is quite compatible with the principle of utility to recognize the fact that some kinds of pleasure are more desirable and more valuable than others. It would be absurd that, while in estimating all other things quality is considered as well as quantity, the estimation of pleasure should be supposed to depend on quantity alone.

If I am asked what I mean by difference of quality in pleasures, or what makes one pleasure more valuable than another, merely as a pleasure, except its being greater in amount, there is but one possible answer. Of two pleasures, if there be one to which all or almost all who have experience of both give a decided preference, irrespective of any feeling of moral obligation to prefer it, that is the more desirable pleasure. If one of the two is, by those who are competently acquainted with both, placed so far above the other that they prefer it, even though knowing it to be attended with a greater amount of discontent, and would not resign it for any quantity of the other pleasure which their nature is capable of, we are justified in ascribing to the preferred enjoyment a superiority in quality so far outweighing quantity as to render it, in comparison, of small account.

Now it is an unquestionable fact that those who are equally acquainted with and equally capable of appreciating and enjoying both do give a most marked preference to the manner of existence which employs their higher faculties. Few human creatures would consent to be changed into any of the lower animals for a promise of the fullest allowance of a beast's pleasures; no intelligent human being would consent to be a fool, no instructed person would be an ignoramus, no person of feeling and conscience would be selfish and base, even though they should be persuaded that the fool, the dunce, or the rascal is better satisfied with his lot than they are with theirs. They would not resign what they possess more than he for the most complete satisfaction of all the desires which they have in common with him. If they ever fancy they would, it is only in cases of unhappiness so extreme that to escape from it they would exchange their lot for almost any other, however undesirable in their own eyes. A being of higher faculties requires more to make him happy, is capable probably of more acute suffering, and certainly accessible to it at more points, than one of an inferior type; but in spite of these liabilities, he can never really wish to sink into what he feels to be a lower grade of existence.

—JOHN STUART MILL, *Utilitarianism*

There are a number of tricky logical problems with the position Mill defends here, the complete analysis of which would carry us into some rather dry and technical regions of the theory of utility. But one problem springs instantly from the page at us. If not all pleasures are equal in quality, if some persons of more refined sensibility are better able to judge of the quality of pleasures, then the basic democratic one-person-one-vote thrust of utilitarianism is lost. Instead of giving every person,

In Mill's revision of Utilitarianism, the tastes and opinions of the upper classes would carry more weight in the calculations of pleasures and pains than the tastes and opinions of ordinary men and women. (Left, Hugh Rogers/Monkmeyer; below, Arthur Tress/Photo Researchers)

however low in station or meager in education, an equal voice in the choice of the ends of social policy, special weight shall have to be accorded to the opinions of that educated minority who have tasted the elevated pleasures of the mind—to those who claim, from the height of their culture, that Bach is better than rock, and cordon bleu better than cheeseburgers. The fact is that Mill does indeed exhibit just such an aristocratic bias in his political writings, both in regard to the privileged position of the upper classes within England and also in regard to England's privileged position in her colonies vis-à-vis the "subject races" not yet raised to her own level of culture. The cultural imperialism of Mill, as we may call it, is of course interesting as a fact about the man and his times. But it is also a first-rate example of the way in which an apparently trivial philosophical argument about a technical point can carry with it very large consequences for the most practical questions of politics.

Mill's second revision of his father's faith concerned the rationality and predictability of the laborers, capitalists, and consumers who interacted in the marketplace. The doctrine of laissez-faire, with its emphasis on limited government intervention in the market and a removal of all regulations on trade and commerce, depended upon two assumptions, as we have already seen. The first was that economic actors could be counted on to behave in a rationally self-interested manner, buying as cheaply as possible, taking the highest wages available, always looking for a profit; the second, which depended for its plausibility on the first, was that an economy run along laissez-faire lines and populated by rationally self-interested persons would maximize growth and production and thereby create the greatest happiness possible, within the limits of natural resources and technology, for the greatest number of people. In one of his major works, *The Principles of Political Economy,* Mill denied the first of these two assumptions and thereby laid the theoretical ground work for the rejection of the second.

First let us look at Mill's argument. Then we will consider its significance.

Under the rule of individual property, the division of the produce is the result of two determining agencies: Competition and Custom. It is important to ascertain the amount of influence which belongs to each of these causes, and in what manner the operation of one is modified by the other.

Political economists generally, and English political economists above others, have been accustomed to lay almost exclusive stress upon the first of these agencies; to exaggerate the effect of competition, and to take into little account the other and conflicting principle. They are apt to express themselves as if they thought that competition actually does, in all cases, whatever it can be shown to be the tendency of competition to do. This is partly intelligible, if we consider that only through the principle of competition has political economy any pretension to the character of a science. So far as rents, profits, wages, prices, are determined by competition, laws may be assigned for them. Assume competition to be their exclusive regulator, and principles of broad generality and scientific precision may be laid down, according to which they will be regulated. The political economist justly deems this his proper business: and as an abstract or hypothetical science, political economy cannot be required to do, and indeed cannot do, anything more. But it would be a great misconception of the actual course of human affairs, to suppose that competition exercises in fact this unlimited sway. I am not speaking of monopolies, either natural or artificial, or of any interferences of authority with the liberty of production or exchange. Such disturbing causes have always been allowed for by political economists. I speak of cases in which there is nothing to restrain competition; no hindrance to it either in the nature of the case or in artificial obstacles; yet in which the result is not determined by competition, but by custom or usage; competition either not taking place at all, or producing its effect in quite a different manner from that which is ordinarily assumed to be natural to it.

Since custom stands its ground against competition to so considerable an extent, even where, from the multitude of competitors and the general energy in the pursuit of gain, the spirit of competition is strongest, we may be sure that this is much more the case where people are content with smaller gains, and estimate their pecuniary interest at a lower rate when balanced against their ease or their pleasure. I believe it will often be found, in Continental Europe, that prices and charges, of some or of all sorts, are much higher in some places than in others not far distant, without its being possible to assign any other cause than that it has always been so: the customers are used to it, and acquiesce in it. An enterprising competitor, with sufficient capital, might force down the charges, and make his fortune during the process; but there are no enterprising competitors; those who have capital prefer to leave it where it is, or to make less profit by it in a more quiet way.

—JOHN STUART MILL, *Principles of Political Economy*

Mill is saying that although the behavior of men and women in the market may be *predictable*, it is not *calculable*. The difference is fundamental, so perhaps we should take a moment to explain it more clearly. Suppose I want to open a snack shop, and I am trying to decide whether to locate downtown or in a new mall being built on the edge of town. I know that the mall will have a number of discount outlets selling well-known brands at very low prices. If I can assume that consumers will be motivated solely by a desire to minimize their expenditures for the goods they buy, then I can *calculate* (without any special information about shopping habits in this area) that the mall will be crowded with bargain-hunters. Since I want my snack shop to be where the shoppers are, I will choose the mall.

But if Mill is right (as in fact he is), then a certain proportion of the shoppers will go on shopping downtown, whether out of habit or because they care enough about such nonmonetary things as the familiarity of the stores. There is no way in the world that I can foresee just how many shoppers will be influenced enough by these factors to go downtown instead of to the mall. I can observe shopping behavior in other towns and extrapolate to this case, or do an opinion survey of shoppers, or in some other fashion try to base my prediction on experience. With enough data, I may be able to *predict* what the shoppers will do, so that I can decide where to put my snack shop. But there is no way that I can *calculate* their behavior.

So long as economic actors in the marketplace act in a rationally self-interested way, I can calculate their actions without any prior knowledge of their individual character, without elaborate collections of information about their past behavior. All I need know is that (1) they seek to maximize profits or enjoyments and (2) they will make use of the available information in a rational attempt to achieve that maximization. I can then carry out in my own head the same calculation they will carry out, and so I can calculate their actions. But if they are influenced by what Mill calls *custom*, which is to say by *irrational* tastes, habits, and preferences that deviate from the strict rationality of profit maximization, then I can only predict their behavior on the basis of vast quantities of systematically collected data about their past behavior. I cannot count on the "invisible hand" of the marketplace to direct their economic activities into the most productive areas. Capitalists may refrain, out of irrational habits or aversions, from shifting their capital into sectors of unfulfilled market demand. Consumers may go on shopping at a more expensive store when identical goods are offered more cheaply next door. Workers may fail to quit low-paying jobs and move to better-paying jobs in labor-short industries.

The result will be a breakdown of the automatic mechanisms of the market and a need for scientifically controlled management of the econ-

John Stuart Mill believed that society ought to protect the widest possible expression of individuality, in order to allow the human spirit to discover its innate potentialities. (Ken Karp)

omy by a central authority possessing both the information and the power to implement its judgments. In short, the slight revision which Mill makes in the classical theory of laissez-faire leads directly, although not immediately, to the modern managed economy of welfare-state capitalism.

Mill's third alteration in the radical philosophy of James Mill follows directly from the first, and concerns the government's right to interfere with the private lives of its citizens. In his famous essay, *On Liberty,* Mill argues for an absolute ban on all state or social intervention in the inner life of thoughts and feelings. But in the last chapter of the *Principles,* he takes a somewhat different line. To be sure, he says, *"Laisser-faire . . . should be the general practice: every departure from it, unless required by some great good, is a certain evil."* But in considering permissible departures, Mill concedes a very great deal indeed. Listen to him in this suggestive passage.

We have observed that, as a general rule, the business of life is better per-formed when those who have an immediate interest in it are left to take their own course, uncontrolled either by the mandate of the law or by the meddling of any public functionary. The persons, or some of the persons, who do the work, are likely to be better judges than the government, of the means of attaining the particular end at which they aim. Were we to sup-pose, what is not very probable, that the government has possessed itself of the best knowledge which had been acquired up to a given time by the persons most skilled in the occupation; even then, the individual agents have so much stronger and more direct an interest in the result, that the means are far more likely to be improved and perfected if left to their uncon-trolled choice. But if the workman is generally the best selector of means, can it be affirmed with the same universality, that the consumer, or person served, is the most competent judge of the end? Is the buyer always quali-fied to judge of the commodity? If not, the presumption in favour of the competition of the market does not apply to the case; and if the commodity be one, in the quality of which society has much at stake, the balance of advantages may be in favour of some mode and degree of intervention, by the authorized representatives of the collective interest of the state.

Now, the proposition that the consumer is a competent judge of the commodity, can be admitted only with numerous abatements and excep-tions. He is generally the best judge (though even this is not true universally) of the material objects produced for his use. These are destined to supply some physical want, or gratify some taste or inclination, respecting which wants or inclinations there is no appeal from the person who feels them; or they are the means and appliances of some occupation, for the use of the persons engaged in it, who may be presumed to be judges of the things required in their own habitual employment. But there are other things of the worth of which the demand of the market is by no means a test; things of which the utility does not consist in ministering to inclinations, nor in serving the daily uses of life, and the want of which is least felt where the need is greatest. This is peculiarly true of those things which are chiefly useful as tending to raise the character of human beings. The uncultivated cannot be competent judges of cultivation.

—JOHN STUART MILL, *Principles of Political Economy*

Despite all his qualifications and revisions in the utilitarian creed, Mill remained faithful to its spirit. But powerful intellectual attacks were mounted on laissez-faire liberalism and utilitarianism from both the right and the left. In the next two sections of this chapter, we shall listen to some of the voices of dissent. The attacks began as soon as industrial capitalism and its liberal defenders appeared. In the very first decades of the nineteenth century, Romantic conservative critics of industrialism and socialist critics of the capitalist organization of that industrialism appeared in England and on the continent. But I do not want you to think that this is an ancient dispute, buried in dusty books written by men long dead. The very same argument continues today, and so we shall hear from a few of the contemporary philosophers who have questioned the foundations of both the theory and the practice of traditional liberal social philosophy.

II The Conservative Attack on Capitalism

Living as we do two centuries after industrial capitalism burst its bonds and rose to a position of domination in the economy and society of England, we tend to think of capitalists and capitalism as the Establishment, as the old order, entrenched in its position of superiority even though under attack from socialism and communism. But in its infancy, **capitalism** was a revolutionary social force which assaulted the bastions of landed wealth and power, toppled kings, and thrust a new class into the arena of politics. The philosophy that rationalized this emergence of a new ruling class was also a revolutionary philosophy, and its celebration of prudential rationality, its insistence upon the rights of the individual, its denial of immemorial custom, privilege, and inherited status grated on the philosophical sensibilities of the old order's defenders as much as the accents of the new industrial barons must have grated on their ears.

The conservative counterattack took many literary forms. It appeared in the speeches of Edmund Burke, in the poetry of Shelley, in the essays and history of Carlyle. Needless to say, there is no single "conservative" position, any more than there was or is a single "liberal" or "radical" position. But the critics from the right tended to concentrate their fire

> **Capitalism**   An economic system based on concentration of private ownership of the means of production in relatively few hands, a large class of propertyless workers who work for wages, and production for sale and profit rather than for use. The money invested by the property owners for the purpose of making a profit is called *capital*, hence the system is called capitalism.

on two strong points of the liberal philosophy. These were the nature and role of *reason* in human affairs and the legitimacy of *tradition* as a source of the bonds that united men and women in society. In each case, the conservatives argued that the liberals had got the matter badly wrong and had produced thereby a philosophy that was both false and socially harmful.

The prime target of conservative arguments was the utilitarian conception of human reason. By now you will have noted how often this matter of the nature of reason comes up in philosophical disputes. Cosmologists, epistemologists, moralists, and political theorists all argue about our peculiar capacity to reason, about what role it should play in our personality, in our study of nature, and in our social arrangements. Bentham, Mill, and company had made two claims about reason. First, they said that human beings are fundamentally rational creatures, despite the overlay of irrationality which is from time to time produced by superstition, ignorance, or religious faith. By saying that we are rational, they meant that we have it within our power to deliberate, to weigh alternatives, and to make choices guided by knowledge and calculation. Second, they said that this power of reason had the function of selecting the efficient means for the achievement of those ends which had already been set by desire. So to the utilitarians, and to liberal philosophers in general, "rational agent" essentially meant "prudent agent."

The conservatives denied both of these theses about reason. First of all, they denied that reason should take the ruling place in the soul. The poets insisted that the power of imagination was actually a higher faculty than reason. It had the capacity to put us in touch with eternal truths, with the ideal of beauty, with a deeper reality that mere sensation and calculation could never reveal. They considered the utilitarians' prudent man to be a vulgar, uninspired, diminished creature, capable only of adding up pleasures and pains, profits and losses. The mystery, awe, wonder, majesty, and sanctity of the human experience were reduced by a Bentham to the level of "pleasures," to be traded off against a good meal or a soft bed. One might as well use a Rembrandt masterpiece as a scratch pad or melt down a statue of the Blessed Virgin to make paperweights. Better by far to lift the masses, by even a little, through the exercise of the unquestioned authority of their cultivated betters, rather than reduce all art, all culture, all society to the lowest common denominator of popular taste.

I do not know of any philosopher who has attacked this celebration of reason more wittily, profoundly, and effectively than the modern English conservative Michael Oakeshott. In his essay, "Rationalism in Politics," Oakeshott takes on virtually the entire corpus of Western philosophers as he ridicules their conception of rationality. The principal target of Oakeshott's criticism is the familiar distinction between ends and means, a distinction which can be found in the writings of Aristotle, Hobbes, Bentham, Mill, Kant, and countless other philosophers of widely different theoretical persuasions. When a person acts, according to the most common view, first he identifies the state of affairs he wishes to bring about—his goal or *end*—and then he selects what seems to him, given his beliefs about the world, the best or most efficient way of bringing it about—his *means*. So when I mow my lawn, first I identify my end, which is to shorten the length of the grass on my lawn to a height that looks nice to me and also keeps the grass growing, and then I select the means available to me that seems likely to accomplish my end in the most efficient manner, according to my personal evaluation of the relative values or costs of the different means. In short, I tell my son to get out the lawn mower and mow the lawn. Or, if my son has gone off with his friends, I do it myself.

According to this analysis, my choice of ends is determined either by the mere, unanalyzable fact that I desire some thing (maybe I just *like* the look of short grass), or by some set of moral convictions (I may, for peculiar reasons, think that it is immoral to have long grass), or by the fact that I desire something else which this particular end is a means to getting (I may want to impress my neighbors, and past experience tells me that they are really impressed by a well-kept lawn). My choice of means is determined by my knowledge of the world taken together with what Defense Department planners call a "cost-benefit" calculation. I figure out the most efficient way to achieve my goal, and then decide whether the payoff is worth the price (if I have to mow the lawn myself, I may decide to pass up my neighbor's praise!).

The interesting thing about Oakeshott's position is that he thinks it is literally impossible for anyone to act in this ends-means way! He sometimes talks as though he thinks it is merely a foolish way to act, but his real claim is that we couldn't act that way even if we tried. What is more, though we always fail, the effort invariably makes things worse than they need be. Here is his argument.

> The general character and disposition of the Rationalist are, I think, not difficult to identify. At bottom he stands (he always *stands*) for independence of mind on all occasions, for thought free from obligation to any au-

thority save the authority of 'reason.' His circumstances in the modern world have made him contentious: he is the *enemy* of authority, of prejudice, of the merely traditional, customary or habitual. His mental attitude is at once sceptical and optimistic: sceptical, because there is no opinion, no habit, no belief, nothing so firmly rooted or so widely held that he hesitates to question it and to judge it by what he calls his 'reason'; optimistic, because the Rationalist never doubts the power of his 'reason' (when properly applied) to determine the worth of a thing, the truth of an opinion or the propriety of an action. . . .

He has no sense of the cumulation of experience, only of the readiness of experience when it has been converted into a formula: the past is significant to him only as an encumbrance. He has none of that *negative capability* (which Keats attributed to Shakespeare), the power of accepting the mysteries and uncertainties of experience without any irritable search for order and distinctness, only the capability of subjugating experience; he has no aptitude for that close and detailed appreciation of what actually presents itself which Lichtenberg called *negative enthusiasm*, but only the power of recognizing the large outline which a general theory imposes upon events ... the mind of the Rationalist impresses us as, at best, a finely-tempered, neutral instrument, as a well-trained rather than as an educated mind. Intellectually, his ambition is not so much to share the experience of the race as to be demonstrably a self-made man. And this gives to his intellectual and practical activities an almost preternatural deliberateness and self-consciousness, depriving them of any element of passivity, removing from them all sense of rhythm and continuity and dissolving them into a succession of climacterics, each to be surmounted by a *tour de raison*. His mind has no atmosphere, no changes of season and temperature; his intellectual processes, so far as possible, are insulated from all external influence and go on in the void. And having cut himself off from the traditional knowledge of his society, and denied the value of any education more extensive than a training in a technique of analysis, he is apt to attribute to mankind a necessary inexperience in all the critical moments of life, and if he were more self-critical he might begin to wonder how the race had ever succeeded in surviving. With an almost poetic fancy, he strives to live each day as if it were his first, and he believes that to form a habit is to fail. And if, with as yet no thought of analysis, we glance below the surface, we may, perhaps, see in the temperament, if not in the character, of the Rationalist, a deep distrust of time, an impatient hunger for eternity and an irritable nervousness in the face of everything topical and transitory.

Every science, every art, every practical activity requiring skill of any sort, indeed every human activity whatsoever, involves knowledge. And, universally, this knowledge is of two sorts, both of which are always involved in any actual activity. It is not, I think, making too much of it to call them two sorts of knowledge, because (though in fact they do not exist separately) there are certain important differences between them. The first sort of knowledge I will call technical knowledge or knowledge of technique. In every art and science, and in every practical activity, a technique is involved. In many activities this technical knowledge is formulated into rules which are, or may be, deliberately learned, remembered, and, as we say, put into practice; but whether or not it is, or has been, precisely formulated, its chief characteristic is that it is susceptible of precise formulation, although special skill and insight may be required to give that formulation. The technique (or part of it) of driving a motor car on English roads is to be found in the Highway Code, the technique of cookery is contained in the cookery book, and the technique of discovery in natural science or in history is in their rules of research, of observation and verification. The second sort of knowledge I will call practical, because it exists only in use, is not reflective and (unlike technique) cannot be formulated in rules. This does not mean, however, that it is an esoteric sort of knowledge. It means only that the method by which it may be shared and becomes common knowledge is not the method of formulated doctrine. And if we consider it from this point of view, it would not, I think, be misleading to speak of it as traditional knowledge. In every activity this sort of knowledge is also involved; the mastery of any skill, the pursuit of any concrete activity is impossible without it. . . .

Now, as I understand it, Rationalism is the assertion that what I have called practical knowledge is not knowledge at all, the assertion that, properly speaking, there is no knowledge which is not technical knowledge. The Rationalist holds that the only element of *knowledge* involved in any human activity is technical knowledge, and that what I have called practical knowledge is really only a sort of nescience which would be negligible if it were not positively mischievous. The sovereignty of 'reason', for the Rationalist, means the sovereignty of technique.

—MICHAEL OAKESHOTT, *Rationalism in Politics*

The second utilitarian thesis about reason got equally short shrift from the conservatives. Though they denied the primacy of reason, they insisted that reason could do more than merely select efficient means to any end desire might throw up before us. That, they thought, was a shopkeeper's conception of reason, a bookkeeper's notion of what it meant to be rational. "Two tickles on this side of the ledger, a twinge on that. Let us see how it balances out." Was this the highest peak to which we could aspire in the exercise of our rational powers? Hardly. Reason was far better employed in a reflection upon the truths of revealed religion, in a just appreciation of the wise ordering of statuses and classes in established society, in a contemplation of the eternal form of beauty.

Conservative critics were especially vigorous in their defense of the traditions which the utilitarians lumped together as "superstitions." A tradition is a way of acting, a style of personality, a form of human relationships, which has been enacted and reenacted over many generations, and has acquired through long usage an authority that exceeds any justification a calculating reason can produce. To a utilitarian, tradition is simply a polite name for thoughtless repetition, for the doing once more of something that could not be justified the first time. This harsh view of tradition assumes that we can know enough about our social affairs to make reliable calculations of the best institutions and policies. But if our capacity to discover the underlying nature of society is limited at best; if the power of reason within each of us is only a feeble check against powerful, destructive passions lurking beneath the surface of civilization; if the experiences of past generations are a fund of unspoken wisdom on which the present can draw through the reenactment of the old ways; if all of this be the case, then tradition will be our best guide rather than our worst. It will preserve for us what is soundest in the history of the human race, while also containing, through its authority, those antisocial passions which mere calculative reason cannot adequately suppress.

One way to bring the dispute between the liberals and the conservatives into focus is to embody their abstract philosophies in concrete human form, to try to imagine what the ideal utilitarian liberal would be like and what the ideal conservative would be like. This is a risky business, and I will probably end up by offending both liberals and conservatives, but let me have a go at it anyway. I think it will help you to see what is at stake. The ideal utilitarian liberal can be imagined as a solid, cautious, open-minded, prudent businessperson. She is self-made, having earned her present position by hard work, self-denial, and a shrewd calculation of advantage. She is not public-spirited, if by that is meant a desire to help others at the expense of herself. But since her own interests are best advanced in the marketplace by satisfying the desires of her customers, she manages to do good for others in the process of doing well by herself.

The ideal conservative is an aristocrat, born into a family with wealth, tradition, and a name to uphold. He is quirky, individualistic, disdainful of the opinions of anyone not in his own social class, but fiercely proud of his honor and determined to uphold it at all costs. He scorns calculation, and considers a good head for business to be a somewhat degrading trait. He has a cultivated mind and is at ease with great art and great literature, though he does not work at it like a dry professor. His morals

The utilitarian businessperson is hard-headed, efficient, practical. The aristocrat is quirky, individual, snobbish, disdainful of the practicalities of everyday life. (Above, Irene Springer; left, Tom Hollyman/Photo Researchers)

are sometimes a trifle loose, but his word is his bond, and in a war he can be counted on to stand his position until the death. His life has style, a certain flamboyance, and it is his own style, not purchased at a clothing store or copied from the pages of a magazine.

Each one—the capitalist and the aristocrat—has strengths, and each has weaknesses. The capitalist is practical, open to experiment, willing to try new ways to solve intractable problems. She is flexible, capable of compromise, able to deal with men and women of all classes and backgrounds. She is respectful of the manners and mores of others (for she never knows when they will be her customers). If you need a railroad constructed, a new technology exploited, or a dispute settled between labor and management, she is your woman.

But the same instrumental calculation that stands the capitalist in such good stead when she is faced with a problem of resource management can be her downfall when hard choices of honor and morality come her way. The utilitarian mentality tends to lead to the subversion of principle in the interest of some "larger" end. Benjamin Franklin said in his autobiography that the *appearance* of honesty was more important in business than honesty itself, and such an attitude easily degenerates into an obsessive concern with public relations, with the salability of a policy or a product rather than its soundness. Liberals are long on practical proposals for benevolent social management, but short on backbone when it comes to defending basic principles against attack.

The conservative's strengths and weaknesses are the mirror opposites of the capitalist's. The conservative is set in his ways, unwilling to experiment with new industrial or social programs, uninterested in compromise, unable to accommodate himself to the manners of those from different social backgrounds. But he has the capacity to take offense, to feel that his honor has been insulted, and when that happens he will stand and fight, not out of a rational calculation of future advantage but simply from an irrational conviction that certain things are "not done."

These sentiments were expressed with great elegance a century and a half ago by the brilliant French historian and observer of social affairs, Alexis de Tocqueville. In his eloquent book, *The Old Régime and the French Revolution*, de Tocqueville analyzed the paradoxical connection between the presence of an aristocracy in the old regime and the preservation of true—though not in the liberal sense *rational*—freedom. This selection from his book should provide us with some second thoughts about our own tendency to identify class inequality with a loss of freedom.

Many of the prejudices, false ideas, and privileges which were the most serious obstacles to the establishment of a healthy, well-ordered freedom had the effect of maintaining in the minds of Frenchmen a spirit of independence and encouraging them to make a stand against abuses of authority. The nobility had the utmost contempt for the administration properly so called, though now and again they addressed petitions to it. Even after the surrender of their former power they kept something of their ancestral pride, their traditional antipathy to servitude and subordination to the common law. True, they gave little thought to the freedom of the populace at large and were quite ready to let the authorities rule those around them with a heavy hand. But they refused to let that hand weigh on themselves and were prepared to run the greatest risks in the defense of their liberties if and when the need arose. When the Revolution broke out, the nobility, destined as they were to be swept away with the throne, still maintained in their dealings with the King an attitude vastly more arrogant and a freedom of speech far greater than those of the Third Estate, who were soon to overthrow the monarchy. Almost all the safeguards against the abuse of power which the French nation had possessed during its thirty-seven years of representative government were vigorously demanded by the nobles. When we read the *cahiers* they presented to the Estates-General, we cannot but appreciate the spirit and some of the high qualities of our aristocracy, despite its prejudices and failings. It is indeed deplorable that instead of being forced to bow to the rule of law, the French nobility was uprooted and laid low, since thereby the nation was deprived of a vital part of its substance, and a wound that time will never heal was inflicted on our national freedom. When a class has taken the lead in public affairs for centuries, it develops as a result of this long, unchallenged habit of pre-eminence a certain proper

ALEXIS DE TOCQUEVILLE (1805–1859) was a French writer, politician, and commentator on public affairs. After a visit to the United States in 1831, he wrote a two-volume study of American politics and national character, *Democracy in America*, which remains to this day the most penetrating analysis of the distinctive American contribution to democratic culture. Tocqueville was one of a number of mid-nineteenth-century writers who believed that complete social and economic equality could be a threat to individual liberty.

pride and confidence in its strength, leading it to be the point of maximum resistance in the social organism. And it not only has itself the manly virtues; by dint of its example it quickens them in other classes. When such an element of the body politic is forcibly excised, even those most hostile to it suffer a diminution of strength. Nothing can ever replace it completely, it can never come to life again; a deposed ruling class may recover its titles and possessions but nevermore the spirit of its forebears. . . .

. . . We must be chary of regarding submission to authority as *per se* a sign of moral abjection—that would be using a wrong criterion. However subservient was the Frenchman of the old régime to the King's authority there was one kind of subservience to which he never demeaned himself. He did not know what it was to bend the knee to an illegitimate or dubious authority, a government little honored and sometimes heartily despised, which it is well to truckle to because it has power to help or harm. This degrading form of servitude was something quite unknown to our forefathers. Their feeling for the King was unlike that of any other modern nation for its monarch, even the most absolute; indeed, that ancient loyalty which was so thoroughly eradicated by the Revolution has become almost incomprehensible to the modern mind. The King's subjects felt towards him both the natural love of children for their father and the awe properly due to God alone. Their compliance with his orders, even the most arbitrary, was a matter far less of compulsion than of affection, so that even when the royal yoke pressed on them most heavily, they felt they still could call their souls their own. To their thinking, constraint was the most evil factor of obedience; to ours, it is the least. Yet is not that type of obedience which comes of a servile mind the worst of all? Indeed, we should be ill advised to belittle our ancestors; and would do better to regain, even if it meant inheriting their prejudices and failings, something of their nobility of mind.

—ALEXIS DE TOCQUEVILLE,
The Old Régime and the French Revolution

Incidentally, Mill read Tocqueville and sought to incorporate his insights into the utilitarian position. Whether he succeeded is a question that I leave to you to decide.

III *The Socialist Attack on Capitalism*

The conservative reaction to industrialism and liberalism was powerful, and it gave rise in the social sciences to an enormous body of impressive theory and research. But more powerful still was the attack from the left.

KARL MARX (1818–1883) is the founder of modern socialism. Born in Prussia, he studied philosophy, and in his twenties joined a circle of young radical social critics and philosophers known as the Young Hegelians. After a number of years as a pamphleteer and intellectual agitator in Germany and France, Marx moved to London to escape political persecution. Once in England, he settled into a rather quiet life of scholarship, reflection, writing, and political organization. Throughout a lifetime of collaboration with Friedrich Engels (1820–1895), Marx systematically elaborated a full-scale economic, political, philosophical, historical, and moral critique of the industrial capitalist system which had developed first in England and then throughout the rest of Europe.

As a young man, Marx was inflamed with the revolutionary conviction that the capitalist order was on the brink of total collapse. After the failure of the workers' uprisings in 1848, and the reactionary turn of most continental governments, Marx developed a deeper and more long-term analysis of the internal weaknesses of capitalism. Though his writings fill many volumes, there can be no doubt that the masterpiece of his life was the book called, simply, *Capital*.

Unlike many of his followers, Marx was always ready to alter his theories in the face of new evidence. Although he was certain in his youth that socialism could only come by way of a violent revolutionary overthrow of capitalist society and government, later in his life he concluded that in such countries as England and America socialism might come through the relatively peaceful avenue of political agitation and election.

The misery of the workers in the early factories, the squalor of the slums in which they and their families suffered, the gross contrast between their poverty and the wealth of the entrepreneurs provoked a flood of scathing condemnations of the new industrial order. Some of the criticisms were merely cries from the heart, but especially in France, a number of philosophers and economists made an effort to discover the underlying causes of the suffering created by capitalism. It was the German Karl Marx, however, who mounted the most sustained, thoroughgoing, and intellectually impressive critique of the institutions, economic theories, and philosophical rationalizations of industrial capitalism.

The genius of Marx's critique was that it met the liberal philosophy head on at its strongest point, and turned its own arguments against itself. Liberalism and laissez-faire claimed to be rational doctrines, stripped of all superstitious mystification. The conservatives had denied the primacy of reason and attempted instead to elevate imagination or tradition to the first place. But Marx accepted the challenge of liberalism. Industrial capitalism, he insisted, was not rational. Instead, it was profoundly irrational, and its claims to rationality, expressed in its economic theory and in its philosophy, were no more than an ideological rationalization designed to conceal the inner illogic of capitalism and thereby preserve a system which favored the interests of a few at the expense of the lives of many.

Marx argued that industrial capitalism was irrational in two different ways. First, it was instrumentally irrational. That is to say, it systematically chose inefficient means to attain the ends it claimed to set for itself.

Marxism   The economic, political, and philosophical doctrines first set forth by Karl Marx and then developed by his disciples and followers. Although Marx himself considered his theories scientific, his followers have often treated them as a form of secular religion. The principal doctrines are: first, that capitalism is internally unstable and prone to fall into economic crises; second, that the profits of capitalist enterprises derive from the exploitation of the workers, who receive in wages less than they produce; third, that as capitalism develops, workers will tend to become more self-aware of their situation, and hence more likely to overthrow capitalism by force; and fourth, that the society that comes into existence after capitalism is destroyed will be socialist and democratic in its economic and political organization.

The triumphant claim of Smith and the other capitalist apologists had been that a free market profit system would make maximally efficient use of the resources and technology available to a society at any moment, and generate new economic production more expeditiously than any system of government management or tradition. Marx agreed that capitalism was unequaled at the task of production, but the very same capitalism was unable to solve the even more important problem of distributing what its factories had produced. In a capitalist system, production is for profit, not for use. If the capitalist cannot make a good return on his investment, he is forced to close up shop, even though there may be men and women in the society crying for the goods he produces. By the same token, as long as he is making a good profit, he goes on churning out goods regardless of whether they are high on society's list of genuine needs. The market is the distribution mechanism, which means that only consumers with cash in hand can buy what the capitalists have produced. But in order for the capitalist to make a high profit, he must keep his wages down, for—Marx argues—profits come out of the difference between the value of what the workers produce and the wages they are paid by their employers. So the same capitalist who cuts his workers' wages to the bone finds no one in the market with money to buy his products.

Competition with other capitalists pushes each producer to cut prices and increase volume, in an attempt to seize a larger share of the market. The result is a cycle of overproduction, leading to layoffs, recession, depression, general misery, and then an upswing into new overproduction. Now, ever since people have been on this earth, natural disasters have afflicted them, blighting their crops, flooding their homes, striking them down with disease. But the depressions produced periodically in the nineteenth and twentieth centuries by capitalism were not natural disasters; they were man-made disasters, arising out of the inner irrationality of the capitalist system. Hunger resulted not from crop failures, but from the inability of the market system to distribute what had been produced. There was famine in the midst of plenty, until in America during the Great Depression of the 1930s, farmers were literally forced to plow piglets under with their tractors while millions hovered on the brink of malnutrition and actual starvation. These "inner contradictions" of capitalism, as Marx called them, were living evidence of the irrationality of that social system which the utilitarians had proclaimed the reign of reason.

Even this terrible instrumental irrationality of capitalism, however, was merely a means, as it were, to the substantive irrationality, the debasing inhumanity of capitalism as it was actually lived by industrial workers. You have all heard the term **alienation**. These days it has become a catchword, and is used to apply to everything from psychic disorder to mere boredom. The term was first used by the German philosopher Georg F. W. Hegel and was taken over by Marx to describe what happens to men and women who labor under capitalism. Marx held that humans are by nature productive animals who live in this world by intelligently, purposefully transforming nature, in cooperation with their fellow humans, into commodities that can satisfy their needs and desires. In the process of production, men and women "externalize" themselves; that is, they make what was first a mere idea in their minds external to themselves in the form of an object or state of affairs which they create by their labor. The most important act of such self-externalizing creation is birth itself, but the same structure of creativity can be seen in the farmer's planning, planting, tending, and harvesting of a field of grain, in the carpenter's conceiving, cutting, fashioning, and finishing of a piece of furniture, and also in an artist's sculpting of a statue or a poet's forming of a sonnet.

Men and women need productive, fulfilling labor in order to be truly happy, Marx thought. He rejected the utilitarian notion that happiness consists simply in the satisfaction of desire. But the process of "externalization," by which men and women embody themselves in their creations, in their transformations of nature and in their interactions with one another, can be corrupted and perverted. If the products of our labor are taken out of our control, if the very laboring process itself is turned into a kind of submission to superior force, then what we make will come to appear to us not as fulfillments of our needs but as oppressive enemies thwarting our human nature. What has been externalized will become *alien*. In short, healthy externalization will become destructive *alienation*.

> **Alienation**   Alienation, according to Marx, is the condition of being at war with one's own nature, the products of one's labor, and one's fellow workers. Marx argued that capitalism undermines the human capacity for creative and productive work, making men and women unhappy in their work, dissatisfied in their leisure, and unable to fulfill their human potential. Marx derived the concept of alienation from German philosophers of the early nineteenth century.

Capitalism systematically frustrates our need for satisfying labor in every possible way, according to Marx. There is plenty of labor, to be sure. But it is not autonomous labor, it is not labor directed at satisfying genuine human needs, it is not healthful, fulfilling labor; it is competitive labor that sets worker against worker, worker against capitalist, and capitalist against capitalist. The very productivity of capitalism makes it a hell on earth, for at the moment in history when we first achieved the technology to raise ourselves above famine, sickness, and misery, the inner contradictions of our system of property plunged us into depths of suffering worse than anything that was known in the Middle Ages.

Here is just a short selection from Marx's essay on alienated labor from the unpublished and unfinished papers which are known today as the *Economic-Philosophic Manuscripts of 1844.*

What constitutes the alienation of labour? First, that the work is *external* to the worker, that it is not part of his nature; and that, consequently, he does not fulfill himself in his work but denies himself, has a feeling of misery rather than well-being, does not develop freely his mental and physical energies but is physically exhausted and mentally debased. The worker, therefore, feels himself at home only during his leisure time, whereas at work he feels homeless. His work is not voluntary but imposed, *forced labour*. It is not the satisfaction of a need, but only a *means* for satisfying other needs. Its alien character is clearly shown by the fact that as soon as there is no physical or other compulsion it is avoided like the plague. External labour, labour in which man alienates himself, is a labour of self-sacrifice, of mortification. Finally, the external character of work for the worker is shown by the fact that it is not his own work but work for someone else, that in work he does not belong to himself but to another person.

—KARL MARX, *Economic-Philosophic Manuscripts of 1844*

What could be done about the irrationality and dehumanization of capitalism? Marx's answer, as you all know, was a revolution, a socialist revolution made by the workers against the capitalists. The revolution, Marx believed, would accomplish several things. First, it would overthrow the system of ownership of the means of production which, under capitalism, placed in the hands of a few the accumulated technology, factories, raw materials, and machinery that had been produced collectively by the labor of generations of working men and women. Second, it would replace the system of production for profit in the marketplace by a system of production for the satisfaction of human needs. Men and

ОТСТРОИМ НА СЛАВУ!

Marx condemns capitalism for inflicting alienating work on the masses. He insists that unalienated work is the fulfillment of human existence, and holds out the hope that such work will be available to all men and women under socialism. Would you prefer a world with no work, or one with demanding, satisfying work? (Left, Art Resource; below, Georg Gerster, Ralpho/ Photo Researchers)

women would collectively determine what they needed, and put their talents to work to produce it. The mere accident of profitability would no longer be permitted to govern decisions about capital investment and economic growth. It might be, for example, that a large profit could be made in the United States by building luxury housing for which there was no burning need, but that little or no profit could be made from the production of well-made, gracefully designed, low-cost housing. No matter. If the low-cost housing were needed, it would get first call on the available building materials and construction work force. Finally, the capitalist system of distribution through the market would be replaced by a rational and humane system of distribution for human need. Under capitalism, the ruling slogan might be "From each as much as you can get; to each as little as you can get away with giving." Under **socialism,** however, the ruling slogan would be "From each according to his ability; to each according to his work." When the final stage of communism was reached, Marx said, the slogan on society's banner would be "From each according to his ability; to each according to his need."

Collective ownership of the means of production, production for use rather than for profit, distribution for need rather than for ability to pay. With these changes, socialism would overcome the instrumental and substantive irrationality of capitalism, and eliminate the alienation of human beings from their product, their labor, their own human nature, and their fellow workers.

Marx wrote in the middle of the nineteenth century, and it is now more than one hundred years later. The last major depression was a half-century ago. In the major industrial nations, despite continuing inequalities of wealth, the workers enjoy a standard of living beyond Marx's wildest dreams. Governments have stepped in with active policies of budget management and monetary control to dampen the boom-to-bust swings which Marx saw as proof of the unstable inner nature of capitalism. De-

Socialism   An economic and social system based on collective social ownership of the means of production, rational planning of economic investment and growth, roughly equal distribution of goods and services, and production for the satisfaction of human need rather than for private profit. Modern socialism dates from the teachings of the French socialists of the early nineteenth century, but the leading socialist philosopher is the German, Karl Marx.

spite the fact that half the world calls itself Marxist, despite the existence of something purporting to be communism in the Soviet Union, in the People's Republic of China, and in a dozen smaller nations, hasn't Marx simply been proved wrong by the passage of time and the flow of events? Is his critique of capitalism relevant today?

No question generates more heated dispute in economics, in political science, or in philosophy. One of the social critics who has defended a modern version of Marx's argument is the German-born philosopher Herbert Marcuse. Marcuse (1898–1979) was educated at Berlin and Freiburg, and then joined the Institute for Social Research at Frankfurt. He came to the United States in 1934 to escape the Nazi persecution of Jews and intellectuals. He taught at Brandeis University for many years, and then at the University of California at San Diego. Marcuse belongs to a group of twentieth-century social thinkers who have sought to fuse the social insights of Marx with the psychological insights of Freud in an attempt to arrive at an integrated critical social theory. In *One-Dimensional Man*, which is perhaps his most influential book, Marcuse insists that the managed economy and increased material well-being of workers under modern capitalism do not in the slightest diminish the fundamental substantive and instrumental irrationality that Marx perceived more than a century ago. He argues that the satisfaction of the needs of workers under advanced capitalism is apparent rather than real. Through the manipulation of desire in advertising, in popular culture, in television, and in education, workers are conditioned to like what they get rather than to insist on getting what they would truly like. To avoid inflation and recession, capitalism pours wasteful trillions into needless defense spending while inner cities rot and human potential goes unfulfilled. The very smoothness of the surface of modern capitalist society is only an added measure of irrationality, for whereas nineteenth-century capitalism was visibly inhuman, and thereby at least made manifest its own inadequacy, modern capitalism has successfully concealed its inhumanity from the very persons it dehumanizes. To call that progress is to suppose that slaves have been made free when they finally are forced to love their chains. This selection comes from the introduction to Marcuse's book. It sets the stage for his critique of capitalist society, philosophy, and ideology.

> Does not the threat of an atomic catastrophe which could wipe out the human race also serve to protect the very forces which perpetuate this dan-

ger? The efforts to prevent such a catastrophe overshadow the search for its potential causes in contemporary industrial society. These causes remain unidentified, unexposed, unattacked by the public because they recede before the all too obvious threat from without—to the West from the East, to the East from the West. Equally obvious is the need for being prepared, for living on the brink, for facing the challenge. We submit to the peaceful production of the means of destruction, to the perfection of waste, to being educated for a defense which deforms the defenders and that which they defend.

If we attempt to relate the causes of the danger to the way in which society is organized and organizes its members, we are immediately confronted with the fact that advanced industrial society becomes richer, bigger, and better as it perpetuates the danger. The defense structure makes life easier for a greater number of people and extends man's mastery of nature. Under these circumstances, our mass media have little difficulty in selling particular interests as those of all sensible men. The political needs of society become individual needs and aspirations, their satisfaction promotes business and the commonwealth, and the whole appears to be the very embodiment of Reason.

And yet this society is irrational as a whole. Its productivity is destructive of the free development of human needs and faculties, its peace maintained by the constant threat of war, its growth dependent on the repression of the real possibilities for pacifying the struggle for existence—individual, national, and international. This repression, so different from that which characterized the preceding, less developed stages of our society, operates today not from a position of natural and technical immaturity but rather from a position of strength. The capabilities (intellectual and material) of contemporary society are immeasurably greater than ever before—which means that the scope of society's domination over the individual is immeasurably greater than ever before. Our society distinguishes itself by conquering the centrifugal social forces with Technology rather than Terror, on the dual basis of an overwhelming efficiency and an increasing standard of living. . . .

The fact that the vast majority of the population accepts, and is made to accept, this society does not render it less irrational and less reprehensible. The distinction between true and false consciousness, real and immediate interest still is meaningful. But this distinction itself must be validated. Men must come to see it and to find their way from false to true consciousness, from their immediate to their real interest. They can do so only if they live in need of changing their way of life, of denying the positive, of refusing. It is precisely this need which the established society manages to repress to the degree to which it is capable of "delivering the goods" on an increasingly large scale, and using the scientific conquest of nature for the scientific conquest of man.

—HERBERT MARCUSE, *One-Dimensional Man*

Marcuse's critique of American society raises political and moral questions, of course, but it also raises very deep metaphysical issues which have been the subject of philosophical debate ever since the time of Plato. Marcuse knows that Americans are, at least legally speaking, free to accept or reject the economic and social arrangements which he condemns as "one-dimensional." He is even willing to concede that most Americans, if asked by a pollster, would say that they like the consumer goods they buy with their money and the amusements with which they fill up their leisure hours. But Marcuse insists that despite their legal freedom and their apparent contentment with the politics and culture of American society, Americans are really fundamentally *unfree*, because their reasoning has been corrupted and their very desires twisted by the repressive institutions of capitalist society.

Does it make any sense to say that a person is unfree when she thinks she is free? Can a person really *not* desire something although consciously she believes that she does desire it? Bentham and the utilitarians say not. Desire is a conscious state of mind which I am immediately and unmistakably aware of. I may be wrong to believe that the thing I desire is going to give me pleasure, but I cannot be wrong about whether I really do desire it. What is more, the utilitarians go on, happiness or pleasure is also a conscious state of mind, and I can simply not be mistaken about whether I am happy. Other people may be wrong about how I feel—I may have the peculiar habit of frowning when I feel good—but I myself can never be wrong about my own happiness.

Plato doesn't agree, and neither does Marcuse. Both of them, and many other philosophers as well, hold that a man or woman can actually be unhappy without knowing it. People deceive themselves, they lie to themselves, they sometimes refuse to recognize the misery they are experiencing, because it is too hard to face the fact of that misery. And deceiving themselves about their own happiness, men and women can be slaves to passion, to ideology, to habit, or to fantasy, while all the time imagining that they are free.

This is a powerful argument, but a dangerous one. As we have already seen, the simple psychology of Bentham serves as a foundation for the democratic political philosophy of the liberal movement. Once we

Workers wait in line for unemployment compensation. The law making benefits available to those who have been thrown out of work by the capitalist system is one of the foundation stones of the Welfare State. (Charles Gatewood)

start arguing that ordinary men and women cannot judge whether they are truly happy, it is only a short step to the conclusion that some wise and powerful dictator had better make their decisions for them. That way lies tyranny and the totalitarianism of the twentieth-century state. But if we reject the notion of false pleasures and self-deception, then we lose all critical purchase on our society. We are forced to accept the superficial notion that whatever *seems* pleasant to people really is enjoyable. We rule out the possibility that men and women grow in self-knowledge.

My own judgment is that Plato, Marx, Marcuse, and the rest are correct in their fundamental claim that people can be unhappy and yet not "know" it—not admit it even to themselves. But like all powerful critical arguments, this one is dangerous and must be used carefully. Solid empirical evidence is needed (such as the evidence used by a psychiatrist in diagnosing mental illness) before we are justified in claiming that people are deceiving themselves about their own states of happiness. And even after we have made a solidly based judgment, we may still have no right to *force* people to do what will really make them happy.

The Main Points in Chapter Three

1. John Stuart Mill devoted his life to applying the principle of Utilitarianism to social questions. In the course of his writings, he revised the principle in three ways:
   a. He distinguished lower and higher pleasures.
   b. He recognized the role of habit or custom in economic life.
   c. He denied the right of the state to interfere in the private lives of men and women.

2. The Utilitarians defended the free market or *laissez-faire* principle that consumers and producers should be free to make bargains in the marketplace without government interference.

3. Conservatives like Edmund Burke and Alexis de Tocqueville attacked the new capitalist society for destroying old and cherished ways of life, and for elevating self-interested reason above tradition and reverence for institutions.

4. Socialists like Karl Marx criticized capitalism for exploiting the working class, for corrupting the work process so that it became a source of pain and suffering rather than fulfillment, and for driving the economy into ever-greater business crises. Marx claimed that a socialist revolution would put an end to capitalism by placing ownership and control of the society's means of production in the hands of the working class.

CONTEMPORARY APPLICATION:

The Welfare State

The first great question of all social philosophy can be stated quite simply in three short words: Who gets what? How shall the food, clothing, shelter, medical care, entertainment, luxury goods, automobiles, television sets, and other goods and services produced by our society be divided up? How much shall each person get, and how shall his or her share be determined?

At the turn of the century, the sharing out of the social product was pretty well decided by the working of the market. Workers got whatever they could afford to buy with their wages, capitalists lived off their profits, landowners had their rents, and what you ended up with was almost entirely a matter of how much you received in wages, profits, rents, or interest. There was no income tax, or much else in the way of taxes, for that matter, and the federal government was not in the business of providing medical care, investment capital, agricultural subsidies, rent subsidies, research and development seed money, or retirement income.

As we approach the end of the twentieth century, all that has changed. In the United States, and also in virtually every other modern industrial nation in the world, the government exercises great influence in determining how the social product shall be divided up. The market still has a central role in our country, of course, but it has long since ceased to be the only determinant of the pattern of distribution. Indeed, for many of us, the federal government (and state government as well) plays a larger role than the market in deciding how much we actually get to consume.

Think for just a moment of all the obvious and not so obvious ways in which the government helps to decide how much we actually get. If I am a wage-earner, my employer must pay me at least the minimum hourly wage. A portion of my salary will be automatically deducted for social security, and another portion will be deducted for state and federal income taxes, all before I ever see my earnings. Some of what I pay in taxes will return to me in the form of police protection, fire protection, and a large military establishment, whether I want those things or not. My medical bills will be paid for in part by Medicare and Medicaid. If I am not earning much, I may receive food stamps. If I am a student, I may receive my education from the state. If I am a farmer, the prices at which I can sell my crops will be partially set by the state, and the government may pay me not to plant some of my land. If I own an apartment house, the local government may fix the rent I can charge. And if I own a factory, virtually every aspect of my business will fall under one or another set of government regulations.

The totality of all these taxes, subsidies, deductions, payments, regulations, restrictions, permissions, and refunds has come to be called the *Welfare State.* No issue of modern social philosophy is more important, more controversial, and more directly related to our daily lives than the question of whether the welfare state is the right or the wrong way to run a society.

Each of the great traditions of social thought—liberal, conservative, and socialist—has a good deal to say about the rights and wrongs of the welfare state, but in the course of the past century, the positions have gotten so confused and tangled up that it is a little hard, anymore, to say just exactly what counts as a liberal position, a conservative position, or a radical position.

As we have seen, the nineteenth-century liberals—John Stuart Mill, his father James Mill, and the other utilitarians—argued strongly that the market should be allowed to decide who gets what, without control or intervention by the state. Their reasons were both practical and moral: the market, they said, does a more efficient and a more humane job of allocating resources and sharing out the social product than any human institution ever could. Millions of individuals vote every day with their dollars, indicating by their purchases what they want and what they don't want. Private companies respond to the pressure of demand by hiring or firing workers, opening or closing factories, and shifting their capital into whatever line of production meets consumer desires. Those who meet the public demand prosper; the others go under and make way for someone with a better sense of what the people want. In a democratic free market, undistorted by government intervention, men and women receive a reward that is directly related to what they contribute to others.

In the short run, the liberals said, the workings of the market might seem cruel or impersonal—workers thrown out of work for no fault of their own, businesses going bankrupt as consumer tastes shift, small family farms failing as agriculture becomes more industrialized and more efficient. But over time, this apparent harshness works to the benefit of us all. The workers who lose their jobs are making goods nobody wants, and that means that somewhere in the society, consumers are being forced to pay higher prices than necessary for what they buy. The decline of the family farm means lower food prices and more abundant food supplies throughout the society. The capital freed up when a business goes bankrupt can be shifted to another sector where human needs are as yet unmet.

So, taking all in all, the liberals insisted that the division of the social product is best left to the impersonal, efficient, decentralized workings of the free market.

There have been many defenders of the laissez-faire, or free, market theory in the past several centuries, but none of them has given us a more vivid picture of the dangers of state regulation and collective interference with individual freedom than the novelist and philosopher Ayn Rand. Rand's ethical theory, which she called Objectivism, asserted the absolute freedom and independence of the individual, whose moral obligations, she claimed, were based on promises or contracts freely entered into. Rand expounded her theories both in essays and in a number of enormously popular novels.

The following selection is from the most important of Rand's novels, *Atlas Shrugged*. The selection we read here is a story told by a man who had been a worker in an automobile company. A few words of background are needed to explain what Rand is doing.

Karl Marx was actively involved in the practical politics of the socialist movement in nineteenth-century Europe, in addition to being the principal socialist theoretician. In 1875, two branches of the German socialist movement were planning to join forces, and Marx was asked to comment on a draft proposal for a joint statement of principles. Since the meeting of the two groups was to take place in the town of Gotha, the statement came to be known as the Gotha Program. In the course of his critique, Marx wrote a paragraph containing a phrase that became the slogan of the communist movement around the world. "In a higher phase of communist society," he said, " . . . the narrow horizon of bourgeois right can be crossed in its entirety and society [can] inscribe on its banner: From each according to his ability, to each according to his need!"

This slogan, which expresses in the most extreme form the proposition that society as a whole should care for each of its members, is the target of Rand's brilliant satire.

Atlas Shrugged

Ayn Rand

"Well, there was something that happened at that plant where I worked for twenty years. It was when the old man died and his heirs took over. There were three of them, two sons and a daughter, and they brought a new plan to run the factory. They let us vote on it, too, and everybody—almost everybody—voted for it. We didn't know. We thought it was good. No, that's not true, either. We thought that we were supposed to think it was good. The plan was that everybody in the factory would work according to his ability, but would be paid according to his need. We—what's the matter, ma'am? Why do you look like that?"

"What was the name of the factory?" she asked, her voice barely audible.

"The Twentieth Century Motor Company, ma'am, of Starnesville, Wisconsin."

"Go on."

"We voted for that plan at a big meeting, with all of us present, six thousand of us, everybody that worked in the factory. The Starnes heirs made long speeches about it, and it wasn't too clear, but nobody asked any questions. None of us knew just how the plan would work, but every one of us thought that the next fellow knew it. And if anybody had doubts, he felt guilty and kept his mouth shut—because they make it sound like anyone who'd oppose the plan was a child-killer at heart and less than a human being. They told us that this plan would achieve a noble ideal. Well, how were we to know otherwise? Hadn't we heard it all our lives—from our parents and our schoolteachers and our ministers, and in every newspaper we ever read and every movie and every public speech? Hadn't we always been told that this was righteous and just? Well, maybe there's some excuse for what we did at that meeting. Still, we voted for the plan—and what we got, we had it coming to us. You know, ma'am, we are marked men, in a way, those of us who lived through the four years of that plan in the Twentieth Century factory. What is it that hell is supposed to be? Evil—plain, naked, smirking evil, isn't it? Well, that's what we saw and helped to make—and I think we're damned, every one of us, and maybe we'll never be forgiven. . . .

"Do you know how it worked, that plan, and what it did to people? Try pouring water into a tank where there's a pipe at the bottom draining it out faster than you pour it, and each bucket you bring breaks that pipe an inch wider, and the harder you work the more is demanded of you, and you stand slinging buckets forty hours a week, then forty-eight, then fifty-six—for your neighbor's supper—for his wife's operation—for his child's measles—for his mother's wheel chair—for his uncle's shirt—for his nephew's schooling—for the baby next door—for the baby to be born—for anyone anywhere around you—it's theirs to receive, from diapers to dentures—and yours to work, from sunup to sundown, month after month, year after year, with nothing to show for it but your sweat, with nothing in sight for you but their pleasure, for the whole of your life, without rest, without hope, without end. . . . From each according to his ability, to each according to his need. . . .

"We're all one big family, they told us, we're all in this together. But you don't all stand working at an acetylene torch ten hours a day—together, and you don't all get a bellyache—together. What's whose ability and which of whose needs comes first? When it's all one pot, you can't let any man decide what his own needs are, can you? If you did, he might claim that he needs a yacht—and if his feelings is all you have to go by, he might prove it, too. Why not? If it's not right for me to own a car until I've worked myself into a hospital ward, earning a car for every loafer and every naked savage on earth—why can't he demand a yacht from me, too, if I still have the ability not to have collapsed? No? He can't? Then why can he demand that I go without cream for my coffee until he's replastered his living room? . . . Oh well . . . Well, anyway, it was decided that nobody had the right to

judge his own need or ability. We *voted* on it. Yes, ma'am, we voted on it in a public meeting twice a year. How else could it be done? Do you care to think what would happen at such a meeting? It took us just one meeting to discover that we had become beggars—rotten, whining, sniveling beggars, all of us, because no man could claim his pay as his rightful earning, he had no rights and no earnings, his work didn't belong to him, it belonged to 'the family,' and they owed him nothing in return, and the only claim he had on them was his 'need'—so he had to beg in public for relief from his needs, like any lousy moocher, listing all his troubles and miseries, down to his patched drawers and his wife's head colds, hoping that 'the family' would throw him the alms. He had to claim miseries, because it's miseries, not work, that had become the coin of the realm—so it turned into a contest among six thousand panhandlers, each claiming that *his* need was worse than his brother's. How else could it be done? Do you care to guess what happened, what sort of men kept quiet, feeling shame, and what sort got away with the jackpot?

"But that wasn't all. There was something else that we discovered at the same meeting. The factory's production had fallen by forty per cent, in that first half-year, so it was decided that somebody hadn't delivered 'according to his ability.' Who? How would you tell it? 'The family' voted on that, too. They voted which men were the best, and these men were sentenced to work overtime each night for the next six months. Overtime without pay—because you weren't paid by time and you weren't paid by work, only by need.

"Do I have to tell you what happened after that—and into what sort of creatures we all started turning, we who had once been human? We began to hide whatever ability we had, to slow down and watch like hawks that we never worked any faster or better than the next fellow. What else could we do, when we knew that if we did our best for 'the family,' it's not thanks or rewards that we'd get, but punishment? We knew that for every stinker who'd ruin a batch of motors and cost the company money— either through his sloppiness, because he didn't have to care, or through plain incompetence—it's we who'd have to pay with our nights and our Sundays. So we did our best to be no good.

"There was one young boy who started out, full of fire for the noble ideal, a bright kid without any schooling, but with a wonderful head on his shoulders. The first year, he figured out a work process that saved us thousands of man-hours. He gave it to 'the family,' didn't ask anything for it, either, couldn't ask, but that was all right with him. It was for the ideal, he said. But when he found himself voted as one of our ablest and sentenced to night work, because we hadn't gotten enough from him, he shut his mouth and his brain. You can bet he didn't come up with any ideas, the second year.

"What was it they'd always told us about the vicious competition of the profit system, where men had to compete for who'd do a better job than his fellows? Vicious, wasn't it? Well, they should have seen what it was like when we all had to compete with one another for who'd do the worst job possible. There's no surer way to destroy a man than to force him into a spot where he has to aim at *not* doing his best, where he has to struggle to do a bad job, day after day. That will finish him quicker than drink or idleness or pulling stick-ups for a living. But there was nothing else for us to do except to fake unfitness. The one accusation we feared was to be suspected of ability. Ability was like a mortgage on you that you could never pay off. And what was there to work for? You knew that your basic pittance would be given to you anyway, whether you worked or not—your 'housing and feeding allowance,' it was called—and above that pittance, you had no chance to get anything, no matter how hard you tried. You couldn't count on buying a new suit of clothes next year—they might give you a 'clothing allowance' or they might not, according to whether nobody broke a leg, needed an operation or gave birth to more babies. And if there wasn't enough money for new suits for everybody, then you couldn't get yours either.

"There was one man who'd worked hard all his life, because he'd always wanted to send his son through college. Well, the boy graduated from high school in the second year of the plan—but 'the family' wouldn't give the father any 'allowance' for the college. They said his son couldn't go to college, until we had enough to send everybody's sons to college—and that we first had to send every-body's children through high school, and we didn't even have enough for that. The father died the following year, in a knife fight with somebody in a saloon, a fight over nothing in particular—such fights were beginning to happen among us all the time.

"Then there was an old guy, a widower with no family, who had one hobby: pho-nograph records. I guess that was all he ever got out of life. In the old days, he used to skip meals just to buy himself some new recording of classical music. Well, they didn't give him any 'allowance' for records—'personal luxury,' they called it. But at that same meeting, Millie Bush, somebody's daughter, a mean, ugly little eight-year-old, was voted a pair of gold braces for her buck teeth—this was 'med-ical need,' because the staff psychologist had said that the poor girl would get an inferiority complex if her teeth weren't straightened out. The old guy who loved music, turned to drink, instead. He got so you never saw him fully conscious any more. But it seems like there was one thing he couldn't forget. One night, he came staggering down the street, saw Millie Bush, swung his fist and knocked all her teeth out. Every one of them.

"Drink, of course, was what we all turned to, some more, some less. Don't ask how we got the money for it. When all the decent pleasures are forbidden, there's always ways to get the rotten ones. You don't break into grocery stores after dark and you don't pick your fel-low's pockets to buy classical symphonies or fishing tackle, but if it's to get stinking

drunk and forget—you do. Fishing tackle? Hunting guns? Snapshot cam-eras? Hobbies? There wasn't any 'amuse-ment allowance' for anybody. 'Amuse-ment' was the first thing they dropped. Aren't you always supposed to be ashamed to object when anybody asks you to give up anything, if it's something that gave you pleasure? Even our 'to-bacco allowance' was cut to where we got two packs of cigarettes a month—and this, they told us was because the money had to go into the babies' milk fund. Ba-bies was the only item of production that didn't fall, but rose and kept on rising—because people had nothing else to do, I guess, and because they didn't have to care, the baby wasn't their burden, it was 'the family's.' In fact, the best chance you had of getting a raise and breathing easier for a while was a 'baby allowance.' Either that, or a major disease.

"It didn't take us long to see how it all worked out. Any man who tried to play straight, had to refuse himself everything. He lost his taste for any pleasure, he hated to smoke a nickel's worth of to-bacco or chew a stick of gum, worrying whether somebody had more need for that nickel. He felt ashamed of every mouthful of food he swallowed, wonder-ing whose weary nights of overtime had paid for it, knowing that his food was not his by right, miserably wishing to be cheated rather than to cheat, to be a sucker, but not a blood-sucker. He wouldn't marry, he wouldn't help his folks back home, he wouldn't put an ex-tra burden on 'the family.' Besides, if he still had some sort of sense of responsibility, he couldn't marry or bring children into the world, when he could plan nothing, promise nothing, count on nothing. But the shiftless and the irresponsible had a field day of it. They bred babies, they got girls into trouble, they dragged in every worthless relative they had from all over the country, every unmarried pregnant sister, for an extra 'disability allowance,' they got more sicknesses than any doctor could disprove, they ruined their clothing, their furniture, their homes—what the hell, 'the family' was paying for it! They found more ways of getting in 'need' than the rest of us could ever imagine—they developed a special skill for it, which was the only ability *they* showed.

"God help us, ma'am! Do you see what we saw? We saw that we'd been given a law to live by, a *moral* law, they called it, which punished those who observed it—for observing it. The more you tried to live up to it, the more you suffered; the more you cheated it, the bigger reward you got. Your honesty was like a tool left at the mercy of the next man's dishonesty. The honest ones paid, the dishonest collected. The honest lost, the dishonest won. How long could men stay good under this sort of a law of goodness? We were a pretty decent bunch of fellows when we started. There weren't many chiselers among us. We knew our jobs and we were proud of it and we worked for the best factory in the country, where old man Starnes hired nothing but the pick of the country's labor. Within one year under the new plan, there wasn't an honest man left among us. *That* was the

evil, the sort of hell-horror evil that preachers used to scare you with, but you never thought to see alive. Not that the plan encouraged a few bastards, but that it turned decent people into bastards, and there was nothing else that it could do—and it was called a moral ideal!

"What was it we were supposed to want to work for? For the love of our brothers? What brothers? For the bums, the loafers, the moochers we saw all around us? And whether they were cheating or plain incompetent, whether they were unwilling or unable—what difference did that make to us? If we were tied for life to the level of their unfitness, faked or real, how long could we care to go on? We had no way of knowing their ability, we had no way of controlling their needs—all we knew was that we were beasts of burden struggling blindly in some sort of place that was half-hospital, half-stockyards—a place geared to nothing but disability, disaster, disease— beasts put there for the relief of whatever whoever chose to say was whichever's need.

"Love of our brothers? That's when we learned to hate our brothers for the first time in our lives. We began to hate them for every meal they swallowed, for every small pleasure they enjoyed, for one man's new shirt, for another's wife's hat, for an outing with their family, for a paint job on their house—it was taken from us, it was paid for by our privations, our denials, our hunger. We began to spy on one another, each hoping to catch the others lying about their needs, so as to cut their 'allowance' at the next meeting.

We began to have stool pigeons who informed on people, who reported that somebody had bootlegged a turkey to his family on some Sunday—which he'd paid for by gambling, most likely. We began to meddle into one another's lives. We provoked family quarrels, to get somebody's relatives thrown out. Any time we saw a man starting to go steady with a girl, we made life miserable for him. We broke up many engagements. We didn't want anyone to marry, we didn't want any more dependents to feed.

"In the old days, we used to celebrate if somebody had a baby, we used to chip in and help him out with the hospital bills, if he happened to be hard-pressed for the moment. Now, if a baby was born, we didn't speak to the parents for weeks. Babies, to us, had become what locusts were to farmers. In the old days, we used to help a man if he had a bad illness in the family. Now—well, I'll tell you about just one case. It was the mother of a man who had been with us for fifteen years. She was a kindly old lady, cheerful and wise, she knew us all by our first names and we all liked her—we used to like her. One day, she slipped on the cellar stairs and fell and broke her hip. We knew what that meant at her age. The staff doctor said that she'd have to be sent to a hospital in town, for expensive treatments that would take a long time. The old lady died the night before she was to leave for town. They never established the cause of death. No, I don't know whether she was murdered. Nobody said that. Nobody would talk about it at all. All I know is that I—and that's what I can't forget!—I, too, had caught myself wishing that she would die. This—may God forgive us!—was the brotherhood, the security, the abundance that the plan was supposed to achieve for us!"

In this next selection, Robert Goodin defends the welfare state on straight moral grounds. It is our obligation, he says, to extend the same support for the vulnerable and needy throughout society that we would offer to members of our own family. Goodin rejects the individualistic ethic of Rand in favor of a principle of social responsibility. Although Rand and Goodin use very different *styles* of writing to defend their positions, they are really talking right at each other. It is up to you to decide where you think the truth lies.

Vulnerabilities and Responsibilities:
An Ethical Defense of the Welfare State
ROBERT E. GOODIN

The aim of this article is to broaden our sense of social responsibility. It is first and foremost an argument in favor of state welfare services. . . .

My argument starts from what I take to be one of our firmest moral intuitions, one that we would be loath to sacrifice in this process of reflective equilibrium. That is the intuition that we have especially strong responsibilities toward our families, friends, clients, and compatriots. Charity, we seem strongly to believe, not only does but *should* begin at home. Our primary responsibilities are toward those who stand in some special relationship to us. Strangers get, and are ordinarily thought to deserve, only what (if anything) is left over. . . .

In what follows, I shall *not* be arguing that we lack any such responsibilities toward family and friends. Neither shall I be denying the strength of such claims. What I shall be arguing is that there is *nothing special* about those responsibilities. There are many others with precisely the same basis—and, depending on circumstances, perhaps even the same strength—as those responsibilities that

SOURCE: Robert Goodin, "Vulnerabilities and Responsibilities: An Ethical Defense of the Welfare State." *The American Political Science Review*, 79 (September 1985), 775–787.

we have always regarded as particularly binding. The upshot of this argument, if it is successful, is that we are not justified in our present practice of serving one set of claimants systematically to the exclusion of the other.

The theory ordinarily offered to account for the moral importance of these intuitively appealing special responsibilities deals in terms of self-assumed obligations. That analysis figures most famously in H.L.A. Hart's classic essay, "Are There Any Natural Rights?" which first introduced the concepts of special rights and duties into modern moral philosophy. "I think it is true of all special duties," Hart (1955, p. 185) wrote, "that they arise from previous voluntary acts."
. . .

The great appeal of the model of self-assumed obligations is that it explains so neatly what is "special" about our special rights, duties, obligations, and responsibilities. Special obligations are distinguished from general ones in two ways. First, whereas everyone has the same general duties, special obligations vary from person to person: I have special responsibilities that you do not. Second, whereas general duties are owed to everyone equally, special obligations are owed to specific others: I have different responsibilities to different people. The analysis of special obligations as self-assumed obligations accounts for both features beautifully. According to that analysis, I have some obligations that others do not because I have assumed them and others have not; my obligations vary because I have assumed obligations with respect to some people but not others . . .

The model I want to counterpose to that traditional one traces our special responsibilities to the peculiar vulnerabilities of specific others to our actions and choices. It is their vulnerability, not our promises or any other voluntary act of will on our part, that imposes upon us special responsibilities with respect to them. The promissory obligations that figure so centrally in the traditional account are, on this analysis, just a special case of vulnerability. If I promised and others are depending on me in consequence, then I am obliged to do as I promised—not because I promised, but merely because they are depending on (i.e., are vulnerable to) me. . . .

The best quick demonstration of the superiority of the vulnerability model is this. Imagine someone who is utterly helpless. The model of self-assumed obligations says you have only such responsibilities with respect to that person as you voluntarily assume. You might agree to do all sorts of nice things for that person. It would be terribly kind of you to do so, and of course once you have assumed responsibilities it would be obligatory at that point for you to discharge them. But, within this model, you are initially under absolutely no obligations to agree to do all (or any) of those favors. You are morally at liberty to press your bargaining advantage to the hilt, and to exploit mercilessly the other's weakness. You can, and morally you *may*, force that person to agree to arrangements that are highly inequitable, to say the least. For examples, if any are needed, reflect upon the classic cases of "unconscionable contracts": peddling useless drugs to desperately ill patients at inflated prices, or charging $1000 for a hamburger when you find yourself enjoying a monopoly on food at some disaster site.

Now, according to the model of self-assumed obligations, parties in strong bargaining positions like these would be violating none of their moral responsibilities by pressing their advantage to the hilt. The vulnerability model, in contrast, regards it as the height of immorality for them to exploit the other's weakness in this way. The same thing that would enable the stronger to drive a hard bargain with (and, within the model of self-assumed obligations, to evade altogether any responsibility for) the weaker would, within the vulnerability model, impose a heavy responsibility upon the stronger to look after the weaker. In such cases, the implications of the two models diverge clearly. And surely our considered moral judgments, backed up by all our "background theories," side with the vulnerability model on this score. . . .

The aim of this essay is to demonstrate that we have a broader range of social responsibilities than we traditionally acknowledge. . . .

The argument for broader responsibilities goes like this. We all acknowledge strong responsibilities toward our own families, friends, and certain others. Once we start examining the sources of those responsibilities, we discover there is nothing "special" about them. It is the vulnerability of the others, rather than any voluntary act of will on our part, that generates those responsibilities. There are many more people vulnerable to us, individually or especially collectively, than stand in any of the standard "special relationships" to us. If my analysis of the true basis of those standard responsibilities is correct, then we have strictly analogous (and, potentially, equally strong) responsibilities toward all those others as well. Aid to vulnerable strangers is thereby justified on the same basis as aid rendered to our own parents or children. . . .

The *raison d'etre* of the welfare state clearly is to discharge in part the responsibility I have here been discussing, namely, to protect vulnerable members of society. The early British initiatives—old-age pensions, health and unemployment insurance, minimum wage policies, and the like—were all aimed explicitly at "protecting the weakest and most vulnerable elements in society, such as the aged poor, the unemployed workman, the sweated worker" (Robson, 1976, p. 21). . . . It is clear that we have a strong moral responsibility to protect those who are vulnerable to our actions and choices. The only remaining question is whether the welfare state is the best way of doing so. Of course, any particular welfare state may fail for reasons peculiar unto itself.

It is important, therefore, to separate out and concentrate on what is generic to the welfare state as such.

For purposes of this discussion, I shall assume the defining features of the welfare state—and the features that must therefore be justified in any defense of it—are as follows. The welfare state necessarily entails *compulsory, collective provision for certain basic needs as a matter of right*. Welfare state provision is said to be compulsory and collective to distinguish it from private, voluntary charity; as distinct from more thoroughgoing egalitarian regimes, it provides only for people's basic needs; and as distinct from the old Poor Law, the welfare state allows beneficiaries to claim their entitlements as a matter of right.

The principal challenge facing any defense of the welfare state must surely be to show why protecting these vulnerable people should be a collective rather than an individual responsibility. There are basically two individualistic options available here. The first focuses upon the responsibilities of needy individuals themselves, while the second focuses upon the responsibilities of their families and friends.

Certainly it is true that people are even more vulnerable in even more ways to their own actions and choices than they are to those of the collectivity. For that reason, they should indeed bear primary responsibility for attending to their own needs. The state's responsibility is in the nature of a secondary, back-up responsibility, activated only when those with primary responsibility have failed to discharge it. Why they have failed is morally irrelevant: my analysis of responsibilities is forward-looking (asking only "Who is best able to help now?") rather than backward-looking (asking "Who is to blame for this situation?"). All that matters is that these individuals are now at risk of failing to have their most basic needs satisfied. That in itself is quite enough to activate secondary responsibility on the part of others to protect them.

The second individualistic option is to admit any need for someone to bear second responsibilities in such a case, but to lodge those responsibilities with some other private individuals rather than with the state. Specifically, this approach suggests that if people are unable to provide for themselves, it should be left to their families and friends to do so. That, curiously, is what "self-reliance" has come to mean in contemporary social policy debates (Goodin, 1985b). No doubt families and friends do, on my account, have strong moral responsibilities to provide assistance in such situations, and at its best, this system is no doubt preferable to state provision: material assistance from families and friends might betoken a deeper affection, in a way that state assistance necessarily cannot. The question is not whether families and friends should help out those in need. It is instead whether those in need should be forced to rely upon their families and friends for such support.

At this point, there is a strong case to be made for welfare-state provision as a kind of back-up to the back-up. An important part of this case is brutally empirical.

One of the primary obstacles to an effective system of family responsibility for needy members is that needy people are ordinarily found in needy families, who are in no position to make any great sacrifices (Goodin, 1985b; Steiner, 1981, p. 114). There is also a principled objection to such policies, however, which would prove decisive even if these empirical facts were otherwise.

This principled objection harks back to the standards of an acceptable dependency relationship laid down above. Dependency might be acceptable if: 1) it were symmetrical; or 2) basic needs were not at stake; or 3) no one were to enjoy discretionary control over needed resources. *Ex hypothesi*, we are here discussing an asymmetrical relationship where the subordinate's basic needs are indeed at stake.

The only thing that could make such a relationship morally acceptable would be for the agent upon whom the subordinate depends not to have discretionary control over those needed resources. Where that agent is a person's family or friends, that condition cannot possibly be met; family and friends must inevitably enjoy discretionary control over resources that are, in the final analysis, still their own. Where the subordinate is dependent instead upon the state, however, it is possible to vest that person with a legal entitlement to assistance. Once such laws have been enacted, state officials (unlike families, friends, or private charities) lack any discretion in deciding whether or not to honor claims of needy petitioners (Goodin, 1985b; Smith, 1949,

1955; Titmuss, 1971). The welfare state, defined as an institution which meets people's basic needs as a matter of right, is therefore a morally necessary adjunct to other more individualistic responses to the problems of vulnerability and dependency in our larger community.

REFERENCES

GOODIN, R. E., "Self-reliance Versus the Welfare State," *Journal of Social Policy*, 14 (1985), 25–47.

HART, H. L. A., "Are There Any Natural Rights?" *Philosophical Review*, 64 (1955), 175–191.

ROBSON, W. A., *Welfare State and Welfare Society*, London: Allen and Unwin, 1976.

SMITH, A. D., *Public Assistance as a Social Obligation*, 63 HARV. L. REV. 266–288 (1949).

SMITH, A. D., *The Right to Life*. Chapel Hill: University of North Carolina Press, 1955.

STEINER, G. H., *The Futility of Family Policy*, Washington, D.C.: Brookings Institution, 1981.

TITMUSS, R. M., "Welfare Rights, Law and Discretion," *Political Quarterly* 42 (1976), 113–132.

Study Questions

1. The government programs created or expanded by the Congress during the 1960s have transformed American society. Medicare, Medicaid, Food Stamps, Aid to Dependent Children, Head Start, and countless other programs now provide a major part of the family income for millions of Americans. Like all government programs, these so-called Welfare State programs are funded by taxes collected from individuals and businesses. Do you think these programs are wise? unwise? morally justified? morally unjustified? Why?

2. The central issue underlying all social philosophy is simply how the goods and services produced in our society should be distributed. Do you think someone should receive food, clothing, and shelter if that person does not work? What about those too young, too old, or too sick to work? What about those who want to work but can't find jobs? What about those who don't work because they are rich?

3. Both the nineteenth-century laissez-faire defenders of capitalism and their socialist critics were looking at a free market economy of small firms, very little restriction on business activity, and no labor unions. Do their theories have anything to tell us about the economy we see today? What?

4. In public debates about foreign policy, Americans repeatedly refer to governments in Latin America, Africa, or Asia as "marxist." What does that mean? What relation, if any, does that use of the term have to the theories of Karl Marx?

5. The top managers of big American corporations earn about twenty times as much as their employees. Is that sharply pyramidal pattern of distribution justified? Why? Why not? What would happen if the ratio were changed from twenty-to-one to ten-to-one?

4

POLITICAL PHILOSOPHY

JEAN-JACQUES ROUS-SEAU (1712–1778) is one of the most paradoxical figures in modern European letters. Born in Geneva, Switzerland, he spent his early years in a succession of homes (his mother having died only a few days after his birth). At the age of sixteen he converted to Catholicism, though he seems not to have been devout in any orthodox manner. After trying his hand at such tasks as music teacher and tutor, Rousseau finally found his true calling, which was to be a writer, a man of letters.

Rousseau's writings fall into two groups which seem entirely to contradict each other in their teachings. His autobiographical *Confessions*, his novels *Émile* and *La Nouvelle Heloise*, and his *Discourse on the Sciences and the Arts* all set forth in the most moving and powerful way the sentimental doctrine that our nature is inherently good, that civilization is the great corrupter, that feeling rather than reason is the proper guide to life, and that men and women will be naturally moral if only the impediments of cultivated life can be cleared away. But in his greatest work, *Of the Social Contract*, Rousseau argues in a spare and rigorously logical way for the proposition that the just state and morality itself arise from the exercise of our rational powers. Rousseau is thus an apostle both of sentiment—of feeling, of tears and sympathy— and also of reason.

Rousseau was a highly sensitive man; as his novels and his autobiography make clear, he was also a deeply troubled man, and in the last two years of his life, he appears to have suffered progressively more serious mental disorder, culminating in genuine insanity. In the world of fiction, he is the first and perhaps the greatest of the sentimentalists; countless eighteenth- and nineteenth-century novels echo his celebration of the feeling heart and the natural goodness of human nature. In political philosophy, he is a classic articulator of the doctrine of the social contract, on which modern democratic theory is built.

I   Rousseau and the Theory of the Social Contract

The literary world loves to gossip, and in Jean-Jacques Rousseau, the *enfant terrible* of eighteenth-century letters, it found a subject of endless speculation and titillation. Not since the great medieval logician Abelard married his young ward, Heloise, and got castrated for his trouble, has there been a philosopher whose personal turmoil contrasted so perfectly with the clarity and rigor of his thought. Rousseau's life and writings offer us an endless series of paradoxes and contradictions. He is the greatest apostle of what the eighteenth century called "sentiment," the feeling heart, the weeping eye, the rhapsodical outpouring of unstructured emotion. And yet his works deeply influenced that stern champion of pure reason, Immanuel Kant. Rousseau celebrated nature, the pastoral countryside; he condemned civilization and city life as a corrupter and destroyer of man's innate goodness. And yet he was born in Geneva, one of the great city-states of the eighteenth century and spent some of his most productive years in the capital of all Europe, Paris. His political philosophy, his novels, even his famous autobiography, at once so revealing and so misleading, all conspire to create for us the image of the eternal adolescent, in rebellion against the grown-up world, chafing against the restrictions of discipline and responsibility. Yet surprisingly, Rousseau did not begin to make his mark in the world of European letters until close to his fortieth year, and the most fruitful decade of his life, his forties, is the time when most philosophers and authors put behind them their youthful fantasies and accept the compromises of adult maturity.

Rousseau was born in 1712 in the extremely Calvinist city of Geneva. His youth and young adulthood were chaotic. His mother died almost immediately after his birth, his rather irresponsible father looked after him only fitfully until his tenth birthday, and not at all thereafter. He had little formal education, even by the standards of his day, and throughout his twenties and thirties he drifted about, trying to make his mark as a music theoretician among other things. Finally, at the age of thirty-eight, he entered a contest held by the Academy of the French city of Dijon. The topic was a popular one in enlightenment circles at that time—namely, whether the revival of the sciences and arts after their decline during the Middle Ages had helped to corrupt or to purify morals. Rousseau defended the unpopular position that the revival of ancient culture had corrupted morals! He won first prize, and his name was made; so too was his reputation as an iconoclast, a destroyer of received opinions and accepted doctrines.

Rousseau nursed a veritable storehouse of resentments throughout his lifetime, and as he grew older and more famous, he also grew more paranoid. The high point of his madness generated one of the great teapot tempests of the cultivated world and demonstrated, if indeed any demonstration was needed, that even philosophers are not immune from childish bickering. The story, in brief, is this. Rousseau's writings in the late 1750s and early 1760s had brought him into considerable disfavor with the governments of Switzerland and France, both because of his attacks on organized orthodox religion and because of his dangerous republican political sympathies. At that time there was close contact and communication between the literary worlds of England and France. David Hume, the great Scottish philosopher, had many friends in the circle of French *philosophes*, as they were called, and he offered to arrange a deal to help Rousseau. It was the practice for kings to give pensions to prominent literary and artistic figures, and Hume wanted to work out such a pension for Rousseau from the English King George III. Rousseau came to England, but he was convinced that Hume was actually secretly plotting against him to destroy his reputation. So he began to make scurrilous attacks on Hume's name and writings in letters to a number of the prominent people of literary London. Now David Hume was one of the sweetest, gentlest, most decent human beings imaginable except where one subject was concerned—his own literary reputation. You could attack his morals, ridicule his fat, bear-shaped body, tease him at a dinner party, or laugh at him in a salon, and he would merely respond with a smile or a gentle witticism. But criticize the quality and originality of his writings, and you aroused him to fury! So Hume struck back with a series of letters of his own, defending himself and attacking Rousseau. Jean-Jacques, now convinced that his life was in danger, leaped into a carriage, fled from the country house where Hume had arranged for him to stay, and raced toward the English Channel to catch a boat back to France before Hume and his supposed fellow conspirators could finish him off. Meanwhile, all literary Europe roared with laughter and wrote Rousseau off as a madman.

Could such a creature actually write philosophy? Could he indeed! Judgments differ among philosophers, as much as they do among the compilers of all-time baseball or football teams, but in my personal judgment, Jean-Jacques Rousseau is the greatest political philosopher who has ever lived. His claim to immortality rests upon one short book, *Of the Social Contract*, an essay scarcely more than a hundred pages long. In that brief, brilliant work, Rousseau formulates the fundamental question of the philosophy of the state, and makes a valiant although ulti-

"First of all, I would like to express my gratefulness to all those wonderful ancestors of mine who helped to make this glorious day possible."

W. Miller; © 1969 The New Yorker Magazine, Inc.

mately unsuccessful effort to solve it. Why such fame, you might ask, if he failed to solve the problem? In philosophy, as in the sciences, the most important step frequently is to ask the right question, and although philosophers had been analyzing the nature of the state for more than 2000 years before Rousseau, he was the first to see exactly what the problem was and to recognize how difficult it would be to solve.

In the last chapter, we took a look at some of the ways in which philosophers have answered the general question, What is the good society? We saw that moral problems of the just distribution of wealth are central to this subject. In a way, social philosophy, as Plato suggested long ago, is ethics writ large—it is ethics in a social, rather than an individual, setting. But there are a very special set of questions associated with the study of the *state*, and these are best explored separately from the general investigations of ethics and social philosophy.

Political philosophy is, before all else, the philosophical study of the state, so before we go any farther, we had best determine what we mean by a *state* and what philosophical problems are raised by states. Everywhere we look, across historical time and around the globe, men and women are organized into social groupings within defined territorial limits or borders. Within each one of these geographical units, there is some smaller group of people who rule, give orders, run things, use force to get others to obey—some group who make and enforce laws. This smaller group is what we call **the state.** Sometimes the group that rules consists of a single person and his or her personal followers: a king or queen, a general or dictator, a priest or pope, plus a group of loyal underlings. Sometimes the group consists of a hereditary class, such as a military aristocracy. The group may be a political clique or party which has led a successful revolution against the previous rulers. It may even, as in our own country, be a large group of men and women who have been chosen in an election by a much larger group of citizens. But whoever makes the laws, gives the commands, and enforces them on everyone living within that territory *is* the state.

States may exist for any number of purposes: they may exist to carry out the tenets of a religious faith, to maintain general peace and security, to see to the well-being of some or all of the people within the territory, or to ensure justice and tranquility. The state may even exist merely for the purpose of lining the pockets and satisfying the desires of itself, regardless of what the rest of the population wants or needs. There are so many different purposes for which states have existed that it is not much use to look for some basic or underlying function which all states

The United States was the first state actually to be brought into existence by a social contract. We call it our Constitution. (Brown Brothers, Sterling, Pa.)

perform insofar as they are states. Philosophers express this fact by saying that the state cannot be defined **teleologically.** That simply means that we cannot explain what a state is in terms of the goals (*telos* is Greek meaning end or goal) at which it aims. But all states, regardless of who comprises them and no matter what purposes they pursue, have *two* characteristics in common. Once you understand these two characteristics, you will know what a state *is* and also what the fundamental problem is of political philosophy.

First, states everywhere and always use force to obtain obedience to their commands. Sometimes force takes the form of armed troops, police, jails, and death rows. Sometimes merely the threat of force is enough to bring recalcitrant citizens into line. Economic threats can be used as effectively as the whip or the club. But behind the judge there always stands the police, and they are not there for ceremony only.

Force alone does not make a group of people into a state, however, for a band of robbers, an invading army, even a lone gunman holding you up on a dark street all use force to make you obey, and no one would call robbers, an army, or a mugger "the state." The second, more important, mark of the state is that as it issues its commands and shows its sword, it also claims to have the *right* to command and the *right* to be obeyed. Now a mugger does not claim the *right* to rob you. He says, "Your money or your life!"; he does not say, "Your money, for I have a right to it." But when the state sends you a bill for taxes, or commands you to report for induction into the armed forces, or orders you to stop at red lights and drive only with a valid license, it claims to have a right to your obedience. In the language of political philosophy, the state claims to be *legitimate*.

There is a wonderful scene in one of Shakespeare's plays (*Henry IV, Part 1*) in which a group of conspirators are planning their attack on the forces of the king. One of the group is a flamboyant Welsh chieftain named Glendower, who claims to have some magical powers in addition to some usable troops. At one point, in an effort to impress his fellow conspirators with the wonderfulness of his powers, he brags, "I can call spirits from the vasty deep." The leader of the conspiracy, Hotspur, is not very impressed, and he answers, "Why so can I, and so can any man/ but will they come when you do call them?" The point, of course, is that it is one thing to make a claim, and quite another to get anybody to believe it.

Now the really remarkable thing about human beings is that they are so prone to accept the claims of legitimacy made by states that rule the territories in which they live. From time to time, people rebel against the state, and a few philosophers called **anarchists** have denied the state's claim to have a right to rule. But by and large, when states make laws and claim the right to enforce them, people believe their claim and obey *even when they aren't actually being forced to do so*. Those last few words

---

Legitimate Authority   Legitimate authority is the right to give commands that others have a moral obligation to obey. States claim legitimate authority when they say that they have a right to pass laws which citizens or subjects *ought* to obey, regardless of whether they are in danger of being caught for not obeying. Democratic states base their claim to legitimate authority on the fact that they are elected by the people whom they rule, and therefore speak with the voice of the people.

Devout Catholic kissing the ring of Pope John XXXIII. The Roman Catholic Church demands obedience from its communicants, as did the absolute monarchs of their subjects. The distinctive mark of eighteenth-century social contract theorists is their rejection of such demands for obedience. (Fabian/Sygma)

are crucial, of course, for most of us "obey" a gunman who holds us up or an army that invades our city and points its guns at us. We "obey" because we don't want to get shot. Cynics might say that that is really the only reason anyone ever obeys the law, but all the historical and sociological evidence points in the opposite direction. Save in the most unusual circumstances, men and women obey the law more faithfully than the threat of punishment requires. They obey from habit, to be sure, but they also obey because they genuinely believe that the state has the right to command them. After all, they think, it is *the law.* How often has each of us done something or refrained from doing something merely because the law says that we must or mustn't? How, save by playing on this belief in the legitimacy of the law, could a single official or police officer control the behavior of a large crowd? How could several thousand overworked employees of the Internal Revenue Service collect taxes from 200 million Americans? How could a lieutenant lead a platoon of frightened soldiers into withering enemy fire? How, indeed, could an old and feeble king bend young, vigorous, ambitious dukes, princes, and generals to his will?

The belief in the legitimacy of the authority of the state is the glue that holds a political society together. It is, more even than armies or police or jails, the means by which the state gets its laws obeyed. So we may sum up the universal characteristics of states by saying that the state is *a group of people who claim the right to enforce obedience to their commands within a territory and succeed in getting most of the people in the territory to accept that claim.* A group of people who make a claim of this sort are said to be claiming *political authority.* So a state is a group of people who claim political authority and have their claim accepted by most of those against whom the claim is made.

Well, states claim political authority, and they get their claims accepted. But it is one thing to get other people to accept something you say; it is quite another to be right. I may claim to be a doctor, and if enough people believe me, I can open an office and start prescribing medicine. But that doesn't make me a doctor. My "patients" may fail to notice that I am not curing them, but even that does not make me a doctor. So too, a group may claim the right to rule, and the people may accept their claim, but that does not make their claim *true.*

The fundamental question of all political philosophy is obviously: When does a group calling itself the state really have a *right* to command? Or, since that way of putting the question seems to assume that states sometimes have such a right, we can ask: Does any group of persons ever have the right to command?

The same question can be turned around to focus our attention on the person doing the obeying rather than the people doing the commanding. From my point of view as citizen, a state is a group of people who command me. If I believe that I have an obligation to obey their commands, then I consider them as constituting a legitimate state. Otherwise, I consider them tyrants. To the citizen, the fundamental question of political philosophy is: Do I ever have an obligation to obey the commands issued by some group calling itself the state?

In ancient and medieval times, the citizen's obligation to the ruler was considered to be limited and conditioned upon the ruler's just performance of his or her sovereign duties. But in the sixteenth and seventeenth centuries, in response to fundamental shifts in the relative power of the aristocracy, the monarchy, and the new middle class, the theory began to be put forward that the authority of the ruler was absolute. The king, it was said, was the sole possessor of the ultimate political authority—**sovereignty,** as it was called. All others in the society were unconditionally obligated to obey his commands. Usually, a religious justification was advanced for this claim—the king was considered God's representative on earth—but sometimes the theory of an original agreement or contract was also appealed to.

The unqualified claim of absolute kingly authority was unacceptable to the philosophers of the Enlightenment. A person who bows her head to God or her knee to the king merely makes herself the slave of another. In the words of Immanuel Kant, who was, as we have seen, deeply influenced by Rousseau, submission to the commands of another means a loss of autonomy, a denial of one's own reason.

So for the political philosophers of the seventeenth and eighteenth centuries, the question of obligation to the state became a new and more complicated question: Is there any way in which I can submit to the commands of a legitimate state without giving up my freedom and autonomy? It was the special genius of Rousseau that he saw this question more clearly than anyone before him, and expressed it with greater precision and force. Here are the words in which he framed the problem, taken from the sixth chapter of *The Social Contract*:

> Where shall we find a form of association which will defend and protect with the whole common force the person and the property of each associate, and by which every person, while uniting himself with all, shall obey only himself and remain as free as before?

For the philosophers of the state who struggled with the question of legitimate authority in the seventeenth and eighteenth centuries, the standard solution to the problem was the device which they call the **social contract.** The authority of the state, it was argued, could only be founded upon an agreement among all the persons who were to be ruled

Social Contract A voluntary, unanimous agreement among all the people of a society to form themselves into a united political community, and to obey the laws laid down by the government they collectively select. In seventeenth- and eighteenth-century political theory, the legitimacy claims of the state are said to rest on an actual or hypothetical social contract.

by the state. The idea of a contract, of course, was taken from the law, where it applied to an agreement between two parties for their mutual advantage. A buyer and seller in the marketplace made a contract with one another, according to which the seller would supply goods in such and such a quantity, and of so and so quality, and the buyer would pay so much money for them at a particular time. The heart and soul of a contract is what the lawyers called a *quid pro quo* or a "this for that"; each side must stand to benefit from the deal in order to make the contract binding. The right of either party to have the contract enforced on the other derives from *two* things: first, each party has freely promised to abide by the contract, and so is bound by his or her word; second, each party benefits from the contract, and so has an obligation to return the benefit to the other according to the agreed terms.

The social contract theorists, as they have become known, conceived the idea of tracing political obligation back to a contract or social agreement between the citizen and all the other members of the society. If each citizen could be imagined to have actually made such an agreement, then the riddle of legitimate state authority would be solved. First, it would then be possible to explain why, and under what conditions, the citizen had a duty to obey the law. Very simply, he would have a duty to obey laws made by a state which he had freely contracted or agreed to bring into existence. If he said to the judge, "Who are you to command me? Who are you to threaten me with punishment if I fail to obey?" the judge would answer, "I am a representative of that state which you yourself promised to obey, when you signed the social contract." And if the citizen, still resistant, went on to ask, "What have I received from my fellow citizens that I should keep the agreement I made with them?" the judge could answer, "You have received peace, social order, even-handed justice, and the benefits of a civilized society."

But even more important, if the citizen asked, "How can I obey this state I have brought into existence without forfeiting any autonomy and giving up my freedom?" the judge could answer, "In this state, and only in this state, those who obey remain free. For the state that makes the laws consists not of *some* of the people who live in this nation, but of all the people. The commands you obey are the very commands which you, as a citizen, have issued in your role as a law-maker. In this state, the law-obeyers and the law-makers are one! Through the device of a social contract, the people become the rulers." Indeed, since the traditional word for ruler is "sovereign," the social contract theory is a doctrine of people's sovereignty, or, as it is usually known, **popular sovereignty.**

A meeting of the Jacobin club, a radical group that ruled France for a time during the Revolution. Maximilien Robespierre, the most famous revolutionary, was a leader of the Jacobin club in 1791–1792. (New York Public Library Picture Collection)

(That doesn't mean that people like it! It means that the people are sovereign. This is what Lincoln meant when he said that we live under a government that is by the people, as well as of and for the people.)

Here is how Rousseau describes the social contract. This passage directly follows the question quoted earlier:

The articles of this contract are so unalterably fixed by the nature of the act that the least modification renders them vain and of no effect; so that they are the same everywhere, and are everywhere tacitly understood and admitted, even though they may never have been formally announced; until, the social compact being violated, each individual is restored to his original rights, and resumes his native liberty, while losing the conventional liberty for which he renounced it.

The articles of the social contract will, when clearly understood, be found reducible to this single point: the total alienation of each associate, and all his rights, to the whole community; for, in the first place, as every individual gives himself up entirely, the condition of every person is alike; and being so, it would not be to the interest of any one to render that condition offensive to others.

Nay, more than this, the alienation being made without any reserve, the union is as complete as it can be, and no associate has any further claim to anything: for if any individual retained rights not enjoyed in general by all, as there would be no common superior to decide between him and the public, each person being in some points his own judge, would soon pretend to be so in everything; and thus would the state of nature be continued and the association necessarily become tyrannical or be annihilated.

Finally, each person gives himself to all, and so not to any one individual; and as there is no one associate over whom the same right is not acquired which is ceded to him by others, each gains an equivalent for what he loses, and finds his force increased for preserving that which he possesses.

If, therefore, we exclude from the social contract all that is not essential, we shall find it reduced to the following terms:

Each of us places in common his person and all his power under the supreme direction of the general will; and as one body we all receive each member as an indivisible part of the whole.

From that moment, instead of as many separate persons as there are contracting parties, this act of association produces a moral and collective body, composed of as many members as there are votes in the assembly, which from this act receives its unity, its common self, its life, and its will. This public person, which is thus formed by the union of all other persons, took formerly the name of "city," and now takes that of "republic" or "body politic." It is called by its members "State" when it is passive, "Sovereign" when in activity, and whenever it is compared with other bodies of a similar kind, it is denominated "power." The associates take collectively the name of "people," and separately, that of "citizens," as participating in the sovereign authority, and of "subjects," because they are subjected to the laws of the State. But these terms are frequently confounded and used one for the other; and it is enough that a man understands how to distinguish them when they are employed in all their precision.

—JEAN-JACQUES ROUSSEAU, *The Social Contract*

Two problems arise immediately. First, it is going to be difficult to get everyone together when laws need to be made. How can the people obey only themselves if they don't personally make the laws? The usual solution both in political theory and in political practice is to institute a system of elected representatives. But Rousseau will have none of that. If the state is not kept small enough for everyone to participate in law making, then so far as he is concerned, tyranny replaces liberty. Of course, that means that all citizens, and not just a few professionals, are going to have to pay attention to public affairs. But that is the price of freedom, Rousseau insists. As he says later on in *The Social Contract,*

As soon as men cease to consider public service as the principal duty of citizens, and rather choose to serve with their purse than with their persons, we may pronounce the State to be on the very verge of ruin. Are the citizens called upon to march out to war? They pay soldiers for the purpose, and remain at home. Are they summoned to council? They nominate deputies, and stay at home. And thus, in consequence of idleness and money, they have soldiers to enslave their country, and representatives to sell it.

It is the hurry of commerce and of the arts, it is the greedy thirst of gain, and the effeminate softness and love of comfort, that occasion this commutation of money for personal service. Men give up a part of the profits they acquire in order to purchase leisure to augment them. Give money, and you will soon have chains. The word "finance" is a term of slavery; it is unknown in the true city. In a State truly free, the citizens do all with their own arms and nothing with their money; and, instead of purchasing exemption from their duty, they would even pay for fulfilling it themselves. My ideas on this subject are indeed very different from those commonly received; I even think the *corvées* are less an infringement upon liberty than taxes.

The better a State is constituted, the more do public affairs intrude upon private affairs in the minds of the citizens. Private concerns even become considerably fewer, because each individual shares so largely in the common happiness that he has not so much occasion to seek for it in private resources. In a well-conducted city, each member flies with joy to the assemblies; under a bad government, no one is disposed to bend this way thither, because no one is interested in proceedings where he foresees that the general will will not prevail, and in the end every man turns his attention to his own domestic affairs. Good laws lead on to better, and bad ones seldom fail to generate still worse. When once you hear some one say, when speaking of the affairs of the State, "What is it to me?" you may give over the State for lost.

It was the decline of patriotism, the activity of private interest, the immense extent of States, the increase of conquests, and the abuses of govern-ment, that suggested the expedient of having deputies or representatives of the people in the assemblies of the nation. These representatives are the body to which, in certain countries, they have dared to give the name of the "Third Estate," as if the private interest of the two other orders deserved the first and second rank, and the public interest should be considered only in the third place.

Sovereignty cannot be represented for the same reason that it cannot be alienated; its essence is the general will, and that will must speak for itself, or it does not exist: it is either itself or not itself: there is no intermedi-ate possibility. The deputies of the people, therefore, are not and cannot be their representatives; they can only be their commissioners, and as such are not qualified to conclude anything definitively. No act of theirs can be a law, unless it has been ratified by the people in person; and without that ratification nothing is a law. The people of England deceive themselves when they fancy they are free; they are so, in fact, only during the election of members of parliament: for, as soon as a new one is elected, they are again in chains, and are nothing. And thus, by the use they make of their brief moments of liberty, they deserve to lose it.

The second problem is how to make decisions when there is disagree-ment. The natural solution that springs to our minds is to take a vote and let the majority rule. We have become so accustomed to deciding questions by majority vote that it sometimes seems as though little chil-dren learn to vote in school before they learn how to count the votes. But Rousseau had the clarity of mind to see that majority rule presented a very serious obstacle to freedom. I might promise, in the original unani-mous contract, to abide by the vote of the majority. But in so doing, I seem simply to be agreeing to a sort of voluntary slavery. If I have voted against a proposed law, believing that it is a bad law, contrary to the national interest, then how can I be said to "obey only myself and remain as free as before," when I am forced to submit to it? Rousseau has an extremely subtle answer to this question. First read what he has to say, and then we can talk about it a bit.

There is one law only which, by its nature, requires unanimous consent; I mean the social compact: for civil association is the most voluntary of all acts; every man being born free and master of himself, no person can under any pretense whatever subject him without his consent. To affirm that the son of a slave is born a slave is to pronounce that he is not born a man.

Should there be any men who oppose the social compact, their opposi-tion will not invalidate it, but only hinder their being included: they are

foreigners among citizens. When the State is instituted, residence constitutes consent; to inhabit a territory is to submit to the sovereignty.

Except in this original contract, a majority of votes is sufficient to bind
all the others. This is a consequence of the contract itself. But it may be
asked how a man can be free and yet forced to conform to the will of others.
How are the opposers free when they are in submission to laws to which
they have never consented?

I answer that the question is not fairly stated. The citizen consents to
all the laws, to those which are passed in spite of his opposition, and even
to those which sentence him to punishment if he violates any one of them.
The constant will of all the members of the State is the general will; it is by
that they are citizens and free. When any law is proposed in the assembly
of the people, the question is not precisely to enquire whether they approve
the proposition or reject it, but if it is comformable or not to the general
will, which is their will. Each citizen, in giving his suffrage, states his mind
on that question; and the general will is found by counting the votes. When,
therefore, the motion which I opposed carries, it only proves to me that I
was mistaken, and that what I believed to be the general will was not so. If
my particular opinion had prevailed, I should have done what I was not
willing to do, and, consequently, I should not have been in a state of
freedom.

Something very tricky is going on in this passage. How can I be free
when I don't get what I voted for? Earlier in *The Social Contract*, Rousseau put his point even more dramatically. A citizen who refuses to obey
the general will, he said, must be compelled to do so. "This in fact only
forces him to be free." What on earth can Rousseau have meant?

The full answer would take a book by itself, but we can say a few
things to clear away some of the mystery. Rousseau believed that the
people had a right to make laws only as long as they were genuinely
attempting to legislate in the public interest rather than in their own

The General Will   A term invented by Jean-Jacques Rousseau to
describe the decision by the citizens of a republic to set aside their
private and partisan concerns, and instead collectively aim at the
general good. According to Rousseau, to say that a society "has a
general will" is to say that all the members of the society are public-
spiritedly aiming at the general good in their political actions and
deliberations. Rousseau was very pessimistic about the possibility of
ever achieving a general will.

President Ronald Reagan ad-
dressing a joint session of
Congress. The social contract
which we in the United
States call the Constitution
vests the authority of the
people in these representative
individuals, and stipulates
how it shall be divided up so
that no branch of govern-
ment becomes so powerful as
to endanger our liberty. (Art
Stein/Photo Researchers)

individual and private interests. Now, if the majority could be counted
on always to be right about the general good, then no one in the minority
would want his or her view to become law. For if I want what is for the
general good, and if the majority is always right about the general good,
and if I am in the minority, then what I mistakenly wanted is *not* for the
general good, and hence not what I really want. And if freedom is getting
what you really want, then only by being forced to abide by the majority
can I really be free!

There is a flaw in the argument, of course. The majority may always
aim at the general good, but it does not always aim accurately. More
often than not, even when every citizen is seeking what is best for all,
the truth will be seen only by one citizen or a few. Rousseau confused
aiming at and hitting the target.

Americans have a vested interest in the theory of the social contract,
with all its flaws, because we are the first nation ever actually to bring
itself into existence as a state by means of a real, historical, explicit contract. We call it our Constitution, but what the Founding Fathers actually
wrote was the first operative social contract. When it was ratified in 1788,
there came into being for the first time in Western history a state truly
founded upon a contract.

Although the theory of the social contract has dominated liberal political theory since the seventeenth century, it has been subjected to a

number of powerful criticisms. The most obvious objection is that, save for the special case of the United States, no actual state has ever been brought into existence by such an explicit contractual agreement among the citizens-to-be. Hence, the theory does not provide any justification at all for the claims of even the most "democratic" governments. David Hume was one of the earliest anticontract writers to make this point. In an essay entitled "Of the Original Contract," he presents the following critique:

> Philosophers . . . assert, not only that government in its earliest infancy arose from consent or rather the voluntary acquiescence of the people; but also, that, even at present, when it has attained its full maturity, it rests on no other foundation. They affirm, that all men are still born equal, and owe allegiance to no prince or government, unless bound by the obligation and sanction of a promise. And as no man, without some equivalent, would forgo the advantages of his native liberty, and subject himself to the will of another; this promise is always understood to be conditional, and imposes on him no obligation, unless he meet with justice and protection from his sovereign. These advantages the sovereign promises him in return; and if he fail in the execution, he has broken, on his part, the articles of engage-ment, and has thereby freed his subject from all obligations to allegiance. Such, according to these philosophers, is the foundation of authority in every government, and such the right of resistance, possessed by every sub-ject.
>
> But would these reasoners look abroad into the world, they would meet with nothing that, in the least, corresponds to their ideas, or can warrant so refined and philosophical a system. On the contrary, we find, every where, princes, who claim their subjects as their property, and assert their independent right of sovereignty from conquest or succession. We find also, every where, subjects who acknowledge this right in their prince, and suppose themselves born under obligations of obedience to a certain sovereign, as much as under the ties of reverence and duty to certain parents. These connections are always conceived to be equally independent of our consent, in Persia and China; in France and Spain; and even in Holland and England, wherever the doctrines above-mentioned have not been carefully incul-cated. Obedience or subjection becomes so familiar, that most men never make any enquiry about its origin or cause, more than about the principle of gravity, resistance, or the most universal laws of nature. Or if curiosity ever move them; as soon as they learn, that they themselves and their ances-tors have, for several ages, or from time immemorial, been subject to such a form of government or such a family; they immediately acquiesce, and acknowledge their obligation to allegiance. Were you to preach, in most

parts of the world, that political connections are founded altogether on voluntary consent or a mutual promise, the magistrates would soon imprison you, as seditious, for loosening of the ties of obedience; if your friends did not before shut you up as delirious for advancing such absurdities. It is strange, that an act of the mind, which every individual is supposed to have formed, and after he came to the use of reason too, otherwise it could have no authority; that this act, I say, should be so much unknown to all of them, that, over the face of the whole earth, there scarcely remain any traces or memory of it.

But the contract, on which government is founded, is said to be the *original contract*; and consequently may be supposed too old to fall under the knowledge of the present generation. If the agreement, by which savage men first associated and conjoined their force, be here meant, this is acknowledged to be real; but being so ancient, and being obliterated by a thousand changes of government and princes, it cannot be supposed to retain any authority. If we would say any thing to the purpose, we must assert, that every particular government, which is lawful, and which imposes any duty of allegiance on the subject, was, at first, founded on consent and a voluntary compact. But besides that this supposes the consent of the fathers to bind the children even to the most remote generations, (which republican writers will never allow) besides this, I say, it is not justified by history or experience, in any age or country of the world.

Almost all the governments, which exist at present, or of which there remains any record in story, have been founded originally, either on usurpation or conquest, or both, without any pretence of a fair consent, or voluntary subjection of the people. When an artful and bold man is placed at the head of an army or faction, it is often easy for him, by employing, sometimes violence, sometimes false pretences, to establish his dominion over a people a hundred times more numerous than his partisans. He allows no such open communication, that his enemies can know, with certainty, their number or force. He gives them no leisure to assemble together in a body to oppose him. Even all those, who are the instruments of his usurpation, may wish his fall; but their ignorance of each other's intention keeps them in awe, and is the sole cause of his security. By such arts as these, many governments have been established; and this is all the *original contract*, which they have to boast of.

—DAVID HUME, *Of the Original Contract*

But the mere historical absence of a contract is not the worst of the problems confronting social contract theories. Even if a group of men and women had indeed contracted together, some time in the dim past, to submit themselves to the collective will of all, that would still leave those of us in the present generation without any reason for obeying the commands of the state. After all, I am not bound by the marriage contracts or the business contracts made by my ancient ancestors; why should I be bound by whatever political contracts they may have made?

To this, the social contract theorists answer that each of us, upon reaching the legal age of adulthood, implicitly signs his or her name to that original contract by remaining in the country, living under its laws, and entering actively into its legal arrangements. John Locke, the spiritual father of our Constitution, especially emphasizes the owning of property in this selection from his most famous political work, the *Second Treatise of Government.*

Every man being, as has been shown, naturally free, and nothing being able to put him into subjection to any earthly power but only his own consent, it is to be considered what shall be understood to be sufficient declaration of a man's consent to make him subject to the laws of any government. There is a common distinction of an express and a tacit consent, which will concern our present case. Nobody doubts but an express consent of any man entering into any society makes him a perfect member of that society, a subject of that government. The difficulty is, what ought to be looked upon as a tacit consent, and how far it binds, *i.e.,* how far any one shall be looked on to have consented, and thereby submitted to any government, where he has made no expressions of it at all. And to this I say that every man that hath any possession or enjoyment of any part of the dominions of any government doth thereby give his tacit consent, and is as far forth obliged to obedience to the laws of that government during such enjoyment as any one under it; whether this his possession be of land to him and his heirs for ever, or a lodging only for a week; or whether it be barely travelling freely on the highway; and in effect it reaches as far as the very being of any one within the territories of that government.

To understand this the better, it is fit to consider that every man when he at first incorporates himself into any commonwealth, he, by his uniting himself thereunto, annexes also, and submits to the community those possessions which he has or shall acquire that do not already belong to any other government; for it would be a direct contradiction for any one to enter into society with others for the securing and regulating of property, and yet to suppose his land, whose property is to be regulated by the laws of the society, should be exempt from the jurisdiction of that government to which he himself, and the property of the land, is a subject. By the same act, therefore, whereby any one unites his person, which was before free, to any commonwealth, by the same he unites his possessions, which was before free, to it also; and they become, both of them, person and possession, subject to

JOHN LOCKE (1632–1704) had a philosophical career which was, in a sense, the reverse of David Hume's. Locke's great works were not published until close to his sixtieth year, and they were received almost immediately with great acclaim. During the troubled times in England which followed the restoration of the Catholic monarchy (in 1660) after the English Civil War, Locke sided with the moderate faction which sought to limit the power of the king and bring the throne under some control by Parliament. In 1689, one year after the so-called Glorious Revolution which established a limited monarchy in England, Locke published a pair of long essays on the subject of the foundations of the authority of the state. The second of these essays, known now as the *Second Treatise of Government*, is the most important single document in the literature of constitutional democracy. Appearing when it did, the *Second Treatise* naturally was interpreted as a justification for the new regime of William and Mary, for it defended the sort of limited monarchy, hedged round with parliamentary restraints, which the English people adopted as their form of government in 1688. Actually, we now know that the two *Treatises* were written in the early 1680s, some years before the change in government took place.

The next year, 1690, Locke published a massive work on the foundations of human knowledge, the *Essay Concerning the Human Understanding*. (See Chapter 7.) The *Essay* is the foundation of the school of philosophy known as empiricism. Locke's arguments profoundly affected Berkeley, Hume, and the other British philosophers who followed him. The work was very soon translated into French and had a major influence as well on continental thought. A century later, Immanuel Kant was to acknowledge it as one of the most important influences on his own thinking.

the government and dominion of that commonwealth as long as it hath a being. Whoever therefore from thenceforth by inheritance, purchases, permission, or otherwise, enjoys any part of the land so annexed to, and under the government of that commonwealth, must take it with the condition it is under, that is, of submitting to the government of the commonwealth under whose jurisdiction it is as far forth as any subject of it.

But since the government has a direct jurisdiction only over the land, and reaches the possessor of it (before he has actually incorporated himself in the society), only as he dwells upon, and enjoys that: the obligation any one is under, by virtue of such enjoyment, to submit to the government, begins and ends with the enjoyment; so that whenever the owner, who has given nothing but such a tacit consent to the government, will by donation, sale, or otherwise, quit the said possession, he is at liberty to go and incorporate himself into any other commonwealth, or to agree with others to begin a new one (*in vacuis locis*) in any part of the world they can find free and unpossessed. Whereas he that has once by actual agreement and any express declaration given his consent to be of any commonweal is perpetually and indispensably obliged to be and remain unalterably a subject to it, and can never be again in the liberty of the state of nature; unless, by any calamity, the government he was under comes to be dissolved, or else by some public acts cuts him off from being any longer a member of it.

—JOHN LOCKE, *Second Treatise of Government*

You may wonder how a person can enter into a contract by "tacit consent." Don't I have to actually *say* that I am making a contract in order to do so? Locke here is relying on the ancient legal principle that when a person, over a period of time, acts in such a way as to give other persons a reasonable expectation that she will continue so to act, and if she benefits from that unspoken understanding, then she has made a "quasi-contract," which the law will enforce just as it will an explicit, spoken contract.

But Locke's argument depends on the assumption that a citizen can pick up and leave if he or she is dissatisfied with the laws of the state under which he or she lives. In Locke's day (the late 1600s) that was still possible. The Pilgrims who came to America, and many millions who followed them, were exercising precisely that option. Today, however, emigration requires visas and passports, no matter where you want to go. Every square foot of inhabitable earth is claimed by some state or other, so that the most anyone can do is to go from the rule of one state to the rule of another. Under this condition, it is harder and harder to see what truth there is in the theory of the implicit, or tacit, contract.

II *Fascism and the Organic State*

The liberal theory of the state dominates early modern political theory, but the nineteenth and twentieth centuries have seen the rise to intellectual prominence and political importance of significant alternatives on both the right and the left of the political spectrum. (In Chapter Three, you encountered this same phenomenon of the central liberal philosophy flanked by right-wing and left-wing countertheories. That is really the basic story of social and political thought in the West for the last two hundred years.) In this section, we will look at the historically most important right-wing attack on liberal philosophy—fascism. In order to prepare the way, we must go all the way back to the late eighteenth century and consider a criticism of the liberal conception of society and the state articulated by the English philosopher Edmund Burke. Burke argued that the notion of a contract, and with it the notion of a society of rationally self-interested pleasure maximizers, could not do justice to the true nature of the human experience. A business partnership might be founded upon a contract, entered into by a pair of self-interested entrepreneurs who estimated that they would profit from the deal. But it was monstrous and inhumane, Burke insisted, to suppose that the association of men and women in the ongoing social intercourse of life rested upon a similar calculation. It was equally absurd, he said, to reduce a citizen's submission to the majesty of the state to such a contract. Loyalty, honor, love of one's nation, all disappear in the double-entry bookkeeping of the social contract theories. Here, in a passage from his essay attacking the French Revolution, is Burke's most famous statement of the anticontract conception of society and the state.

> Society is indeed a contract. Subordinate contracts for objects of mere occasional interest may be dissolved at pleasure—but the state ought not to be considered as nothing better than a partnership agreement in a trade of pepper and coffee, callico or tobacco, or some other such low concern, to be taken up for a little temporary interest, and to be dissolved by the fancy of the parties. It is to be looked on with other reverence; because it is not a partnership in things subservient only to the gross animal existence of a temporary and perishable nature. It is a partnership in all science; a partnership in all art; a partnership in every virtue, and in all perfection. As the ends of such a partnership cannot be obtained in many generations, it becomes a partnership not only between those who are living, but between those who

EDMUND BURKE (1729–1797) is the father of modern conservative political thought, and its most eloquent spokesman. During his long political career in England, he defended a moderate position on political liberties and the rights of the American colonies, but turned violently against the French Revolution, which he saw as a subversion of the just and natural order of human society. In a moving message to his constituency, Burke defended the duty of a representative to vote his conscience, even against the wishes of the electorate which had put him in office.

are living, those who are dead, and those who are to be born. Each contract of each particular state is but a clause in the great primeval contract of eternal society, linking the lower with the higher natures, connecting the visible and invisible world, according to a fixed compact sanctioned by the inviolable oath which holds all physical and all moral natures, each in their appointed place. This law is not subject to the will of those, who by an obligation above them, and infinitely superiour are bound to submit their will to that law. The municipal corporations of that universal kingdom are not morally at liberty at their pleasure, and on their speculations of a contingent improvement, wholly to separate and tear asunder the bands of their subordinate community, and to dissolve it into an unsocial, uncivil, unconnected chaos of elementary principles. It is the first and supreme necessity only, a necessity that is not chosen but chooses, a necessity paramount to deliberation, that admits no discussion, and demands no evidence, which alone can justify a resort to anarchy. This necessity is no exception to the rule; because this necessity itself is a part too of that moral and physical disposition of things to which man must be obedient by consent or force; but if that which is only submission to necessity should be made the object of choice, the law is broken, nature is disobeyed, and the rebellious are outlawed, cast forth, and exiled, from this world of reason, and order, and peace, and virtue, and fruitful penitence, into the antagonist world of madness, discord, vice, confusion, and unavailing sorrow.

—EDMUND BURKE, *Reflections on the French Revolution*

This passage is an early expression of what later came to be known as the "organic" theory of the state. A business partnership or contractual association is a coming together of independent individuals, each of whom has his or her own interests, desires, plans, and standards of judgment. The association combines their efforts but it does not merge them into a single entity. Even a marriage, which in the eyes of the law is a contract, cannot obliterate the distinction between the husband and wife, though the usual talk of "making two one" sounds as though it does.

According to another philosophical tradition, however, society is more accurately compared to a living organism than to a business partnership. In an organism, the "parts" are merged into, and exist for, the whole. The feet, heart, hands, brain, and liver do not have separate interests, plans, or purposes. Indeed, when one organ of the body starts aggrandizing itself at the expense of the others, doctors suspect that the body is sick. An organism is an interconnected system of parts, all of which subserve the interests of the total living thing. There is proper subordination, not equality, among the parts. The brain gives orders which the nerves transmit to the muscles. If the survival of the organism requires it, a part may be amputated or removed, for each part exists only for the whole, not for itself.

Ever since Plato drew a double analogy between body and soul, and soul and state, some philosophers have said that a society is really like an organism. Men and women take their existence and their purpose from their role in the totality; the ruler, like the brain, gives the orders which the subordinate members of the whole must obey. Sacrifice for the good of the state, not self-interested calculation of personal advantage, is the fundamental principle of the organic state. Just as a healthy individual has a coherent personality that gives form and style to his life, so a healthy state has a culture that unites its people and gives their social life a distinctive style. Societies may enter into alliances with one another, just as individuals may enter into contracts with one another. But no alliance between disparate social organisms can overcome the organic wholeness of each.

In the early expressions of this theory, by de Tocqueville, Burke, and others, great emphasis is placed upon the traditions of the society, on its religious faith, and on its hierarchical political and social structure. As Oakeshott makes clear (though he is writing in our own century), the entry of new men and women onto the political scene is a violation of those traditions, a potentially destructive intrusion into the settled style of the politics of society. But in the nineteenth century, great social and economic changes destroyed the old preindustrial patterns of life and politics. First, the rising capitalist class, then the new working class formed by industrialism, thrust into the political life of nation after nation.

At the same time, the political rearrangements produced by Napoleon's wars released cultural forces which had been pent up by the old imperial order. Nationalities—that is to say, peoples with a common language, culture, and history—began to insist upon political independence. Czechs, Poles, Slovaks, Hungarians, Serbians, Rumanians, Estonians, Lithuanians, Croatians—each group with its special style of culture and society—demanded the chance to determine their own destinies. In the nineteenth century, there was a great surging up of interest in the music and literature of the people, and with it a rejection of the tradition of high Latin culture going back to the time of the Roman Empire. The Grimms' fairy tales, the études of Chopin, the rediscovery of Aryan or Teutonic culture—all were manifestations of this same search for the indigenous culture of the peoples of Central Europe.

In the early years of this movement, the doctrine of the folk or people was a progressive and liberating influence in Europe. But the turning point was the unimaginable upheaval of World War I. In the aftermath of that "war to end all wars," the political unity of Europe was permanently shattered and its economic health gravely damaged. The search for cultural unity took on the darker color of political absolutism. Economic depression and social disintegration fostered a powerful desire for unity, together with a hatred of foreigners and a rejection of the individualistic doctrines of liberalism. The most famous form of this new organicism, of course, was the National Socialism of Adolf Hitler in Germany. But a full decade before Hitler's rise to power, Benito Mussolini gave the doctrine a name, **fascism,** and a home, Italy. Mussolini cannot really be called a political philosopher, but he stated the fundamental teachings of fascism as clearly and unambiguously as any political leader ever has. In this lengthy section from Mussolini's *The Doctrine of Fascism,* we find

Fascism   The twentieth-century political movement begun in Italy in
1919 by Mussolini, which emphasized the primacy of the nation or
people, opposed left-wing political movements, and sought a rebirth
of the ancient glory of the Italian people. Subsequently, the term
fascist has been broadly applied to right-wing popular movements
which celebrate military power and use the police power of the state
to suppress dissent or opposition. The word derives from the Latin
term for a bundle of sticks bound together, a *fasces*, which served as
the symbol of Mussolini's party.

all the key elements of fascism: the exaltation of the state, the antiliberal-
ism, the totalitarianism, and the celebration of war rather than peace,
struggle rather than accommodation.

Fascism is a religious conception in which man is seen in his immanent relationship with a superior law and with an objective Will that transcends the
particular individual and raises him to conscious membership of a spiritual
society. Whoever has seen in the religious politics of the Fascist regime
nothing but mere opportunism has not understood that Fascism besides
being a system of government is also, and above all, a system of thought.

   Fascism is a historical conception, in which man is what he is only in so
far as he works with the spiritual process in which he finds himself, in the
family or social group, in the nation and in the history in which all nations
collaborate. From this follows the great value of tradition, in memories, in
language, in customs, in the standards of social life. Outside history man is
nothing. Consequently Fascism is opposed to all the individualistic abstrac-
tions of a materialistic nature like those of the eighteenth century; and it is
opposed to all Jacobin utopias and innovations. It does not consider that
"happiness" is possible upon earth, as it appeared to be in the desire of
the economic literature of the eighteenth century, and hence it rejects all
teleological theories according to which mankind would reach a definitive
stabilized condition at a certain period in history. This implies putting oneself outside history and life, which is a continual change and coming to be.
Politically, Fascism wishes to be a realistic doctrine; practically, it aspires to
solve only the problems which arise historically of themselves and that of
themselves find or suggest their own solution. To act among men, as to act
in the natural world, it is necessary to enter into the process of reality and
to master the already operating forces.

   Against individualism, the Fascist conception is for the State; and it is
for the individual in so far as he coincides with the State, which is the con-

BENITO MUSSOLINI (1883–1945) was the founder and leader of the Italian fascist movement. He ruled Italy, first as premier, later as dictator, from 1922 until his overthrow in 1943. Two years later he was captured by Italian underground fighters and assassinated. Mussolini was the first fascist leader in Europe, though he took a back seat to Adolf Hitler in the German-Italian alliance which started and waged the European portion of World War II. Like Hitler, Mussolini was an enemy of the liberal politics, lifestyle, and economic policies which flourished in much of Europe and America after World War I. Italy was a devoutly religious country, and Mussolini concluded an agreement with the papacy which gained him the support, or at least the acquiescence, of that major force in Italian life.

science and universal will of man in his historical existence. It is opposed to classical Liberalism, which arose from the necessity of reacting against absolutism, and which brought its historical purpose to an end when the State was transformed into the conscience and will of the people. Liberalism denied the State in the interests of the particular individual; Fascism reaffirms the State as the true reality of the individual. And if liberty is to be the attribute of the real man, and not of that abstract puppet envisaged by individualistic Liberalism, Fascism is for liberty. And for the only liberty which can be a real thing, the liberty of the State and of the individual within the State. Therefore, for the Fascist, everything is in the State, and nothing human or spiritual exists, much less has value, outside the State. In this sense Fascism is totalitarian, and the Fascist State, the synthesis of unity of all values, interprets, develops and gives strength to the whole life of the people.

Outside the State there can be neither individuals nor groups (political parties, associations, syndicates, classes). Therefore Fascism is opposed to Socialism, which confines the movement of history within the class struggle and ignores the unity of classes established in one economic and moral reality in the State; and analogously it is opposed to class syndicalism. Fascism recognizes the real exigencies for which the socialist and syndicalist movement arose, but while recognizing them wishes to bring them under the control of the State and give them a purpose within the corporative system of interests reconciled within the unity of the State.

Individuals form classes according to the similarity of their interests, they form syndicates according to differentiated economic activities with these interests; but they form first, and above all, the State, which is not to be thought of numerically as the sum-total of individuals forming the majority of a nation. And consequently Fascism is opposed to Democracy, which equates the nation to a majority, lowering it to the level of that majority; nevertheless it is the purest form of democracy if the nation is conceived, as it should be, qualitatively and not quantitatively, as the most powerful idea (most powerful because most moral, most coherent, most true) which acts within the nation as the conscience and the will of a few, even of One, which ideal tends to become active within the conscience and the will of all—that is to say, of all those who rightly constitute a nation by reason of nature, history or race, and have set out upon the same line of development and spiritual formation as one conscience and one sole will. Not a race, nor a geographically determined region, but as a community historically perpetuating itself, a multitude unified by a single idea, which is the will to existence and to power: consciousness of itself, personality.

This higher personality is truly the nation in so far as it is the State. It is not the nation that generates the State, as according to the old naturalistic concept which served as the basis of the political theories of the national States of the nineteenth century. Rather the nation is created by the State, which gives to the people, conscious of its own moral unity, a will and therefore an effective existence. The right of a nation to independence derives not from a literary and ideal consciousness of its own being, still less from a more or less unconscious and inert acceptance of a *de facto* situation, but from an active consciousness, from a political will in action and ready to demonstrate its own rights: that is to say, from a state already coming into being. The State, in fact, as the universal ethical will, is the creator of right.

The nation as the State is an ethical reality which exists and lives in so far as it develops. To arrest its development is to kill it. Therefore the State is not only the authority which governs and gives the form of laws and the value of spiritual life to the wills of individuals, but it is also a power that makes its will felt abroad, making it known and respected, in other words, demonstrating the fact of its universality in all the necessary directions of its development. It is consequently organization and expansion, at least virtually. Thus it can be likened to the human will which knows no limits to its development and realizes itself in testing its own limitlessness.

The Fascist State, the highest and most powerful form of personality, is a force, but a spiritual force, which takes over all the forms of the moral and intellectual life of man. It cannot therefore confine itself simply to the functions of order and supervision as Liberalism desired. It is not simply a mechanism which limits the sphere of the supposed liberties of the individual. It is the form, the inner standard and the discipline of the whole person; it saturates the will as well as the intelligence. Its principle, the central inspiration of the human personality living in the civil community, pierces into the depths and makes its home in the heart of the man of action as well as of the thinker, of the artist as well as of the scientist: it is the soul of the soul.

Fascism, in short, is not only the giver of laws and the founder of institutions, but the educator and promoter of spiritual life. It wants to remake, not the forms of human life, but its content, man, character, faith. And to this end it requires discipline and authority that can enter into the spirits of men and there govern unopposed. Its sign, therefore, is the Lictors' rods, the symbol of unity, of strength and justice.

—BENITO MUSSOLINI, *The Doctrine of Fascism*

III Marx's Theory of the State

To Karl Marx and his lifelong collaborator Friedrich Engels, the liberal social contract theory of the state was merely a convenient fiction designed to justify the rise to power of the new capitalist class. In order to understand the Marxist conception of the state, we must get at least a preliminary picture of Marx's doctrine of **historical materialism.**

As we saw in Chapter Three, Marx began with the fact of the sheer misery of the working class in England during the first part of the nineteenth century and added to this the instability of industrial capitalism as he observed it. Out of these elements, and the philosophical theories he had studied in his youth, Marx constructed a full-scale theory about the human condition, society, and history. The theory explained past history, analyzed the situation of industrial capitalism in the mid-nineteenth century, and predicted the future course of economic, social, and political developments. Simplifying somewhat, we can see Marx's theory as consisting of three parts: a theory of human nature; a theory of social organization; and a theory of social change, historical development, and revolution.

You have already studied Marx's theory of human nature in Chapter Three. The keynote is the concept of *alienation*. Human beings are considered by Marx to be socially productive creatures who find fulfillment and happiness through the free, productive, healthful exercise of their natural powers in cooperative labor with their fellow men and women. Capitalism thwarts that exercise, causing an alienation of men and women from the product of their labor, from the labor itself, from their own human nature, and from their fellow workers. The result is misery in the midst of plenty, unreason in the midst of technical rationality.

The second element of Marx's theory is his conception or model of social and economic organization. At first inspection, society at any one time seems an unorganized beehive of multifarious activities, without any system, pattern, or rationale. Agriculture, the arts, science, industry, government, religion, entertainment, marketing, war, charity, crime—the things men and women do are endless in number and variety. Merely to list all the categories of jobs being performed by someone or other is to lose oneself in a confusion of diversity. But Marx saw order in the chaos. He argued that in order to make sense of social life, we must distinguish a certain group of activities which are basic to the survival and reproduction of the human race. Each day, men and women work to transform nature into the food, clothing, and shelter they need to live. These economic activities form the base, or foundation, on which all else in the society rests. In order to distinguish the productive economic activities from the philosophical theorizing which his German idealist predecessors had made so much of, Marx called the productive elements of society its *material base*. In calling the base "material," he did not mean to suggest that it consisted of physical bodies rather than human thoughts, purposes, and plans, for even productive activities are intelligent, purposeful activities involving "ideas." Rather, Marx wanted to emphasize the fundamental role of economic production as opposed to philosophy, religion, or art.

The material base of a society consists of three subelements. The first is the *means* of production—the raw materials, land, and energy resources with which men and women work. The second is the *forces* of production, which includes the factories, machinery, technology, industrial knowledge, and accumulated skills of those who transform the means of production by their labor. The third and by far the most important subelement of the material base is what Marx called the *social relationships of production*. Since everything in Marx's theory depends on this last element, we must take a few paragraphs to explain it in some detail.

Human beings are productive creatures, to be sure. But according to Marx, they are *socially* productive creatures. Men and women divide the labor among themselves, differentiating the process of production into a series of subjobs or specialties and then parceling these pieces of the total productive process out among different workers. Some people raise grain, others dig iron ore out of the ground. Others bake the grain into bread, and still others work the ore into tools and weapons. This *division of labor* requires also a system of exchange, for no one can live on the products of his or her own labor alone. The farmer needs the products of the carpenter, the carpenter needs the products of the metal worker, and the metal worker needs the grain grown by the farmer. The market is the system by which a never-ending chain of trades, or purchases and sales, distributes the products of labor among the members of the society.

Although productive activity is cooperative, in the sense that there is a division of function and an exchange of products, it is by no means harmonious, equitable, or universally beneficent. Very early in human history, according to Marx, some men by force of arms succeed in seizing control over the vital means of production. They take the land, the streams, the mines, and the forests, and they prevent others from using them. Once these men have successfully asserted ownership of the means of production, they are in a position to extract a ransom from the rest of the men and women in the society. Pay me half of all you grow, the landholder says to the farmer, or I will not allow you to farm the land. The farmer has no choice, for if he does not farm, he starves. So two classes of people crystallize out of the social situation: the ruling class, which controls the means of production, and the underclass, which is forced to give up a part of the product of its labor in order to survive.

At first, of course, the naked force which holds the underclass down is obvious to all. But as time passes and generations succeed one another, sheer custom and familiarity confer legitimacy on what was originally mere might. The rulers pass on the control of the means of production

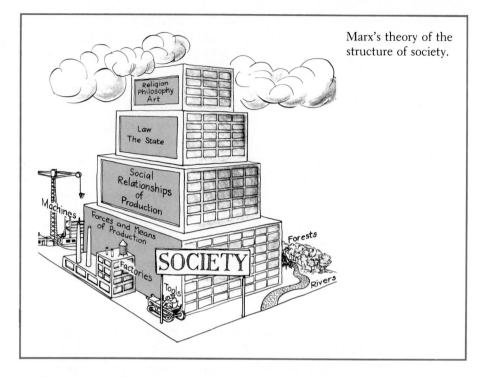

Marx's theory of the structure of society.

to their sons and daughters, who grow up believing that it is theirs by right. The free time which the rulers have—because they eat and drink and wear what they do not have to produce—permits them to develop a culture and style of life quite different from that of the laboring majority. Small wonder that even those in the underclass soon come to believe that the rulers are "different." They may not have been originally, but their descendants have certainly become so! As regular patterns of work, exchange, land ownership, and personal subordination develop, the rulers hold periodic courts to settle disputes that may have arisen in the enactment of those patterns. The decisions of these courts become the law of the land. Needless to say, the decisions rarely threaten the interests of the rulers, for it is they who convene the courts, they who sit on the bench, and they who enforce the orders of the courts with their soldiers. Nor is it surprising that the religious men and women of the society bless the rulers and their dominance. Churches are economically unproductive institutions, and they can survive only by sharing in that portion of the product which the rulers have taken from the laborers.

The system of relationships connecting those who control the means of production and those who do not is called the **social relationships of**

Proletariat/Bourgeoisie In Marx's writings, the *proletariat* is the urban population of wage-earning workers. The *bourgeoisie* is the middle class consisting of factory owners, shop-keepers, bankers, financiers, and their associates. The term proletariat comes from the old Latin word for the lowest class of people in Rome. Bourgeoisie comes from the medieval term *bourg*, meaning walled city. Burghers, or bourgeois, were the inhabitants of a walled city—by extension, the merchants and master craftsmen who formed the economic elite of the city, as opposed to the aristocracy, whose wealth and power was based on landholdings.

production. It is the basic fact about a society, and from it grow such other, secondary facts as the structure of the law, the dogmas of the dominant religion, the underlying themes of the art and literature, and also *the form and organization of the state.* Marx calls these subordinate or secondary features of a society its *superstructure,* conveying by this metaphor the notion that a society rests on, or is built on, that portion of it which is the "base." A more modern way of putting the same idea would be to say that the means, forces, and social relationships of production are the independent variables in a society and that the law, politics, art, religion, and philosophy are the dependent variables.

In the superstructure, the state occupies a central place, for it is the instrument the ruling class uses to maintain its domination of the rest of the society. As the character of the social relationships of production changes, so does the character of the state. Under feudalism, which is a system of production based on ownership of land, the state is controlled by the landed aristocracy, which employs it to maintain control of the agricultural workers (or "serfs") and to regulate the relationships between the great land holders (or "lords") and their subordinate tenants (or "vassals"). This same system of landholding also forms the basis for the military organization of the society, thereby combining the control of the means of production with the supply of the force to maintain that control. In an industrial system of production, where capital rather than land is central to the productive process, the class that owns the capital (the "capitalists") also controls the state. As Marx and Engels say in their most famous work, *The Communist Manifesto,* "The executive of the modern state is but a committee for managing the common affairs of the whole bourgeoisie."

Political philosophers claim that they are disinterestedly pursuing

A May Day celebration in Red Square, Moscow. The Bolsheviks came to power in Russia in 1917 as the leaders of a coalition of peasants, workers, and intellectuals. Very quickly, they established a state whose centralized power surpassed that of the old pre-Revolutionary Czars. (Sovfoto)

eternal truth when they write their treatises, essays, and dialogues, but Marx pointed to the curious fact that in each era, quite intelligent and reasonable philosophers just happened to argue for precisely that system of politics and law which best served the interests of the ruling class. Aristotle enunciated the dictum that man is a rational animal, and then proceeded to conclude that because some men are more rational than others, nature has obviously created "natural slaves" and "natural masters." That Greek society was at that time built on slave labor was, presumably, irrelevant. St. Thomas Aquinas contemplated the infinite, and came to the conclusion that God had intended a hierarchical organization of the universe remarkably similar to the feudal system then flourishing in Aquinas' Europe. John Locke examined the law of nature, and deduced from it a justification for the contractual freedom and legal equality necessary to the growth of the rising capitalist class of England. In an early essay intended as a review of a book by Bruno Bauer, Marx took the Declaration of the Rights of Man and the Citizen which had been proclaimed by the French Revolution and showed in a clause-by-clause analysis that it was nothing more than a rationalization for bourgeois capitalism.

The same analysis could be given for Marx's own philosophy, as he himself realized. His theory of historical materialism was a justification for the working-class revolution which he hoped for, predicted, and confidently expected. The intellectual superstructure, as a reflection of the economic or material base, could not be expected to achieve a transhistorical truth. At best, it could give expression to the real social relationships of production and distribution through which men and women, day by day, labored to transform nature into the means for human life.

The third part of Marx's theory was his account of the way in which societies change over time. At any given moment, we may speak of the ruling class and the underclass. But as new technology develops, as the division of labor is carried farther and farther, slow shifts take place in the material base. Within the feudal order, capitalism begins to grow. New ways of production and exchange give rise to new systems of relationships. At first, the changes seem minute by comparison with the overwhelming preponderance of economic activity. But little by little, more men and women are drawn into the new patterns of economic activity. The economically progressive group, or class, is at first disadvantaged, for the rules have all been made to favor the dominant class. But as the real economic power of the progressive class grows, it begins to demand a place in the ruling circles of the society. It wants laws changed to help rather than hinder its economic interests. It wants a share of the power that comes from controlling the means of production.

Now Marx was an optimist, if by that we mean that he thought the human race was heading toward better times. But he was not a fool. It was perfectly obvious to him that whenever a growing class challenged the dominance of a ruling class, there was going to be violence. There was no way that capitalists could compromise their interests with the landed aristocrats of the old order; one of them was going to have to go. According to Marx and Engels, the two centuries of civil war and social upheaval beginning with the English Civil War, continuing on through the French and American revolutions, and ending with the American Civil War, were simply the protracted struggle between the landed aristocracy of the precapitalist order and the capitalist class which controlled the new industrial means of production.

In much the same way, he predicted the new rising class of industrial workers, the proletariat, would one day do battle with the ruling class, the capitalists. Out of that revolutionary struggle would emerge a post-

capitalist society in which a new system of social relationships of production would replace the old. No longer would there be a small group that
controlled the means of production and a large group forced to work for
it in an unjust, exploitative, alienated manner. Instead, the entire society
would collectively take control of the means of production, and the division of labor would serve the interests of all, not merely the interests of
the few. Under this new system of society, called socialism, there would
be no domination of one person by another. Hence, there would be no
need for a *state*, for the function of the state in every previous society
had been to enforce the domination of the ruling class. There would, of
course, be some sort of central direction of economic activity, for in a
highly complex industrial economy, a sophisticated coordination of millions of workers would be indispensable. But this would merely be an
"administration of things," not the "domination of men."

What then would become of the state? The answer, Engels stated,
was that it would cease to exist as any unnecessary organ ceases to exist.
It would "wither away." Here is Engels' analysis of the future of the state
after the proletarian revolution.

> The proletariat takes control of the State authority and, first of all, converts
> the means of production into State property. But by this very act it destroys
> itself, as a proletariat, destroying at the same time all class differences and
> class antagonisms, and with this, also, the State. Past and present Society,
> which moved amidst class antagonisms, had to have the State, that is, an
> organization of the exploiting class for the support of its external conditions
> of production, therefore, in particular, for the forcible retention of the ex-
> ploited class in such conditions of oppression (such as slavery, serfdom,
> wage-labor), as are determined by the given methods of production. The
> State was the official representative of the whole of Society, its embodiment
> in a visible corporation; but it was only in so far as it was the State of that
> class which, in the given epoch, alone represented the whole of society. In
> ancient times it was the State of the slave owners—the only citizens of the
> State; in the middle ages it was the State of the feudal nobility; in our own
> times it is the State of the capitalists. When ultimately, the State really be-
> comes the representative of the whole of society, it will make itself superflu-
> ous. From the time when, together with class domination and the struggle
> for individual existence, resulting from the present anarchy in production,
> those conflicts and excesses which arise from this struggle will all disap-
> pear—from that time there will, therefore, be no need for the State. The
> first act of the State, in which it really acts as the representative of the whole
> of Society, namely, the assumption of control over the means of production
> on behalf of society, is also its last independent act as a State. The interfer-

ence of the authority of the State with social relations will then become superfluous in one field after another, and finally will cease of itself. The authority of the Government over persons will be replaced by the administration of things and the direction of the processes of production. The State will not be 'abolished'; it will wither away. It is from this point of view that we must appraise the phrase, "a free popular State"—a phrase which, for a time, had a right to be employed as a purely propaganda slogan, but which in the long run is scientifically untenable. It is also from this point of view that we must appraise the demand of the so-called anarchists that the State "should be abolished overnight."

—FRIEDRICH ENGELS,
Herr Eugen Dühring's Revolution in Science

Engels wrote these words more than a century ago (in 1878). Since then, something calling itself a "proletarian revolution" has taken place in a dozen countries, including two of the largest in the world. Were Marx and Engels correct? Has the state withered away?

The question is a tricky one, because neither Russia nor China was an advanced bourgeois capitalist industrial society at the time of its communist revolution. Nevertheless, a number of modern political philosophers, sympathetic with Marx but skeptical of much of his theory, have argued that even in a truly socialist society, the state will not disappear. Marx and Engels based their prediction on the expectation that after the revolution, there would be no further class divisions within society. But the evidence of Russia (and to some extent, of China) suggests that even when the means of production are, technically speaking, owned by everyone collectively, there still springs up a distinction between those who

Collective farming in the Soviet Union. Despite the forced collectivization of Soviet farms, during which millions of Russian peasants were killed, agriculture remains the weak link in the Russian economy. (Sovfoto)

labor and those who manage, those who are on the receiving end of decisions and those who issue the orders. In the Soviet Union, this distinction has given rise to systematic inequalities in the distribution of wealth, educational opportunities, status, and power.

Mao Tse-Tung, the political and philosophical leader of the Chinese revolution, was throughout his long career especially concerned about this tendency for class distinctions to reappear after the official elimination of private ownership of the means of production. The People's Republic of China has tried a number of tactics to overcome the tendency, including the quite unusual practice of requiring technical experts and industrial managers to spend time in the fields or on the production line doing ordinary labor. It remains to be seen whether Marx's dream of a classless society can be achieved. And even if it can be, we shall still have to wait to see whether in such a society, the state will wither away.

The Main Points in Chapter Four

1. The central issue of political philosophy is the legitimacy of the authority of the state. Jean-Jacques Rousseau, in the eighteenth century, posed the question clearly and forcefully in his essay, *Of the Social Contract.*

2. Rousseau asked: How can a state be created that has the right to command, while citizens retain their freedom and autonomy? His answer was: by means of a SOCIAL CONTRACT—an agreement among all the citizens to create a state and submit themselves to its authority.

3. Conservatives like David Hume criticized the theory of the social contract on the ground that there never had been, and never would be, such a general agreement to bring a state into existence.

4. Fascists like Benito Mussolini in Italy, in the 1920s and 30s, argued that the state is a living, organic whole, not a contract, and that citizens should place the welfare of the state above their own welfare. Fascists also attacked the liberal theory of the state for setting reason above instinct and passion.

5. Marx described the state as an instrument of the ruling capitalist class. He predicted that in a true socialist society, there would be no domination of one class by another, and therefore the state as such would disappear, being replaced by rational administration in the general interest.

Mandatory Testing for AIDS

Nowhere in our society is the conflict between the rights of the individual and the authority of the state more powerfully joined than in the debate about mandatory testing for the AIDS virus. Never in the entire history of medical science has there been a disease as deadly as AIDS. The Black death, smallpox, even cancer kill only a portion of those who develop the disease, but every man, woman, and child who contracts AIDS dies, despite the heroic efforts of our most advanced hospitals and clinics.

There have always been afflictions, of course. Famine, when the rains didn't come, famine when they came too often, fire, plague, even—in the dawn of the human race—the slow, silent advance of the glaciers in the Ice Age. But in the past two centuries, we have conquered famine, flood, and all of the traditional plagues that beset mankind. Now, when people die of hunger, it is not because we cannot produce enough food, but because our social and economic systems will not permit us to feed the hungry with the food we have. Smallpox has been virtually wiped off the face of the earth. Even cancer is yielding to the wonders of modern chemotherapy. So it is especially frightening for us to be confronted by a completely fatal illness for which we can find no cure, no vaccine.

At first, the AIDS virus seemed to be limited to only three clearly defined segments of the American population: homosexuals, intravenous drug users, and those who had originally come from the Caribbean island of Haiti. It was easy for those who didn't fall into any of these groups to suppose that the problem was someone else's, not theirs'. But as the virus broke out into the general public—as viral or bacterial agents generally do in the epidemic spread of a disease—it finally dawned on the non-homosexual, non-drug using, non-Haitian part of the public that AIDS is a terrible threat to *all* of us.

Since the disease, thank the heavens, is not highly infectious, requiring exchange of bodily fluids for its transmission, it is obvious that its spread might be slowed, or even stopped, if everyone carrying the virus could be identified. But since it appears that many more people carry

the virus than ever develop the disease, and since even those who develop the disease may do so only after years of being virus-carriers, chemical testing would be required to identify potential transmitters.

So we have come, slowly but inevitably, to proposals for mandatory—
required—testing of large populations, in order to identify those carrying
the virus.

But these proposals pose the most far-reaching problems of a political
sort. Does the state have the right to invade the privacy of individuals
by requiring them to be tested? Do individuals have a right to refuse to
be tested when they may, unknown to themselves, be carrying and
spreading a deadly disease? How far may the state go in its demands that
individuals be subjected to testing? Will mandatory testing backfire, by
driving those who fear they have the virus into hiding?

These issues are debated in the four selections combined here. We
begin with a very useful survey of the issue from *Time* magazine, followed by a pair of position statements opposed to mandatory testing. We
conclude with excerpts from a speech by William Bennett, Secretary of
Education under President Reagan, who argues in favor of mandatory
testing.

This issue is so immediate, so volatile, that even though these selections have been taken from the latest sources available at the time this
book goes to press, their facts may be out-of-date before it comes into
your hands. Nevertheless, unless medical science finds a cure or vaccine
for AIDS very soon, the underlying question is sure to be of the first
importance no matter when you are reading this chapter. I hope, for all
our sakes, AIDS is soon history.

Putting AIDS to the Test

Amy Wilentz

TOUGH QUESTIONS ABOUT THE MERITS OF MASS SCREENING

For David Souleles, 21, a psychology student at the University of California at Irvine, the issue of whether to be tested for exposure to the AIDS virus is a simple one. Souleles, a homosexual, openly acknowledges the possibility that he may have been infected with the virus through previous sexual contact. But now he practices what has become known as "safe sex," and, he says, "the information that I'll receive from the test is not going to help me become more safe. If I find out I'm positive, there's nothing I can do about it anyway. It's kind of pointless."

Today the decision is up to Souleles. But as the AIDS toll continues to mount, a number of state and local politicians around the country are calling for widespread, mandatory AIDS antibody testing. These demands have spurred vigorous opposition from gay-rights activists, civil rights lawyers and public-health officials. They urge, instead, voluntary testing that includes what have been called the "three Cs": informed consent, confidentiality and counseling. This week both views will be represented in Atlanta as medical experts from across the nation gather for a conference sponsored by the Centers for Disease Control to debate the value of mass AIDS testing. Among the questions to be discussed: How far should the Government go in supporting and even requiring the test? How effective would mass testing really be in containing the spread of the virus?

Hundreds of thousands of Americans are already required by the Federal Government to submit to AIDS testing. By the end of this year, the military will have screened 3 million service members. Last month the State Department began testing its more than 8,000 Foreign Service personnel, and in March, the Labor Department plans to begin administering the test to some 60,000 young Job Corps applicants. A few states may be moving toward mandatory testing. Some examples: in Georgia, a committee of the legislature has approved a bill that proposes permitting the exchange of information regarding AIDS victims among health-care professionals. In Illinois, legislation is pending that would require state officials to withhold marriage licenses if a prospective spouse tests positive for the AIDS antibody.

Although a recent poll indicates the

SOURCE: *Time*, March 2, 1987. Reprinted by permission of the publisher.

general public seems to favor compulsory testing, especially of those in high-risk groups, experts question its wisdom. "For both sound public-health reasons and civil rights reasons, we are very much opposed to any type of mandatory testing," says Dr. Stephen Joseph, New York City's health commissioner. Experience with other diseases, he says, shows that without an effective cure for AIDS, such a policy would be useless. "Until treatment was available, mandatory testing and [sexual] contact tracing did nothing to stem the spread of syphilis."

Then, too, gay-rights activists question whether the record keeping and identification that testing would entail could remain confidential. Concern about being publicly branded positive for AIDS antibodies is so great among high-risk groups that mandatory testing would probably force such people into hiding. Thus those most likely to carry the disease would be least likely to find out whether they had been infected.

Civil liberties lawyers are also concerned about the threat of discrimination based on compulsory-testing results. (For this reason, most voluntary AIDS tests offered today are done anonymously.) Once identified as a carrier of the AIDS virus, an individual runs the risk of losing friends, employment, housing and insurance. In New York City, 314 AIDS discrimination complaints were filed in 1986 alone. Says Nan Hunter, a staff attorney for the American Civil Liberties Union: "The antibody test is not like other medical blood tests. People don't lose their jobs because they have B-positive blood."

Another and more immediate reason mandatory testing will not work, according to many researchers, is that the results of the blood test most commonly administered can be misleading. A positive result on the ELISA (for enzyme-linked immunosorbent assay) screening test means that an individual has been exposed to the AIDS virus and has developed antibodies to it, not necessarily that a person has—or will fall victim to—the disease. Scientists assume, but have not proved, that those who test positive are still carrying the virus and can transmit it. Moreover, additional testing is needed to confirm a positive result. Negative results can also be deceiving. Since the virus apparently takes from six to twelve weeks to provoke antibody production, an individual may have been exposed and still not show antibodies.

The annual cost of all this testing, including the ELISA, confirmation tests and counseling, would probably be counted in the billions. But the personal and emotional costs of testing are immeasurable. "The test tends to rip people's lives apart," says Dooley Worth, who leads a support group of high-risk women, many of them former intravenous drug users, in Manhattan. "I've even seen couples who are both negative break up because of questions raised from just getting the test." For those who test positive, the psychological effect is devastating. And critics of mass testing question the ethics of informing people who are practicing safe sex, like Student Souleles, that they have been exposed. "You're handing people an explosion in their lives," says Judith Cohen, a University of California at San Francisco epidemiologist. Says Souleles: "The risks outweigh the benefits of finding out. I can deal with it fine on this level."

A more positive approach, and one that will do more to stop the spread of the AIDS virus, say critics of testing, is education. "Our problem is not finding out who's infected," says New York Commissioner Joseph, "but educating everyone about the risks. Everyone—young, old, gay, straight—has to consider AIDS as a personal message." Pat Christen of the San Francisco AIDS Foundation agrees. "It's not up to me to test everyone to see that you don't get infected. It's up to you to protect yourself."

Secondary Infection

EDITORIAL

The ravages of AIDS are not confined to the body physical. Since the start of the terrible epidemic in this country five years ago, AIDS has attacked the body politic with successive waves of fear, loathing and panic, which threaten to do lasting damage to society long after effective medical therapies are found. As yet there is no vaccine in the works for the syndrome of social intolerance, moral majoritarianism and repressive conformity that has become a secondary infection of the disease.

In the name of prophylaxis, officials at the Federal Centers for Disease Control are proposing that everyone admitted to a hospital for whatever reason, everyone applying for a marriage license, everyone treated during pregnancy or for sexually transmitted diseases, be given the AIDS virus antibody test. The net they cast would catch millions of people—most of whom may never get sick with the disease—and brand them as pariahs, perhaps lose them their jobs and their passports, and confine them for life to a medically defined ghetto of medieval dimensions. Already the government is testing current and prospective Foreign Service and military personnel; corporations are running their own programs; and local authorities are considering a variety of measures to "screen" undesirables out of society.

At the present level of scientific knowledge about AIDS, testing has no purpose except as a social screen, a method of harassment and a worthless weapon in the war against drugs. The government has an important role to play in preventing the spread of the disease—through mass

SOURCE: *The Nation* Reprinted by permission of the publisher.

education, the provision of condoms and the encouragement of attitudes that make furtive and destructive personal be-

havior unnecessary. Antibody testing, as the government doctors want it, will have the opposite effect.

Where the A.C.L.U. Stands on AIDS

IRA GLASSER

The American Civil Liberties Union has been severely criticized for its opposition to compulsory testing for AIDS and to government efforts to identify and trace all sexual contacts of those suspected of harboring the AIDS virus.

It has been wrongly asserted that this organization has opposed "obviously good" public health measures in order reflexively to protect the right of privacy.

Actually, the A.C.L.U. sees no conflict between civil liberties and sound public health policies. Nor is it alone. Public health officials overwhelmingly oppose mandatory testing and contact-tracing. They believe that such programs would make it harder, not easier, to limit the spread of acquired immune deficiency syndrome.

People understandably panic when they first confront the policy issues related to acquired immune deficiency syndrome. The disease is fatal, it has no cure or even a successful treatment and it is

communicable. Worse, it is heavily stigmatized by prejudice toward homosexuality. In a situation of panic, and with an easily-identifiable scapegoat group available, people often grasp at what seem to be simple and clear-cut answers—even if those answers are wrong.

So the assumption is intuitively made that forced testing will be effective in preventing the spread of the AIDS virus. In fact, this is a field in which coercion would almost certainly backfire.

Our only protection against AIDS now is preventing the spread of the virus. Successful prevention efforts depend on reaching as many people as possible with accurate information about the disease and on persuading them to make appropriate changes in their behavior. Mandatory testing would not achieve that end. It would only drive people away from health authorities, which is the reason that most public health officials oppose it.

What public health officials want is more voluntary testing. And they want to be able to assure people who do come in that they will not face punitive sanctions

---

SOURCE: *The New York Times*, May 23, 1987, sec. A, p. 27.

Ira Glasser is executive director of the American Civil Liberties Union.

like quarantine, or have their names entered into a government computer, or suffer the loss of jobs or housing or health insurance. Such consequences subvert the very efforts we need most strongly to promote. One of the greatest tragedies of AIDS is that so many have died because this disease and basic information about it have been forced into a medical underground. We desperately need to bring people forward not drive them away.

It is for these reasons that the conflict between civil liberties and public health is often more perceived than real. The Centers for Disease Control, part of the United States Public Health Service, has just drafted a major set of recommendations for AIDS-related testing programs. Its major finding is that all such testing should remain voluntary. The Surgeon General of the United States has taken the same position, as has the American Public Health Association and virtually every public health official in the country.

The American Civil Liberties Union's policy on AIDS is consistent with public health interests. We favor broad access to testing on a voluntary basis, anonymously if possible but with confidentiality assured. We have filed lawsuits both to pro-tect individual rights and to force government to do more to educate the public about the risks of AIDS. We have also called for strong anti-discrimination laws to help counter the stigma and prejudice that has crippled much of the prevention work.

We do not apologize for our concern for traditional rights. Privacy is not something to be easily set aside during moments of hysteria. Nor is it merely an abstract legal principle, to be debated and dissected by lawyers. Widespread mandatory testing of the general population, where the incidence of AIDS is still very small, would inevitably result in a large number of false positives, perhaps as much as 28 percent, according to a forthcoming study from the Harvard School of Public Health. The consequences to those people falsely identified are not trivial and should concern us all.

Unfounded fear often leads us to abandon our concern for individual rights and to embrace policies that falsely promise deliverance. Mandatory testing and contact-tracing will not deliver us from the threat of AIDS. To argue otherwise is counter-productive to both public health and civil liberties.

AIDS: Education and Public Policy

WILLIAM J. BENNETT

I think we need to begin to ask some hard questions, and to debate some of the hard choices, surrounding AIDS—questions like whether mandatory testing might be advisable under certain circumstances, whether "contact tracing" might not be necessary, and whether or not spouses or lovers have a right to be informed if their partner is found to be infected with AIDS.

The Surgeon General, as well as a number of public health professionals, has called for expanded testing. Testing is necessary to track the spread of the disease and to determine the effectiveness of measures taken to combat it; and testing is also necessary to identify those who are infected, so they can act in ways that will reduce the likelihood that they will infect others. According to Dr. Robert Redfield, a specialist in infectious diseases at Walter Reed, "the most important education message is to encourage widespread testing."

Testing could be expanded in a variety of ways. Voluntary testing could be even more strongly encouraged, and facilitated. I believe it should be. And I think there is a good case to be made for pro-

posals to make testing a requirement for hospital admissions; to require testing as a part of the treatment at clinics, perhaps particularly at those serving "high risk" populations; to make it a requirement for securing marriage licenses, and for those seeking admission to this country; and/or to require an AIDS test for all persons convicted of a crime upon imprisonment, and prior to release.

All of these possibilities, and others, deserve to be explored. Is the failure of most States to offer even optional AIDS screening at venereal disease clinics sensible? I don't think so. In these States, anyone who comes to a clinic with a suspected venereal disease will be tested for a wide range of sexually transmitted ailments—but rarely for AIDS. That doesn't make sense. Many States require a blood test for syphilis to obtain a marriage license—but no test for AIDS is required. And where testing has taken place, only a handful of States offer to contact previous sexual partners of people known to be infected with the virus—what is known as contact tracing. Shouldn't these individuals be contacted?

Why is there so much resistance to AIDS testing? Why is there so much resistance to at least limited disclosure to, say, public health officials and sex part-

SOURCE: Address by William J. Bennett, United States Secretary of Education, Washington, D.C. April 30, 1987.

ners, of testing results? There seem to be three main arguments—or assumptions. First, it is said that the disclosure of AIDS test results would invade the privacy of the tested individuals. Second, it is feared that disclosure would lead to discrimination against those individuals in housing, employment, education, insurance, and other benefits. And third, it is argued that disclosure of test results would undermine the willingness to undergo voluntary testing or even to cooperate with mandatory testing, thus working to the detriment of AIDS research and the protection of other individuals.

These arguments are offered in good faith. But I think it is time we looked more seriously at the countervailing arguments. There are strong arguments for more testing, both for the sake of acquiring epidemiological knowledge and for the sake of protecting individuals; and there are strong arguments for considering superseding, in certain circumstances, the principle of confidentiality. After all, confidentiality, even in the medical profession, does not outweigh all other considerations. The American Medical Association's Principles of Medical Ethics recognize that a physician may reveal otherwise confidential information if this is necessary to protect the welfare of another individual or the community. Several State court cases have recognized that such disclosures are not a breach of the physician's fiduciary duty, if the disclosures are necessary to protect the public. Some of these cases have upheld disclosures by a physician concerning a patient's disease to the patient's spouse.

While these cases did not involve AIDS, their logic would seem to apply, at least in the absence of a State statute to the contrary.

Another significant line of cases indicates that physicians have not only the authority, but an affirmative duty, to notify third parties (such as attendants, family members, and other individuals) of the risk of infection from a patient and that physicians may be held liable for breach of this duty. Indeed, according to Dr. Roy Schwarz, the American Medical Association's assistant executive vice president for medical education and science, "When someone has the potential of transmitting the disease to someone who isn't infected, the second party has the right to know." I agree.

Now, these are not simply medical or legal issues. They are issues of public policy, which require honest, open, and thoughtful debate. Such a debate would have to weigh competing principles and considerations, taking into account the claims of individual privacy *and* the well-being of other individuals, and the health of the public. I believe such a debate would lead us to reject, for example, the California law that makes it illegal to divulge results of AIDS tests to anyone without written permission. This law, as I understand it, means that a doctor delivering a baby cannot tell other medical personnel, including the child's pediatrician, that the mother has AIDS, and that the baby may be at risk, unless the mother consents. It means a physician cannot inform past or present sex partners, unless the infected individual consents. Does this law sensibly balance the competing claims of the privacy of the patient and the well-being of others? I don't think so. I note that the American College of Obstetricians and Gynecologists has recently called for expanded testing among high risk women, pointing out that under some current State laws, a doctor could not, for example, inform a pediatrician and public health authorities about a new mother's AIDS test results.

Similarly, I doubt whether an open and honest debate would leave us in accord with a New York State policy which resulted in fifty prisoners who were afflicted with AIDS being released on parole without the State requiring disclosure of their condition to their spouses or lovers. As reported in *The New York Times*, one parole officer said, "I had one [parolee] assigned to me who simply didn't care. The guy was given about a year to live, and he was in total despair. He told me he was going to have sex with as many prostitutes as he could get his hands on, just to get even. What do I do, since he isn't violating his parole? He can kill someone, and we can't do anything

about it." I doubt that this is the kind of public policy we are ready to condone, or ready to support.

Cases like these need to be addressed. We need to ask: Are we thinking through the costs, as well as the benefits, of these kinds of policies? Do we not need more testing? Is voluntary testing sufficient? How do we balance a desire to protect the confidentiality of AIDS carriers against our obligation to protect the health of other individuals? Can we not see to it that testing, tracing and the sharing of information can be conducted within strict safeguards to ensure that such measures and information are used solely as compelling public health considerations dictate? More generally: Are we doing everything we should be doing by way of public health and public policy measures to discourage and impede the spread of this terrible disease? Of course, there are limits to what we can do. But we must do what we can; and we cannot let the fact that many of these questions are difficult, and many of the choices hard, deter us from facing up to them.

Study Questions

1. Suppose that your philosophy class decides to have an end-of-semester party. How should you decide who is to pay, how much they will pay, and what the party will be? Should the professor decide? Should the richest students decide? Should the strongest decide? The smartest? The best looking? Should everyone have a voice in planning the party? Why? Why not? What can the theory of the social contract tell us about group decisions?

2. Leaving aside the colonists who were alive during the writing and ratifying of the Constitution, no Americans have entered into a social contract, although naturalized citizens are called on to swear allegiance to the constitution already in existence. In light of these facts, is any of us morally obligated to abide by the constitution? Why? Why not?

3. In his Inaugural Address in January, 1961, President John F. Kennedy said to the nation, "Ask not what your country can do for you. Ask rather what you can do for your country." Was Kennedy a fascist? Why? Why not?

4. As I write these study questions, AIDS is terrorizing the nation, transforming our sexual practices, and placing heavy burdens on our medical facilities. By the time you read these study questions, the problem will be much worse. In the face of the threat of AIDS, do individuals who may be spreading the disease have the right to protect their privacy by refusing to be tested for the virus? If we institute widespread mandatory testing, do we risk losing something more important even than our lives, namely our freedom? How SHOULD the United States respond to the medical threat of AIDS?

5. From the biologist's point of view, AIDS is a big success story for the virus, as well as a major threat to humans. Every epidemic represents a success for the disease organism. Does one species of life have the right to wipe out another species of life? How does stamping out the AIDS virus differ from hunting the buffalo to extinction?

5

*PHILOSOPHY OF ART

PLATO (427?–347 B.C.) is one of the immortal geniuses of philosophy. Born in Athens to a wealthy and politically influential aristocratic family, he was closely associated as a young man with Socrates, who died when Plato was in his late twenties. When the democracy was restored, Plato's family fell out of favor, and his hostility to democratic government is reflected in a number of his works. At some time after Socrates' death, perhaps as much as fifteen years or more, Plato started to write dialogues in which moral, political, religious, cosmological, logical, and other subjects were explored. In the early dialogues, Socrates is always the principal speaker, and there is some reason to suppose that Plato's picture of Socrates' personality and doctrines bears a close resemblance to the actual historical man who was his teacher. Later on, however, the dialogues clearly come more and more to reflect Plato's own philophical investigations, and in the works that he composed last, Socrates disappears altogether as a character.

Retreating from public life, Plato founded a school at his home in Athens. The home was called the "Academy," and the word has since then meant a school or university. Many of the most gifted philosophers of the day worked or studied at the Academy, including the other great genius of ancient thought, Aristotle. Eventually, the Academy became an independent institution, and it continued in existence for almost 900 years before it was finally closed by the Roman emperor Justinian in 529 A.D.

Plato's greatest work was the *Republic*, a dialogue on the nature of justice, but much of his work in later life was devoted to mathematics and cosmology, and members of the Academy made significant contributions to formal logic and to such mathematical fields as solid geometry.

I   Plato's Attack on the Poets

Here is a short parable: There was a singer with a clear, strong, beautiful voice, whose songs were so lovely that people would come from miles around to hear him sing. The singer was a thoughtful, compassionate man whose heart was troubled by the poverty and misery of the people for whom he sang. After much reflection, he concluded that the people should rise up and change their condition. And he realized that his songs, because of their loveliness, were a distraction to the people, making them forget for the moment the real causes of their misery. He decided to tell the people what he had discovered, but alas, they would only listen to him when he sang. So he wrote a song about the misery of the people and the dangerousness of lovely songs. But because he was a great singer, his song was a lovely song, and the people, listening to it, were soothed and distracted from their misery, and so did nothing.

Plato was just such a singer of philosophical songs, and nothing is more poignant or paradoxical than his attitude toward the great works of art which he himself created. You have several times met Socrates in these pages, always in his role as the principal character in Plato's Dialogues (his "philosophical songs"). But Plato, the artist himself, is not to be confused with the dramatic character who sometimes speaks for him in his dialogues, any more than the real historical Socrates should be confused with that character. Socrates wrote nothing himself, as Plato's own portrait of him tells us; but Plato wrote a great deal, and so he was forced to ask himself, as every artist must, whether artistic creation is good or evil, whether a life spent in the forming of artworks is a life well-spent, what indeed the function of art is in human life and society, and whether there is a place for art in the good society.

Since Plato's Dialogues, at least as we encounter them today, are classified as philosophical works rather than as works of art, it might be worth saying a few words about what sets them off from all the other philosophical works which no one would dream of calling "artistic." A philosophical dialogue is easy enough to write, if all you care about is getting the arguments down on paper. Just put your own theories in the mouth of one character—call her Ms. Wise—and whatever objections you can think of in the mouth of a second character—"The Fool," per-haps—and then write the whole thing down as though it were a play. The result will not exactly be beautiful, but as long as it has two charac-ters in it, you can call it a dialogue. A number of great and not-so-great philosophers have actually written some of their philosophy in roughly this way, including the seventeenth-century Dutch metaphysician Baruch Spinoza, who was no artist at all, and the eighteenth-century Irish cleric George Berkeley, who wasn't either.

But Plato's Dialogues are quite another thing altogether. Their artis-tic brilliance results from Plato's ability to do three things at the same time, and to do them all superbly. First, his dialogues are not shadowbox-ing, or put-up jobs. Plato constructs real arguments, in which Socrates' opponents score points and make philosophical moves that are genuinely persuasive. We have already seen how Plato puts into the mouth of Cal-licles an argument against the practice of philosophy which many readers have considered overpowering. Second, the characters in the dialogues are not cardboard figures, two-dimensional pop-ups with name tags at-tached. They are fully realized human beings, with feelings, passions, characteristic ways of speaking. Some of them run on in great long speeches; others are mulish, grudging, giving nothing in an argument and resisting even the most obvious implications of their own state-ments. Some are dignified old men, full of years and self-confident in an awareness that they are nearing the end of life with their honor unsul-lied; others are eager, ambitious young men, out to score a quick knock-out over Socrates and make their reputations. Most of the characters in the dialogues were apparently modeled after real people, and the original readers presumably could judge how skillfully Plato had caught their characters in his portraits. But for those of us who read the dialogues two millennia later, it matters only that they are completely successful artistic creations.

Finally, Plato accomplishes the most difficult creative feat of all—he makes the personalities and speech of his characters actually exemplify, and thereby provide evidence for, the philosophical theories he is trying to expound. His characters are not merely believable; they are just what they ought to be, given the philosophy they are expressing, if Plato's own theories are true. This fit between character and belief is designed by Plato as an expression of the central thesis of his philosophy: the doctrine that the metaphysical order of the universe is mirrored in the inner psychic order of the soul. Plato bases his philosophy upon a distinction between *appearance* and *reality*, a distinction that turns up over and over in many different guises throughout his works (indeed, we can quite accurately say that although the distinction *appears* in many different forms, it is *really* always the same distinction, and that is just one more example, Plato would say, of the distinction between appearance and reality). For example, a straight stick looks bent when half of it is put in water (because of the refraction of light). Sugar may seem good to a diabetic even though it would really make him sick. A tricky argument may look correct, but really be invalid. A devil may appear to be an angel of the Lord, but really be a messenger from Satan. It may seem smart to cheat on an exam, even though it is really wrong. Popular opinion may sound wise, but really be foolish.

In all these cases, and countless others besides, there is an image, a belief, an action, a feeling, which seems to be right, true, good, accurate, veridical, or healthy but is really wrong, false, evil, misleading, fallacious, or harmful. The ability to tell the difference between the two is always, according to Plato, a matter of some sort of knowledge, and the power or part of the soul whose job it is to make that distinction is *reason*. Reason tells us that the stick is really straight, even though it looks bent; reason tells the diabetic not to eat the apparently good sugar; reason finds the flaw in the valid-looking argument; and reason shows us when the easy way—cheating, or going along with popular opinion—is in the end the harmful, destructive way.

As these examples suggest, knowledge of reality, and the ability to distinguish it from misleading appearance, is more than just "book learning." You can study the principles of optics in the classroom, but you need some common sense and the power of observation to tell when to apply the formulas to a real stick in some real water. The diabetic patient can carefully write down his doctor's instructions not to eat candy, but he needs a quite different kind of knowledge and a much stronger power of reason to apply those instructions when temptation appears in the guise of a rich, tasty dessert. Socrates needed more than just a "philosophical" understanding of justice to resist the chance to escape from his punishment by the Athenians and instead remain, calm and resigned, to drink the hemlock.

According to Plato, a woman who has some true opinions but does not really understand what makes them true will *look* wise as long as she doesn't get into morally difficult or complicated situations, but she will not *really be* wise. We are liable to confuse her good habits and her true opinions with real knowledge until we see her come unstuck in a crunch. Then we will realize that we were deceived and that what we took for real wisdom was only its appearance. So too, a man who mouths current arguments without really having thought them through for himself will sound very knowledgeable until we press him with some hard questions. Then we will discover that his knowledge is only appearance. Worst of all, according to Plato, a person who has no systematic grasp of the true good for humanity will not be able to tell what is going to make her truly happy, and so will do what looks pleasant but is ultimately harmful. She will allow herself to be flattered into betraying a trust, or beguiled away from the hard work that brings real satisfaction, or fightened by imagined evils into shameful or dishonorable deeds.

Plato weaves his philosophical theory about appearance and reality together with his psychological insights into human character to produce a series of persuasive and fundamentally true portraits in his Dialogues. (Needless to say, he deliberately intends the dramatic persuasiveness of his characters—their appearance—to reveal, rather than conceal, the truth about their souls—their reality.)

One example may make all this a bit clearer. In the dialogue entitled *Gorgias,* you will remember, there are three characters who argue with Socrates. The first is the title role, a traveling public speaker and teacher named Gorgias; the second is a young disciple named Polus; and the third is the hot-headed, brilliant Callicles. Now Plato sees Gorgias as one of those decent human beings who personally would not do anything shameful or wicked, but who does not really have rational knowledge of the right moral principles. In fact, although in his own life he is an upright person, the philosophy he expounds is totally false. Plato thinks that Gorgias is dangerous, because his pupils tend to do as he says, not as he does. Instead of imitating the decency and honorableness of Gorgias'

Plato criticized art for misrepresenting reality. Here are three paintings by the Frenchman Claude Monet, the American Adolph Gottlieb, and the Spaniard Pablo Picasso. All three would claim that they are successfully capturing some aspect of reality that a photograph fails to reveal. (Clockwise from top: Baltimore Museum of Art, The Core Collection; Dallas Museum of Art, Dallas Art Association purchase; The Museum of Modern Art, N.Y. Mrs. Simon Guggenheim Fund)

private life, his pupils listen to his relativistic moral arguments and act on them in the law courts and public life of Athens. Plato presents Gorgias as a man who is stuffily self-confident, easily trapped into logical contradictions, but personally horrified at the thought that anyone would take his philosophy as an excuse for dishonorable behavior. Plato lets him off rather easily in the dialogue, because he respects Gorgias' personal decency as a human being, while nevertheless condemning the confusion of his thought. When Polus, the young disciple, enters the argument in Gorgias' place, the tone changes immediately. Polus is one of those impressionable young men who have been misled by Gorgias' statements and insufficiently impressed by Gorgias' actual character. Polus argues better than Gorgias, because he is not restrained—as Gorgias is—by a well-developed sense of what is fitting and proper to maintain in a moral argument. Gorgias cannot bring himself to say something he knows to be wrong merely to make a point in a debate, but Polus is not so hesitant. Nevertheless, since he is merely repeating things he has heard in current conversation, without any deep thought, he is easily refuted by Socrates. But Plato permits Socrates to make fun of Polus, thereby expressing his moral evaluation of Polus as compared with Gorgias. When Callicles jumps into the debate to replace Polus, a real tension develops between him and Socrates. Callicles really believes, as he says, that might makes right, that there are no universal rational principles binding the weak and the strong, the ordinary and the extraordinary, to a single standard of conduct. This total confusion (as Plato sees it) is mirrored in the disorder of Callicles' soul. He rants, he shouts, he grows abusive, he loses whatever dignity he may have possessed. In short, his personality exhibits precisely that breakdown of true reason which his philosophy also reveals. The dialogue becomes, at one and the same time, an argument between two philosophies and a contrast between two personalities. The truth of Socrates' position is shown as much by his composure, his ironic self-deprecation, his inner peace, as it is by the forcefulness of his arguments.

Now let me connect up the parable at the beginning of the chapter with Plato's theory of appearance and reality and this long example from the *Gorgias* of Plato's artistic skill. Strange and paradoxical as it may seem, Plato actually believed, on the basis of his theoretical distinction between appearance and reality, that artistic creations were *appearances* and that as such they led us away from knowledge and away from a proper inner harmony of the soul. And like the singer in the parable, Plato expressed this conviction in a series of artistic works of such beauty that the attention of his audience is turned away from the message rather than toward it!

Our first selection in this chapter is, once again, from the *Republic.* It contains Plato's reasons for believing that art is misleading, harmful and, therefore, that it ought not to be permitted a place in the ideal society he is sketching. In much of this selection, Plato seems to be talking about what philosophers call **metaphysics,** or the study of the forms and nature of being, as much as about art. This interconnection of the different branches of philosophy is typical of the work of the great philosophers, and you should not be misled by the organization of this book into supposing that philosophy consists of a number of separate subfields locked away in watertight compartments. Indeed, the distinction between appearance and reality also bears directly on John Stuart Mill's claim, in the last chapter, that some pleasures are higher or truer or better than others. Plato held the same view, and he defended it precisely by saying that some pleasures are *more real* than others.

Plato's objections to art focus on two distinct but related questions: First, does art give us knowledge, or does it mislead us about the nature of reality? and, second, does art help us to achieve a proper, harmonious inner psychic order, or does it stir up our emotions and destroy the rule of reason within the personality? Plato convicts art on both counts. Art leads us away from reality rather than toward it, he claims, and it destroys our psychic harmony rather than reinforcing it. These twin issues, of the truthfulness of art and the psychological effect of art on the audience, run through all the philosophies of art that we shall be examining in this chapter.

Can you tell me what is meant by representation in general?

. . . shall we proceed as usual and begin by assuming the existence of a single essential nature or Form for every set of things which we call by the same name? . . .

Then let us take any set of things you choose. For instance there are

---

Metaphysics   In modern philosophy, the study of the most fundamental principles of the nature of things. The term derives from an early description of the set of essays by Aristotle, called by him "First Philosophy," which came after the Physics in an edition of Aristotle's works. (*ta meta ta physica,* or after the Physics.)

any number of beds or of tables, but only two Forms, one of Bed and one of Table. . . .

And we are in the habit of saying that the craftsman, when he makes the beds or tables we use or whatever it may be, has before his mind the Form of one or other of these pieces of furniture. The Form itself is, of course, not the work of any craftsman. . . .

Now what name would you give to a craftsman who can produce all the things made by every sort of workman?

He would need to have very remarkable powers!

Wait a moment, and you will have even better reason to say so. For, besides producing any kind of artificial thing, this same craftsman can create all plants and animals, himself included, and earth and sky and gods and the heavenly bodies and all the things under the earth in Hades.

That sounds like a miraculous feat of virtuosity.

Are you incredulous? Tell me, do you think there could be no such craftsman at all, or that there might be someone who could create all these things in one sense, though not in another? Do you not see that you could do it yourself, in a way?

In what way, I should like to know.

There is no difficulty; in fact there are several ways in which the thing can be done quite quickly. The quickest perhaps would be to take a mirror and turn it round in all directions. In a very short time you could produce sun and stars and earth and yourself and all the other animals and plants and lifeless objects which we mentioned just now.

Yes, in appearance, but not the actual things.

Quite so; you are helping out my argument. My notion is that a painter is a craftsman of that kind. You may say that the things he produces are not real; but there is a sense in which he too does produce a bed.

Yes, the appearance of one.

And what of the carpenter? Were you not saying just now that he only makes a particular bed, not what we call the Form or essential nature of Bed?

Yes, I was.

If so, what he makes is not the reality, but only something that resembles it. It would not be right to call the work of a carpenter or of any other handicraftsman a perfectly real thing. . . .

We must not be surprised, then, if even an actual bed is a somewhat shadowy thing as compared with reality.

True.

Now shall we make use of this example to throw light on our question as to the true nature of this artist who represents things? We have here three sorts of bed: one which exists in the nature of things and which, I imagine, we could only describe as a product of divine workmanship;

another made by the carpenter; and a third by the painter. So the three kinds of bed belong respectively to the domains of these three: painter, carpenter, and god.

Yes.

Now the god made only one ideal or essential Bed, whether by choice or because he was under some necessity not to make more than one; at any rate two or more were not created, nor could they possibly come into being.

Why not?

Because, if he made even so many as two, then once more a single ideal Bed would make its appearance, whose character those two would share; and that one, not the two, would be the essential Bed. Knowing this, the god, wishing to be the real maker of a real Bed, not a particular manufacturer of one particular bed, created one which is essentially unique.

So it appears.

Shall we call him, then, the author of the true nature of Bed, or something of that sort?

Certainly he deserves the name, since all his works constitute the real nature of things.

And we may call the carpenter the manufacturer of a bed?

Yes.

Can we say the same of the painter?

Certainly not.

Then what is he, with reference to a bed?

I think it would be fairest to describe him as the artist who represents the things which the other two make.

Very well, said I; so the work of the artist is at the third remove from the essential nature of the thing?

Exactly.

The tragic poet, too, is an artist who represents things; so this will apply to him: he and all other artists are, as it were, third in succession from the throne of truth.

Just so.

We are in agreement, then, about the artist. But now tell me about our painter: which do you think he is trying to represent—the reality that exists in the nature of things, or the products of the craftsman?

The products of the craftsman.

As they are, or as they appear? You have still to draw that distinction.

How do you mean?

I mean: you may look at a bed or any other object from straight in front or slantwise or at any angle. Is there then any difference in the bed itself, or does it merely look different?

It only looks different.

Well, that is the point. Does painting aim at reproducing any actual object as it is, or the appearance of it as it looks? In other words, is it a representation of the truth or of a semblance?

Of a semblance.

The art of representation, then, is a long way from reality; and apparently the reason why there is nothing it cannot reproduce is that it grasps only a small part of any object, and that only an image. Your painter, for example, will paint us a shoemaker, a carpenter, or other workman without understanding any one of their crafts; and yet, if he were a good painter, he might deceive a child or a simple-minded person into thinking his picture was a real carpenter, if he showed it to them at some distance.

. . . the content of this poetical representation is something at the third remove from reality, is it not?

Yes.

On what part of our human nature, then, does it produce its effect?

What sort of part do you mean?

Let me explain by an analogy. An object seen at a distance does not, of course, look the same size as when it is close at hand; a straight stick looks bent when part of it is under water; and the same thing appears concave or convex to an eye misled by colours. Every sort of confusion like these is to be found in our minds; and it is this weakness in our nature that is exploited, with a quite magical effect, by many tricks of illusion, like scene-painting and conjuring.

. . . Instead of trusting merely to the analogy from painting, let us directly consider that part of the mind to which the dramatic element in poetry appeals, and see how much claim it has to serious worth. We can put the question in this way. Drama, we say, represents the acts and fortunes of human beings. It is wholly concerned with what they do, voluntarily or against their will, and how they fare, with the consequences which they regard as happy or otherwise, and with their feelings of joy and sorrow in all these experiences. That is all, is it not?

Yes.

And in all these experiences has a man an undivided mind? Is there not an internal conflict which sets him at odds with himself in his conduct, much as we were saying that the conflict of visual impressions leads him to make contradictory judgments? However, I need not ask that question; for, now I come to think of it, we have already agreed that innumerable conflicts of this sort are constantly occurring in the mind. But there is a further point to be considered now. We have said that a man of high character will bear any stroke of fortune, such as the loss of a son or of anything else he holds dear, with more equanimity than most people. We may now ask: will he feel no pain, or is that impossible? Will he not rather observe due measure in his grief?

Yes, that is nearer the truth.

Now tell me: will he be more likely to struggle with his grief and resist it when he is under the eyes of his fellows or when he is alone?

He will be far more restrained in the presence of others.

Yes; when he is by himself he will not be ashamed to do and say much that he would not like anyone to see or hear.

Quite so.

What encourages him to resist his grief is the lawful authority of reason, while the impulse to give way comes from the feeling itself; and, as we said, the presence of contradictory impulses proves that two distinct elements in his nature must be involved. One of them is law-abiding, prepared to listen to the authority which declares that it is best to bear misfortune as quietly as possible without resentment, for several reasons: it is never certain that misfortune may not be a blessing; nothing is gained by chafing at it; nothing human is matter for great concern; and, finally, grief hinders us from calling in the help we most urgently need. By this I mean reflection on what has happened, letting reason decide on the best move in the game of life that the fall of the dice permits. Instead of behaving like a child who goes on shrieking after a fall and hugging the wounded part, we should accustom the mind to set itself at once to raise up the fallen and cure the hurt, banishing lamentation with a healing touch.

Certainly that is the right way to deal with misfortune.

And if, as we think, the part of us which is ready to act upon these reflections is the highest, that other part which impels us to dwell upon our sufferings and can never have enough of grieving over them is unreasonable, craven, and faint-hearted.

Yes.

Now this fretful temper gives scope for a great diversity of dramatic representation; whereas the calm and wise character in its unvarying constancy is not easy to represent, nor when represented is it readily understood, especially by a promiscuous gathering in a theatre, since it is foreign to their own habit of mind. Obviously, then, this steadfast disposition does not naturally attract the dramatic poet, and his skill is not designed to find favour with it. If he is to have a popular success, he must address himself to the fretful type with its rich variety of material for representation.

Obviously.

We have, then, a fair case against the poet and we may set him down as the counterpart of the painter, whom he resembles in two ways: his creations are poor things by the standard of truth and reality, and his appeal is not to the highest part of the soul, but to one which is equally inferior. So we shall be justified in not admitting him into a well-ordered commonwealth, because he stimulates and strengthens an element which threatens to undermine the reason. As a country may be given over into the power of its worst citizens while the better sort are ruined, so, we shall say, the dramatic poet sets up a vicious form of government in the individual soul: he gratifies that senseless part which cannot distinguish great and small, but regards the same things as now one, now the other; and he is an image-maker whose images are phantoms far removed from reality.

Quite true.

—PLATO, *Republic*

One final word on the paradox of the parable of the singer before we move on to the views of other philosophers. Plato feared that art would lead us away from reality, rather than toward it. Considering how famous Plato has become, how widely his works have been read and studied in both the West and the East, it is tempting to dismiss his fears as foolish. But the fact is that in a peculiar way, Plato's own success is evidence that he was right. Through the dramatic power of Plato's art, Socrates has become an immortal figure of Western thought. When we read the Dialogues today, all of us—students and trained philosophers alike—instinctively cast Socrates as the hero and his opponents as the villains of the drama. This encourages us to accept Socrates' (and Plato's) doctrines without properly criticizing them or evaluating them. In other words, we treat Socrates in exactly the way that the ancient Athenians treated Gorgias and the other popular speakers. We are swayed by Plato's art rather than persuaded by his arguments. Now, Socrates took what we today would call a conservative political position, and his opponents—at least according to some scholars—were the "liberals" of their society. Strange as it may seem, many modern philosophers whose own political opinions are liberal still treat Socrates as the good guy and Gorgias or Protagoras or Thrasymachus or Callicles as the bad guys. In short, they are so beguiled by the beauty of Plato's song that they do not reflect, calmly and rationally, on its words. That is just the danger Plato saw and warned of when he banned the artists from his ideal Republic.

II *Aristotle's Defense of the Poets*

Plato was not yet thirty when Socrates died. Later in life, he founded a school or center for mathematical, cosmological, and philosophical investigation called the Acacemy. Far and away the most distinguished "student" at the Academy, if we can speak of students at all, was a man named Aristotle. There are many students of philosophy who consider

ARISTOTLE (384–322 B.C.) is the most in-fluential figure in the history of Western philosophy. Born in Stagira, a Greek colony on the Aegean Sea, he came to Athens as a very young man to study with Plato in the school known as the Academy. He remained a student and member of the Academy for twenty years, leaving only in 347 B.C. on Plato's death. Eventually, he founded his own school, where he lectured on a range of subjects so broad that he must have been virtually a one-man faculty. In addition to his major philosophical discoveries in the fields of logic, metaphysics, and the theory of knowledge, Aristotle did an enormous amount of empirical work on problems of astronomy, biology, comparative politics, and anatomy.

Aristotle is remembered today for his philosophy, but during his middle life, after leaving Plato's Academy and before founding his own school, he spent seven years as a tutor to the young prince who was to become Alexander the Great. Alexander, heir to the throne of Macedonia, eventually conquered the entire Greek world, and pushed his military campaigns as far east as India. Aristotle persuaded Alexander to send back biological specimens and other data from his explorations.

Although much of Aristotle's work has been surpassed by later investigators in the 2000 years and more since his death, some of his writings, particularly those in the areas of psychology and the theory of art, remain as suggestive and useful today as they were in ancient times.

Aristotle the greatest philosopher of all. St. Thomas Aquinas, the medieval theologian who figures so prominently in the development of Catholic doctrine, had so high an opinion of Aristotle that he referred to him simply as "the philosopher," as if there were no other. When you think about it, the odds must be simply astronomical against such a sequence of teachers and students as Socrates, Plato, and Aristotle.

Aristotle was not at all gifted artistically as Plato was, though in his youth he tried his hand at writing some dialogues. His temperament was rather that of a scientist, and the writings which we have today by him are actually treatises or lecture notes for the teaching he did at the Academy. Because they were written for a specialized audience rather than for the general public, they are very condensed, rather dry, and sometimes hard to follow if you aren't already pretty well up on what Aristotle is talking about. The range of Aristotle's investigations was simply staggering. In addition to his great work in logic, he wrote on systematic comparative political science, moral philosophy, cosmology, psychology, biology, astronomy, and physics, and he even developed several proofs for the existence of a "prime mover," or God. In Athens at that time, the public theater was an important part of the religious and civic as well as cultural life of the people, and the annual performances of the tragedies written by the great Greek playwrights were a focus of public interest. Aristotle wrote a short treatise on the subject of tragedy. We know that little work today as *The Poetics,* and despite its brevity, it is much read and quoted, for it has had a wide and deep influence throughout the ages on philosophical theories about art.

For our purposes, Aristotle's treatise is interesting because of its defense of art against the twofold attack of his teacher, Plato. Recall the charge that Plato had leveled against poetry: it leads us away from truth, and it disorders the soul. Aristotle does not say a great deal about these two criticisms, but he indicates rebuttals to both. First, consider the claim that art misleads us by offering nothing more than imperfect copies of the world of the senses, which is itself no better than an imperfect copy or realization of the ideal standards of beauty, goodness, and justice which Plato calls the Forms or Ideas. If I want to know the true nature of a circle, I had better turn my eyes away from physical objects and reflect instead upon the pure definitions of mathematical forms. It is bad enough that my inadequate intelligence sometimes needs the aid of wheels, coins, and other imperfectly round objects which I encounter in life. I will simply stray farther from the truth if I fix my eyes on a picture of a wheel. The same is true for the knowledge of the human soul. True or ideal justice has never been achieved by a living man or woman, so I can learn very little about the eternal standard of justice through an examination of the lives of even the noblest men and women. What can a tragedian do, save conjure up for me on the stage an admittedly imperfect imitation of an admittedly imperfect character. I might as well try to get a feel for fine cowhide by looking at a photograph of imitation leather!

Not so, Aristotle replies. Plato is right in insisting that we should seek a knowledge of the unchanging, universal forms of justice, beauty, and goodness, but he is wrong in supposing that art merely provides us with imperfect copies of particular instances of those universal forms. Great artists have the ability, through their art, to grasp the universal that lies within the particular, and to present it to us in such a way that we achieve a greater knowledge than we would otherwise have. When Shakespeare creates for us the character of Hamlet (needless to say, this is my example, not Aristotle's), he shows us, through the particularities of the vacillations and inner conflicts of one young prince, some universal truths about fathers and sons, sons and mothers, intellect and will, thought and action. Plato to the contrary notwithstanding, we are wiser for seeing a performance of *Hamlet* than we would be were we to travel back in time and meet the real man on whom the play is based.

The dispute between Plato and Aristotle is partly a disagreement about art, of course, but it is, at a deeper level, a disagreement about metaphysics. Plato seems to have held that the universal, eternal, unchanging Forms actually exist independently of the particular, time-bound, changing objects and events which fitfully and inadequately embody them. (I say, "seems to have held," because this is a subject on which scholars differ.) In other words, Plato believed that there is a reality which transcends the appearances of the senses and the world of space, time, and physical things. True knowledge was for him, therefore, a rational understanding of that transcendent realm of universal Forms. Aristotle, on the other hand, held that the universal Forms were completely embodied in the particular things of the world of space and time. True knowledge did indeed consist of a grasp of those forms, and Plato was certainly right that we must penetrate the changing particularity of this and that moment or event in order to get at the universal truths. But because the universals were embodied in the particulars—because true circularity was to be found within actual circular things, true rationality within actual rational creatures, true beauty within actual works of art, our attention should be focused even more intently on those particular

A representation of the graveyard scene from Shakespeare's great tragedy, *Hamlet.* Terrible though the events of the play are, Aristotle would claim that in watching them unfold, we are purged of powerful and potentially destructive emotions. (The Bettmann Archive)

instances rather than directed entirely away from them toward an independent realm of eternal Forms.

Aristotle's answer to Plato's second charge rests on a point of psychology rather than metaphysics. Plato was afraid that tragedy would arouse uncontrollable passions in the audience and thereby disarrange the proper harmony of the soul. It would weaken the ascendency of the rational forces within the personality and release erotic and aggressive elements that were destructive and deluding. Aristotle argued that just the opposite was the case. Since those harmful passions are present anyway, far better to release them in the controlled setting of the drama than to bottle them up entirely. In art, we experience those terrible feelings vicariously, through our identification with the characters in the play. When they suffer, triumph, love, hate, rage, and mourn, we in the audience do also. When the play ends, we are purged of the pent-up passions without having expressed them in the terrible deeds that the playwright has depicted on the stage. We leave the theater calmed, not aroused.

All this seems thin, bloodless, "academic" until we realize that exactly the same debate now rages in America about violence and sex in our movies and television shows. Does the portrayal of violence make our children more prone to act violently in their real lives, or does it drain away the violence that lies within all of us, giving it a safe, harmless outlet? Does sado-masochistic pornography stimulate its viewers to commit sex crimes, or does it divert passions which otherwise would lead to rape or mutilation?

The following brief selections from Aristotle's *Poetics* will give you some sense of his approach to the analysis and justification of art, but they will hardly settle such a host of difficult and controversial questions. In the remainder of this chapter, we shall take a look at a number of other conceptions of the nature and rationale of art. Perhaps somewhere in this debate you will find your own answer to Plato's question: Does art have a legitimate place in the good society?

From what we have said it will be seen that the poet's function is to describe, not the thing that has happened, but a kind of thing that might happen, i.e. what is possible as being probable or necessary. The distinction between historian and poet is not in the one writing prose and the other verse—you might put the work of Herodotus into verse, and it would still be a species of history; it consists really in this, that the one describes the

Catharsis   Literally, a cleansing or purging. Aristotle uses the term to describe the effect on us of powerful dramatic performances. By watching a play whose events arouse fear and pity within us, he thought, we are purged of those emotions, so that we leave the theater liberated or cleansed. The opposing view is that such plays (and, by extension, movies and television programs) arouse in us feelings we otherwise wouldn't have, and shouldn't have, such as aggressive and sexual feelings.

thing that has been, and the other a kind of thing that might be. Hence poetry is something more philosophic and of graver import than history, since its statements are of the nature rather of universals, whereas those of history are singulars. . . .

. . . A tragedy, then, is the imitation of an action that is serious and also, as having magnitude, complete in itself; in language with pleasurable accessories, each kind brought in separately in the parts of the work; in a *dramatic*, not in a narrative *form*; with incidents arousing pity and fear, wherewith to accomplish its catharsis of such emotions. . . .

We assume that, for the finest form of Tragedy, the Plot must be not simple but complex; and further, that it must imitate actions arousing fear and pity, since that is the distinctive function of this kind of imitation. It follows, therefore, that there are three forms of Plot to be avoided. (1) A good man must not be seen passing from happiness to misery, or (2) a bad man from misery to happiness. The first situation is not fear-inspiring or piteous, but simply odious to us. The second is the most untragic that can be; it has no one of the requisites of Tragedy; it does not appeal either to the human feeling in us, or to our pity, or to our fears. Nor, on the other hand, should (3) an extremely bad man be seen falling from happiness into misery. Such a story may arouse the human feeling in us, but it will not move us to either pity or fear; pity is occasioned by undeserved misfortune, and fear by that of one like ourselves; so that there will be nothing either piteous or fear-inspiring in the situation. There remains, then, the intermediate kind of personage, a man not pre-eminently virtuous and just, whose misfortune, however, is brought upon him not by vice and depravity but by some error of judgment, of the number of those in the enjoyment of great reputation and prosperity; e.g. Oedipus, Thyestes, and the men of note of similar families. The perfect Plot, accordingly, must have a single, and not (as some tell us) a double issue; the change in the hero's fortunes must be not from misery to happiness, but on the contrary from happiness to misery; and the cause of it must lie not in any depravity, but in some great error on his part; the man himself being either such as we have described, or better, not worse, than that . . .

The tragic fear and pity may be aroused by the Spectacle; but they may also be aroused by the very structure and incidents of the play—which is the better way and shows the better poet. The Plot in fact should be so framed that, even without seeing the things take place, he who simply hears the account of them shall be filled with horror and pity at the incidents; which is just the effect that the mere recital of the story in *Oedipus* would have on one. To produce this same effect by means of the Spectacle is less artistic, and requires extraneous aid. Those, however, who make use of the Spectacle to put before us that which is merely monstrous and not productive of fear, are wholly out of touch with Tragedy; not every kind of pleasure should be required of a tragedy, but only its own proper pleasure.

The tragic pleasure is that of pity and fear, and the poet has to produce it by a work of imitation; it is clear, therefore, that the causes should be included in the incidents of his story. Let us see, then, what kinds of incident strike one as horrible, or rather as piteous. In a deed of this description the parties must necessarily be either friends, or enemies, or indifferent to one another. Now when enemy does it on enemy, there is nothing to move us to pity either in his doing or in his meditating the deed, except so far as the actual pain of the sufferer is concerned; and the same is true when the parties are indifferent to one another. Whenever the tragic deed, however, is done within the family—when murder or the like is done or meditated by brother on brother, by son on father, by mother on son, or son on mother— these are the situations the poet should seek after.

—ARISTOTLE, *Poetics*

III *Art for Art's Sake*

Plato claims that art is harmful, both intellectually and emotionally. Aristotle replies that art teaches and purges, that it aids us in acquiring knowledge of universal truths and in maintaining the proper internal order of our psyches. Though they seem to disagree fundamentally, nevertheless they are united in believing the art should be judged according to the positive or negative value of its effects on us. Most philosophers who have reflected on the value of art have judged it in this way, as useful or harmful for some purpose. But one group of defenders of art, repelled by the merely instrumental conception of art, developed the view that art needs no justification outside itself, that art should be encouraged, valued, cherished for itself alone. The slogan of this group, who lived and wrote in the nineteenth century, was "art for art's sake," and before going on to several of the more prominent philosophical defenses of art, it might be interesting to spend a few moments looking at the "art for art's sake" doctrine.

The central notion that we need here is a distinction, long current in philosophy, between what is sometimes called *instrumental value* and *instrinsic value*. Human beings are purposive creatures. They have goals or ends or purposes which they pursue by choosing what seem to them to be appropriate means. (As you know, Michael Oakeshott dissents from this view of human action. There probably isn't any statement ever made, and certainly not an interesting or important statement, which every philosopher would agree to—not even the statement that philosophy is a worthwhile enterprise!) Very often, when we describe something as valuable, or useful, or good, we simply mean that it is especially helpful to us in achieving some purpose or getting to some goal that we have. If I call a car a good car, I probably mean that it runs smoothly, or rarely breaks down, or uses relatively little gas. In short, I mean that it is a useful means or *instrument* for doing what I want to do, which may be to get somewhere fast, or safely, or cheaply, or reliably. If I say that a good education is the most valuable gift that parents can give their child, I probably mean that in the modern world, a good education will be more useful to that child in achieving his or her goals than anything else. Someone who replies that strong character is even more valuable than a good education will probably mean that certain strengths of personality turn out to make more difference in the adult world than formal book learning or credits and degrees.

A good car is good *for* doing something; an education is valuable as a means *to* something; character will be a source of strength *for* some end. All these, and countless other things besides, are valuable as means or instruments, which is to say that they have **instrumental value.** Now, if you stop and think about it for a moment, it should be obvious that you will never consider something valuable *as a means* unless there is something else that you consider just plain valuable in itself. If there is nothing you want for *itself*, nothing you like or desire or consider worthy *in and of itself*, then it would make no sense to value other things simply as "useful." Suppose, for example, that you are quite happy right where you are and have no desire whatsoever to go anywhere else. A friend comes along and says, "Now that road there is a really great road. You

> **Intrinsic Value/Instrumental Value**   To say that something has *intrinsic value* is to say that it is valuable, good, worthwhile, purely for itself alone, regardless of what it may produce or lead to. Some people say that pleasure has intrinsic value, others that beauty does, still others that moral goodness does. *Instrumental value* is the value something has as a means, or instrument, for producing or getting something else. A tool or instrument that is useful for some purpose is said to be instrumentally valuable.

ought to take a ride down it." You say, "Why should I take a ride down it? I don't want to go where it leads." And she answers, "It doesn't matter! It's such a great road, you ought to take it anyway." Well, your friend is either joking, or she is crazy. As the old saying goes, a bargain isn't a bargain unless it is a bargain for you. And a road isn't a good road for you unless it is a good road to somewhere you want to go.

Or you might go into a hardware store to buy a hammer so that you can hang some pictures. But even if the store has nothing better than a mediocre hammer and a really great sale on saws, the sensible thing to do is to buy the hammer. You don't want "a good tool." You want a tool that is *good for* whatever you want to do, which in this case is to hang some pictures.

By contrast, things which are good in themselves, rather than being good for something else, are said to have **intrinsic value.** That simply means that their merit, value, goodness, or whatever is possessed by them independently of anything else in the world. One way to make this point about something that has intrinsic value is to say that it would be valuable even if nothing else in the world existed. A road has only instrumental value, for if there were nothing in the world but that road—and in particular, if there were no place at the other end of it—who would value it as a road? Similarly, if there were no nails, no pictures to hang, nothing to hit, who would value a hammer? But when something has intrinsic value, it retains that value even in the absence of other objects, places, events, or states of affairs with regard to which it might be useful.

Is there anything at all that has intrinsic value? Well, we might argue that unless *something* has intrinsic value, then nothing has instrumental value. If one thing is useful for getting another, and that other is not valuable in itself, but simply useful for getting a third thing, and so on and on, we get into what is sometimes called "an infinite regress." It is like the ancient Hindu theory that the world rests on the back of an elephant, which stands on the back of a giant sea turtle, which swims in an enormous ocean. The obvious question is, what is the ocean in? So something must have intrinsic value, if anything is to have any sort of value at all.

We have already encountered two philosophical candidates for the title of things having intrinsic value, although we didn't use that language when we met them. Immanuel Kant said that humanity is an end in itself, and that is another way of claiming that *humanity* has intrinsic value. And Jeremy Bentham said that the only good thing is *pleasure,* by which he obviously meant that pleasure was the only thing that is intrinsically valuable. In the nineteenth century, Walter Pater, Clive Bell, and Oscar Wilde, all of them British, argued that art has intrinsic value, that it is valuable in and of itself. Wilde carried this view to such lengths that he ended by reversing the usual order of priority between life and art. Instead of saying, as most philosophers have, that art is valuable insofar as it contributes to life, Wilde argued that life acquired value by contributing to art! In this selection from his book, *Intentions*, Wilde summarizes his doctrine. Incidentally, Wilde was a gifted and successful playwright, as well as a thoughtful philosopher of art. You probably know the old joke that those who can, do, and those who can't, teach. Sometimes a third line is added: and those who cannot even teach, philosophize. But in this chapter, most of the philosophers we read are also able practitioners of some form of artistic creation.

CYRIL. . . . But in order to avoid making any error I want you to tell me briefly the doctrines of the new aesthetics.

VIVIAN. Briefly, then, they are these. Art never expresses anything but itself. It has an independent life, just as Thought has, and develops purely on its own lines. It is not necessarily realistic in an age of realism, nor spiritual in an age of faith. So far from being the creation of its time, it is usually in direct opposition to it, and the only history that it preserves for us is the history of its own progress. Sometimes it returns upon its footsteps, and revives some antique form, as happened in the archaistic movement of late Greek Art, and in the pre-Raphaelite movement of our own day. At other times it entirely anticipates its age, and produces in one century work that it takes another century to understand, to appreciate and to enjoy. In no case does it reproduce its age. To pass from the art of a time to the time itself is the great mistake that all historians commit.

The second doctrine is this. All bad art comes from returning to Life and Nature, and elevating them into ideals. Life and Nature may sometimes be used as part of Art's rough material, but before they are of any real service to art they must be translated into artistic conventions. The moment Art surrenders its imaginative medium it surrenders everything. As a method Realism is a complete failure, and the two things that every artist should avoid are modernity of form and modernity of subject matter. To us, who live in the nineteenth century, any century is a suitable subject for art except our own. The only beautiful things are the things that do not concern us. It is, to have the pleasure of quoting myself, exactly because Hecuba is nothing to us that her sorrows are so suitable a motive for a tragedy. Besides, it is only the modern that ever becomes old-fashioned. M. Zola sits

OSCAR WILDE (1854–1900) was a brillant Irish playwright and novelist whose super-aesthetic mannerisms typified the movement known as "art-for-art's-sake." He wrote *The Picture of Dorian Gray,* which was made many years later into a truly scary horror film, and the much revived play *The Importance of Being Earnest.* In Gilbert and Sullivan's delightful light opera, *Patience,* the character of Bunthorne is a take-off on Wilde.

down to give us a picture of the Second Empire. Who cares for the Second Empire now? It is out of date. Life goes faster than Realism, but Romanticism is always in front of Life.

The third doctrine is that Life imitates Art far more than Art imitates Life. This results not merely from Life's imitative instinct, but from the fact that the self-conscious aim of Life is to find expression, and that Art offers it certain beautiful forms through which it may realise that energy. It is a theory that has never been put forward before, but it is extremely fruitful, and throws an entirely new light upon the history of Art.

It follows, as a corollary from this, that external Nature also imitates Art. The only effects that she can show us are effects that we have already seen through poetry, or in paintings. This is the secret of Nature's charm, as well as the explanation of Nature's weakness.

The final revelation is that Lying, the telling of beautiful untrue things, is the proper aim of Art. But of this I think I have spoken at sufficient length. And now let us go out on the terrace, where "droops the milk-white peacock like a ghost," while the evening star "washes the dusk with silver." At twilight nature becomes a wonderfully suggestive effect, and is not without loveliness, though perhaps its chief use is to illustrate quotations from the poets. Come! We have talked long enough.

—OSCAR WILDE, *Intentions*

IV *Romanticism*

The most powerful and influential aesthetic movement of the past several centuries, both in England and on the continent of Europe, is undoubtedly **romanticism.** In the late eighteenth century, poets, painters, and philosophers of art rebelled against the style and tenets of the neoclassicism which had until then dominated the theory and practice of art. **Neoclassicism** exalted order, proportion, reason, and the subordination of the creative artist to objective principles of aesthetic taste. In England especially, neoclassicism looked back to the calm gravity of the art and language of the great period of Roman culture known—after the Emperor Caesar Augustus—as the Augustan Age. The English romantic poets overturned all the entrenched tenets of neoclassical art, and in doing so carried out a revolution whose effects are still being felt today even beyond the confines of the world of art and literature.

The key to the romantic rebellion was two reversals or denials of the traditional doctrine. First, the romantics denied the supremacy of *reason* in art and life. Instead, they insisted that the power of creative *imagination* was the highest human faculty. From Plato on, philosophers and students of art had insisted that reason is our primary organ of knowledge, our source for whatever truth we can attain. The romantics granted the power of reason to accumulate knowledge of the ordinary, or work-a-day sort. But for deep insight into the inner being of humanity and nature, for a grasp of that eternal, unchanging realm beyond the world of the senses, artistic imagination was necessary.

The second reversal was the substitution of the subjective for the objective as the test and source of true knowledge. Philosophers traditionally had dismissed the subjective, the particular, the individual, as lacking in value or cognitive significance. What mathematics or philosophy or science could validate as universally and objectively true, indepen-

> **Romanticism** The late eighteenth-century and nineteenth-century movement in art and literature that stressed the powerful expression of feeling and the free play of imagination over the observation of formal limits on artistic creativity. The term comes originally from the late medieval term *romance*, meaning a poem, play, or story written in the local popular language, such as French, rather than in Latin.

A portrayal by the French romantic painter Delacroix, of Jacob wrestling with the angel of the Lord. See the Book of Genesis, Chapter 32. (New York Public Library Picture Collection)

dently of the momentary subjective state of the individual investigator, could be accepted as established. But the intense fleeting feeling of the lone artist could not possibly serve as a conduit of important truth. The romantics turned this traditional view on its head. They insisted that the most intense and momentary emotional states of the most extraordinary individuals were our glimpse of the infinite, our window on eternity.

Plato was suspicious of poets and the poetic impulse, because he believed that the act of artistic creation had more than a touch of madness about it. Poets were, in popular Greek opinion, possessed by the gods, and certainly their moments of inspiration bore little resemblance to the quiet rational progress of dialectical philosophical argument. Art, Plato said, could not put us in touch with the eternal because it was irrational. The romantics turned Plato completely around and asserted that art *could* put us in touch with the eternal precisely *because* it was ecstatic, subjective, emotionally intense, and in that sense irrational. The great irony of the romantics is that they considered themselves neo-Platonists!

One of the finest statements of the romantic philosophy is, as you might expect, a poem, namely, the ode by William Wordsworth entitled "Intimations of Immortality from Recollections of Early Childhood." I would have liked to use it as our selection, but since this is a philosophy text, I have instead selected a portion of the preface which Wordsworth wrote for a book of verse entitled *Lyrical Ballads*. Ask your English teacher to read Wordsworth's ode with you.

> ... All good poetry is the spontaneous overflow of powerful feelings: and though this be true, Poems to which any value can be attached were never produced on any variety of subjects but by a man who, being possessed of more than usual organic sensibility, had also thought long and deeply. For our continued influxes of feelings are modified and directed by our thoughts, which are indeed the representatives of all our past feelings; and, as by contemplating the relation of these general representatives to each other, we discover what is really important to men, so, by the repetition and continuance of this act, our feelings will be connected with important subjects, till at length, if we be originally possessed of much sensibility, such habits of mind will be produced, that, by obeying blindly and mechanically the impulses of those habits, we shall describe objects, and utter sentiments, of such a nature, and in such connexion with each other, that the understanding of the Reader must necessarily be in some degree enlightened, and his affections strengthened and purified. ...
>
> However exalted a notion we would wish to cherish of the character of a Poet, it is obvious, that while he describes and imitates passions, his employment is in some degree mechanical, compared with the freedom and power of real and substantial action and suffering. So that it will be the wish of the Poet to bring his feelings near to those of the persons whose feelings he describes, nay for short spaces of time, perhaps, to let himself slip into an entire delusion, and even confound and identify his own feelings with theirs; modifying only the language which is thus suggested to him by a consideration that he describes for a particular purpose, that of giving pleasure. Here, then, he will apply the principle of selection which has been

WILLIAM WORDSWORTH (1770–1850) was one of the leading poets of the English romantic movement. In his youth, he traveled to France and became an enthusiastic supporter of the revolution. After fathering an illegitimate child by a French woman, Marie Anne Vallen, he returned to England and eventually settled in Somerset, near Samuel Coleridge. During the last years of the old century and the first years of the new, Coleridge and Wordsworth wrote a series of poems, entitled *Lyrical Ballads*, which remain among the classic works of romanticism.

In middle life, Wordsworth turned against the liberal views of his youth and became increasingly conservative. He continued to write poetry throughout his lifetime, but never achieved the heights of his early work. In 1843, he was named Poet Laureate of England, succeeding Robert Southey.

already insisted upon. He will depend upon this for removing what would otherwise be painful or disgusting in the passion; he will feel that there is no necessity to trick out or to elevate nature: and, the more industriously he applies this principle, the deeper will be his faith that no words, which *his* fancy or imagination can suggest, will be to be compared with those which are the emanations of reality and truth.

But it may be said by those who do not object to the general spirit of these remarks, that, as it is impossible for the Poet to produce upon all occasions language as exquisitely fitted for the passion as that which the real passion itself suggests, it is proper that he should consider himself as in the situation of a translator, who does not scruple to substitute excellencies of another kind for those which are unattainable by him; and endeavours occasionally to surpass his original, in order to make some amends for the general inferiority to which he feels that he must submit. But this would be to encourage idleness and unmanly despair. Further, it is the language of men who speak of what they do not understand; who talk of Poetry as of a matter of amusement and idle pleasure; who will converse with us as gravely about a *taste* for Poetry, as they express it, as if it were a thing as indifferent as a taste for rope-dancing, or Frontiniac or Sherry. Aristotle, I have been told, has said, that Poetry is the most philosophic of all writing: it is so: its object is truth, not individual and local, but general, and operative; not standing upon external testimony, but carried alive into the heart by passion; truth which is its own testimony, which gives competence and confidence to the tribunal to which it appeals, and receives them from the same tribunal. Poetry is the image of man and nature. The obstacles which stand in the way of fidelity of the Biographer and Historian, and their consequent utility, are incalculably greater than those which are to be encountered by the Poet who comprehends the dignity of his art. The Poet writes under one restriction only, namely, the necessity of giving immediate pleasure to a human Being possessed of that information which may be expected from him, not as a lawyer, a physician, a mariner, an astronomer, or a natural philosopher, but as a Man. Except this one restriction, there is no object standing between the Poet and the image of things; between this, and the Biographer and Historian, there are a thousand.

—WILLIAM WORDSWORTH, *Preface to the Lyrical Ballads*

V *Tolstoy's Religious Defense of Art*

The romantics follow Plato, Aristotle, and most other philosophers of art in assigning instrumental value to art, but their conception of its instrumentality leads them to emphasize the unusual rather than the ordinary, the outstanding rather than the commonplace. The characteristic romantic image of the artist is the gifted, tortured genius, alone in his garret, unappreciated by the multitudes but nevertheless tearing great works of art quivering from his breast.

Just about the most completely opposite conception of art and the artist was put forward by another great literary figure, the Russian novelist Leo Tolstoy. You have all heard of Tolstoy's immortal novel, *War and Peace,* though in all likelihood very few of you have plowed your way through that immensely long book. Tolstoy is an extraordinary figure in

COUNT LEO TOLSTOY (1828–1910) is one of the immortal geniuses of European literature. He and Feodor Dostoyevsky have, in their novels, given us matchless pictures of Russian life in the nineteenth century. In his youth, Tolstoy served in the czar's army, seeing action as the commander of a battery in the Crimean War (1854–56). He retired to his family's estates, and began his career as a writer. His masterpiece, *War and Peace,* was published in 1866. It is a panoramic story of Russian life and thought during the great struggle of Russia against Napoleon.

In 1876, Tolstoy underwent a profound spiritual conversion to a form of Russian Orthodox Christianity that emphasized the virtues of the simple life and hard, physical labor. He worked alongside the peasants in the fields of his estates, while continuing to write novels and essays. Among the works of this later period in his life are *Anna Karenina,* which was begun before his conversion and completed in 1877; *The Death of Ivan Ilyich;* and the essay on the nature of art from which the selection in this book is taken.

literature and philosophy. He was born in 1828, into the Russian aristocracy and served in the army as a young man. When he was only thirty-eight he published *War and Peace,* his great novel of Russian life and thought during the period of the Napoleonic wars. Some time later, he underwent a deep religious conversion and adopted a life of poverty and peasant simplicity. Out of his conversion emerged a new, simplified Christian faith and a rejection of the cultivated aesthetic sensibilities which he himself had contributed to in his earlier writings. Thirty years after the publication of *War and Peace,* in 1896, Tolstoy gave formal philosophical expression to his new conception of art and life in an essay entitled *What is Art?*

Tolstoy argues that there are two basic means by which human beings communicate with one another. The first is speech, by which men and women communicate their *thoughts*; the second is art, by which they communicate their *feelings*. Each of us has the capacity to communicate feelings by arousing them in others. We not only tell our listeners that we are sad, we actually arouse feelings of sadness in them, sometimes by reporting what it is that has made us sad, sometimes by the tone of our voice, sometimes by looks, gestures, or other means of expression. Feelings are infectious. When one person laughs, others laugh too. When one cries, others cry. Tolstoy describes art in this way:

> To evoke in oneself a feeling one has experienced, and having evoked it in oneself, then, by means of movements, lines, colors, sounds, or forms expressed in words, so to transmit that feeling that others may experience the same feeling—this is the activity of art.
>
> Art is a human activity consisting in this, that one man consciously, by means of certain external signs, hands on to others feelings he has lived through, and that other people are infected by these feelings and also experience them.

The stronger the degree of infectiousness of art, the better the art is, Tolstoy maintains. And the fundamental source of infectiousness—the quality in the artist which enables him or her to spark a contagion of feeling in the audience—is not reason nor imaginative brilliance, nor metaphysical insight, nor extraordinary creativity, but simply *sincerity*. Honesty of feeling is directly apprehended and responded to by an artist's audience.

So far as the content of the work of art is concerned, Tolstoy—as you might expect—turns the usual canons of aesthetic judgment upside down. Common subjects are best, for they will enable the artist to reach the largest audience. The purpose of art (Tolstoy is an instrumentalist, remember) is to unite humanity through shared feeling. Art that relies on specialized knowledge or highly refined taste will exclude rather than include, divide rather than unite. If a work of art is so specialized that men and women can respond to it emotionally only after long training and cultivation, then it will mark off the few from the many and place obstacles in the way of a union of all humanity.

If sincerity and universality of emotional appeal are the criteria of greatness in art, then obviously some so-called artistic "masterpieces" are going to get pretty low marks. Sure enough, Tolstoy downgrades some of the works of music, literature, and painting that had been held up for generations as perfect examples of great art, and in their place offers peasant stories, folk music, and other arts of the common people.

There is one last element in Tolstoy's aesthetic theory which we have not yet mentioned—namely, the *religious* dimension of art. In the following selection from *What is Art?* Tolstoy draws upon his analysis of art as a means for the communication of feeling and as an instrument for uniting human beings in a universal community, in order to lay the foundations for a religious justification of art.

> In every period of history, and in every human society, there exists an understanding of the meaning of life which represents the highest level to which men of that society have attained, an understanding defining the highest good at which that society aims. And this understanding is the religious perception of the given time and society. And this religious perception is always clearly expressed by some advanced men, and more or less vividly perceived by all the members of the society. Such a religious perception and its corresponding expression exists always in every society. If it appears to us that in our society there is no religious perception, this is not because there really is none, but only because we do not want to see it. And we often wish not to see it because it exposes the fact that our life is inconsistent with that religious perception.
>
> Religious perception in a society is like the direction of a flowing river. If the river flows at all, it must have a direction. If society lives, there must be a religious perception indicating the direction in which, more or less consciously, all its members tend. . . .
>
> I know that according to an opinion current in our times religion is a superstition which humanity has outgrown, and that it is therefore assumed that no such thing exists as a religious perception, common to us all, by which art, in our time, can be evaluated. I know that this is the opinion current in the pseudo-cultured circles of today. People who do not acknowledge Christianity in its true meaning because it undermines all their social privileges, and who, therefore, invent all kinds of philosophic and aesthetic theories to hide from themselves the meaninglessness and wrongness of their lives, cannot think otherwise. These people intentionally, or sometimes unintentionally, confusing the conception of a religious perception think that by denying the cult they get rid of religious perception. But even the

These two paintings illustrate the difference between the vibrant immediacy of folk art and the formalism of high art. (The Baltimore Museum of Art; Smithsonian Institution)

very attacks on religion and the attempts to establish a life-conception contrary to the religious perception of our times most clearly demonstrate the existence of a religious perception condemning the lives that are not in harmony with it.

If humanity progresses, i.e., moves forward, there must inevitably be a guide to the direction of that movement. And religions have always furnished that guide. All history shows that the progress of humanity is accomplished not otherwise than under the guidance of religion. But if the race cannot progress without the guidance of religion—and progress is always going on, and consequently also in our own times—then there must be a religion of our times. So that, whether it pleases or displeases the so-called cultured people of today, they must admit the existence of religion—not of a religious cult, Catholic, Protestant, or another, but of religious perception—which, even in our times, is the guide always present where there is any progress. And if a religious perception exists among us, then our art should be appraised on the basis of that religious perception; and, as has always and everywhere been the case, art transmitting feelings flowing from the religious perception of our time should be chosen from all the indifferent art, should be acknowledged, highly esteemed, and encouraged, while art running counter to that perception should be condemned and despised, and all the remaining indifferent art should neither be distinguished nor encouraged. . . .

Christian art, i.e., the art of our time, should be catholic in the original meaning of the word, i.e., universal, and therefore it should unite all men. And only two kinds of feeling do unite all men: first, feelings flowing from the perception of our sonship to God and of the brotherhood of man; and next, the simple feelings of common life, accessible to every one without exception—such as the feeling of merriment, of pity, of cheerfulness, of tranquillity, etc. Only these two kinds of feelings can now supply material for art good in its subject matter. . . .

Beethoven's *Ninth Symphony* is considered a great work of art. To verify its claim to be such, I must first ask myself whether this work transmits the highest religious feeling. I reply in the negative, for music in itself cannot transmit those feelings; and therefore I ask myself next, Since this work does not belong to the highest kind of religious art, has it the other characteristic of the good art of our time—the quality of uniting all men in one common feeling: does it rank as Christian universal art? And again I have no option but to reply in the negative; for not only do I not see how the feelings transmitted by this work could unite people not specially trained to submit themselves to its complex hypnotism, but I am unable to imagine to myself a crowd of normal people who could understand anything of this long, confused, and artificial production, except short snatches which are lost in a sea of what is incomprehensible. And therefore, whether I like it or not, I am compelled to conclude that this work belongs to the rank of bad art. It is curious to note in this connection that attached to the end of this very symphony is a poem of Schiller's which (though somewhat obscurely) expresses this very thought, namely, that feeling (Schiller speaks only of the feeling of gladness) unites people and evokes love in them. But though this poem is sung at the end of the symphony, the music does not accord with the thought expressed in the verses; for the music is exclusive and does not unite all men, but unites only a few, dividing them off from the rest of mankind.

And just in this same way, in all branches of art, many and many works considered great by the upper classes of our society will have to be judged. By this one sure criterion we shall have to judge the celebrated *Divine Comedy* and *Jerusalem Delivered,* and a great part of Shakespeare's and Goethe's works, and in painting every representation of miracles, including Raphael's *Transfiguration,* etc.

Whatever the work may be and however it may have been extolled, we have first to ask whether this work is one of real art or a counterfeit. Having acknowledged, on the basis of the indication of its infectiousness even to a small class of people, that a certain production belongs to the realm of art, it is necessary, on the basis of the indication of its accessibility, to decide the next question. Does this work belong to the category of bad, exclusive art, opposed to religious perception, or to Christian art uniting people? And having acknowledged an article to belong to real Christian art, we must then, according to whether it transmits the feelings flowing from love to God and man, or merely the simple feelings uniting all men, assign it a place in the ranks of religious art or in those of universal art.

Only on the basis of such verification shall we find it possible to select from the whole mass of what in our society claims to be art those works which form real, important, necessary spiritual food, and to separate them from all the harmful and useless art and from the counterfeits of art which surround us. Only on the basis of such verification shall we be able to rid ourselves of the pernicious results of harmful art and to avail ourselves of that beneficent action which is the purpose of true and good art and which is indispensable for the spiritual life of man and of humanity.

—LEO TOLSTOY, *What Is Art?*

VI *Marcuse and the Uses of Negation*

Plato says that art is negative, disruptive, antirational and, therefore, that it ought to be banned from the good society. Aristotle, Wordsworth, and Tolstoy all in their different ways say that good art is positive, constructive, and ought to play an important role in social life. Wilde, Bell, and the art-for-art's-sake movement insist that art is intrinsically rather than instrumentally valuable and, therefore, deserves a central place in human life regardless of its consequences. You might think that we had exhausted the possibilities so far as the function of art is concerned, but our last theory of art puts these elements together in a startling, apparently contradictory way. Herbert Marcuse argues that great art is negative, destructive, irrational and, *therefore*, is a valuable element in human life! Why on earth would anyone praise art for having precisely the qualities that other philosophers have considered worthy of condemnation? To put the question in its most paradoxical form, what is positive about being negative?

HERBERT MARCUSE (1898–1979) was born in Berlin. He was one of the original members of the famous Frankfurt School of Social Research which flourished in Germany in the years before World War II. After fleeing to the United States to escape the Nazis, Marcuse became a major voice on the left. During the 1960s, he was the most widely quoted radical critic of American capitalist society. His best known books include *Eros and Civilization* and *One-Dimensional Man*.

Marcuse begins his argument with a puzzle that doesn't at first seem to have anything to do with art. Why is it that the most dramatic, outrageous, powerful words and ideas so rapidly become domesticated and acceptable in America today, *without changing anything along the way?* Radicals call America imperialist, and decent people everywhere are horrified. Several years later, Senator J. William Fulbright refers in passing to America's imperialist foreign policy on a television interview program and none of the newsmen thinks it worth commenting on. Black militants shout "Power to the people!" and "nice folks" cringe in their beds. Next season, "Power to the people!" is a liberal Democratic campaign slogan, and soon thereafter a Richard Nixon campaign promise. Avant-garde artists violate every canon of artistic sensibility in a last-ditch effort to repudiate the plastic culture of Madison Avenue capitalism, and Madison Avenue reproduces their most outrageous productions as decorations for its advertisements. Woodstock begins as a cry of protest against Middle America and ends as the name of a bird in *Peanuts.* How can this be? Is nothing sacrilegious? Can modern American society absorb anything into itself with changing? Must every protest turn into this year's fad and next year's ancient history?

To answer these questions, Marcuse draws on the psychological theory of the origins of the ego and of civilization which Sigmund Freud set forth in *Civilization and its Discontents,* and which Marcuse revised and developed in *Eros and Civilization.* Freud argued that the objective, "un-get-over-able" constraints of the real world force each infant to, as he put it, substitute the reality principle for the pleasure principle. Because the physical world won't always fit itself to our desires, and also

Repression/Sublimation   Two terms from the psychological theories of Sigmund Freud referring to the primitive operations of the human mind. *Repression* is the forcible pushing out of consciousness of desires, wishes, thoughts, or feelings that the mind considers bad, dangerous, or otherwise unacceptable. According to Freud, what is repressed does not go away, but remains, with all its emotional power, in the unconscious portion of the mind. *Sublimation* is the redirecting of sexual or aggressive energies into socially or morally acceptable channels—for example, aggressive energies directed away from physical violence and into philosophical arguments, or sexual energies diverted from immediate sexual activity into flirting.

because we all inevitably get into interpersonal conflicts, particularly those fueled by sexual desire, we are forced to regulate or deny entirely some of our strongest desires. The psychic means for the regulation, Freud suggested, are repression, sublimation, and fantasy, of which repression is the first and most important. Thus is generated the realm of the "unconscious," populated by wishes, impulses, desires, loves, and hatreds which cannot be expressed and acted out in the real world. Civilization itself, our organized collective life, rests upon a foundation of repression, for not even the most miraculous technical wonders or the most flexible social arrangements can gratify the infantile wishes that lie beneath the conscious surface in every adult man and woman.

Two features of the content and structure of the unconscious are crucial to Marcuse's analysis. First, the unconscious is timeless. The thwarted desires and fears which reside there retain their power across decades of real-world time, returning again and again irrespective of changes in the world which originally thwarted them. A mother who loses her child grieves, mourns, and eventually becomes reconciled to the loss. Time heals her wounds, and the objective passage of events places the loss further and further behind her. The child whose mother dies before he or she can cope with the loss may repress the grief and anger, so that half a century later, the anger at the mother's desertion will recur as strongly, albeit in transmuted forms. In particular, all of us carry with us unrelinquished infantile desires for the sorts of total, immediate, ecstatic satisfaction which as tiny babies we imagined we could, in our omnipotence, command.

Second, the content of the unconscious has a thoroughly ambivalent character. In the unconscious is to be found everything that reality (either natural or social) has decreed to be bad, inefficient, worthless, dirty, ugly, hostile, shameful. But the wishes and desires that fill the unconscious retain their power, even though they have been denied fulfillment. Part of the self—the part that identifies with society, reality, adulthood, and the world—hates, loathes, feels shame for what is repressed. That is the part of the self that cannot acknowledge a fascination with its own feces, or sexual desire for objects deemed socially inappropriate, or laziness, or messiness, or the urge to inflict pain and suffering. But another part of the self secretly delights in the content of the repressed. And what is more, it delights in the repressed *because* it is repressed. So we have the men and women who can only enjoy illicit sex; or, rather less dramatically, we find the familiar folk-character of the perpetual child who refuses to grow up—Pan, Til Eulenspiegel, and Peter Pan.

Marcuse accepts Freud's fundamental claim that repression is essential to civilization. But in a brilliant deployment of one of Marx's key notions, he revises Freud's theory of repression by introducing a distinction between necessary repression and surplus repression. Necessary repression is simply that kind and amount of repression that is required at any stage of social development in order to carry on the struggle for existence. It involves, for example, denying ourselves part of the harvest even when we are hungry so that we have seed for the next planting; it involves forcing ourselves to continue laboring at painful tasks because of our rational recognition that hunger, disease, danger, and death may result if we let up too soon. But some repression, Marcuse argues, is not required by the objective constraints of reality. Rather, it is required by the specific system of domination and submission that exists in society at that moment in history. In short, some repression serves only to protect the favored position of the rulers by restraining the subjects from rising up and overthrowing their masters. That repression is "surplus repression," and human progress consists in eliminating surplus repression while simultaneously decreasing the amount of necessary repression through technological advance. Indeed, Marcuse argues, at a time when our technology should permit us considerably to relax the bonds of necessary repression, through the shortening and lightening of the workday, through the relaxation of work discipline, and so forth, surplus repression grows greater and greater so that the total burden of repression suffered in modern industrial society is not appreciably lighter than that suffered in technically less advanced societies. The purpose of that ever-increasing sector of surplus repression is, Marcuse claims, to maintain the ever more manifestly unjustifiable dominance of the ruling sectors of our society.

The concept of surplus repression is one of those brilliant insights which are too often rejected by hard-headed social scientists because they prove difficult to quantify or operationalize. How would we measure the relative proportions of necessary and surplus repression in an individual psyche? Indeed, how could we ever show of a single instance of repression that it was unnecessary, and hence surplus? I don't know the answer to these questions, but I remain convinced that Marcuse has his finger on a fundamental fact here, and that to the extent that it is fuzzy or imprecise, we should struggle to clarify it rather than use the unclarity as an excuse for rejecting it.

Now, with the notion of surplus repression, and the theory of the unconscious, we can sketch Marcuse's theory of the function of negative thinking and thereby approach his analysis of the function of art. Briefly, his position is this: The repressed content of the unconscious in all of us exists as a permanent psychic pool or source of opposition to the established order of society. We all construct powerful defenses against this repressed content within ourselves, using such familiar mechanisms as denial, projection, and transference. When a rebellious member of society violates some taboo, by uncovering a part of the body that is supposed to be concealed, or by using, in public, language that is supposed to be used only in private, or by defying canons of dress, decorum, or deference, he or she provokes a response that is exaggerated all out of proportion. The rest of us recoil from the temporary and perhaps insignificant breach of the rules of repression because it provokes the ever-present desire within us to liberate ourselves from the same rules, and we can control that desire only by clamping down on the transgressor. A struggle over bare nipples or long hair or even an insolent, slouching way of standing becomes a struggle between the repressed content and the forces of civilization.

If all the actual repression were necessary repression, then it would be clear that the rebel should be contained, however sympathetically we might acknowledge that he or she speaks for a part of each of us. Marcuse's claim, however, is precisely that not all of the repression is necessary, that some of it is surplus, unnecessary, and that in the interest of human happiness it ought to be eliminated. But—and this is the key to his entire theory, so far as I can see—in order to generate sufficient emotional energy in enough people to conquer the surplus repression inflicted by our society, it is necessary to tap the ubiquitous, irrational, infantile desire for a release from all repression. To put it bluntly, you must promise people an impossible liberation from necessary repression in order to get them to struggle for the elimination of the merely surplus repression. To get us to the barricades, it is not enough to say, "Workers of the world, unite! After the revolution you shall suffer only necessary repression." Instead, you must say, "Workers of the world, unite! After the revolution you shall be free." And each projects his or her own fantasy of absolute freedom, a daydream both inevitable and unfulfillable.

The revolutionary role of negative, oppositional styles of artistic expression is precisely to tap the reservoir of repressed desires, to draw on the permanent opposition within us to necessary repression, and thereby to fuel the fight against surplus repression. The artist's image of libera-

　　　　　　　　　　　　　　　　　　　　　　　　　　　　　　　　　　　　　PHILOSOPHY OF ART

The Pornographic Book.

tion is necessary, and illusory. The particular content of the rebellion against the established order of aesthetic canons is not crucial. In one social setting, the expletive "damn" will have as much effect as total nudity in another. The point is that no matter what is permitted, there remains both a repressed content that is denied and a longing to express it that can be tapped. The fight always appears to be about the particular artistic rule that has been broken, but it is always really about the existence of repression itself. If the rebellion is successful, surplus repression is reduced, but that success is always perceived as a failure by the participants themselves, because they must sooner or later relinquish their fantasy of total liberation.

The social function of art is thus to keep alive the possibility of what Marcuse calls **transcendence.** By transcendence, he does not mean, as Plato or Wordsworth might, the passing from this world of space, time, and objects to a higher, eternal realm of forms or ideals entities. Rather, he means the imaginative leap beyond the given social world, with its repressions, oppressions, and reality-oriented sacrifices, to the conception of possible future social orders in which some of the repressed libidinal energy has been liberated. In thus adding a second "dimension" to our existence, Marcuse claims, art helps us to escape the one dimensionality of present society. But it is not art's job to draw us blueprints of the future. It must simply keep alive those repressed dreams of liberation and gratification whose energies, blocked but not diminished, will fuel the revolutions that reduce surplus repression and bring us closer to conditions of genuine human happiness.

In this last selection of the chapter, we listen to Marcuse talking about the "negative" function of great art. Despite the difficulty of his philosophical language, I think you will be able to see here some of the themes I have been discussing in the last few pages.

> The achievements and the failures of this society invalidate its higher culture. The celebration of the autonomous personality, of humanism, of tragic and romantic love appears to be the ideal of a backward stage of the development. What is happening now is not the deterioration of higher culture into mass culture but the refutation of this culture by the reality. The reality surpasses its culture. Man today can do *more* than the culture heros and half-gods; he has solved many insoluble problems. But he has also betrayed the hope and destroyed the truth which were preserved in the sublimations of higher culture. To be sure, the higher culture was always in contradiction with social reality, and only a privileged minority enjoyed its blessings and represented its ideals. The two antagonistic spheres of society have always coexisted; the higher culture has always been accommodating, while the reality was rarely disturbed by its ideals and its truth.
>
> Today's novel feature is the flattening out of the antagonism between culture and social reality through the obliteration of the oppositional, alien, and transcendent elements in the higher culture by virtue of which it consti-

tuted *another dimension* of reality. This liquidation of *two-dimensional* culture takes place not through the denial and rejection of the "cultural values," but through their wholesale incorporation into the established order, through their reproduction and display on a massive scale. . . .

In contrast to the Marxian concept, which denotes man's relation to himself and to his work in capitalist society, the *artistic alienation* is the conscious transcendence of the alienated existence—a "higher level" or mediated alienation. The conflict with the world of progress, the negation of the order of business, the anti-bourgeois elements in bourgeois literature and art are neither due to the aesthetic lowliness of this order nor to romantic reaction—nostalgic consecration of a disappearing stage of civilization. "Romantic" is a term of condescending defamation which is easily applied to disparaging avant-garde positions, just as the term "decadent" far more often denounces the genuinely progressive traits of a dying culture than the real factors of decay. The traditional images of artistic alienation are indeed romantic in as much as they are in aesthetic incompatibility with the developing society. This incompatibility is the token of their truth. What they recall and preserve in memory pertains to the future: images of a gratification that would dissolve the society which suppresses it. . . .

The tension between the actual and the possible is transfigured into an insoluble conflict, in which reconciliation is by grace of the oeuvre as *form:* beauty as the "promesse de bonheur." In the form of the oeuvre, the actual circumstances are placed in another dimension where the given reality shows itself as that which it is. Thus it tells the truth about itself; its language ceases to be that of deception, ignorance, and submission. Fiction calls the facts by their name and their reign collapses; fiction subverts everyday experience and shows it to be mutilated and false. But art has this magic power only as the power of negation. It can speak its own language only as long as the images are alive which refuse and refute the established order. . . .

Whether ritualized or not, art contains the rationality of negation. In its advanced positions, it is the Great Refusal—the protest against that which is. The modes in which man and things are made to appear, to sing and sound and speak, are modes of refuting, breaking, and recreating their factual existence. But these modes of negation pay tribute to the antagonistic society to which they are linked. Separated from the sphere of labor where society reproduces itself and its misery, the world of art which they create remains, with all its truth, a privilege and an illusion.

In this form it continues, in spite of all democratization and popularization, through the nineteenth and into the twentieth century. The "high culture" in which this alienation is celebrated has its own rites and its own style. The salon, the concert, opera, theater are designed to create and invoke another dimension of reality. Their attendance requires festive-like preparation; they cut off and transcend everyday experience.

Now this essential gap between the art and the order of the day, kept open in the artistic alienation, is progressively closed by the advancing technological society. And with its closing, the Great Refusal is in turn refused; the "other dimension" is absorbed into the prevailing state of affairs. The works of alienation are themselves incorporated into this society and circulate as part and parcel of the equipment which adorns and psychoanalyzes the prevailing state of affairs. Thus they become commercials—they sell, comfort, or excite.

—HERBERT MARCUSE, *One-Dimensional Man*

The Main Points in Chapter Five

1. Plato criticized the poets of classical Greece on the ground that they presented mere imitations or copies of reality that took their listeners farther away from the truth. He thus raised a question—about the value or purpose of art—that has been debated ever since.

2. Plato's great disciple and pupil, Aristotle, defended the poets, saying that through their tragedies we are able to experience powerful emotions of anger and pity, and purge our souls of them.

3. In the nineteenth and twentieth centuries, a number of artists rejected the notion that art must justify itself, saying that art is valuable simply for its own sake—that it is *intrinsically* valuable.

4. Against the art-for-art's-sake school, we may counterpose a number of theories about what art is good for, what it can accomplish that other forms of human activity can not. *Romanticism*, for example, claims that art puts us in touch with a realm that transcends the sphere of ordinary life. The Romantics conceived of the artist as an unusual individual whose powerful creative imagination sets him or her off from the general run of humanity.

5. In contrast to the Romantics, the great Russian novelist Tolstoy said that true art is the expression of what is universal in human experience, and in that way has the religious purpose of uniting us and bringing us into relation to God.

6. The most unusual defense of art in the history of the debate comes from twentieth-century social theorists like Herbert Marcuse who defend art as an expression of the *negative,* the *oppositional,* in human personality and society. Art, Marcuse claims, is thus a medium of social revolution.

Pornography and Art

Twenty-three hundred years ago, Plato began the debate over the role of the arts in a good society, and the argument has raged without stop ever since. In recent decades, the focus of the debate in the United States has been pornography and obscenity, with complicated legal questions of constitutional rights getting tangled up with the more traditional disagreements about the good and bad effects of art. A great deal of attention, of course, has been concentrated on the impact of explicit sexuality and violence on the young. For every psychologist who testifies that boys and girls are made more violent or more sexually promiscuous by what they see on television, in movies, and on the newsstands, there is another one ready to prove that such vicarious sexual or violent experience actually drains away destructive passions and leaves children less prone to commit antisocial acts. It all sounds very much like a modern-dress replay of the dispute between Plato and Aristotle!

Frequently, the psychological and legal arguments dominate the discussion so completely that we lose sight entirely of the original issue, which is the proper role or function for art. But sometimes, even today, the debate rises to an impressive level of philosophical generality. Our first pair of readings is actually a legal opinion handed down by a judge in a famous obscenity trial and the dissenting opinion of another member of the same bench who saw the matter differently. At issue was the long, complex, experimental novel *Ulysses* by the twentieth-century Irish author James Joyce. In an effort to capture the complexity and immediacy of daily experience, Joyce experimented with what has come to be known as "stream of consciousness" exposition. As his characters go about their business on a single day in Dublin, Ireland, we hear the flow of their inner thoughts and associations, in addition to their public conversation. Not surprisingly, their thoughts are less inhibited, more concerned overtly with sex, than is their outer behavior.

The novel was published in Paris in 1922, having already caused a considerable stir there. A decade later, the novel was imported into the

United States, where the distributor was charged with disseminating obscene materials. The ensuing trial was enlivened, as were subsequent trials of other supposedly obscene materials, by expert testimony from literary critics, who were called upon to give their professional judgment as to the intention of the author. Although the justices made no reference to classical philosophy in their official opinions, it is obvious that they had in mind exactly the same sorts of considerations that exercised Plato and Aristotle, among others.

What is the proper role, or function, of art? Does a work of art injure us or improve us when it provokes strong sexual or aggressive feelings? Should art be judged by its effects on us? Ought there to be one standard for literary works written with "elevated" artistic intentions and a different standard for works written purely to arouse? Does it matter, indeed, what the author's intention was, or should we attend only to the effect of the work on its readers? All of these traditional issues in the philosophy of art, and others besides, were raised by the justices in the case. Here are their opinions.

The Ulysses Case Opinions

Judge Woolsey: I have read "Ulysses" once in its entirety and I have read those passages of which the Government particularly complains several times. In fact, for many weeks, my spare time has been devoted to the consideration of the decision which my duty would require me to make in this matter.

"Ulysses" is not an easy book to read or to understand. But there has been much written about it, and in order prop-

erly to approach the consideration of it it is advisable to read a number of other books which have now become its satellites. The study of "Ulysses" is, therefore, a heavy task.

The reputation of "Ulysses" in the literary world, however, warranted my taking such time as was necessary to enable me to satisfy myself as to the intent with which the book was written, for, of course, in any case where a book is claimed to be obscene it must first be determined, whether the intent with which it was written was what is called, according to the usual phrase, pornographic—

SOURCE: From U.S. District Court opinion, *One Book Called Ulysses*, rendered December 6, 1933, in the Southern District of New York.

that is, written for the purpose of exploiting obscenity.

If the conclusion is that the book is pornographic that is the end of the inquiry and forfeiture must follow.

But in "Ulysses," in spite of its unusual frankness, I do not detect anywhere the leer of the sensualist. I hold, therefore, that it is not pornographic.

In writing "Ulysses," Joyce sought to make a serious experiment in a new, if not wholly novel, literary genre. He takes persons of the lower middle class living in Dublin in 1904 and seeks not only to describe what they did on a certain day early in June of that year as they went about the City bent on their usual occupations, but also to tell what many of them thought about the while.

Joyce has attempted—it seems to me, with astonishing success—to show how the screen of consciousness with its ever-shifting kaleidoscopic impressions carries, as it were on a plastic palimpsest, not only what is in the focus of each man's observation of the actual things about him, but also in a penumbral zone residua of past impressions, some recent and some drawn up by association from the domain of the subconscious. He shows how each of these impressions affects the life and behavior of the character which he is describing.

What he seeks to get is not unlike the result of a double or, if that is possible, a multiple exposure on a cinema film which would give a clear foreground with a background visible but somewhat blurred and out of focus in varying degrees.

To convey by words an effect which obviously lends itself more appropriately to a graphic technique, accounts, it seems to me, for much of the obscurity which meets a reader of "Ulysses." And it also explains another aspect of the book, which I have further to consider, namely, Joyce's sincerity and his honest effort to show exactly how the minds of his characters operate.

If Joyce did not attempt to be honest in developing the technique which he has adopted in "Ulysses" the result would be psychologically misleading and thus unfaithful to his chosen technique. Such an attitude would be artistically inexcusable.

It is because Joyce has been loyal to his technique and has not funked its necessary implications, but has honestly attempted to tell fully what his characters think about, that he has been the subject of so many attacks and that his purpose has been so often misunderstood and misrepresented. For his attempt sincerely and honestly to realize his objective has required him incidentally to use certain words which are generally considered dirty words and has led at times to what many think is a too poignant preoccupation with sex in the thoughts of his characters.

The words which are criticized as dirty are old Saxon words known to almost all men and, I venture, to many women, and are such words as would be naturally and habitually used, I believe, by the types of folk whose life, physical and mental, Joyce is seeking to describe. In respect of the recurrent emergence of the theme of sex in the minds of his characters, it must always be remembered that his locale was Celtic and his season Spring.

Whether or not one enjoys such a technique as Joyce uses is a matter of taste on which disagreement or argument is futile, but to subject that technique to the standards of some other technique seems to me to be little short of absurd.

Accordingly, I hold that "Ulysses" is a sincere and honest book and I think that the criticisms of it are entirely disposed of by its rationale.

Furthermore, "Ulysses" is an amazing *tour de force* when one considers the success which has been in the main achieved with such a difficult objective as Joyce set for himself. As I have stated, "Ulysses" is not an easy book to read. It is brilliant and dull, intelligible and obscure by turns. In many places it seems to me to be disgusting, but although it contains, as I have mentioned above, many words usually considered dirty, I have not found anything that I consider to be dirt for dirt's sake. Each word of the book contributes like a bit of mosaic to the detail of the picture which Joyce is seeking to construct for his readers.

If one does not wish to associate with such folk as Joyce describes, that is one's own choice. In order to avoid indirect contact with them one may not wish to read "Ulysses"; that is quite understandable. But when such a real artist in words, as Joyce undoubtedly is, seeks to draw a true picture of the lower middle class in a European city, ought it to be impossible for the American public legally to see that picture?

To answer this question it is not sufficient merely to find, as I have found above, that Joyce did not write "Ulysses" with what is commonly called pornographic intent, I must endeavor to apply a more objective standard to his book in order to determine its effect in the result, irrespective of the intent with which it was written.

The statute under which the libel is filed only denounces, in so far as we are here concerned, the importation into the United States from any foreign country of "any obscene book." ... It does not marshal against books the spectrum of condemnatory adjectives found, commonly, in laws dealing with matters of this kind. I am, therefore, only required to determine whether "Ulysses" is obscene within the legal definition of that word.

The meaning of the word "obscene" as legally defined by the Courts is: tending to stir the sex impulses or to lead to sexually impure and lustful thoughts. ...

Whether a particular book would tend to excite such impulses and thoughts must be tested by the Court's opinion as to its effect on a person with average sex instincts—what the French would call *l'homme moyen sensuel*—who plays, in this branch of legal inquiry, the same role of hypothetical reagent as does the "reasonable man" in the law of torts and "the man learned in the art" on questions of invention in patent law.

The risk involved in the use of such a reagent arises from the inherent tendency of the trier of facts, however fair he may intend to be, to make his reagent too much subservient to his own idiosyncrasies. Here, I have attempted to avoid this, if possible, and to make my reagent herein more objective than he might otherwise be, by adopting the following course:

After I had made my decision in regard to the aspect of "Ulysses," now under consideration, I checked my impressions with two friends of mine who in my opinion answered to the above stated requirement for my reagent.

These literary assessors—as I might properly describe them—were called on separately, and neither knew that I was consulting the other. They are men whose opinion on literature and on life I value most highly. They had both read "Ulysses," and, of course, were wholly unconnected with this cause.

Without letting either of my assessors know what my decision was, I gave to each of them the legal definition of obscene and asked each whether in his opinion "Ulysses" was obscene within that definition.

I was interested to find that they both agreed with my opinion: that reading "Ulysses" in its entirety, as a book must be read on such a test as this, did not tend to excite sexual impulses or lustful thoughts but that its net effect on them was only that of a "somewhat tragic and very powerful commentary on the inner lives of men and women. . . .

Judge Manton: I dissent. . . . Who can doubt the obscenity of this book after a reading of the pages referred to, which are too indecent to add as a footnote to this opinion? Its characterization as obscene should be quite unanimous by all who read it. . . .

Ulysses is a work of fiction. It may not be compared with books involving medical subjects or description of certain physical or biological facts. It is written for alleged amusement of the reader only. The characters described in the thoughts of the author may in some instances be true, but, be it truthful or otherwise, a book that is obscene is not rendered less so by the statement of truthful fact. . . . nor can that case be taken to mean that the book is to be judged as a whole. If anything, the case clearly recognizes that the statute forbade it to be carried in the mails. Congress did not intend that the question as to the character of the paper should depend upon the opinion or belief of the person who, with knowledge or notice of its contents, assumed the responsibility of putting it in the mails of the United States. The evils that congress sought to remedy would continue and increase in volume if the belief of the accused as to what was obscene, lewd, and lascivious were recognized as the test for determining whether the statute has been violated. Every one who uses the mails of the United States for carrying papers or publications must take notice of what, in this enlightened age, is meant by decency, purity, and chastity in social life, and what must be deemed obscene, lewd, and lascivious.

Congress passed this statute against obscenity for the protection of the great mass of our people; the unusual literator can, or thinks he can, protect himself.

The people do not exist for the sake of literature, to give the author fame, the publisher wealth, and the book a market. On the contrary, literature exists for the sake of the people, to refresh the weary, to console the sad, to hearten the dull and downcast, to increase man's interest in the world, his joy of living, and his sympathy in all sorts and conditions of men. Art for art's sake is heartless and soon grows artless; art for the public market is not art at all, but commerce; art for the people's service is a noble, vital, and permanent element of human life.

The public is content with the standard of salability; the prigs with the standard of preciosity. The people need and deserve a moral standard; it should be a point of honor with men of letters to maintain it. Masterpieces have never been produced by men given to obscenity or lustful thoughts—men who have no Master. Reverence for good work is the foundation of literary character. A refusal to imitate obscenity or to load a book with it is an author's professional chastity.

Good work in literature has its permanent mark; it is like all good work, noble and lasting. It requires a human aim—to cheer, console, purify, or ennoble the life of people. Without this aim, literature has never sent an arrow close to the mark. It is by good work only that men of letters can justify their right to a place in the world.

Under the authoritative decisions and considering the substance involved in this appeal, it is my opinion that the decree should be reversed.

Now let us turn to two contemporary thinkers who take up the debate over pornography in a deliberately philosophical manner. We begin with an attack on censorship by the late poet, novelist, social critic, and philosopher Paul Goodman. Goodman was trained at the University of Chicago in the philosophy of Plato and Aristotle, a fact that shows in everything he wrote subsequently. Goodman faces the issue of pornography head on, by challenging the usually unexamined assumption that it is harmful to arouse powerful sexual passions. He also points out, quite rightly, that there is something absurd and insulting in saying both that Joyce was a great writer and that he did not intend to arouse the feelings that his novel so obviously and successfully arouses! Such a defense is a little like defending a great magician by saying that she didn't mean to fool us.

Pornography, Art, and Censorship

PAUL GOODMAN

Present thinking about obscenity and pornography is wrongheaded and damaging. In order to protect vital liberties, the higher, more intellectual courts often stand out against the police, the postmasters, and popular prejudice; yet since they don't give the right reasons, the issues are never settled. And worse, the courts lend themselves to the sexual attitude which, at this moment in our history, creates the very "hardcore" pornography that is objected to. That is, the court corrupts, it helps the censors corrupt. It ought to give light and provide leadership, and instead it stands in the way of progress. And worst of all, finally, by misunderstanding the nature of art and speech, the court emasculates them and prevents them from playing their indispensable social role. . . .

Judge Woolsey's method in clearing *Ulysses* is as follows: he defines the obscene as the pornographic, as "tending to stir the sex impulses or to lead to sexually impure and lustful thoughts," and he proceeds to show that the book does neither but "is a sincere and serious attempt to

devise a new literary method for the observation and description of mankind." Let us postpone the literary criticism till the next section, but here stop short at the definition of obscenity.

The notion that sexual impulse or stirring sexual impulse is a bad thing comes from an emotional climate in which it was generally agreed that it would be better if sexuality did not overtly exist, when people bathed and slept fully clothed, and a bull was called a he-cow. Then anything which was sexual in public, as by publication of "detailed representation in words or pictures," violated society's self-image and was certainly obscene. In our times such a notion cannot define obscenity. The pornographic is not *ipso facto* the obscene. As Judge Jerome Frank pointed out in 1949, "No sane man thinks that the arousing of normal sexual desires is socially dangerous." We lived in a culture where all High Thought insists on the beauty and indeed hygienic indispensability of sexual desires, and where a vast part of commerce is busy in their stimulation. . . .

Let me proceed to a philosophical question raised by these decisions, which is, in my opinion, even more important for our society than the sexual matter: what is the nature of speech and art? To protect their "serious" books, the courts

SOURCE: Paul Goodman, selections from "Pornography, Art, and Censorship," from *Commentary* (March 1961). Copyright © 1961 by Paul Goodman. Reprinted from *Utopian Essays and Practical Proposals*, by Paul Goodman, by permission of Random House, inc.

attempt to distinguish speech as communication of an idea or even as talking
about a subject, from speech as an action
doing something to its speaker, subject,
and hearer. This is the tactic of Woolsey
when he devotes most of his opinion to
Joyce's "new method for the observation
and description of mankind" . . .

Woolsey's doctrine is insulting to the
artist. He says that the book did "not tend
to excite lustful thoughts, *but* the net effect was a tragic and powerful commentary" (italics mine). Surely the author
wants to say, "It is lustful among other
things, and *therefore* its net effect is
tragic."

In our culture an artist is expected to
move the reader; he is supposed to move
him to tears, to laughter, to indignation,
to compassion, even to hatred; but he
may not move him to have an erection
or to mockery of public figures making a
spectacle of themselves. Why not? By
these restrictions we doom ourselves to
a passionless and conformist community.
Instead of bracketing off the "classics," as
especially the British courts do—indeed,
the legal definition of a classic seems to

be a "nonactionable obscenity"—let us
pay attention to the classical pornography and we shall see that it is not the
case, as the court feels obliged to prove,
that a work has a "net" social use despite
its sexual effect, but rather that the pornography, in a great context and spoken
by a great soul, *is* the social use. Aristo-
phanic comedy was still close to a sea-
sonal ritual to encourage rebelliousness
and lead to procreation. Rabelais is disgraceful like a giant baby, and this *is* the
Renaissance. Catullus teaches us the callous innocence of highborn youth, free of
timidity and pettiness; and Tom Jones is
a similar type, with a dash of English sen-
timentality. If we may believe their pre-
ludes, both the *Arabian Nights* and the
Decameron are cries of life in the face of
death; and in our times Jean Genet, one
of our few fine writers, is pornographic
and psychopathic because only so, he
tells us, can he feel that he exists in our
inhuman world. But apart from these
lofty uses, there are also famous pornographic books made just for fun, since sex
is a jolly subject.

By and large, the anticensorship side of the debate has had the good
publicity in recent decades. Very few people want to defend censorship
of political, religious, or moral opinions, and it is difficult to say exactly
when a novel, a play, or a movie ceases to be "political" and becomes
simply a commercial exploitation of sex and violence. In our last selection
in this chapter, however, we encounter a serious, thoughtful defense of
censorship from a thinker who, like Plato, takes the moral health of the
body politic as the highest good. The key to Walter Berns' defense of
censorship is his provocative question: "What if, contrary to what is now
so generally assumed, shame is natural to man . . . ?" In other words,

what if it is natural to be aroused by sex and violence, *and equally natural to feel the moral emotion of shame for being aroused?* What if the primary role of society is not to release our natural impulses, but to restrain them, not to make us shameless but to strengthen, direct, and use our shame for humanly good purposes! In that case, it will be no defense of pornographic books that we all have a "natural" desire to read them. Quite to the contrary, that fact will simply make it all the clearer that society must help us to control that ugly side of our souls.

I have deliberately given the procensorship side of the debate the lion's share of space here because I suspect that your sympathies will lie with Paul Goodman. As John Stuart Mill pointed out, there is much to be gained from forcing ourselves to face arguments that contradict our own opinions.

Pornography vs. Democracy: The Case for Censorship

WALTER BERNS

The case against censorship is very old and very familiar. Almost anyone can formulate it without difficulty. One has merely to set the venerable Milton's *Areopagitica* in modern prose, using modern spelling, punctuation, and examples. This is essentially what the civil libertarians did in their successful struggle, during the past century, with the censors. The unenlightened holder of the bishop's imprimatur, Milton's "unleasur'd licencer" who has never known "the labour of book-writing," became the ignorant policeman or the bigoted school board member who is offended by "Mrs. Warren's Profession," or the benighted librarian who refuses to shelf *The Scarlet Letter,* or the insensitive customs official who seizes *Ulysses* in the name of an outrageous law, or the Comstockian vigilante who glues together the pages of every copy of *A Farewell to Arms* she can find in the bookstore. The industrious learned Milton, insulted by being asked to "appear in Print like a punie with his guardian and his censors hand on the back of his title to be his bayle and surety," was

SOURCE: Walter Berns, "Pornography vs. Democracy: The Case for Censorship," *The Public Interest* (Winter 1971). Reprinted by permission of the author and the Public Affairs Conference Center, Kenyon College.

replaced by Shaw, Hawthorne, Joyce, or Hemingway, and those who followed in their wake, all victims of the mean-spirited and narrow minded officials who were appointed, or in some cases took it upon themselves, to judge what others should read, or at least not read. The presumed advantage of truth when it grapples with falsehood became the inevitable victory of "enduring ideas" in the free competition of the market. With these updated versions of old and familiar arguments, the civil libertarians have prevailed.

They prevailed partly because of the absurdity of some of their opposition, and also because of a difficulty inherent in the task their opponents set for themselves. The censors would proscribe the obscene, and even assuming, as our law did, that obscene speech is no part of the speech protected by the First Amendment to the Constitution, it is not easy to formulate a rule of law that distinguishes the non-obscene from the obscene. Is it the presence of four-letter words? But many a literary masterpiece contains four-letter words. Detailed descriptions of sexual acts? James Joyce provides these. Words tending to corrupt those into whose hands they are likely to fall? But who is to say what corrupts or, for that matter, whether anything corrupts or, again, what is meant by corruption? Is it an appeal to a "prurient interest" or is it a work that is "patently offensive"? If that is what is meant by the obscene, many a "socially important work," many a book, play, or film with "redeeming social value," would be lost to us. The col-

lege professors said so, and if college professors do not know the socially important, who does? Be that as it may, they succeeded in convincing the Supreme Court, and the result was the complete rout of the "forces of reaction." To the college professors, therefore, as well as to the "courageous" publishers and the "public-spirited" attorneys who had selflessly fought the cases through the courts, a debt of gratitude is owed by the lovers of Shaw, Hawthorne, Joyce and Hemingway—and others too numerous to detail here. In the same spirit one might say that never has there been such a flourishing of the arts in this country. . . .

Just as it is no simple task to formulate a rule of law that distinguishes the non-obscene from the obscene, it is still more difficult to distinguish the obscene from the work of genuine literary merit. In fact, it is impossible—and our failure to understand this may be said to be a condition, if not a cause, of our present situation. Our laws proscribe obscenity as such and by name, and we are unwilling to admit that great literary and dramatic works can be, and frequently are, obscene. In combination these two facts explain how it came about that we now have, with the sanction of the law, what is probably the most vulgar theatre and literature in history. The paradox is readily explained. The various statutes making up the law have made obscenity a criminal thing, and our judges assume that if a work of art is really a work of art, and not vulgar rubbish, it cannot be obscene. Thus, Judge Woolsey, in his celebrated opinion in the *Ulysses* case, recounts how he had asked two literary friends whether the book was obscene within the legal definition, which he had explained to them, and how they had both agreed with him that it was not. But of course *Ulysses* is obscene. Not so obscene as an undoubted masterpiece, Aristophanes' "Assembly of Women," for example, which would not be a masterpiece—which would not be anything— were its obscenity removed, but obscene nevertheless.

The trouble stems from the fact that the Tarrif Act of 1930 would exclude "obscene" books from the country, and Judge Woolsey, being a sensible man, did not want this to happen to *Ulysses*. So he fashioned a rule to protect it. But the same rule of law protects *The Tropic of Cancer*, because according to the rule's necessarily clumsy categories, the latter is no more obscene than the former, however it compares on another scale and whatever the aesthetic distances separating its author, Henry Miller, and James Joyce as writers. Eventually, and for the same reason, the protection of the law was extended to *Trim, MANual,* and *Grecian Guild Pictorial,* the homosexual magazines involved in a case before the Supreme Court in 1962, and then to *Fanny Hill. . . .*

Underlying this unfortunate development is the familiar liberal idea of progress. Rather than attempt to inhibit artists and scientists, the good polity will grant them complete freedom of expression and of inquiry, and will benefit collectively by so doing. What is good for the arts and sciences is good for the polity: this proposition has gone largely unquestioned among us for 200 years now. The case for censorship rests on its denial, and can be made only by separately examining its parts. What is good for the arts and sciences? What is good for the polity? The case for censorship arises initially out of a consideration of the second question.

The case for censorship is at least as old as the case against it, and, contrary to what is usually thought today, has been made under decent and even democratic auspices by intelligent men. To the extent to which it is known today, however, it is thought to be pernicious or, at best, irrelevant to the enlightened conditions of the 20th century. It begins from the premise that the laws cannot remain indifferent to the manner in which men amuse themselves, or to the kinds of amusement offered them. . . .

We turn to the arts—to literature, films, and the theatre, as well as to the graphic arts . . . for the pleasure to be derived from them, and pleasure has the capacity to form our tastes and thereby to affect our lives. It helps determine the kind of men we become, and helps shape the lives of those with whom and among whom we live. So one can properly ask: Is it politically uninteresting whether men derive pleasure from performing their duties as citizens, fathers, and husbands or, on the other hand, from watching their laws and customs and institutions being ridiculed on the stage? Whether the passions are excited by, and the affections drawn to, what is noble or what is base?

Whether the relations between men and women are depicted in terms of an eroticism wholly divorced from love and calculated to destroy the capacity for love and the institutions, such as the family, that depend on love? Whether a dramatist uses pleasure to attach men to what is beautiful or to what is ugly? We may not be accustomed to thinking of these things in this manner, but it is not strange that so much of the obscenity from which so many of us derive our pleasure today has an avowed political purpose. It would seem that the pornographers know intuitively what liberals have forgotten, namely, that there is indeed a "causal relationship ... between word or pictures and human behavior." At least they are not waiting for behavioral science to discover this fact.

The purpose is sometimes directly political and sometimes political in the sense that it will have political consequences intended or not. This latter purpose is to make us shameless, and it seems to be succeeding with astonishing speed. Activities that were once confined to the private scene—to the "ob-scene," to make an etymological assumption— are now presented for our delectation and emulation in center stage. Nothing that is appropriate to one place is inappropriate to any other place. No act, we are to infer, no human possibility, no possible physical combination or connection, is shameful. ... Nothing prevents a dog from enjoying sexual intercourse in the marketplace, and it is unnatural to deprive men of the same pleasure, either actively or as voyeurs in the theatre. Shame

itself is unnatural, a convention devised by hypocrites to inhibit the pleasures of the body. We must get rid of our "hang-ups."

THE IMPORTANCE OF SHAME

But what if, contrary to what is now so generally assumed, shame is natural to man, in the sense of being an original feature of human existence? What if it is shamelessness that is unnatural, in the sense of having to be acquired? What if the beauty that men are capable of knowing and achieving in their living with each other derives from the fact that man is naturally a "blushing creature," the only creature capable of blushing? ...

To speak in a manner that is more obviously political, there is a connection between self-restraint and shame, and therefore a connection between shame and self-government or democracy. There is, therefore, a political danger in promoting shamelessness and the fullest self-expression or indulgence. To live together requires rules and a governing of the passions, and those who are without shame will be unruly and unrulable; having lost the ability to restrain themselves by observing the rules they collectively give themselves, they will have to be ruled by others. Tyranny is the natural and inevitable mode of government for the shameless and self-indulgent who have carried liberty beyond any restraint, natural and conventional.

Such, indeed, was the argument made by political philosophers prior to the 20th century, when it was generally understood that democracy, more than any other form of government, required self-restraint, which it would inculcate through moral education and impose on itself through laws, including laws governing the manner of public amusements. It was the tyrant who could usually allow the people to indulge themselves. Indulgence of the sort we are now witnessing did not threaten his rule, because his rule did not depend on a citizenry of good character. Anyone can be ruled by a tyrant, and the more debased his subjects the safer his rule. A case can be made for complete freedom of the arts among such people, whose pleasures are derived from activities divorced from their labors and any duties associated with citizenship.

One who undertakes to defend censorship in the name of the arts is obliged to acknowledge that he has not exhausted his subject when he has completed that defense. What is missing is a defense of obscenity. What is missing is a defense of the obscenity employed by the greatest of our poets—Aristophanes and Chaucer, Shakespeare and Swift—because it is impossible to believe, it is unreasonable to believe, that what they did is indefensible; and what they did, among other things, was to write a good deal of obscenity. Unfortunately, it would require a talent I do not possess to give a sufficient account of it.

They employed it mainly in comedy, but their purpose was not simply to make us laugh. Comedy, according to Aristotle, makes us laugh at what is ludicrous in ugliness, and its purpose is to teach, just as tragedy teaches by making us cry before what is destructive in nobility. The latter imitates what is higher, the former what is lower, but they are equally serious; Aristotle discussed both, and Shakespeare, for example, was a comic as well as a tragic poet.

Those aspects of his soul that make man truly human and distinguish him from all other beings—higher or lower in the natural order of things—require political life. And no great poet ever denied this. Man's very virtues, as well as their counterparts, his vices, require him to be governed and to govern; they initiate demands that can be met only in political life—but the poet knows with Rousseau that the demands of human virtue cannot be fully met in political life because they transcend political life. The poet knows the beauty of that order beyond the polity; he reminds us that there is an order outside the conventional and that we are part of that natural order, as well as of the conventional. Shakespeare knows with Rousseau that there is a tension between this natural order and the conventional or legal order, and his purpose is to resolve it, at least for some men, at the highest possible level. These men must first be shown that this world of convention is not the only world, and here is where obscenity may play a part—that beyond Venice there is Portia's Belmont, the utopia where the problems that plague Venice do not exist. Obscenity can be used to ridicule the conventional. But it is used in the name of the natural, that order outside the conventional according to which the conventional may be criticized and perhaps, if only to an extent, reformed. Obscenity in the hands of such a poet can serve to *elevate* men, elevate them, the few of them, above the conventional order in which all of us are forced to live our mundane lives. Its purpose is to teach what is truly beautiful—not what convention holds to be beautiful—and to do so by means of pleasure, for obscenity can be pleasurable.

How to express in a rule of law this distinction between the justified and the unjustified employment of obscenity is no simple task. That I have admitted and willingly concede. I have also argued that it cannot be done at all on the premise from which our law has proceeded. I have, finally, tried to indicate the consequences of a failure to maintain the distinction in the law: not only will we no longer be able to teach the distinction between the proper and the improper, but we will no longer be able to teach—and will therefore come to forget—the distinction between art and trash. Stated otherwise, censorship, because it inhibits self-indulgence and supports the ideal of propriety and impropriety, protects politi-

cal democracy; paradoxically, when it faces the problem of the justified and unjustified use of obscenity, censorship also serves to maintain the distinction between art and trash and, therefore, to protect art and, thereby, to enhance the quality of this democracy. We forgot this. We began with a proper distrust of the capacities of juries and judges to make sound judgments in an area that lies outside their professional competence; but led by the Supreme Court we went on improperly to conclude that the judgments should not be made because they cannot be made, that there is nothing for anyone to judge. No doubt the law used to err on occasion; but democracy can live without "Mrs. Warren's Profession," if it must, as well as without *Fanny Hill*— or to speak more precisely, it can live with the error that consigns "Mrs. Warren's Profession" to under-the-counter custom along with *Fanny Hill*. It remains to be seen whether the true friend of democracy will want to live in the world without under-the-counter custom, the world that does not know the difference between "Mrs. Warren's Profession" and *Fanny Hill*.

Study Questions

1. There is overwhelming evidence that art, in some form or other, occurs in every human society, however technologically primitive or advanced. In short, art is *natural* to human beings. Does that, by itself, prove that art is a good thing? Might something that is natural and universal nevertheless be a bad thing, something to be repressed or stamped out?

2. It is easy enough to see in what sense a realistic painting is a representation, or image, or mere appearance, of the object it pictures. But what representational relation, if any, does music bear to the world? We are accustomed to separating out some artistic activities as belonging to what is called the *fine arts*. That distinction, however, only dates back to the fifteenth and sixteenth centuries. Is there any important difference between ballet, opera, classical music, poetry, sculpture, and painting on the one hand, and fairy tales, folk songs, rock music, macrame, basket weaving, and leather work on the other?

3. One of the principal charges against pornography is that its sole purpose is to arouse prurient desires in its readers or viewers. In defense of the civil rights of pornographers, some people respond that pornography has a political or social purpose. But what is wrong with arousing prurient desires?

4. Most pornography in American society portrays women in a degrading fashion, and that fact has led many feminists to argue that pornography violates the rights of women, and should be banned. Now, pornography, almost without exception, is bad art, whatever else it is. But suppose we are confronted with a great work of art that is also morally objectionable, because of its representation of women, or Jews, or the Irish, or working people, or because of its attack on religion, or on democracy. Should our *moral* objections take precedence over our *aesthetic* judgments?

5. If Marcuse is correct, art performs a valuable social function precisely by being negative, offensive, a reproach to decent people. If that is true, then don't we destroy art's positive function by *tolerating* it?

6

PHILOSOPHY OF RELIGION

SØREN KIERKEGAARD (1813–1855) was the founder and most brilliant spokesman of the style of philosophizing known as "existentialism." His life was devoted to an unending inward reflection on human existence and the terror and uncertainty which each of us experiences in the face of his or her own death. Kierkegaard was deeply religious, though he rejected what he felt to be the superficial, self-satisfied Lutheranism of his native Denmark. In a series of books, some on philosophical topics, others more directly religious in their focus, he redefined the nature of faith, making it radically subjective and totally alien to the processes of ordinary systematic reason.

Kierkegaard was a witty, brilliantly provocative writer. His works abound in complex ironies which are challenges to the reader. He seems always to seek to unsettle his readers, to put us off balance and thereby force us to examine our lives as Kierkegaard had examined his own. One of his many literary devices to achieve this was the practice of publishing his books under pseudonyms. The *Philosophical Fragments*, for example, was published with its author listed as "Johannes Climacus." Farther down on the page, there appeared the statement, "Responsible for publication: S. Kierkegaard." By this and other devices, Kierkegaard hoped to block any attempt by his readers to classify his position and pigeonhole him, for Kierkegaard was convinced that such techniques of systematic professional philosophy were merely ways of defusing a book and making it safe.

As he himself pessimistically predicted, Kierkegaard has fallen into the hands of professors and systematizers, and even his challenge to established philosophy has itself come to be treated merely as one more philosophy, namely, Existentialism. Kierkegaard would have laughed, or perhaps he would have wept, to see his struggle with death and eternity reduced to an "ism."

I Kierkegaard's Encounter With Faith

Søren Kierkegaard was born in 1813 to a father fifty-six and a mother forty-four. His early life and education were very closely supervised by his father, who demanded both a scholarly mastery of classical languages and a highly charged imaginative appreciation of the literature his young son read. The young Søren had laid upon him the full weight of the guilt which extreme Pietist Protestantism so often inflicted upon its communicants. Although Kant and Kierkegaard thus had roughly the same sort of religious upbringing, Kierkegaard completely lacked Kant's quiet inner confidence and peace. He reacted first against the torment of his religious training by plunging himself into a life of physical self-indulgence, eating, drinking, dressing the dandy. But these distractions could not free him from the black gloom which hung over him, and he decided finally to return to his studies and become a pastor.

   The dramatic turning point in Kierkegaard's private life was his engagement, and then the breaking of it, to seventeen-year-old Regine Olson. Kierkegaard wrote endlessly of his feelings for Regine, of the philosophical significance of marriage, love, and the problems of such a life commitment, but one cannot help thinking that she was more important to him as a subject for meditation than as a real, live woman. After pouring out a series of essays and books on aesthetic, moral, and religious topics, Kierkegaard died at the relatively early age of forty-two.

Kierkegaard's inner emotional life, his lifelong struggle with religious faith, and his reaction to the dominant Hegelian philosophy of his day are all so intimately intertwined that it is very difficult to speak of any one without immediately bringing in all three. There is hardly space in an introductory text of this sort to explore the subject fully, but a few systematic remarks may be helpful to you. I especially want you to develop an interest in Kierkegaard because, in my opinion, he is, after the immortal Plato, the most gifted artist among all the important philosophers who have come down to us in the Western tradition. If you pick up one of his books, many of which are easily available in paperback editions, you will find him profound, troubling, witty, touching, and in the end deeply rewarding.

The passionate center of Kierkegaard's thought and life is his confrontation with the ever-present terror of existential dread—the obsessive, unavoidable fact of my own impending death, the infinity of the universe and the meaninglessness of my own brief life in comparison. Every man, woman, and child faces these terrible, fundamental facts of the human condition. We may deny them, flee from them, repress them, distract ourselves to escape from them, but always they are there, at the edge of consciousness, waiting to return in the darkness of night. The first lesson Kierkegaard teaches us, both in his books and by his life, is that this dread of death and meaninglessness must be faced, confronted, not shoved aside again and again. If I may speak personally—and the greatest honor we can pay to Kierkegaard is precisely to be honest, each one of us, about our own encounter with the fear of death—I first came face to face with this dread as a teenager. I was obsessed with fears of death, and the more I thrust them from my mind, the more intensely they returned. In my case, the fear was not of pain, or age, or sickness, but simply of nonbeing. The more I turned the thought over in my mind, the closer my own eventual death seemed to come, until finally I would seize any distraction to divert my attention from what was, and of course still is, an unavoidable fate.

For Kierkegaard, the dread of death was both heightened and complicated by the hope of eternal life which the religion of his fathers held out to him. All of you have heard the expression, "Trust in the Lord." But how many of you have actually asked yourselves what it means to "trust in the Lord"? What does it mean to "believe in" God, to have faith in Him?

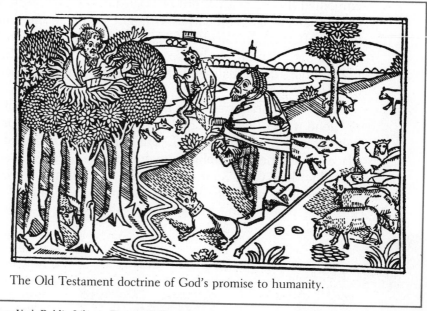

The Old Testament doctrine of God's promise to humanity.

New York Public Library Picture Collection

Well, what it *doesn't* mean is believing *that* God exists! In our increasingly nonreligious society, when a person says that she "believes in God," we automatically assume that she means that she believes there is such a thing as God. But in the Judeo-Christian religious tradition, particularly in the extreme individualistic Protestant sort of Christianity that was Kierkegaard's heritage, the phrase "belief in God" has quite a different meaning. To believe in God, to trust in Him, to have faith in Him, means to believe that He will keep His promise to humanity; it is to have faith that He will keep the pact, or covenant, that He made with the beings He created. That pact is testified to first in what we call the Old Testament, and then again in a renewed form in the New Testament.

The promise, of course, is the promise of salvation, of a life after death, of true happiness, of fruitfulness, of a union of the soul with God. (Needless to say, long books could be written on the various interpretations that Jews, Christians, and Muslims have placed upon this notion of a covenant with God. The version I am summarizing here is something like what Kierkegaard would have learned and brooded upon.) According to the Old Testament, God made a promise to Noah, He repeated it to Abraham, He renewed it again and again, despite the failure of the Hebrews to keep His Law and follow His commands. Finally, God embodied that Law (or Word or Logos) in the Person of Jesus Christ, in order that His offer of salvation might be made once more. With the birth, suffering, and death of Jesus, God sealed His free gift of eternal life. As the price of that blessedness, He asked only faith, an unstinting, unconditioned, unqualified belief by us that He would keep His promise of this free gift.

Other Christian traditions had emphasized the role of right behavior, or "good works," either as part of the price of salvation or else as worldly evidence of one's true belief. But the Pietist strain of Protestantism placed a very heavy emphasis upon the pure possession of that unconditioned faith in God. So it was that for Kierkegaard, the central religious problem quite naturally became the problem of **faith.**

A drawing, by the great seventeenth-century Dutch artist Rembrandt, of Abraham preparing to sacrifice his only son, Isaac, at God's command. In one of his most powerful books, *Fear and Trembling*, Kierkegaard interpreted the story of Abraham and Isaac as an evidence of Abraham's perfect faith in the Lord. (New York Public Library Picture Collection)

> **Faith**   In Christianity, trust that God will keep the promise He made to the Israelites in the Old Testament and renewed to all mankind in the New Testament (hence, "trust in the Lord"). Originally, the promise was to make the Israelites fruitful and populous. In the New Testament, the promise is of life eternal in heaven. According to some Christians, men and women are unable to have and sustain this trust without the miraculous help of God.

You might think, on first reflection, that the Christian message would be a very welcome message indeed! After all, life is short, bedeviled by suffering, terminated by the absolute finality of unavoidable death. It was good enough news to be told, in the Old Testament, that God would grant life everlasting to those who kept His commandments. But we are weak, imperfect creatures, and it soon became clear that doing God's bidding was a task too hard for us, even with the promise of salvation to lead us on. He took upon Himself, in the Person of His Son, the atonement for *our* sins, and offered to us the priceless pearl of salvation for the merest asking. All we needed do was believe that we would receive it. What could possibly be better news than that? Small wonder that this message was called the Gospel, which means "good news." Small wonder too that those who spread the message were called evangelists, which means "bringers of good news."

But strange to tell, the glad tidings of God's free gift have brought fear, dread, doubt, torment, and tortured self-examination to countless hearers, among them Søren Kierkegaard. The gift is so great, the price so small—and yet, the price of faith must be paid freely, unhesitatingly, without doubts or second thoughts. Therein lie the seeds of terror. Do I truly believe? Is my faith pure? Can I trust in the Lord, or is there lurking deep within my heart a doubt that so great a gift will be conferred on so undeserving a creature as myself? Out of this inner hell Kierkegaard tore the writings by which we remember him. His doubts and fears concerned his very *existence* as an individual, mortal creature longing to believe in God's promise, not the abstract, impersonal logical relationships among disembodied forms, or "essences." Hence, Kierkegaard's way of thinking has come to be called **existentialist.** Indeed, Kierkegaard is universally acknowledged to be the first true existentialist philosopher. Whether he would have appreciated such a categorization and sterilization of his inner torment is of course not so clear.

In his lifelong struggle with the problem of faith, Kierkegaard did battle with three enemies, against whom he turned not only his considerable philosophical and theological gifts, but also a brilliant, convoluted, ironic wit. The first of his enemies was the established Christianity of his own day, the solid, comfortable, Sunday-sermon Lutheranism of nineteenth-century Denmark. Like so many passionate prophets before him, Kierkegaard accused the established church of mouthing empty formulae which were neither lived nor understood. Sin, redemption, damnation, salvation—all were the subjects of elegant sermons and pious attitudes which did not for a moment interfere with the secular, weekday activities of this world. Kierkegaard once observed that just as it is hard to jump up in the air and land exactly on the spot from which one began, so too it is harder to become a Christian when one has been born a Christian. He meant that those who were born into Christianity, who were baptized, confirmed, and raised in the official emptiness of its dogmas and rituals, might actually find it more difficult to take the message of Christianity seriously than would a pagan to whom the divine promise came as wonderful, terrible, astonishing news. Kierkegaard devoted many of his books to a sustained effort to breathe new existential significance into the familiar phrases and concepts of Christian theology.

His second enemy was the complacent middle-class culture of his society, the "bourgeois" culture of solid tradesmen and lawyers—sound, self-confident people who disdained anyone so odd, so passionate, so disruptive as Kierkegaard. The word "bourgeois" has drifted into our vocabulary these days as a catch-all term for what we in America call "middle-class" life, but in nineteenth-century Europe, it had a much richer, more resonant set of associations. Historically, a "bourgeois," or a "burgher," was simply a resident of a "bourg" or "burg," which in the late Middle Ages was a walled city. By extension, the word came to mean a member of the urban merchant class, and also a "freeman" or citizen of one of the cities whose charter came from the king rather than from the feudal aristocracy. The burghers of the European cities were men of substance, solid citizens, true to their word in business deals, extremely conservative in their family relationships, jealous of their rights as city leaders, forward-looking in commerce, and quite often supporters of a strong monarchy against the ancient and dispersed powers of the landed aristocracy. For the burghers of Copenhagen, religion was first of all a matter of propriety, of respectability, and only then a matter of conscience or salvation. One dressed in one's finest clothes on Sunday and went with one's family to church; one sat in a front pew, purchased at great ex-

A nineteenth-century bourgeois gentleman and lady
friend as the painter Tou-
louse Lautrec saw them.
(The metropolitan Museum of
Art, Bequest of Miss Adelaide
Milton de Groot (1876–1967),
1967.)

pense, where one was seen by one's neighbors. One listened piously to the sermon, which, though heavy on damnation, was conveniently light on social responsibility, and then one returned to one's substantial town-house for a good Sunday dinner.

As you can imagine, the unthinking religiosity, the self-satisfied complacency of the solid citizens of Denmark made Kierkegaard furious. Many of his most spectacular literary tricks and devices, and particularly his extremely heavy irony, are aimed at puncturing that complacency and somehow reaching the real human beings behind those masks.

The final enemy was the official philosophy of Kierkegaard's day, the vast, pompous, elaborate philosophical systems constructed by the disciples and followers of the great German philosopher Georg Hegel. The Hegelian philosophy, as it was expounded by the professors of Europe, put itself forward as the objective, impersonal, purely rational, totally systematic, absolutely final truth about just about everything. It was turgid, jargon-filled and completely self-confident. It claimed to wrap up

"You seem troubled, Brother Timothy. Is anything worrying you? I mean, besides the sins of the world, the vanities of mankind, and that sort of thing."

Stevenson, © 1960 The New Yorker Magazine, Inc.

space, time, eternity, being, history, man, the state, and God in one vast metaphysical synthesis that simultaneously answered all our questions about the universe and also—rather conveniently—demonstrated the superiority of precisely the social and religious system then dominant in European society.

In short, Kierkegaard's three enemies were really one and the same enemy in different disguises. The Christianity of his day was bourgeois Christianity, buttressed and justified by the official philosophical system. The burghers were Establishment Christians, who—though they knew precious little philosophy—were justified and rationalized by that same philosophy. And the philosophy, though it claimed to be the purest product of reason, was a thoroughgoing justification of the reign of the burghers and the ascendency of their religion.

Karl Marx, facing this very same union of religion, philosophy, and the ascendent bourgeoisie, turned his attack on the social and economic consequences, for Marx was a secular man, concerned with this-worldly issues of justice, poverty, and work. Kierkegaard, before all else a man of God, attacked the same union of forces on its religious front. He cared nothing at all for worldly happiness or misery. Rather, he brushed all secular considerations aside and instead demanded that the good Christians of Denmark begin to pay to eternal life as much attention as they regularly gave to a daily profit.

Kierkegaard's onslaught was complex and subtle and, hence, is impossible to summarize in a few paragraphs. Two ideas lie at the heart of his religio-philosophical message, and we can at least take a first step toward understanding them. These notions are the inwardness, or subjectivity, of truth, and the irrational, unarguable "leap of faith." Now, that sounds more like a Hegelian mouthful than a bit of biting wit, so let us take a look at each.

The Hegelian philosophers put their doctrines forward as *rational* and *objective*. They were, in a way, like today's scientists. All of you have noticed, I imagine, that there is a very big difference in the teaching style and approach of science professors as compared with professors of literature or philosophy. In a literature class, you are encouraged to express your own "interpretation" of Dickens or Mailer or Shakespeare. In a philosophy class—I hope!—you are prompted to think out your own position, to develop your own arguments, and to defend whatever point of view you think closest to the truth. But nobody teaches calculus or physics that way! Can you imagine a physics quiz with questions like "Write a ten-minute essay on your impressions of Boyle's law" or "Take a position for or against relativity and defend it—in your answer, make reference to the text." Hardly! Scientists quite confidently assume that their knowledge is objective, and that what they teach is a matter neither of "opinion" nor of personality. In the same way, the Hegelian philosophers represented themselves as objective, rational discoverers of the truth. Their private fears, hopes, terrors, and joys were no more a part of their philosophy, they thought, than would a modern biochemist's neuroses be a part of her theory of DNA. To be sure, readers might be curious, in a gossipy way, about the personal lives of the great philosophers, just as we today like to read stories about Albert Einstein. But no one would suppose for a moment that there was any important scientific connection between those delightful or depressing glimpses into the scientist's private life and the scientific truth of his theories.

In a total reversal of the received philosophical-scientific opinion of his day, Kierkegaard argued that Truth is Subjectivity. In other words, he denied the objective impersonality of truth and insisted, instead, that all truth must be inward, dependent upon the subject, particular rather than universal, personal rather than interpersonal or impersonal.

When Kierkegaard says that Truth is Subjectivity, he is denying the ancient philosophical doctrine that the truth of an idea or a statement consists in its conformity to an independent object. When I say, "That is a very good picture of Jim," I mean that the picture looks like Jim, that it resembles, or copies, or conforms to the objective nature of Jim's body. When I say, "It is true that Sacramento is the capital of California," I mean that the real world—California, in this case—actually has the characteristics that my statement says it has. In other words, truth is conformity to the objective state of things in the world. Or, Truth is Objectivity. If this familiar conception of truth is correct, then the truth of a statement or belief depends only on the relationship between the statement or belief and the world, *not* on the relationship between the statement or belief and the person who thinks it. If Truth is Objectivity, then it doesn't matter, so far as truth is concerned, whether I believe Sacramento to be the capital of California passionately, calmly, tentatively, with all my heart, or simply because a friend told me so.

Kierkegaard doesn't care about the capitals of states or nations, of course. He cares about salvation, the Christian message. And when it comes to salvation, *how* you believe is as important as *what* you believe, he thought. The Hegelian system builders wanted to treat the Christian message as though it were merely one subpart of their grand structure of objective knowledge. So "Jesus died for my sins" would be treated by them as more or less on a par with "Space is three dimensional and homogeneous." Each statement would be true if it corresponded correctly to the objective state of things, false otherwise. But that treatment of the promise of salvation as "objective" was precisely wrong, Kierkegaard insisted. Truth does not consist in the proper relationship between the belief and the *object*; rather, it consists in the proper relationship between the belief and the *subject*, the individual human being who holds that belief. *How* he or she holds it is the criterion of its truth. In order for the belief to be true, it must be held passionately, unconditionally, absolutely without inner reservation or doubt.

But—and here we come to the second of Kierkegaard's great ideas, the "leap of faith." That belief in God's promise of eternal life can have no rational justification, no evidence, no proof. Theologians since the time of Aristotle had sought to *prove* the existence of God, to prove the truth of this or that religious doctrine. Sometimes they used evidence of their senses—what they could see, hear, and touch. At other times, they

Modern American fundamentalist protestantism shares with Kierkegaard the belief that true religion is based on faith, not on reason. (Kenneth Murray/Photo Researchers)

erected abstract arguments of pure logic, deducing the absolute, objective truth of Christianity (or Islam, or Judaism). But Kierkegaard believed that all such attempts at rational justification were doomed to total failure. The absolute gap between finite man and infinite God made any rational bridge building between the two on man's part futile. God might reach down to man, though how He could manage that was beyond our comprehension. But man could no more reason his way into the presence of God than a mathematician, by doggedly adding unit to unit, could calculate his way to infinity.

Because reason was inadequate to the task of supporting our belief in God's promise, Kierkegaard said, our only hope was an absolutely irrational, totally unjustifiable leap of faith. I must take the plunge and say, with all my heart, *Credo*—I believe.

Couldn't we perhaps look for a little bit of support from reason? Mightn't reason at least show that God's promise is probable? That the weight of the evidence inclines us toward God's promise? That a reasonable person could tend to believe God's promise?

Not a bit of it! That is just what a fat, solid, smug merchant or a pompous, self-important professor would say. Can't you just imagine the two of them sitting in front of the fire, the burgher after a long day at the counting house, the professor after a day of serious, important lectures. The burgher leans back in his comfortable chair, puffs a bit on his pipe (one wouldn't want to speak too quickly on such matters—it might show a lack of seriousness), and then asks, "Is it your opinion that the weight of the evidence, objectively and impartially considered, inclines us to the view that God has promised us eternal life rather than eternal death?" The professor takes a sip of beer, strokes his beard thoughtfully, and answers, "Well, on the one hand, Hegel, in the *Phenomenology of Mind,* seems to suggest that God does make such a promise; but on the other hand, Kant, in the *Critique of Pure Reason,* argues that we cannot know with certainty that such a promise has been made. In the light of recent research which I understand has been reported in the latest issue of the Berlin *Journal of Metaphysics,* I would judge professionally that the answer is a qualified yes."

Both the subjectivity of truth and the leap of faith are central to the writings of Kierkegaard. The *Concluding Unscientific Postscript to the Philosophical Fragments* is Kierkegaard's major systematic exposition of his philosophical theology. The title, in typical Kierkegaardian fashion, is an elaborate joke. The *Philosophical Fragments* was short—not quite one hundred pages. The *Postscript,* on the other hand, ran to more than five hundred pages. By calling his most important work a mere "postscript" to the *Fragments,* a lengthy p.s. to a short letter, so to speak, Kierkegaard was laughing at the self-important philosophers of his day. The word "unscientific," of course, is another dig at the Hegelian systematizers, who called everything they did "scientific."

The *Philosophical Fragments* deals with the contrast between secular truth and religious truth, between the objective and the subjective, between reason and faith, between wisdom and salvation. Kierkegaard imagines all these contrasts as gathered together into the person of Socrates, who is the greatest of all teachers, and Jesus, who is not a teacher in the rational sense, but the Saviour. Kierkegaard's argument goes like this (yes indeed, Kierkegaard uses arguments to show us that arguments cannot be used in matters of faith! I leave it to you to determine whether

> **Existentialism**   The philosophical doctrine, associated originally with Søren Kierkegaard, according to which our being as subjective individuals (our *existence*) is more important than what we have in common objectively with all other human beings (our *essence*). Of primary concern for Kierkegaard was his relationship to God. Later existentialists emphasized the individual's creation of himself or herself through free individual choices.

there is a contradiction in his mode of procedure). Secular knowledge of morality is something that can be learned through rational self-reflection. Teachers like Socrates help us to bring our moral knowledge to consciousness by probing questions that force us to justify our beliefs. But since in some sense this moral knowledge already lies within each of us, a teacher—even so great a teacher as Socrates—is merely helpful; if we had to, we could get along without one. As philosophers say, a teacher is "accidental" rather than "essential." But salvation is a matter of the fate of my soul. It is a matter of my *existence*, not merely of my state of knowledge. And salvation is not something I can acquire on my own if I am forced to do so. Salvation requires that God reach down and lift me up to His Kingdom. Somehow, the gulf between myself and God must be crossed. Thus salvation is totally different from the acquisition of wisdom, for there is no gulf to be crossed on the road to wisdom. I need only look carefully and critically enough inside myself.

Jesus is God's instrument for bridging the gulf between Himself and myself. Jesus is the Saviour. And since salvation concerns my *existence*, the actual, historical reality of Jesus is all-important. You see, it doesn't really matter to me whether Socrates ever actually lived. Once I have learned from Plato's Dialogues how to engage in Socratic questioning, it would make no difference if I were to discover that the Dialogues were a hoax and that there never had been any Socrates. But if God never actually became Man in the form of Jesus Christ, if Christ never died for my sins, then I am damned rather than saved. The mere Idea of the Saviour isn't enough. I need to be absolutely certain that God did actually become Man, that He really died for my sins, that God did renew His free gift to me through His only begotten Son.

But just because I need so desperately to know that Jesus really lived, I am hopelessly at a loss for evidence or argument sufficient to my need. Can I rest comfortably in the belief that I have been promised eternal life, when the evidence for my belief is merely probable, merely the sort of evidence that an historian or a philosopher can produce? No, too much is at stake: Salvation is everything; it is eternity of life rather than death. I am reduced by my terror and my need to infinite concern for something that defies rational grounding. In short, I am reduced to an absolute *leap of faith*.

This passage comes from a portion of the *Postscript* entitled "The Subjective Thinker." The focus of Kierkegaard's argument is the contrast between my relationship to some other human thinker, such as Socrates, and my relationship to the divine Saviour, Jesus.

The mode of apprehension of the truth is precisely the truth. It is therefore untrue to answer a question in a medium in which the question cannot arise. So for example, to explain reality within the medium of the possible, or to distinguish between possibility and reality within possibility. By refraining from raising the question of reality from the aesthetic or intellectual point of view, but asking this question only ethically, and here again only in the interest of one's own reality, each individual will be isolated and compelled to exist for himself. Irony and hypocrisy as opposite forms, but both expressing the contradiction that the internal is not the external, irony by seeming to be bad, hypocrisy by seeming to be good, emphasize the principle anent the contemplative inquiry concerning ethical inwardness, that reality and deceit are equally possible, and that deceit can clothe itself in the same appearance as reality. It is unethical even to ask at all about another person's ethical inwardness, in so far as such inquiry constitutes a diversion of attention. But if the question is asked nevertheless, the difficulty remains that I can lay hold of the other's reality only by conceiving it, and hence by translating it into a possibility; and in this sphere the possibility of a deception is equally conceivable. This is profitable preliminary training for an ethical mode of existence: to learn that the individual stands alone.

It is a misunderstanding to be concerned about reality from the aesthetic or intellectual point of view. And to be concerned ethically about another's reality is also a misunderstanding, since the only question of reality that is ethically pertinent, is the question of one's own reality. Here we may clearly note the difference that exists between faith *sensu strictissimo* on the one hand (referring as it does to the historical, and the realms of the aesthetic, the intellectual) and the ethical on the other. To ask with infinite interest about a reality which is not one's own, is faith, and this constitutes a paradoxical relationship to the paradoxical. Aesthetically it is impossible to raise such a question except in thoughtlessness, since possibility is aesthetically higher than reality. Nor is it possible to raise such a question ethically, since the sole ethical interest is the interest in one's own reality. The analogy between faith and the ethical is found in the infinite interest, which suffices to distinguish the believer absolutely from an aesthetician or a thinker. But the believer differs from the ethicist in being infinitely interested in the reality of another (in the fact, for example, that God has existed in time). . . .

Precisely in the degree to which I understand a thinker I become indifferent to his reality; that is, to his existence as a particular individual, to his having really understood this or that so and so, to his actually having realized his teaching, and so forth. Aesthetic and speculative thought is quite justified in insisting on this point, and it is important not to lose sight of it. But this does not suffice for a defense of pure thought as a medium of communication between man and man. Because the reality of the teacher is properly indifferent to me as his pupil, and my reality conversely to him, it does not by any means follow that the teacher is justified in being indifferent to his own reality. His communication should bear the stamp of this consciousness, but not directly, since the ethical reality of an individual is not directly communicable (such a direct relationship is exemplified in the paradoxical relation of a believer to the object of his faith), and cannot be understood immediately, but must be understood indirectly through indirect signs.

When the different spheres are not decisively distinguished from one another, confusion reigns everywhere. When people are curious about a thinker's reality and find it interesting to know something about it, and so forth, this interest is intellectually reprehensible. The maximum of attainment in the sphere of the intellectual is to become altogether indifferent to the thinker's reality. But by being thus muddle-headed in the intellectual sphere, one acquires a certain resemblance to a believer. A believer is one who is infinitely interested in another's reality. This is a decisive criterion for faith, and the interest in question is not just a little curiosity, but an absolute dependence upon faith's object.

The object of faith is the reality of another, and the relationship is one of infinite interest. The object of faith is not a doctrine, for then the relationship would be intellectual, and it would be of importance not to botch it, but to realize the maximum intellectual relationship. The object of faith is not a teacher with a doctrine; for when a teacher has a doctrine, the doctrine is *eo ipso* more important than the teacher, and the relationship is again intellectual, and it again becomes important not to botch it, but to realize the maximum intellectual relationship. The object of faith is the reality of the teacher, that the teacher really exists. The answer of faith is therefore unconditionally yes or no. For it does not concern a doctrine, as to whether the doctrine is true or not; it is the answer to a question concerning a fact: "Do you or do you not suppose that he has really existed?" And the answer, it must be noted, is with infinite passion. In the case of a human being, it is thoughtlessness to lay so great and infinite a stress on the question whether he has existed or not. If the object of faith is a human being, therefore, the whole proposal is the vagary of a stupid person, who had not even understood the spirit of the intellectual and the aesthetic. The object of faith is hence the reality of the God-man in the sense of his existence. But existence involves first and foremost particularity, and this is why thought must abstract from existence, because the particular cannot be thought, but only the universal. The object of faith is thus God's reality in existence as a particular individual, the fact that God has existed as an individual human being.

Christianity is no doctrine concerning the unity of the divine and the human, or concerning the identity of subject and object; nor is it any other of the logical transcriptions of Christianity. If Christianity were a doctrine, the relationship to it would not be one of faith, for only an intellectual type of relationship can correspond to a doctrine. Christianity is therefore not a doctrine, but the fact that God has existed.

The realm of faith is thus not a class for numskulls in the sphere of the intellectual, or an asylum for the feeble-minded. Faith constitutes a sphere all by itself, and every misunderstanding of Christianity may at once be recognized by its transforming it into a doctrine, transferring it to the sphere of the intellectual. The maximum of attainment within the sphere of the intellectual, namely, to realize an entire indifference as to the reality of the teacher, is in the sphere of faith at the opposite end of the scale. The maximum of attainment within the sphere of faith is to become infinitely interested in the reality of the teacher.

—Søren Kierkegaard,
Concluding Unscientific Postscript to the Philosophical Fragments

II Can We Prove That God Exists?

When students are introduced to the study of philosophy, one of the standard moves is to go through what are usually referred to as the "proofs of the existence of God." This is a set of arguments, developed over the past 2000 years by many different philosophers, which purport to demonstrate that there is, or exists, an infinite, omnipotent, omniscient, benevolent creator of the universe who goes by the name of God. When I teach an introduction to philosophy, I try to slip the proofs for the existence of God in just before Christmas in the fall semester, and just before Easter in the spring semester. It seems fitting, somehow.

Is anyone ever convinced by the proofs? Well you may ask! I have, from time to time, started off my presentation of them by asking how many members of the class believe in God. I mean by that, of course, how many believe that there is a God, not how many believe that He will keep His promise of eternal life. Anyway, I count the hands, and then I present one of the proofs. Usually, I try out what is called the Cosmological Argument, and sometimes I go right into the real number one proof, which is called the Ontological Argument. (We'll get to these in a minute. Don't despair!) After running through the proof, I ask whether there are any objections or criticisms. Usually there aren't any (how many students are going to tell their professor that they think he is crazy?). Then I ask for another show of hands on those who believe in God. Now, it is the most peculiar thing, but even though no one ever objects to my proofs or raises any doubts, not a single person is ever converted to the faith by them! I don't think I have convinced a single, solitary nonbeliever in all the years I have been proving the existence of God. Next I run through the standard refutations for the proofs. (In philosophy, there is an argument against just about everything that there is an argument for.) Same result. I never make agnostics out of the believers, any more than I have made believers out of the agnostics.

When you stop and think about it, there is really something wonderful and mad about a finite, mortal man or woman undertaking to *prove* that God exists. It is as though the philosopher rears up on her hind legs and says, "God! You may be out there, You may exist, but unless You fit into my syllogisms, unless You follow from premises, unless You are a theorem in my system, I won't acknowledge Your existence!" When it comes to sheer effrontery, to what the Greeks called *hubris* and the Jews call *chutzpah*, there just isn't anything to match it.

Philosophers have never been known for their humility, and a fair number of great ones have had a shot at proving the existence of God. Aristotle tried it, and so did St. Thomas Aquinas. Occam had a proof, Descartes had several, Spinoza came up with some, and even William

Argument from Design   The attempt to prove the existence of God by demonstrating the high degree of organization and purposive order in the universe, and arguing that such design must be the product of an intelligent, powerful, purposeful creator. The argument is very old, but had a wide popularity in the eighteenth century.

Argument from Design

Premise: The purposive organization of man-made objects is evidence of the intelligence and purpose of the maker.

Premise: The world contains many natural objects (animals, plants, the human eye, and so on) whose organization is clearly purposive and the world itself is purposively organized.

Conclusion: By analogy, there must exist a maker of the universe who has made it according to a plan. That world-maker, or Creator, is God.

Cosmological Argument

Premise: We know, by the evidence of our senses, that in the world some things are moved.

Premise: Everything that is moved must be caused to move by something else.

Argument: If each thing that moves is in turn moved by something that itself moves, which in its turn requires a cause of motion that itself moves, then there will nowhere be a first mover, and hence no motion at all. But there is motion.

Conclusion: Hence, there must be a first mover that is not itself moved. That first mover is what we call God.

Ontological Argument

Premise: I possess the idea of a being than which no greater can be conceived. That idea includes within it everything that belongs essentially to such a being.

Premise: To exist in actuality is greater than merely to be possible.

Argument: The idea of that, than which nothing greater can be conceived, includes the idea of its existence, which thus belongs to it necessarily.

Conclusion: Hence, that, than which nothing greater can be conceived, exists, and it is this that we call God.

Proof for the Existence of God

WILLIAM PALEY (1743–1805) was an English churchman whose writings in defense of Christianity were widely read and much admired in the eighteenth and nineteenth centuries. Paley was a defender of utilitarianism in moral philosophy and of the truths of revelation in theology (a position known as *theism*). His book, *Natural Theology* was a systematic presentation of the so-called Argument from Design for the existence of God, an argument which David Hume had vigorously attacked in his *Dialogues Concerning Natural Religion.*

James, the American pragmatist, offered his own rather odd version of reasons for believing in the existence of God. In this section, we are going to take a close look at the three most famous proofs. These aren't all the proofs, by any means, but they will give you a good idea of some of the different tactics that philosophers have used over the ages. The three proofs are called the *Argument from Design,* the *Cosmological Proof,* and the *Ontological Proof.* We will examine the version of the Argument from Design offered by the eighteenth-century English philosopher William Paley, the Cosmological Argument as it was set forth by the great medieval theologian St. Thomas, and the Ontological Argument in its original version as stated by the man who thought it up, the eleventh-century logician St. Anselm. Since David Hume and Immanuel

Kant are the two best proof-for-existence-of-God-refuters who have ever lived, we will look at their refutations together with the proofs. Here we go. Don't be surprised if you hear Kierkegaard laughing at us along the way!

William Paley: The Argument from Design

Our first proof for the existence of God is at once the most obvious, the most natural, the most ancient, the most persuasive, the easiest to understand, and—alas—the philosophically weakest! The **Argument from Design** is quite simple. We observe that certain man-made objects exhibit an internal purposive organization, a fitting of parts to the function of the whole. In a watch, to take the example that Paley himself uses, the various springs and pins and hands are all made precisely to serve the purpose of keeping and telling time. This rational, purposive order in the watch is the direct result of the conscious, rational, purposive activity of its creator, the watchmaker. From the character of the watch, we naturally infer the existence of a watchmaker, whether we actually know her or not. If you show me a watch (or a chair or a painting or even a simple stone axe) and say, "It is so old that no one can remember who made it," I would never dream of saying, "Perhaps no one made it. The intelligence of its creation inheres in its internal organization." The watch is, if you will permit a bad pun, intelligently produced on the face of it. Well, Paley argues (and so have countless other theologians and philosophers over the ages), nature is more wonderfully organized than the most subtle human contrivance. The human eye far exceeds a camera in sensitivity and fidelity of reproduction; the human brain cannot be duplicated by the most sophisticated computer; the merest one-celled microscopic organism exhibits a biochemical complexity and adaptation that taxes the analytic powers of all science. Who can doubt for a moment that nature has its Creator, an intelligence, purposeful, all-powerful Maker, who in His infinite wisdom has adjusted means to end, part to whole, organ to organism, throughout the whole of space and time?

The technical name for this is an *argument from analogy*. You have probably encountered ratios or proportions in high school math—problems like: "Eight is to four as six is to *x*. Solve for *x*." When I was in school, the way to state that mathematically was either like this: 8:4::6:*x*, or else like this: ¾ = ⁶⁄$_x$. The solution, of course is $x = 3$. The same sort of "analogy" turns up in aptitude tests. "Fire engine is to fire department as _____ is to police department." The answer is "police car." The point is that if we already know the relationship between one pair of things (such as the numbers 8 and 4, or a fire engine and the fire department), then when we are presented with only one member of another pair, we may be able to figure out what the other member of the pair is (3 in the math example, or a police car in the other case). Now all this may seem like baby talk to you, but philosophers frequently build powerful arguments from what look like very simple pieces.

Paley and the other arguers from design draw up two sorts of analogies. The first is between an artificially constructed object and its human maker, on the one hand, and a particular organism or bit of natural organization and its divine Creator, on the other. So we get

Watch is to watchmaker as the human eye is to x. x = God.

The other analogy is between an artificially constructed object and its human maker, on the one hand, and the whole universe and its divine Creator, on the other. So this time we get

Watch is to watchmaker as the universe is to x. x = God.

Here is Paley's own statement of the argument. Because he tends to be rather wordy, I have edited it down to the bare bones.

In crossing a heath, suppose I pitched my foot against a *stone*, and were asked how the stone came to be there, I might possibly answer, that for any thing I knew to the contrary it had lain there for ever; nor would it, perhaps, be very easy to show the absurdity of this answer. But suppose I had found a *watch* upon the ground, and it should be inquired how the watch happened to be in that place, I should hardly think of the answer which I had before given, that for any thing I knew the watch might have always been there. Yet why should not this answer serve for the watch as well as for the stone; why is it not as admissible in the second case as in the first? For this reason, and for no other, namely, that when we come to inspect the watch, we perceive—what we could not discover in the stone—that its several parts are framed and put together for a purpose, *e.g.* that they are so formed and adjusted as to produce motion, and that motion so regulated as to point out the hour of the day; that if the different parts had been differently shaped from what they are, or placed after any other manner or in any other order

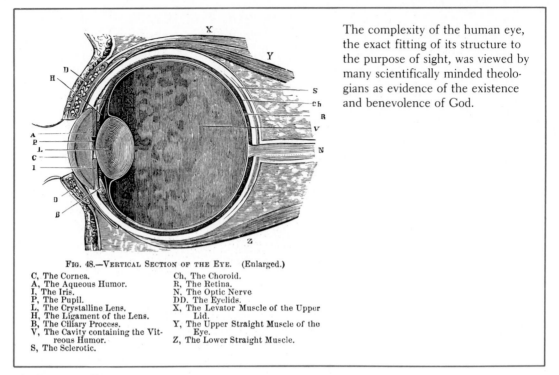

The complexity of the human eye, the exact fitting of its structure to the purpose of sight, was viewed by many scientifically minded theologians as evidence of the existence and benevolence of God.

FIG. 48.—VERTICAL SECTION OF THE EYE. (Enlarged.)

C, The Cornea.
A, The Aqueous Humor.
I, The Iris.
P, The Pupil.
L, The Crystalline Lens.
H, The Ligament of the Lens.
B, The Ciliary Process.
V, The Cavity containing the Vitreous Humor.
S, The Sclerotic.

Ch, The Choroid.
R, The Retina.
N. The Optic Nerve
DD. The Eyelids.
X, The Levator Muscle of the Upper Lid.
Y, The Upper Straight Muscle of the Eye.
Z, The Lower Straight Muscle.

The Bettman Archive

than that in which they are placed, either no motion at all would have been carried on in the machine, or none which would have answered the use that is now served by it. . . .

. . . This mechanism being observed—it requires indeed an examination of the instrument, and perhaps some previous knowledge of the subject, to perceive and understand it; but being once, as we have said, observed and understood, the inference we think is inevitable, that the watch must have had a maker—that there must have existed, at some time and at some place or other, an artificer or artificers who formed it for the purpose which, we find it actually to answer, who comprehended its construction and designed its use. . . .

Were there no example in the world of contrivance except that of the *eye*, it would be alone sufficient to support the conclusion which we draw from it, as to the necessity of an intelligent Creator. It could never be got rid of, because it could not be accounted for by any other supposition which did not contradict all the principles we possess of knowledge—the principles according to which things do, as often as they can be brought to the test of experience, turn out to be true or false. . . .

... If other parts of nature were inaccessible to our inquiries, or even if other parts of nature presented nothing to our examination but disorder and confusion, the validity of this example would remain the same. If there were but one watch in the world, it would not be less certain that it had a maker. If we had never in our lives seen any but one single kind of hydraulic machine, yet if of that one kind we understood the mechanism and use, we should be as perfectly assured that it proceeded from the hand and thought and skill of a workman, as if we visited a museum of the arts, and saw collected there twenty different kinds of machines for drawing water, or a thousand different kinds for other purposes. Of this point each machine is a proof independently of all the rest. So it is with the evidences of a divine agency. The proof is not a conclusion which lies at the end of a chain of reasoning, of which chain each instance of contrivance is only a link, and of which, if one link fail, the whole falls; but it is an argument separately supplied by every separate example. An error in stating an example affects only that example. The argument is cumulative, in the fullest sense of that term. The eye proves it without the ear; the ear without the eye. The proof in each example is complete; for when the design of the part, and the conduciveness of its structure to that design is shown, the mind may set itself at rest; no future consideration can detract any thing from the force of the example.

—WILLIAM PALEY, *Natural Theology*

This argument has an antique sound, of course. It was written 180 years ago, after all. But the principle underlying it is one we use today in interplanetary exploration. When astronauts first walked on the moon, they looked of course for evidences of intelligent life, though they didn't really expect to find such evidences on an atmosphereless body. Now how on earth (or elsewhere) could they possibly tell what would *be* evidence of intelligent life? Having no advance knowledge of the sorts of creatures that might inhabit other parts of the universe, by what signs could the astronauts infer their existence and presence? The answer is obvious. Any sort of device, or instrument, or machine that exhibited some purposive internal organization, and that seemed not to grow naturally in that environment, would permit them to infer by analogy the existence of some (presumably) nonhuman intelligent maker.

Anyone who has been enraptured, bemused, or awestruck by the wonder of nature will appreciate the psychological force of the Argument from Design. Can the order of planets, stars, and galaxies, the underlying simplicity and regularity of natural forces, the exquisitely delicate adjustment of part to part in living things really just *be*? Must there not be some intelligence directing, organizing, creating this vast interconnected universe?

Well, maybe so, but the Argument from Design won't prove it! There are basically two things wrong with the Argument from Design. First, even if it is correct, it doesn't prove what Paley and most other Christian, Jewish, or Muslim theologians want it to prove. And, second, it doesn't really prove much of anything at all. The first point is liable to slip by us because we are so mesmerized by the word "God." In the great Western religions, God is conceived as an infinite, eternal, omnipotent (infinitely powerful), omniscient (all-knowing) creator of the universe. But the most that the Argument from Design can prove, even if it is sound, is that there is a *very* long-lived (not eternal), very powerful (not omnipotent), very wise (not omniscient) world organizer who has worked up the raw materials of space, time, and matter into a reasonably well-integrated machinelike universe. After all, the watchmaker does not create her materials, she merely fashions them to her purposes. And the human eye is not infinitely complex, it is just a good deal more complex than a camera. So if the analogy is taken strictly, we can at best demonstrate the existence of a conscious, purposeful, powerful, very knowledgeable, very old worldmaker. But if we label that worldmaker "God," then we may mistakenly slip into identifying him or her or it with the God of the Old and New Testaments, the God of the great Western religions, the God who lays down commandments, punishes the wicked, offers the free gift of eternal life, and so forth. And absolutely nothing in the analogy justifies any of those conclusions.

But the argument isn't very sound, as David Hume pointed out in one of his most brilliant works, the *Dialogues Concerning Natural Religion*. Hume actually wrote the dialogues in the 1750s, twenty years before his death in 1776, but he was prevailed upon by his friends (including the economist and philosopher Adam Smith) to withhold them from publication, because the forcefulness of their attack on received religious opinions would open Hume to condemnation. Eventually, they were brought out posthumously in 1779 by his nephew. The work is a three-person discussion of all the principal arguments for the existence of God, in which first one character and then another comes to the fore. In the subtlety of their development and pacing, the *Dialogues* have something of the quality of a Baroque trio, and I think it may fairly be said that Hume is the only great philosopher after Plato to use the dialogue form to its full literary effect. The work is in twelve parts, and this selection comes from Part Two. The speaker is the skeptic, Philo:

In reality, CLEANTHES, continued he, there is no need of having recourse to that affected scepticism, so displeasing to you, in order to come at this determination. Our ideas reach no farther than our experience: We have no experience of divine attributes and operations: I need not conclude my syllogism: You can draw the inference yourself. And it is a pleasure to me (and I hope to you too) that just reasoning and sound piety here concur in the same conclusion, and both of them establish the adorably mysterious and incomprehensible nature of the supreme Being. . . .

What I chiefly scruple in this subject, said PHILO, is not so much, that all religious arguments are by CLEANTHES reduced to experience, as that they appear not to be even the most certain and irrefragable of that inferior kind. That a stone will fall, that fire will burn, that the earth has solidity, we have observed a thousand and a thousand times; and when any new instance of this nature is presented, we draw without hesitation the accustomed inference. The exact similarity of the cases gives us a perfect assurance of a similar event; and a stronger evidence is never desired nor sought after. But wherever you depart, in the least, from the similarity of the cases, you diminish proportionably the evidence; and may at last bring it to a very weak *analogy*, which is confessedly liable to error and uncertainty. After having experienced the circulation of the blood in human creatures, we make no doubt that it takes place in Titius and Maevius: But from its circulation in frogs and fishes, it is only a presumption, though a strong one, from analogy, that it takes place in men and other animals. The analogical reasoning is much weaker, when we infer the circulation of the sap in vegetables from our experience that the blood circulates in animals; and those, who hastily followed that imperfect analogy, are found, by more accurate experiments, to have been mistaken.

If we see a house, CLEANTHES, we conclude, with the greatest certainty, that it had an architect or builder; because this is precisely that species of effect, which we have experienced to proceed from that species of cause. But surely you will not affirm, that the universe bears such a resemblance to a house, that we can with the same certainty infer a similar cause, or that the analogy is here entire and perfect. The dissimilitude is so striking, that the utmost you can here pretend to is a guess, a conjecture, a presumption concerning a similar cause; and how that pretension will be received in the world, I leave you to consider. . . .

Were a man to abstract from every thing which he knows or has seen, he would be altogether incapable, merely from his own ideas, to determine what kind of scene the universe must be, or to give the preference to one state or situation of things above another. For as nothing, which he clearly conceives, could be esteemed impossible or implying a contradiction, every chimera of his fancy would be upon an equal footing; nor could he assign any just reason, why he adheres to one idea or system, and rejects the others, which are equally possible.

Again; after he opens his eyes, and contemplates the world, as it really is, it would be impossible for him, at first, to assign the cause of any one event; much less, of the whole of things or of the universe. He might set his fancy a rambling; and she might bring him in an infinite variety of reports and representations. These would all be possible; but being all equally possible, he would never, of himself, give a satisfactory account for his preferring one of them to the rest. Experience alone can point out to him the true cause of any phenomenon.

—DAVID HUME, *Dialogues Concerning Natural Religion*

Although Hume's refutation stands pretty well on its own feet, it also draws upon the more fundamental criticisms which Hume developed of causal reasoning of all sorts. In Chapter Seven, we will have another opportunity to examine the reasons for his skepticism concerning any attempt to infer causes from effects or effects from causes.

St. Thomas Aquinas: The Cosmological Argument

Christian theologians derive their beliefs about God from two sources. The first is *revelation*, consisting of those truths which God has revealed to us through the holy writings of the Old and New Testaments or through His miraculous appearance to particular individuals. Revelation must of course be interpreted, and therein lies the origin of many learned disputes and bloody wars. But everyone agrees that the *fact* of revelation is simply a miracle, to be taken on faith. The second source is *reason*, our natural human power of analysis, argument, observation, and inference. We must wait for revelation. We cannot make it happen, and we cannot predict when or where God will reveal Himself. But reason is our own instrument, and we can deploy it at will to seek out the origins of the universe and the existence and nature of a Creator. The greatest of all the rational theologians, by universal agreement, is the thirteenth-century Christian philosopher St. Thomas Aquinas. His elaboration and codification of the rational metaphysical basis for Christian theology remains to this day the dominant intellectual influence in the Roman Catholic

> **Cosmological Argument** The attempt to prove the existence of God by starting with the mere fact of motion, or change, or the existence of things in the universe, and then arguing that these must have their origin in a being that does not move, or does not change, or does not merely happen to exist. The earliest form of the argument is to be found in the writings of Aristotle.

Church. The philosophy known as Thomism is an enduring monument of medieval intellectual architecture, as impressive in its way as the great Cathedral of Notre Dame in Paris.

Aquinas actually offers five separate proofs for the existence of God in his most important work, the *Summa Theologica*. The first three of these are variations of the same argument, and we shall examine them all together. In each case, Aquinas begins with some fact about the world: the first argument takes off from the fact that things *move* in the world around us; the second from the fact that every event that is observed to take place is made to happen, or caused, by something else that precedes it; the third from the fact that there are at least some things in the world whose existence is not necessary, which are, in metaphysical language, "possible." Aquinas then reasons that the observed motion, or event, or possible thing, is the last in a chain of motions or causes or possible things, and he asserts that such a chain cannot reach back endlessly to prior motions, to earlier causes, to other possible things on which this thing depends for its existence. Somewhere, the chain must end, with a mover that is not itself also moved by something else, with a cause which is not itself caused by yet another cause, with a being whose existence is not merely possible but necessary. That first mover, first cause, or necessary being, is God.

If the task of proving the existence of God weren't such a serious business, we might say that the cosmological argument is a very sophisticated answer to the four-year-old's question, "Where did I come from, Mommy?" Now a straight answer would be, "You came from inside mommy's womb." And after a few more details have been added, that answer usually satisfies a four-year-old. Eventually, the obvious follow-up question will occur to a six- or seven-year-old, namely, "Where did you come from, Mommy?" A somewhat longer story about Grandma and Grandpa should handle that one. But sooner or later, a bright child is going to start brooding on the *real* problem. Maybe I came from Mom

God's creation of Adam, by the great Italian painter Michelangelo. (Alinari/Art Resource)

and Dad, each of whom came in turn from a mother and father; maybe the earliest human mothers and fathers evolved through a combination and mutation and selection from prehuman mammals, who in turn evolved from reptiles, or what have you; and maybe life itself sprang up spontaneously through chance rearrangements of amino acid-like compounds, which in turn emerged from the stuff of which the earth was formed, but *damn it*, somewhere the buck has got to stop! If there isn't anything that was *first*, then how can there be anything at all? If the existence of each particular thing is to be explained by saying that it came from some preceding thing, then we have no explanation at all. We just have a chain that leads so far back into the misty past that finally we get tired of asking, and mistake our fatigue for an answer. In short, an "infinite regress" is no answer at all. We might just as well have answered the very first question by saying, "Shut up and don't ask silly questions!"

ST. THOMAS AQUINAS (1225–1274) is the greatest intellectual figure of the high medieval culture that flourished in Europe during the thirteenth century. Aquinas was an Italian theologian and philosopher who spent his life in the Dominican Order, teaching and writing. His writings, which run to many volumes, set forth in extremely systematic form a full-scale theory of God, man and the universe. The official dogma of the Church, as established by revelation and interpretation of holy scriptures, was combined by Aquinas with the secular metaphysical doctrines of Aristotle and the post-Aristotelian Greek and Roman philosophers.

Aquinas' philosophical synthesis of philosophy and theology became the accepted teaching of the Roman Catholic Church. It is known today as Thomism, and in various forms it continues to exercise a profound intellectual influence both on Church doctrine and on the philosophical work of Catholic and non-Catholic thinkers.

So we might summarize Aquinas' proofs by saying that if the universe makes any sense at all, if it is through and through rational, then there must be a necessary being, a first mover, a first cause. Here are the three proofs as Aquinas stated them. Notice that he doesn't waste any words. He proves the existence of God three times in the space it takes Plato to introduce one of the characters in a dialogue.

. . . The existence of God can be proved in five ways.

The first and more manifest way is the argument from motion. It is certain and evident to our senses, that in the world some things are in motion. Now whatever is moved is moved by another, for nothing can be moved except it is in potentiality to that towards which it is moved; whereas a thing moves inasmuch as it is in act. For motion is nothing else than the reduction of something from potentiality to actuality. But nothing can be reduced from potentiality to actuality, except by something in a state of actuality. Thus that which is actually hot, as fire, makes wood, which is potentially hot, to be actually hot, and thereby moves and changes it. Now it is not possible that the same thing should be at once in actuality and potentiality in the same respect but only in different respects. For what is actually hot cannot simultaneously be potentially hot; but it is simultaneously potentially cold. It is therefore impossible that in the same respect and in the same way a thing should be both mover and moved, *i.e.*, that it should move itself. Therefore, whatever is moved must be moved by another. If that by which it is moved be itself moved, then this also must needs be moved by another, and that by another again. But this cannot go on to infinity, because then there would be no first mover, and consequently, no other mover, seeing that subsequent movers move only inasmuch as they are moved by the first mover; as the staff moves only because it is moved by the hand. Therefore it is necessary to arrive at a first mover, moved by no other; and this everyone understands to be God.

The second way is from the nature of efficient cause. In the world of sensible things we find there is an order of efficient causes. There is no case known (neither is it, indeed, possible) in which a thing is found to be the efficient cause of itself; for so it would be prior to itself, which is impossible. Now in efficient causes it is not possible to go on to infinity, because in all efficient causes following in order, the first is the cause of the intermediate cause, and the intermediate is the cause of the ultimate cause, whether the intermediate cause be several, or one only. Now to take away the cause is to take away the effect. Therefore, if there be no first cause among efficient causes, there will be no ultimate, nor any intermediate, cause. But if in efficient causes it is possible to go on to infinity, there will be no first efficient cause, neither will there be an ultimate effect, nor any intermediate efficient causes; all of which is plainly false. Therefore it is necessary to admit a first efficient cause, to which everyone gives the name of God.

The third way is taken from possibility and necessity, and runs thus. We find in nature things that are possible to be and not to be, since they are found to be generated, and to be corrupted, and consequently, it is possible for them to be and not to be. But it is impossible for these always to exist, for that which can not-be at some time is not. Therefore, if everything can not-be, then at one time there was nothing in existence. Now if this were true, even now there would be nothing in existence, because that which does not exist begins to exist only through something already existing. Therefore, if at one time nothing was in existence, it would have been impossible for anything to have begun to exist; and thus even now nothing would be in existence—which is absurd. Therefore, not all beings are merely possible, but there must exist something the existence of which is necessary. But every necessary thing either has its necessity caused by another, or not. Now it is impossible to go on to infinity in necessary things which have their necessity caused by another, as has been already proved in regard to efficient causes. Therefore we cannot but admit the existence of some being having of itself its own necessity, and not receiving it from another, but rather causing in others their necessity. This all men speak of as God.

—St. Thomas Aquinas, *Summa Theologica*

Hume has an answer to these arguments as well as to the argument from design. In Part IX of his *Dialogues,* he considers a version which reasons from cause and effect to the existence of a first cause, whose existence must therefore be necessary. It is thus a combination of the second and third of Aquinas' proofs. Hume's refutation, put this time into the mouth of the character named Cleanthes, begins with a paragraph that is also a refutation of the third great proof, the ontological argument. More of that a little later.

I shall begin with observing, that there is an evident absurdity in pretending to demonstrate a matter of fact, or to prove it by any arguments *a priori.* Nothing is demonstrable, unless the contrary implies a contradiction. Nothing, that is distinctly conceivable, implies a contradiction. Whatever we conceive as existent, we can also conceive as non-existent. There is no Being, therefore, whose non-existence implies a contradiction. Consequently there is no Being, whose existence is demonstrable. I propose this argument as entirely decisive, and am willing to rest the whole controversy upon it.

It is pretended that the Deity is a necessarily existent Being; and this necessity of his existence is attempted to be explained by asserting that, if we knew his whole essence or nature, we should perceive it to be as impossible for him not to exist as for twice two not to be four. But it is evident, that this can never happen, while our faculties remain the same as at present. It will still be possible for us, at any time, to conceive the non-existence of what we formerly conceived to exist; nor can the mind ever lie under a necessity of supposing any object to remain always in being: in the same manner as we lie under a necessity of always conceiving twice two to be four. The words, therefore, *necessary existence*, have no meaning; or, which is the same thing, none that is consistent.

But farther; why may not the material universe be the necessarily existent Being, according to this pretended explication of necessity? We dare not affirm that we know all the qualities of matter; and for aught we can determine, it may contain some qualities, which, were they known, would make its non-existence appear as great a contradiction as that twice two is five. I find only one argument employed to prove, that the material world is not the necessarily existent Being; and this argument is derived from the contingency both of the matter and the form of the world. "Any particle of matter," it is said, "may be *conceived* to be annihilated; and any form may be *conceived* to be altered. Such an annihilation or alteration, therefore, is not impossible." But it seems a great partiality not to perceive, that the same argument extends equally to the Deity, so far as we have any conception of him; and that the mind can at least imagine him to be nonexistent, or his attributes to be altered. It must be some unknown, inconceivable qualities, which can make non-existence appear impossible, or his attributes unalterable: And no reason can be assigned, why these qualities may not belong to matter. As they are altogether unknown and inconceivable, they can never be proved incompatible with it.

Add to this, that in tracing an eternal succession of objects, it seems absurd to inquire for a general cause or first Author. How can any thing, that exists from eternity, have a cause, since that relation implies a priority in time and a beginning of existence?

In such a chain too, or succession of objects, each part is caused by that which preceded it, and causes that which succeeds it. Where then is the difficulty? But the WHOLE, you say, wants a cause. I answer, that the uniting of these parts into a whole, like the uniting of several distinct counties into one kingdom, or several distinct members into one body, is performed merely by an arbitrary act of the mind, and has no influence on the nature of things. Did I show you the particular causes of each individual in a collection of twenty particles of matter, I should think it very unreasonable, should you afterwards ask me, what was the cause of the whole twenty. This is sufficiently explained in explaining the cause of the parts.

—DAVID HUME, *Dialogues Concerning Natural Religion*

St. Anselm: The Ontological Argument

Here it is, the most famous, the most mystifying, the most outrageous and irritating philosophical argument of all time! Read it carefully and see what you think. *Truly there is a God, although the fool hath said in his heart, There is no God.*

And so, Lord, do thou, who dost give understanding to faith, give me, so far as thou knowest it to be profitable, to understand that thou art as we believe; and that thou art that which we believe. And, indeed, we believe that thou art a being than which nothing greater can be conceived. Or is there no such nature, since the fool hath said in his heart, there is no God? (Psalms xiv. 1). But, at any rate, this very fool, when he hears of this being

SAINT ANSELM (1033–1109) was born in Italy and was trained there for the priesthood. In 1093, he was appointed Archbishop of Canterbury in England by the Norman king William Rufus. His most important philosophical work is the *Proslogion,* in which he set forth a startling and radically new proof for the existence of God. The proof, known now as the Onto-logical Argument, has been defended over the past nine centuries by Descartes, Spinoza, and others. St. Thomas Aquinas, on the other hand, claimed it was not a valid proof, and he rejected it.

This drawing shows the ceremony in which Anselm (standing, with hand raised) was appointed Archbishop of Canterbury by the king.

of which I speak—a being than which nothing greater can be conceived—understands what he hears, and what he understands is in his understanding; although he does not understand it to exist.

For, it is one thing for an object to be in the understanding, and another to understand that the object exists. When a painter first conceives of what he will afterwards perform, he has it in his understanding, but he does not yet understand it to be, because he has not yet performed it. But after he has made the painting, he both has it in his understanding, and he understands that it exists, because he has made it.

Hence, even the fool is convinced that something exists in the understanding, at least, than which nothing greater can be conceived. For, when he hears of this, he understands it. And whatever is understood, exists in the understanding. And, assuredly that, than which nothing greater can be conceived, cannot exist in the understanding alone. For, suppose it exists in the understanding alone: then it can be conceived to exist in reality; which is greater.

Therefore, if that, than which nothing greater can be conceived, exists in the understanding alone, the very being, than which nothing greater can be conceived, is one, than which a greater can be conceived. But obviously this is impossible. Hence, there is no doubt that there exists a being, than which nothing greater can be conceived, and it exists both in the understanding and in reality.

And it assuredly exists so truly, that it cannot be conceived not to exist. For, it is possible to conceive of a being which cannot be conceived not to exist; and this is greater than one which can be conceived not to exist. Hence, if that, than which nothing greater can be conceived, can be conceived not to exist, it is not that, than which nothing is greater can be conceived. But this is an irreconcilable contradiction. There is, then, so truly a being than which nothing greater can be conceived to exist, that it cannot even be conceived not to exist; and this being thou art, O Lord, our God.

So truly, therefore, dost thou exist, O Lord, my God, that thou canst not be conceived not to exist; and rightly. For, if a mind could conceive of a being better than thee, the creature would rise above the Creator; and this is most absurd. And, indeed, whatever else there is, except thee alone, can be conceived not to exist. To thee alone, therefore, it belongs to exist more truly than all other beings, and hence in a higher degree than all others. For, whatever else exists does not exist so truly, and hence in a less degree it belongs to it to exist. Why, then, has the fool said in his heart, there is no God (Psalms xiv. 1), since it is so evident, to a rational mind, that thou dost exist in the highest degree of all? Why, except that he is dull and a fool?

—St. Anselm, *Proslogion*

Ontological Argument   The attempt to prove the existence of God by starting with nothing more than the mere concept of the most perfect being. The argument is extremely controversial, and has been rejected as invalid by many religious philosophers, including the leading medieval proponent of the Cosmological Argument, St. Thomas Aquinas.

Whenever I read the **Ontological Argument,** I have the same feeling that comes over me when I watch a really good magician. Nothing up this sleeve; nothing up the other sleeve; nothing in the hat; presto! A big, fat rabbit. How can Anselm pull God out of an idea? At least the Argument from Design and Cosmological Arguments start from some actual fact about the world, whether it is the apparently purposeful organization of living things, or the motion of bodies in space, or whatever. But the Ontological Argument starts from a mere idea in the mind of the philosopher and undertakes to prove, from that idea alone, that there must actually be something corresponding to the idea. The argument makes no use at all of facts that might be gathered by observation or analysis of the world. Philosophers call an argument of this sort an **a priori** argument. Propositions that can be known to be true without consideration of factual support, merely from an analysis of the concepts involved in the judgments, are called propositions *knowable a priori,* or simply, *"a priori* propositions."

Now, philosophers have for a long time held that there are *a priori* propositions, or propositions whose truth can be known merely from a consideration of their meaning. For example, consider the proposition, "If an aardvark is a mammal, then it bears its young live." Is that true? Well, your first reaction might be to ask yourself whether you know what an aardvark is, or maybe to look it up in the encyclopedia. But stop and think about it for a moment. A mammal is an animal that bears its young live rather than laying eggs. That is what we *mean* when we call something a mammal. This is part of the definition of the word "mammal." So if anything is to be classified as a mammal, it will have to be the sort of thing that bears its young live. Otherwise, we wouldn't call it a mammal; we would call it something else, or even just say that we don't have a word for it. If you think about it, you will realize that you can decide about the truth of my proposition without knowing anything about aardvarks, indeed without ever having heard the word "aardvark" before. Whatever aardvarks are, "If an aardvark is a mammal, then it bears its young live." In short, you can know the truth of the proposition *a priori*, or even more briefly, it is an *a priori* proposition.

But are there any aardvarks? Ah well, that is quite another question. My *a priori* proposition only tells me that if there are any, and if they are mammals, then they bear their young live. It doesn't tell me whether there are any. Indeed, it doesn't even tell me whether aardvarks are mammals. It just says, *if* there are aardvarks and they are mammals, then they bear their young live. Propositions that can be known to be true merely on the basis of the meanings of the words used in them are called **tautologies,** and you can make up tautologies all day long, with no more material to work with than the English language.

The Ontological Argument seems to depend on a tautology too. First, Anselm *defines* the word "God" as meaning "a being than which nothing greater can be conceived." Then, he argues that this concept, of a greatest being, must include the notion that the being cannot be conceived not to exist. In other words, he argues that when we spell out the definition of "God" as "a being than which nothing greater can be conceived," we will find that the definition includes the characteristic "necessarily existing," just as when we spell out the definition of "mammal," we find that it includes the notion "bearing its young live."

Well, "Mammals bear their young live" is a tautology; it is true by definition; we can know it to be true merely by understanding the words used in the statement. It follows from the definition. So too, Anselm claims, "God necessarily exists" is a tautology; it too is true by definition; it too can be known merely through an understanding of the words used in the statement. But there is one enormous difference. The statement about mammals, and all the other ordinary tautologies that have ever been thought up, say nothing about whether something *exists*. Ordinary tautologies just tell us that *if* there are any things fitting a certain definition, *then* they have the following characteristics. If there are mammals, then they bear their young live; if there are any bachelors, then they are unmarried (because "bachelor" means "unmarried man"); if there are any triangles, then they have three angles; and so forth. The Ontological Argument is the only case in which a tautology is used to prove that something—namely, God—exists.

Now of course philosophers who use the Ontological Argument are perfectly well aware that this is a very special and peculiar sort of tautology. If they can prove the existence of God this way, why can't I use the same trick to prove the existence of a perfect horse, or a necessarily existent ox, or a mosquito than which none greater can be conceived? Their answer is that God is different from all the other beings in or out of the universe, and that God's existence is a different sort of existence from the existence of every created thing. God is infinite, all other things are finite; God's existence is necessary, the existence of every other thing is merely contingent; God is perfect, all else is imperfect; and God's existence follows *a priori* from His definition, whereas the existence of every other thing, since it depends ultimately on God and not on itself alone, follows *not* from its own definition but only from God's act of creation.

The Ontological Argument remains to this day one of the most controversial arguments in all of philosophy. Some very devout theologians, including St. Thomas Aquinas, have believed that it was wrong, invalid, a confusion. Several of the greatest philosophers of the seventeenth century, including Descartes and Spinoza, thought it was valid, and developed their own versions of it. In his great *Critique of Pure Reason*, Immanuel Kant offered an elaborate refutation of the argument which for more than a hundred years was thought to have permanently laid it to rest. Just recently, however, there has been a revival of philosophical interest in the Ontological Argument, and philosophers like myself, who grew up thinking that Kant had once and for all finished it off, now find the technical journals full of new versions of the Ontological Argument, in which the latest tools of formal logic are used to give the old warhorse some new life.

Let us wind up this discussion of proofs for the existence of God with Kant's refutation of the Ontological Argument. This is a difficult passage, harder even than the argument itself, which was no breeze. Please don't expect to understand everything Kant is saying. I have been studying Kant for twenty-five years, and I am not sure what he means sometimes. But read through this selection two or three times, with the aid of your professor. Kant always repays hard work, and his treatment of the Ontological Argument is one of his most brilliant efforts.

One bit of explanation before you begin. Kant asks whether the proposition "God exists" is an *analytic* or a *synthetic* proposition. An **analytic proposition,** according to Kant, is a statement which merely spells out, or *analyzes,* what is already contained in the subject of the statement. For example, the proposition "Triangles have three angles" tells us nothing new about triangles. All it does is repeat what is already contained in the idea of a triangle. **Synthetic propositions,** on the other hand, add something to what is contained in the idea of the subject of the proposition. "Bachelors are unhappy" is synthetic (whether or not it is true!), because being unhappy is *not* part of what we mean by being a bachelor. "Bachelors are unmarried" is analytic, however, for being unmarried *is* part of what we mean by being a bachelor. Kant argues, as you will see, that any proposition which asserts the existence of something must be a synthetic proposition. He thinks that this claim successfully undermines the Ontological Argument.

> Notwithstanding all these general considerations, in which every one must concur, we may be challenged with a case which is brought forward as proof that in actual fact the contrary holds, namely, that there is one concept, and indeed only one, in reference to which the not-being or rejection of its object is in itself contradictory, namely, the concept of the *ens realissimum*. It is declared that it possesses all reality, and that we are justified in assuming that such a being is possible (the fact that a concept does not contradict itself by no means proves the possibility of its object: but the contrary assertion I am for the moment willing to allow). Now 'all reality' includes existence; existence is therefore contained in the concept of a thing that is possible. If, then, this thing is rejected, the internal possibility of the thing is rejected—which is self-contradictory.
>
> My answer is as follows. There is already a contradiction in introducing the concept of existence—no matter under what title it may be disguised—into the concept of a thing which we profess to be thinking solely in reference to its possibility. If that be allowed as legitimate, a seeming victory has been won: but in actual fact nothing at all is said: the assertion is a mere tautology. We must ask: Is the proposition that *this* or *that thing* (which, whatever it may be, is allowed as possible) *exists*, an analytic or a synthetic proposition? If it is analytic, the assertion of the existence of the thing adds nothing to the thought of the thing; but in that case either the thought, which is in us, is the thing itself, or we have presupposed an existence as belonging to the realm of the possible, and have then, on that pretext, inferred its existence from its internal possibility—which is nothing but a miserable tautology. The word "reality," which in the concept of the thing sounds other than the word "existence" in the concept of the predicate, is of no avail in meeting this objection. For if all positing (no matter what it may be that is posited) is entitled reality, the thing with all its predicates is already posited in the concept of the subject, and is assumed as actual; and in the predicate this is merely repeated. But if, on the other hand, we admit, as every reasonable person must, that all existential propositions are synthetic, how can we profess to maintain that the predicate of existence cannot be rejected without contradiction? This is a feature which is found only in analytic propositions, and is indeed precisely what constitutes their analytic character.

I should have hoped to put an end to these idle and fruitless disputations in a direct manner, by an accurate determination of the concept of existence, had I not found that the illusion which is caused by the confusion of a logical with a real predicate (that is, with a predicate which determines a thing) is almost beyond correction. Anything we please can be made to serve as a logical predicate; the subject can even be predicated of itself; for logic abstracts from all content. But a *determining* predicate is a predicate which is added to the concept of the subject and enlarges it. Consequently, it must not be already contained in the concept.

"*Being*" is obviously not a real predicate; that is, it is not a concept of something which could be added to the concept of a thing. It is merely the positing of a thing, or of certain determinations, as existing in themselves. Logically, it is merely the copula of a judgment. The proposition, "God is omnipotent," contains two concepts, each of which has its object—God and omnipotence. The small word "is" adds no new predicate, but only serves to posit the predicate *in its relation* to the subject. If, now, we take the subject (God) with all its predicates (among which is omnipotence), and say "God is," or "There is a God," we attach no new predicate to the concept of God, but only posit the subject in itself with all its predicates, and indeed posit it as being an *object* that stands in relation to my *concept*. The content of both must be one and the same; nothing can have been added to the concept, which expresses merely what is possible, by my thinking its object (through the expression "it is") as given absolutely. Otherwise stated, the real contains no more than the merely possible. A hundred real thalers do not contain the least coin more than a hundred possible thalers. For as the latter signify the concept, and the former the object and the positing of the object, should the former contain more than the latter, my concept would not, in that case, express the whole object, and would not therefore be an adequate concept of it. My financial position is, however, affected very differently by a hundred real thalers than it is by the mere concept of them (that is, of their possibility). For the object, as it actually exists, is not analytically contained in my concept, but is added to my concept (which is a determination of my state) synthetically; and yet the conceived hundred thalers are not themselves in the least increased through thus acquiring existence outside my concept.

—IMMANUEL KANT, *Critique of Pure Reason*

III *Freud's Critique of Religion*

Kierkegaard concentrated entirely on *faith,* on the inner passionate concern with the truth of the Christian message. He scorned all rational evidences and arguments as radically inadequate to his religious needs. Anselm, Aquinas, and Paley, together with thousands of other rational theologians and religious philosophers, have looked to *reason* to support their faith, either through *a priori* arguments for the existence of God, or through **a posteriori** arguments founded upon His effects in the world He created. But for Kierkegaard, Anselm, Aquinas, Paley, and all the rest, there can be no real human doubt about the truth and centrality of religion. Even Kant was, in his personal life, a devoted, practicing Christian.

To some men and women, however, religion has seemed to be a fraud, a sham, a delusion foisted by humanity upon itself, or else foisted by priests and holy men on the common people. Karl Marx believed that the proletarian revolution would eliminate established religious institutions along with all the other instruments by which ruling classes have oppressed mankind. Eventually, religion, like the state, would wither away, leaving a society thoroughly secular and thoroughly rational.

Quite apart from formal attacks on religion by philosophers or social reformers, there has been a dramatic decline in the religiosity of Western society during the last century and a half. Even in such countries as Italy, which maintains official ties with the Roman Catholic Church, the influence of religious belief on the everyday lives of men and women has declined. In the United States, religion plays virtually no part in the public affairs of the nation, and only a small portion of the American people place their religious beliefs at the center of their private lives in the way that almost all people did two centuries ago. This progressive secularization of Western society seems to be related to industrialization, to urbanization, to the gradual rise to dominance of scientific modes of dealing with the world, rather than to changes in philosophical arguments. Periodically, religious revivals sweep the country, apparently reversing the tide of secularization. But when the waves recede, the level of religiosity settles at a new low, and the process continues.

One of the most powerful attacks on religious belief comes not from a philosopher but from the father of modern psychoanalytic theory, Sigmund Freud. Freud is famous for the discovery of the unconscious, for his theory of infant sexuality, and for his invention of the method of psychoanalysis. "Lying on the couch" and "going to the shrink" have entered our language as slang for receiving the treatment which Freud developed for emotional problems. Because of his emphasis on the irrational components in the human personality, Freud is sometimes thought of as an enemy of rationalism. Certainly, he was an enemy of the facile and comfortable belief that human beings are rational animals, and that reason can without much trouble establish control over the non-rational forces in the soul. But in a deeper sense, Freud was a rationalist through and through. He believed, as Plato did, that human beings suffer great unhappiness when the irrational elements in the soul control and manipulate the rational elements. He believed too, as Plato did, that self-knowledge was the cure for that unnecessary unhappiness. But Freud parted company with Plato, and with many other students of the human condition as well, in his pessimistic conviction that even a healthy personality would necessarily suffer pain and misery. The problem, as Freud saw it, was that the human condition is fundamentally compromised by disease, by death, and by the unbridgeable gap between the deep desires we all have for erotic gratification and the limited opportunities we have in the real world for the satisfaction of those desires.

Faced with frustration and death, Freud argued, we systematically fool ourselves with fairy tales, dreams, fantasies, and illusions. The greatest of those illusions is religion, and its hold on us is so strong that we persist in believing even in the face of the most powerful negative evidence. We believe in heaven, in God, in a life after death, in reward for virtue and punishment for sin, not because there is the slightest evidence for our beliefs, but because we *want* so much to believe. Religion is indeed an opiate, as Marx had said, but for all humanity, not merely for the working class. To those who ask Freud what he offers in place of religion, he can only answer: the hard truth, however painful it is to face.

Here is Freud's statement of his conception of religion. Notice that even if Freud is right, the issue is not settled, for though we believe because we want to believe rather than because evidence or reasoning justifies our belief, our belief might still be true.

> Religious ideas . . . which are given out as teachings, are not precipitates of experience or end-results of thinking: they are illusions, fulfilments of the oldest, strongest and most urgent wishes of mankind. The secret of their strength lies in the strength of those wishes. As we already know, the terrifying impression of helplessness in childhood aroused the need for protection—for protection through love—which was provided by the father; and the recognition that this helplessness lasts throughout life made it necessary to cling to the existence of a father, but this time a more powerful one. Thus the benevolent rule of a divine Providence allays our fear of the dangers of life; the establishment of a moral world-order ensures the fulfilment of the demands of justice, which have so often remained unfulfilled in human civilization; and the prolongation of earthly existence in a future life provides the local and temporal framework in which these wish-fulfilments shall take

SIGMUND FREUD (1856–1939) was the founder of the branch of medicine and psychological theory known as psychoanalysis. Freud was born in Austria, where he was trained as a neurologist. Through his clinical work on problems of hysterical paralysis, he became interested in the possibility of unconscious mental processes. Working first with the techniques of hypnosis and later with techniques of dream interpretation and word association which he invented, Freud made major discoveries about the workings of the mind. His studies of the unconscious and his emphasis on the central importance of sexuality in the mental life of adults and of children aroused great controversy and brought down on Freud considerable criticism both from the medical community and from the general public. Freud had many pupils and disciples who carried on his research and developed the therapeutic techniques he had devised. Though only a portion of modern-day psychiatrists and psychoanalysts describe themselves as "Freudians," virtually every branch of psychiatry is deeply indebted to Freud's work. In the last years of his life Freud was forced to leave Austria to escape persecution by the Nazis. He died in England.

place. Answers to the riddles that tempt the curiosity of man, such as how the universe began or what the relation is between body and mind, are developed in conformity with the underlying assumptions of this system. It is an enormous relief to the individual psyche if the conflicts of its childhood arising from the father-complex—conflicts which it has never wholly overcome—are removed from it and brought to a solution which is universally accepted.

When I say that these things are all illusions, I must define the meaning of the word. An illusion is not the same thing as an error; nor is it necessarily an error. Aristotle's belief that vermin are developed out of dung (a belief to which ignorant people still cling) was an error; so was the belief of a former generation of doctors that *tabes dorsalis* is the result of sexual excess. It would be incorrect to call these errors illusions. On the other hand, it was an illusion of Columbus's that he had discovered a new sea-route to the Indies. The part played by his wish in this error is very clear. One may describe as an illusion the assertion made by certain nationalists that the Indo-Germanic race is the only one capable of civilization; or the belief, which was only destroyed by psycho-analysis, that children are creatures without sexuality. What is characteristic of illusions is that they are derived from human wishes. In this respect they come near to psychiatric delusions. But they differ from them, too, apart from the more complicated structure of delusions. In the case of delusions, we emphasize as essential their being in contradiction with reality. Illusions need not necessarily be false—that is to say, unrealizable or in contradiction to reality. For instance, a middle-class girl may have the illusion that a prince will come and marry her. This is possible; and a few such cases have occurred. That the Messiah will come and found a golden age is much less likely. Whether one classifies this belief as an illusion or as something analogous to a delusion will depend on one's personal attitude. Examples of illusions which have proved true are not easy to find, but the illusion of the alchemists that all metals can be turned into gold might be one of them. The wish to have a great deal of gold, as much gold as possible, has, it is true, been a good deal damped by our present-day knowledge of the determinants of wealth, but chemistry no longer regards the transmutation of metals into gold as impossible. Thus we call a belief an illusion when a wish-fulfilment is a prominent factor in its motivation, and in doing so we disregard its relations to reality, just as the illusion itself sets no store by verification.

Having thus taken our bearings, let us return once more to the question of religious doctrines. We can now repeat that all of them are illusions and insusceptible of proof. No one can be compelled to think them true, to believe in them. Some of them are so improbable, so incompatible with everything we have laboriously discovered about the reality of the world, that we may compare them—if we pay proper regard to the psychological differences—to delusions. Of the reality value of most of them we cannot judge; just as they cannot be proved, so they cannot be refuted. We still know too little to make a critical approach to them. The riddles of the universe reveal themselves only slowly to our investigation; there are many questions to which science to-day can give no answer. But scientific work is the only road which can lead us to a knowledge of reality outside ourselves.

—SIGMUND FREUD, *The Future of an Illusion*

The Main Points in Chapter Six

1. The nineteenth-century Danish philosopher Søren Kierkegaard struggled throughout his life to come to terms with the Protestant Christianity of northern Europe, focusing in complex ways on such religious concepts as *faith, the saviour, sin,* and *dread.* His many writings were at one and the same time an exploration of the experience of religious faith and a critique of the middle-class society in which he lived.

2. Rejecting the teachings of Hegel, who was the leading philosophical influence of that time, Kierkegaard asserted that truth lies in what is *subjective, inward* and *immediate,* not *objective* and *universal.* Kierkegaard's approach to these central questions of human existence has come to be called Existentialism.

3. For several thousand years, philosophers have argued about whether it is possible to actually prove the existence of a divine and infinite being—God. The arguments designed to prove that God exists have traditionally been grouped under three headings:

   a. The *Argument From Design* seeks to prove that there is a God by pointing to the evidences in nature of purpose or design, and then reasoning that they must be the result of an intelligent, purposive designer, namely God. William Paley, in the late eighteenth century, gave the most elaborate version of this argument, although in one form or another it goes all the way back to ancient times.

   b. The *Cosmological Argument* starts from the fact there is motion in the world, or from the fact that things in the world come into being and pass away, and then reasons that there must be a first cause of motion, or a first unalterable cause of existence, which itself has no higher cause and neither comes to be or passes away.

c. The *Ontological Argument* begins with the mere *concept* of an infinite being, and argues that from a logical analysis of the concept, we can conclude that something corresponding to the concept—an infinite being, or God—*must* exist. The Ontological Argument, which dates from the middle ages, has been the subject of a very vigorous debate in philosophy for the past seven centuries.

4. Certain modern critics, such as the founder of psychoanalysis, Sigmund Freud, have argued that the religious impulse in human beings is an expression of infantile wishes and fantasies, provoked by our unwillingness to face the fact of our insignificance and inevitable death.

CONTEMPORARY APPLICATION

Creationism versus Evolution

In the beginning, religion and science went hand in hand. The early creation myths which form such an important part of most religions are at one and the same time religious accounts of God's relationship to the human race and scientific theories of the origin of the cosmos. As we saw in Chapter 1, early Greek speculations about the nature and origin of our world were one of the two great sources of what we now call Philosophy.

There has always been a certain tension between science and religion, to be sure. The Carthaginian church father Tertullian, who lived and wrote in the early third century after Christ, rejected the "science" of the Greek philosophers with a dramatic declaration of faith: *Credo, quia absurdum est!* I believe *because* it is absurd. Religious faith, he insisted, was utterly divorced from the rational science of the philosophers.

Nevertheless, Tertullian was very much in the minority. For the first eighteen hundred years of the Christian era, the scientific explanation of the natural world—both in the heavens and on earth—seemed perfectly compatible with the teachings of the church and the word of the Bible. Descartes, Leibniz, Locke, and Kant, among the philosophers we have encountered thus far, believed that they could square their religious faith with what reason and the senses told them about the world around them.

In the end, the greatest challenge to this harmony of science with religion came not from physics or chemistry, but from biology. It was the theory of evolution, as developed and taught most effectively by Charles Darwin, that produced a crisis in the ancient relationship between faith and reason.

Darwin himself was a quite pious and unrevolutionary naturalist, whose most impressive work consisted of painstaking observations of a variety of animal and plant species. But his theory of evolution, as set forth in his two most famous books, *The Origin of Species* and *The Descent of Man*, hit nineteenth-century European and American society like an earthquake. Needless to say, the focus of the controversy was Darwin's claim that the human species itself had descended, by a process of evolution and natural selection, from nonhuman species. A great deal was made of the notion that human beings were descended from monkeys, something that Darwin in fact never asserted. But it didn't really matter whether he traced our ancestry back to apes or to some slightly less disreputable sort of creatures. What caused all the fuss was the claim that we are simply a part of nature—not lifted up above the other inhabitants of the earth, not formed in God's image, not separated once and for all from everything else in the universe by our immortal souls—just animals.

As you might expect, reactions to Darwin's revolutionary theories varied. Some religious thinkers insisted that evolution posed no problem for the believing Christian. The story of the Creation at the beginning of the Book of Genesis could, with suitable interpretations, be made quite compatible with the latest evolutionary speculations. Other divines took a slightly different line. Science and the revealed truths of the Bible, they said, were like trains running on separate tracks. Science told us whatever reason and observation could discover about the natural world, and the Bible told us of God's plan for the human race and His divine commandments. So long as we rendered unto God what was God's, we could go on poking about with fossils and such to our heart's content.

But in the heartland of American Christianity, in that portion of the United States known to this day as "the Bible belt," where an unswerving belief in the literal truth of the Bible was the litmus test of true faith, neither of these compromises held any appeal. Fundamentalist Christians, particularly Protestants, rejected evolution as absolutely incompatible with the teachings of their faith.

At first, efforts were made simply to exclude the theory of evolution from the textbooks and classrooms. In several states, including Tennessee, laws were passed making it a crime to teach the theory of evolution in public schools. In 1925, a schoolteacher, John Scopes, was actually prosecuted and convicted under one such law.

In recent years, however, Bible literalists, or fundamentalists, have taken a quite different tack in their fight against evolutionary theories. Evolution, they now insist, is simply one explanation of the origin of species, and the teachings of the Bible, which they label creationism, is a second theory, equally legitimate, which ought in all fairness to be given equal time in public education.

The posing of creationism as an alternative to evolution raises the debate to a level of genuine philosophical significance, for it forces the defenders of the evolutionary teaching to ask themselves exactly what they think science is, what they think religion is, and what relation they think the two ought to bear to one another. It is that debate which we encounter in the pair of selections reproduced here.

The creationism/evolution debate frequently becomes extremely technical, for the creationists, despite their rejection of evolution, know all the ins and outs of the fossil evidence quite as well as the evolutionists. Sometimes, however, as in these selections, the basic issue of religion versus science emerges clearly without the confusing fog of paleontological detail. The first selection is by Dr. Duane T. Gish, the leading spokesperson of the creationist school. Dr. Gish holds a Ph.D. in biochemistry from the University of California at Berkeley and spent two decades doing scientific research at Cornell University and elsewhere before taking up a position as Associate Director of the Institute for Creation Research. His opponent in this confrontation, L. Beverly Halstead, teaches at the University of Reading in England.

Obviously, the creation/evolution debate raises questions which belong in half a dozen branches of philosophy. In the context of the issues we have been discussing in this chapter, it might be especially useful to consider the way in which the debate calls into question the relationship between faith and reason. Are religious faith in the revealed truth of the Bible and rational scientific explanations of the natural world compatible with one another? If the answer is yes, then how do we explain away the apparent conflicts between the story of Genesis and the accounts of cosmologists and biologists? If faith and reason are incompatible, to which shall we give precedence? These selections may start you thinking about the issues.

Evolution? The Fossils Say No!

DUANE T. GISH

The general theory of organic evolution, or the evolution model, is the theory that all living things have arisen by a material-

SOURCE: Duane T. Gish, *Evolution: The Fossils Say No.* Reprinted by permission of Master Book Publishers.

istic evolutionary process from a single source which itself arose by a similar process from a dead, inanimate world. This theory may also be called the molecule-to-man theory of evolution.

The creation model, on the other hand, postulates that all basic animal and plant types (the created kinds) were brought into existence by acts of a supernatural Creator using special processes which are not operative today.

Most scientists accept evolution, not as a theory, but as an established fact. . . . Almost all science books and school and university texts present evolution as an established fact. These considerations alone convince many people that molecule-to-man evolution has actually occurred.

The proponents of evolution theory adamantly insist that special creation be excluded from any possible consideration as an explanation for origins on the basis that it does not qualify as a scientific theory. On the other hand, they would view as unthinkable the consideration of evolution as anything less than pure science. In fact, as already mentioned, most evolutionists insist that evolution must no longer be thought of as a theory, but must be considered to be a fact. In spite of this attitude, however, not only is there a wealth of scientific support for rejecting evolution as a fact, but evolution does not even qualify as a scientific theory according to a strict definition of the latter.

What criteria must be met for a theory to be considered as scientific in the usually accepted sense? . . . A definition of science given by the Oxford Dictionary is:

A branch of study which is concerned either with a connected body of *demonstrated truths* or with *observed facts* systematically classified and more or less colligated by being brought under general laws, and which includes trust-worthy methods for the discovery of new truth within its own domain. [Emphasis added.]

Thus, for a theory to qualify as a scientific theory, it must be supported by events, processes, or properties which can be observed, and the theory must be useful in predicting the outcome of future natural phenomena or laboratory experiments. An additional limitation usually imposed is that the theory must be capable of falsification. That is, it must be possible to conceive some experiment, the failure of which would disprove the theory.

It is on the basis of such criteria that most evolutionists insist that creation be refused consideration as a possible explanation for origins. Creation has not been witnessed by human observers, it cannot be tested experimentally, and as a theory it is nonfalsifiable.

The general theory of evolution also fails to meet all three of these criteria, however. It is obvious, for example, that no one observed the origin of the universe, the origin of life, the conversion of a fish into an amphibian, or an ape into a man. No one, as a matter of fact, has ever observed the origin of a species by naturally occurring processes. Evolution has been *postulated*, but it has never been *observed*. . . .

In view of the above, it is incredible that most leading scientists dogmatically insist that the molecules-to-man evolution theory be taught as a fact to the exclusion of all other postulates. Evolution in this broad sense is unproven and unprovable and thus cannot be considered as fact. It is not subject to test by the ordinary methods of experimental science—observation and falsification. It thus does not, in a strict sense, even qualify as a scientific theory. It is a postulate and may serve as a model within which attempts may be made to explain and correlate the evidence from the historical record, that is, the fossil record, and to make predictions concerning the nature of future discoveries.

Creation is, of course, unproven and unprovable by the methods of experimental science. Neither can it qualify, according to the above criteria, as a scientific theory, since creation would have been unobservable and would as a theory be nonfalsifiable. In the scientific realm, creation is, therefore, as is evolution, a postulate which may serve as a model to explain and correlate the evidence related to origins. Creation is, in this sense, no more religious nor less scientific than evolution. In fact to many well-informed scientists, creation seems to be far superior to the evolution model as an explanation for origins. . . .

The evolutionist's view of man . . . is in direct contrast to the Biblical view of man, found, for example, in Psalm 100, verse 3: "Know ye that the Lord he is God: it is he that hath made us and not we ourselves; we are his people and the sheep of his pasture." The Bible does indeed reveal that there is a living God who has created us and who controls our destiny.

Furthermore, a God who is great enough to create and control this universe is great enough, once having given His revelation to man, to preserve that revelation free from error. This preservation was not dependent upon man, but succeeded in spite of man. In this revelation, found in the first two chapters of Genesis in the Bible, the account of creation is recorded in a grand but concise fashion.

Not all evolutionists are materialistic atheists or agnostics. Many evolutionists believe in God and some even believe the Bible to be the Word of God. They believe that evolution was God's method of creation, that God initiated the process at the molecular level and then allowed it to follow its natural course. The Biblical and scientific evidence, however, tells just as strongly against theistic evolution as it does against any other form of evolution.

The first two chapters of Genesis were not written in the form of parables or poetry but present the broad outlines of creation in the form of simple historical facts. These facts directly contradict evolution theory. The Bible tells us that at one time in history there was a single human being upon the earth—a male by the name of Adam. This in basic contradiction to evolution theory because, according to that theory, populations evolve, not individuals. After God had formed Adam from the dust of the ground, the Bible tells us that He used some portion from Adam's side (in the King James version this translated as "rib") to form Eve. This, of course, cannot be reconciled with any possible evolutionary theory concerning the origin of man.

The New Testament Scriptures fully support this Genesis account. For example, in I Corinthians 11:8 we read, "Man is not of the woman, but the woman of the man." By any natural reproductive process, man is always born of a woman. We all have mothers. This Biblical account can, therefore, be referring only to that unique time in history when God created woman from man, just as described in Genesis 2:21,22.

It is apparent that acceptance of creation requires an important element of faith. Yes, it is true, creationists do have faith, and that faith is vitally important. In Hebrews 11:6 we read "But without faith it is impossible to please Him, for he that cometh unto God must believe that He is, and that He is a rewarder of them that diligently seek Him." This faith is an intelligent faith, supported both by Biblical revelation and the revelation found in nature. While the *theories* and *opinions* of some scientists may contradict the Bible, there is no contradiction between the *facts* of science and the Bible.

Of course, belief in evolution also requires a vitally important element of faith. According to one of the most popular theories on the origin of the universe, all energy and matter of the universe was once contained in a plasma ball of electrons, protons, and neutrons (how it got there, no one has the faintest notion). This huge cosmic egg then exploded—and here we are today, several billion years later, human beings with a three-pound brain composed of 12 billion neurons each connected to about 10 thousand other neurons in the most complicated arrangement of matter known to man. (There are thus 120 trillion connections in the human brain.)

If this is true, then what we are and how we came to be were due solely to the properties inherent in electrons, protons, and neutrons. To believe *this* obviously requires a tremendous exercise of faith. Evolution theory is indeed no less religion nor more scientific than creation.

The question is, then, who has more evidence for his faith, the creationist or the evolutionist? The scientific case for special creation, as we will show in the following pages, is much stronger than the case for evolution. The more I study and the more I learn, the more I become convinced that evolution is a false theory and that special creation offers a much more satisfactory interpretive framework for correlating and explaining the scientific evidence related to origins.

Evolution—The Fossils Say Yes!

L. BEVERLY HALSTEAD

The poster advertising the oft-given lecture (and sometimes debate) by Dr. Duane T. Gish of the Institute for Creation Research, San Diego, carries the title "Evolution: Scholarship *versus* Dogmatism." In this article I shall endeavour to present the case for scholarship.

It is necessary first to admit of a major and fundamental area of agreement with the creationists. I personally do not see how the concept of evolution can be made consistent with that of creation by a personal god, or indeed any sort of god. I agree with Duane T. Gish in his book *Evolution? The Fossils Say No!*

> The reason that most scientists accept the theory of evolution is that most scientists are unbelievers, and unbelieving, materialistic men are forced to accept a materialistic, naturalistic explanation for the origin of all living things.
> Sir Julian Huxley, British evolutionist and grandson of Thomas Huxley, one of Darwin's strongest supporters when he first published his theory, has said that "Gods are peripheral phenomena produced by evolution." What Huxley meant was that the idea of God merely evolved as man evolved from lower animals. . . . Huxley believes that man is just as much a natural phenomenon as an animal or plant; that his body, mind and soul were not supernaturally created but are products of evolution, and that he is not under the control or guidance of any supernatural being or beings, but has to rely on himself and his own powers.

This is one area in which Gish and I agree. . . .

. . . It is very important to illustrate the differences in approach between the scientific and religious standpoints. One of the best examples to illustrate this comes from the Genesis account of the fall. To me there are some inspiring passages in this book. But I first want to set the scene (Gen. 2:15–17).

> And the LORD GOD took the man, and put him into the garden of Eden to dress it and to keep it.
> And the LORD GOD commanded the man, saying, Of every tree of the garden thou mayest freely eat:
> But of the tree of the knowledge of good and evil, thou shalt not eat of it: for in the day that thou eatest thereof thou shalt surely die.

Here we have man being given an instruction by the supreme Authority, and

SOURCE: L. Beverly Halstead, "Evolution—The Fossils Say Yes!" *Science and Creationism*, ed. Ashley Montagu. Reprinted by permission of Ashley Montagu and Oxford University Press.

he was expected to accept this quite un-critically—he was not expected to question it, he was certainly not expected to defy it, he was expected to obey it. Let us consider what this means. Here is a situation where you are placed in an environment where you have everything, all you must not do is think.

Samuel Butler in the last century wrote "The Kingdom of Heaven is the being like a good dog."

A good dog does what he is told, gets a pat on the head, and that is all. This is a prospect that no real human being should ever stand for. But we are very fortunate in this story—we have the hero of this entire episode, the serpent, and he gave very good advice (Gen. 3:5-7).

For GOD doth know that in the day ye eat thereof, then your eyes shall be opened, and ye shall be as gods, knowing good and evil.

And when the woman saw that the tree was good for food, and that it was pleasant to the eyes, and a tree to be desired to make one wise, she took of the fruit thereof, and did eat, and gave also unto her husband with her; and he did eat.

And the eyes of them both were opened.

That, to my mind, is the most inspiring passage in this entire volume.

That was original sin, the defiance of the Lord God was original sin, and this sin is the one which every scientist worthy of the name is dedicated to uphold.

Let us go to the New Testament, the Gospel According to St. John (20:25-29) and note the approach of Thomas.

The other disciples therefore said unto him, We have seen the Lord. But he said unto them, Except I shall see in his hands the print of the nails, and put my finger into the print of the nails, and thrust my hand into his side, I will not believe.

That is where the scientist stands—you should not believe something without evidence. Thomas was one of the early men of a scientific frame of mind.

Evidence, according to this story, was provided.

And after eight days again his disciples were within, and Thomas with them, then came Jesus, the doors being shut, and stood in the midst and said, Peace be unto you.

Then saith he to Thomas, Reach hither thy finger, and behold my hands; and reach hither thy hand, and thrust it into my side and be not faithless, but believing.

And Thomas answered and said unto him, My Lord and my God.

He said that because he had the evidence. Thomas is still the hero, but this is where we come to the serious part.

Jesus said unto him, Thomas, because thou hast seen me, thou hast believed; blessed are they that have not seen, and yet have believed.

That is by far the most subversive statement in this book. And this is something that has characterized Western Civilisation for hundreds of years. You accept what authority says, do not question. And this is something of which

I don't think we can be proud. Of course, people have defied authority throughout the millenia and will continue to do so. The motto of the Royal Society of London is *Nullius in Verba,* which freely translated, means, "We take no man's word for anything." This is a very proud motto for scientists to have. There is no question that any scientist or any man, for that matter, should not ask; there are no areas in which we should not question.

In striking contrast Gish writes, "It is apparent that acceptance of creation requires an important element of faith. Yes, it is true, creationists do have faith, and that faith is vitally important. In *Hebrews* 11:6 we read, 'But without faith it is impossible to please Him, for he that cometh unto God must believe that He is, and that He is a rewarder of them that diligently seek Him.' This faith is an intelligent faith, supported both by Biblical revelation and the revelation found in nature."

This attitude, I claim, seeks to close the mind. Gish and I stand on opposite sides of a divide which will not be crossed; he will not cross to my side and I will not cross to his. There is a fundamental division in the attitude of a believer and the attitude of a scientist. . . . If you are faced with ignorance, it is very difficult to always say, "I do not know." It is much easier to simply invoke the deity to explain the unknown. That is a very comfortable stand to take, but that of science is to say, "I do not know, I cannot explain." It does not mean that the scientist doesn't believe that one day he may be able to explain. One of the techniques of Gish and his colleagues is to ask scientists to explain certain things regarding evolution and the fossil record, and the simple answer, and I will give it now, is that I cannot: I will not be able to explain them although I may be able to in the future. This is not what science is about. Science does not claim to have all the answers. Science is a way of looking at things, and the first approach of a scientist is to doubt and not believe.

Study Questions

1. Have you ever had an experience that you could properly describe as religious? I have in mind not only dramatic experiences like visions and conversions, but also more commonplace, socially embedded experiences such as receiving communion, becoming *bar mitzvah*, serving as a godparent for a young relative, or even simply attending religious services. Think about that experience, and ask yourself: Did it put you in touch, do you think, with a realm outside of, or different from, the everyday world? What significance did the experience have for you? Did it change your life? Why? Why not? What would change your life?

2. Read through the proofs for the existence of God carefully. Think about them. Do any of them convince you? If the answer is no [and it usually is], then what purpose do you think those proofs serve? Would it make a difference to you if the proofs were beefed up, made better? How would Jesus have responded to attempts to prove the existence of God?

3. Let us suppose you reject the proofs for the existence of God, and even reject the claim that there is a God. How then do you explain the fact that there is a universe? Do we need an explanation for the fact that we exist? Why is there in general something, and not nothing?

4. Suppose we make contact with an alien race on a distant planet, and discover that they, like we, worship a divine being who has revealed himself to them in a set of holy writings. Suppose that when we finally learn how to translate their language into ours, it turns out that their holy writings and the New and Old Testaments say roughly the same things. Would that prove that there is a God? Suppose, on the other hand, that they have no cultural practice that looks even remotely like religion. Would that undermine the claims of our religions? Why?

5. How do you suppose Kierkegaard would react to the creationism/evolution controversy? Would he think that we needed more scientific data to settle the dispute? Why? Why not? At the present time, a team of editors is slowly publishing the complete papers of the greatest scientist of the twentieth century, Albert Einstein. If it turns out, down the road, that Einstein secretly believed in Creationism, would that be evidence that it is correct? What *would* be evidence that one or the other theory is correct?

7

THEORY OF KNOWLEDGE

RENÉ DESCARTES (1596–1650) is universally recognized among philosophers as the first great figure of the modern age. Born in a small town in Touraine, France, Descartes was educated by the Jesuits, and he remained throughout his life a devoted Catholic. His early interest was principally in mathematics and physics, two fields in which exciting new work was being done by many continental and English thinkers. In his early twenties, perhaps as the result of a dramatic trio of dreams, Descartes conceived the grandiose plan of formulating an entirely new system of science founded upon mathematics. Though he never accomplished this impossible task, his many contributions to mathematics and physics place him in the forefront of seventeenth-century science.

Descartes' primary concern throughout his life was with problems of methodology, justification, and certainty. His first work was entitled *Rules for the Direction of the Mind,* and in it he sought to establish the proper procedures by which a question could be investigated without the danger of error or confusion. His most famous work, *Meditations on First Philosophy,* was immediately recognized as a dramatic challenge to all established philosophy and science. It was circulated widely throughout Europe, and provoked a series of objections, to which Descartes wrote extended replies. In these objections and replies we can see a number of profound and dramatic debates unfolding, in which such famous thinkers as Hobbes, Gassendi, and Arnauld locked horns with Descartes.

Although Descartes was deeply influenced by the scholastic philosophy which had preceded him, the problems he posed, the questions he raised, and the demands he made for absolute subjective certainty in knowledge served to undermine the influence of the 2000-year-old tradition of Aristotelian philosophizing. Virtually all the great philosophy written during the 150 years following Descartes' death can be seen as an attempt to answer the questions raised by the brilliant, iconoclastic Frenchman.

I   Descartes' Method of Doubt

If you have been working your way through this book carefully, reading
and thinking, discussing the problems it raises with your teacher and
your fellow students, you should by now be getting some feel for what
philosophy is and how philosophers think. And if I have been at all successful, then philosophy ought to seem a fairly sensible sort of business
to you. Perhaps philosophical questions aren't exactly what your mind
would turn to if you had a few spare moments caught in a traffic jam or
if you couldn't sleep late at night, but at least it is easy enough to understand how reasonable men and women might get genuinely worked up
about them. What rules should I use to decide the hard moral choices
that life poses for me? How should the wealth of a society be divided up
among its members? Do I have an obligation to obey the state, even
when I believe that its laws are unjust? What place should painting and
poetry, music and fiction play in a good society? Is there a God? Can I
trust Him to keep His promise of eternal life? These may not be everyone's questions, but they are surely questions worth asking. Some of
them even get asked in political campaigns, in hospital emergency wards,
in law courts, or in the front lines of a war.

In this chapter, the situation changes dramatically. We are going to
take a look at the philosophical attempts to deal with questions that some
of you may think are just plain crazy. Suppose a friend of yours asks

whether you and he really did go to the movies last night or whether he just dreamed it. A little odd, perhaps, but people do have very lifelike dreams; I have myself on a couple of occasions had dreams so real that afterwards I wasn't entirely sure whether they had actually happened or not. You wouldn't think your friend was being *philosophical,* but on the other hand you wouldn't think he was crazy either. Suppose he went on to wonder, in absolute seriousness, whether everything that had ever happened to him was a dream, whether his childhood, his adolescence, his school days, his fights with his parents, his first romance, his first trip away from home, his coming to college, and his standing right there in front of you were *all just dreams.* If he were dead serious, not just kidding around or trying to get a rise out of you, then about now you would start edging toward the phone, trying to figure out how you could call the school psychiatrist without getting your friend too upset. People who really aren't sure whether their whole lives have been dreams "need help," as the saying goes.

Suppose another friend said, as the two of you were waiting for an elevator, that she couldn't really be sure that she needed an elevator to get back down to the first floor. Maybe if she stepped out of the window, she would be able simply to fly down. Suppose, indeed, that she expressed doubt about whether she could ever tell what would happen next—whether she would drown if she held her head under water, whether her finger would burn if she held it in a flame, whether her books would fall down or up if she let go of them. She might even admit that she wasn't sure there was anyone else in the whole world besides herself, though of course there might be a lot of human-looking bodies that made speechlike noises and acted in peoplelike ways. Well, once again, you would probably think that either the whole act was a put-on, or your friend was in the midst of a bad trip, or else that it was time for the shrink. You certainly wouldn't think that she was simply doing philosophy!

From the beginning of the seventeenth century until the present day, some of the most brilliant thinkers ever to grace the cultural and intellectual life of Western civilization have devoted their best philosophical efforts to just such questions as the ones we have been imagining your friends to be asking. And though I would be the first to admit that philosophers have suffered their share of mental illness, there is no reason at all to suspect that any of these great thinkers was mentally unsound when he wrote his philosophy. (Rousseau, as we have seen, was more than a little odd, but we won't be talking about him in this chapter.)

Copyright © 1986 by USA TODAY.

The greatest challenge any teacher of philosophy faces is to present the epistemological theories of the seventeenth- and eighteenth-century theorists of knowledge in such a way that students not only understand the arguments but also understand why in heaven's name sane people worried about such peculiar problems.

The theory of knowledge is the heart and soul of the philosophy that has been written since the beginning of the seventeenth century. All of the most important philosophers—Descartes, Leibniz, Locke, Berkeley, Hume, Kant—set epistemological investigations at the center of their work. If we cannot understand what made them take so seriously the questions that seem odd to us today, then we cannot really understand philosophy as it has been done during the past four centuries. In the second place, the strange-seeming problems of the modern theory of knowledge (in philosophy, anything since 1600 is called "modern") connect directly with one of the dominant cultural and intellectual developments of the postmedieval world—namely, the steady movement toward a radical individualism in religion, in politics, in art, and in literature, as well as in philosophy. Though the epistemological puzzles of seventeenth- and eighteenth-century philosophy seem bizarre or unintuitive on first inspection, they have deeply influenced the way painters painted, the way poets wrote, the way theologians reinterpreted the Word of God, and even the way economists, political scientists, and sociologists have explained our collective social life. So like it or not, we are in for some complicated philosophy in this chapter.

By common agreement, the man who started the new theory of knowledge on its way in philosophy was a Frenchman, born in 1596, named René Descartes. Indeed, though Descartes wrote a number of important works during his fifty-four years, in which mathematics, physics, and other subjects as well as philosophy were discussed, we can even

SIR ISAAC NEWTON (1642–1727) was the greatest physicist of the modern age. Newton did revolutionary work on the laws of optics in addition to inventing the calculus and achieving a theoretical unification of the theories of Galileo and Kepler.

name the precise piece of philosophy that marks the beginning of modern philosophy as we study it today. That honor clearly belongs to a seventy-page work entitled *Meditations on First Philosophy*, published by Descartes in 1641.

The seventeenth century was an age of scientific giants, and among the truly great thinkers whose efforts created what we know today as modern science, only the German Gottfried Leibniz and the Englishman Isaac Newton can stand with Descartes. You have probably already met Descartes, or at least spent some time working with one of his contributions to knowledge, for it was he who invented what is called analytic geometry. (That is why, when you draw a graph and plot points on it, you are said to be using "Cartesian" coordinates.)

Descartes was born three quarters of a century after Martin Luther had begun the Protestant Reformation by nailing his famous theses to the church door in Wittenberg. Descartes himself was, and remained throughout his life, a Roman Catholic, and his early education was received from the Jesuits. Nevertheless, if the essence of the Protestant Reformation was the rejection of the religious authority of the institution of the Church and the emphasis on the primacy of individual conscience, then it is clear that Descartes was, intellectually and emotionally, an extreme protestant. The keynote of his life work was a thoroughgoing rejection of received opinion, established doctrine, and the authority of the ancients, and a thoroughly individualistic insistence upon accepting only those truths which his own reason could certify to be correct.

In his early twenties, Descartes' interest turned to mathematics and physics, fields which at that time were dominated by concepts and methods almost 2000 years old. Exciting new work was being done in both areas, and Descartes, like many young scientific geniuses, moved immediately to the scientific frontier. On the night of November 10, 1619, the 23-year-old Descartes had a series of three dreams which seem to have transformed his life. He spoke and wrote of them ever after as the turning point in his career. I am not going to try my hand at armchair dream interpretation. As Freud made very clear when he first described the psychoanalytic method of interpreting dreams, you cannot figure out what a dream meant to the person who had it unless you can get that person actually to talk to you about the dream. There isn't any code book of dream symbols in which you can look up the meaning of falling, or a mirror, or whatever. But Descartes himself interpreted his dreams as a sign that he was to spend his life establishing a new, unified theory of the universe based upon mathematics—what we today would call mathematical physics.

The important part of Descartes' plan, for our purposes, is not the new science he developed, but his conception of the *method* by which he was to proceed. Descartes devoted a great deal of thought to problems of intellectual and scientific method, and his contributions in this field are, if anything, more revolutionary than his actual mathematical and scientific work itself. Descartes published nothing while he was young, despite the fact that he had made a number of important discoveries in his twenties and thirties. In 1637, when he was past forty, he brought out his first published work, appropriately titled "Discourse on the Method

FRANCIS BACON (1561–1626) was an English empiricist philosopher. Bacon's great work, *Novum Organum*, laid down rules for investigating nature in order to learn the inner nature and workings of physical processes.

of Rightly Conducting the Reason and Seeking for Truth in the Sciences." In this partly autobiographical, partly philosophical work, he lays down a set of four rules which he claims are sufficient to guide the mind in whatever inquiry it may undertake. Here are the rules, as Descartes stated them:

> The first of these was to accept nothing as true which I did not clearly recognize to be so: that is to say, carefully to avoid precipitation and prejudice in judgements, and to accept in them nothing more than what was presented to my mind so clearly and distinctly that I could have no occasion to doubt it.
>
> The second was to divide up each of the difficulties which I examined into as many parts as possible, and as seemed requisite in order that it might be resolved in the best manner possible.

The third was to carry on my reflections in due order, commencing with objects that were the most simple and easy to understand, in order to rise little by little, or by degrees, to knowledge of the most complex, assuming an order, even if a fictitious one, among those which do not follow a natural sequence relatively to one another.

The last was in all cases to make enumerations so complete and reviews so general that I should be certain of having omitted nothing.

—RENÉ DESCARTES, *Discourse on Method*

They don't seem like much when you first read them, do they? Avoid prejudice, don't take anything on faith, be careful, tackle questions a step at a time, be orderly, and so forth. It sounds more like instructions to an army filing clerk or the directions for assembling an outdoor barbecue grill than a great revolution in philosophy. Indeed, Leibniz once remarked rather sarcastically that Descartes' famous "method" boiled down to saying "Take what you need, and do what you should, and you will get what you want." But first impressions are often wrong (as Descartes himself pointed out), and in this case Leibniz was being more clever than wise.

The real importance of Descartes' method lies in *two* of its features and a consequence that follows from those two. Since what follows may be easier to understand if you have some labels to attach to it, let me start by telling you that Descartes' method is both a *method of inquiry* and a *method of doubt,* and that the combined consequence of these two methods is to set in motion a philosophical transformation known as the *epistemological turn.* Now, if you have carefully underlined these three terms in red or yellow or blue, we can try to make some sense out of them.

First, Descartes' method is a *method of inquiry.* In other words, it is a method for finding things out and making sure that you get them right; it is not a method for proving what you already know, or for setting forth your knowledge in the most systematic way. Think for a moment about traditional Euclidean geometry. On the first page of a geometry book (at least this was so when I went to school) you find definitions, axioms, and postulates. These are the simplest, or the most fundamental part of the geometric theory, but they are hardly the first things that a real mathematician would think up if she were doing geometry. Then come the theorems, each one neatly set forth, step by step, from the axioms or previously proved theorems down to what is to be proved, Q.E.D. That may be the way Euclid rearranged his proofs once he had thought them up, but it surely isn't the way he discovered them! Most likely, when he wanted to prove something (say, the theorem that the line bisecting the apex of an isosceles triangle is perpendicular to the base), he drew a diagram, fiddled around with the lines, looked to see whether there was anything that was equal to anything else, worked his way up from the conclusion and down from the premises, until the proof finally fell into place. So his *method of inquiry*—his way of finding something out—was very different from his method of proof or exposition. Descartes' rules for the mind are obviously intended as guides for someone who is trying to solve a problem or analyze a phenomenon. In other words (and this is going to turn out to be very important indeed), he adopts the point of view of someone who does not yet know anything, but is trying by the use of his or her intelligence to discover something, rather than the point of view of a teacher or expert who is quite sure he or she knows something, and is simply trying to explain it to someone else.

Second, Descartes' method is a **method of doubt.** His first rule is "to accept nothing as true which I do not clearly recognize to be so." Just how radical this rule will be depends on how we interpret the phrase "clearly recognize." If Descartes merely wants us to stop and think before we say we are sure, as a quiz show contestant might pause before answering the jackpot question, then obviously that rule is not going to produce any great intellectual revolution. But as you shall see in a few pages, when you read part of the *Meditations on First Philosophy*, Descartes had much more in mind. When he tells us not to accept anything unless we can "clearly recognize" it as true, he means that we should refuse to accept anything, however sure we once were of it, however many people believe it, however obvious it seems, unless we can be *absolutely certain that it is one hundred percent right*. If there is the slightest, the wildest, the farthest-out chance that it just might be false, then we are not to accept it. Now that opens up quite a can of worms! For example, I am quite sure that Washington, D.C., is the capital of the United States of America. If you ask me how I can be so sure, I will tell you that I have read it in history and government books, that I have heard Washington referred to a thousand times on television as "our nation's capital," that I have visited Washington and actually sat for a day in the visitors' gallery of the Senate, and so forth. But does that make it absolutely, one hundred percent certain? Couldn't I be wrong? It isn't likely that I am wrong, but is it logically possible? Maybe the books were wrong; maybe the television commentators were wrong; maybe I was actually in

Philadelphia when I thought I was in Washington; indeed, maybe there is a great conspiracy afoot to fool me into thinking that Washington is the capital. I can't imagine why anyone would go to all that trouble, but it *is* possible. Put it this way: I could write a science fiction story about such a conspiracy, and although you might say it wasn't very plausible, you couldn't say that the story was a total impossibility.

Well, you protest, if Descartes is going to interpret "clearly recognize" like that, then just about everything anyone has ever believed will go out the window! I might as well doubt that there is even a United States, or an earth, or a human race, or space and time and the universe. If I am going to refuse to accept things like that, then maybe I ought to start doubting that two plus two is four. After all, if a giant conspiracy might be underway to trick me into believing that Washington is the capital of the United States, then maybe some mysterious, evil, powerful demon is reaching into my mind and tricking me into thinking that two plus two is four when really it is five. Maybe every time I take two objects and place them next to two more, that demon sneaks one of them away, so that as I count them up, I get only four instead of five, which is the right number!

Strange as it may sound, this is just what Descartes has in mind. When he says accept *nothing* that isn't certain, he means *nothing*. But, you object, that is madness! We have to start somewhere. Why, if I am going to doubt everything that has even the most minute bit of possible uncertainty attached to it, then I might even have to doubt my own existence! Perhaps I don't exist either; maybe that evil demon is fooling me about myself as well as about simple arithmetic! No, says Descartes, with one of the most dramatic reversals in all philosophical literature. Doubt all else, but you cannot doubt your own existence. That, and nothing but that, is the true foundation, the unshakable first principle, the rock on which all the rest of your knowledge shall be raised up. How does he manage to prove that I cannot rationally doubt my own existence, when he has erected a standard of certainty so strict that literally everything else that I have ever believed fails to meet it? You shall see when you read the *Meditations*. I do not want to spoil the effect of the argument by giving it away. Descartes' proof of his own existence is one of the high points in the history of philosophy. It is also, in a way, the high point of unbridled individualism in Western civilization. Imagine a philosopher who proposes to base the entire edifice of scientific, mathematical, and religious knowledge *not* on the collective learning and wisdom of humanity, *not* on the evidence of the laboratory, *not* on the existence of God, *not even* on the first principles of logic, *but simply* on *the fact of his own existence!*

When the method of inquiry is combined with the method of doubt, a transformation in the central nature of philosophy is begun. That transformation, which I am calling the **epistemological turn,** took a century and a half to complete. Not until Kant's *Critique of Pure Reason* was the epistemological turn brought to its end; thereafter, all philosophy was so changed that the very questions philosophers asked, as well as the answers they gave, looked little like what was written before the *Meditations.* The epistemological turn is a very simple, but tricky, notion. Even after you have it, you find it slipping away from you. Like Einstein's notion of relativity, or a Picasso painting, it makes you see familiar things in an entirely new way.

The heart of the E.T. (philosophers these days like to abbreviate things, so let's use E.T. for *epistemological turn*) is a simple reversal in order of two basic questions. From the ancient pre-Socratic cosmologists up to the time of Descartes, philosophers put questions about what exists, about the nature of the universe, before questions about what I can know to exist, about what I can know the nature of the universe to be. That is to say, philosophers considered questions of *being* to take precedence over questions of *knowing.* Aristotle, for example, called the essays in which he discussed questions of being "essays on first philosophy." He didn't mean that these very difficult, very abstract essays were the first sorts of philosophy a student should read. He meant that questions about the nature of being were the logically first, or most fundamental, or most basic questions to be dealt with.

To be sure, Aristotle and many of his predecessors and followers discussed the nature of knowledge. They talked about the nature of the mind, the role of the senses (sight, hearing, touch, and so forth) in knowledge, the role of reasoning, the limits of human knowledge, and countless other topics. But they considered these *epistemological* questions to be secondary, less important than questions about the nature of God, the reality of space and time, and all the other topics dealt with in "first philosophy," or as we call it today, metaphysics. So we can sum up philosophy prior to Descartes by saying that in it, *metaphysics took precedence over epistemology.*

Descartes' two methods—the method of inquiry and the method of doubt—had the effect of reversing this order of precedence. Properly understood and carried out with a consistency and rigor which Descartes himself never achieved, these two methods forced philosophers to set aside questions of being until they had dealt with the questions of knowing. And that fact in turn changed the meaning of the questions about being, so that by the time the revolution begun by Descartes had run its course, old-style metaphysics was finished, and new-style epistemology had taken its place as "first philosophy." Let us see how Descartes' two methods began this transformation.

First, as we have noted, the method of inquiry tells us to adopt the point of view of someone who is ignorant but is trying to learn, rather than the point of view of someone who knows something and is trying to explain. What is more, it teaches us to take questions in an orderly manner, not moving on to the next until we have settled the first. There is an old case in the English common law, going back to the Middle Ages, which illustrates the hidden force of Descartes' rule. Jones sued Smith for damages, claiming that Smith had borrowed a water jug from him and had returned it broken. Smith's defense was a classic of what we now call "stonewalling." "First" he argued, "the jug does not exist; second, I didn't borrow it; third, it was whole when I returned it; and fourth, it was cracked when I borrowed it." Smith wasn't out of his mind. He was simply saying to Jones, "Before I am going to pay you any money, you are going to have to prove every single item in your story. You must prove that the jug even exists; then you must prove that I borrowed it; then you must prove that I didn't return it whole; and then you must prove that it wasn't cracked when I borrowed it, but was cracked when I returned it." Now the legal point of this story is that proving one of these points might be a good deal harder than proving another, and Jones must prove them all in order to collect damages. If he threw the jug away after it was returned broken, then he may have trouble proving that it ever existed. Even if he kept the pieces, he may have trouble proving that it wasn't already cracked when he lent it to Smith. And so on. When the defense in a court case agrees not to dispute some assertion by the prosecution about the facts of the case, it is called "stipulating." Descartes' first rule tells us not to stipulate anything.

For example, at the beginning of his book entitled *Physics*, Aristotle says that the subject matter of physics is motion, or rather things in motion. If anyone wants to deny that there is motion in the world (as some philosophers in fact had denied), then a book on physics is not the right place to argue with him or her. "We physicists," Aristotle writes, "must take for granted that the things that exist by nature are, either all or some of them, in motion. . . . No man of science is bound to solve every kind of difficulty that may be raised, but only as many as are drawn falsely from the principles of the science." But Descartes adopts the opposite view. Before we can do physics, we must prove that there are bodies in motion in space. Once we have established that, we can appeal to the experiments and observations, deductions and proofs, which scientists have developed in their study of nature. But until we have shown that nature exists—until we have, like Jones, proved that there is a jug—we must set aside such investigations. We shall not stipulate the universe.

The second half of Descartes' method—the method of doubt—makes things ten times worse, of course. Having refused to stipulate anything, even the existence of the world, Descartes now insists that the standard of proof be absolute certainty. In a court of law, the jury is asked whether the case has been proved "beyond a reasonable doubt." There is a whole lot of difference between absolute certainty and beyond a reasonable doubt. I am pretty sure that my car won't turn into a boa constrictor and squeeze me to death while I am putting on my seat belt. I am sure enough of it to bet my life on it every day when I drive somewhere. My conviction goes way beyond any reasonable doubt. But if Descartes asks me whether I can be *certain* that my car won't turn into a boa, I must answer that of course I cannot rule it out as absolutely impossible. I can, after all, imagine some weird planet across the galaxy in which cars turn into boa constrictors. In a way, that isn't much stranger than the fact that caterpillars turn into butterflies.

Combining the two methods seems to drive us into the corner which philosophers call "skepticism." If we can't move on to point B until we have proved point A, and if in order to prove point A, we must establish it with absolute certainty, then it looks as though we will have a very hard time proving any point at all. Instead of wandering all over the universe, studying the stars, the planets, the origins of life, the workings of the human body, the laws of society, or the movement of the tides, we are

Epistemological Skepticism   The doctrine that no adequate justification can be given for any of our beliefs about the world, not even for apparently rock-solid beliefs that there is a physical world, that I have a body, that the sun will rise tomorrow, or that fire causes heat. The aim of epistemological skepticism is to focus our attention on the relationship between our beliefs and their justification, not actually to get us to stop believing.

going to be huddled in a corner, trying to figure out how to take step A, so that we can take step B. Now, if your car is working, you go on trips and look at the scenery. But if your car won't run, you open the hood and inspect the motor. So too, if your logical engine is in good working order, then you cruise through the world of knowledge, looking at one interesting field after another; but if your logical engine breaks down— if your rules of inquiry and proof don't permit you to move with ease from one truth to another—then you stop, raise the lid on your mind (which is, after all, your logical engine), and take a good hard look to see what is wrong. In short, you start analyzing and examining the process by which you come to know anything. Epistemology is the study of the way in which we know, the rules by which we reason, the limits of what we can know, and the criteria or standards we use for judging whether a supposed piece of knowledge really is knowledge. If we follow Descartes' rule, we cannot take a scientific or metaphysical trip through the universe until we have checked out our means of transportation—our knowing process itself—and made sure that it will take us where we want to go.

Descartes himself never realized the full magnitude of the revolution that his two methods were to produce. He thought of himself as laying the basis for a new, unified system of scientific knowledge free of all

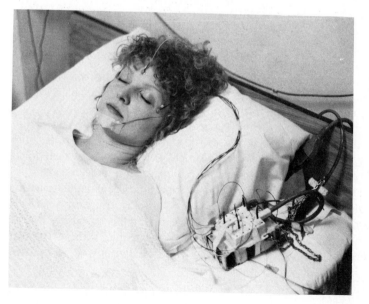

Modern scientists can actually determine when we are dreaming by measuring the electrical impulses in the brain. (Teri Stratford, courtesy Sleep-Wake Disorders Center, Montefiore Medical Center)

reliance on tradition, the wisdom of the ancients, or the old concepts of Aristotelian metaphysics. But he seems still to have supposed that questions of being would take precedence over questions of knowing. In the *Meditations*, after the section which you are about to read, he went on to offer "proofs" for the existence of God, of the physical universe, and of all the other things he had so carefully doubted at the beginning of the essay. It remained for later philosophers, both on the continent of Europe and in Great Britain, to draw out the deeper implications of the process which Descartes started.

Here now are selections from First and Second Meditation.

MEDITATION I

It is now some years since I detected how many were the false beliefs that I had from my earliest youth admitted as true and how doubtful was everything I had since constructed on this basis; and from that time I was convinced that I must once for all seriously undertake to rid myself of all the opinions which I had formerly accepted, and commence to build anew from the foundation, if I wanted to establish any firm and permanent structure in the sciences.

Now for this object it is not necessary that I should show that all of these are false—I shall perhaps never arrive at this end. But inasmuch as reason already persuades me that I ought no less carefully to withhold my assent from matters which are not entirely certain and indubitable than from those which appear to me manifestly to be false, if I am able to find in each one some reason to doubt, this will suffice to justify my rejecting the whole. And for that end it will not be requisite that I should examine each in particular, which would be an endless undertaking; for owing to the fact that the destruction of the foundations of necessity brings with it the downfall of the rest of the edifice, I shall only in the first place attack those principles upon which all my former opinions rested.

All that up to the present time I have accepted as most true and certain I have learned either from the senses or through the senses; but it is sometimes proved to me that these senses are deceptive, and it is wiser not to trust entirely to any thing by which we have once been deceived.

But it may be that although the senses sometimes deceive us concerning things which are hardly perceptible, or very far away, there are yet many others to be met with as to which we cannot reasonably have any doubt, although we recognise them by their means. For example, there is the fact that I am here, seated by the fire, attired in a dressing gown, having this paper in my hands and other similar matters. And how could I deny that these hands and this body are mine, were it not perhaps that I compare myself to certain persons, devoid of sense, whose cerebella are so troubled and clouded by the violent vapours of black bile, that they constantly assure us that they think they are kings when they are really quite poor, or that they are clothed in purple when they are really without covering, or who imagine that they have an earthenware head or are nothing but pumpkins or are made of glass. But they are mad, and I should not be any the less insane were I to follow examples so extravagant.

At the same time I must remember that I am a man, and that consequently I am in the habit of sleeping, and in my dreams representing to myself the same things or sometimes even less probable things, than do those who are insane in their waking moments. How often has it happened to me that in the night I dreamt that I found myself in this particular place, that I was dressed and seated near the fire, whilst in reality I was lying undressed in bed! At this moment it does indeed seem to me that it is with eyes awake that I am looking at this paper; that this head which I move is not asleep, that it is deliberately and of set purpose that I extend my hand and perceive it; what happens in sleep does not appear so clear nor so distinct as does all this. But in thinking over this I remind myself that on many occasions I have in sleep been deceived by similar illusions, and in dwelling carefully on this reflection I see so manifestly that there are no certain indications by which we may clearly distinguish wakefulness from sleep that I am lost in astonishment. And my astonishment is such that it is almost capable of persuading me that I now dream.

Now let us assume that we are asleep and that all these particulars, e.g. that we open our eyes, shake our head, extend our hands, and so on, are but false delusions; and let us reflect that possibly neither our hands nor our whole body are such as they appear to us to be. At the same time we must at least confess that the things which are represented to us in sleep are like painted representations which can only have been formed as the counterparts of something real and true, and that in this way those general things at least, i.e. eyes, a head, hands, and a whole body, are not imaginary things, but things really existent. For, as a matter of fact, painters, even when they study with the greatest skill to represent sirens and satyrs by forms the most strange and extraordinary, cannot give them natures which are entirely new, but merely make a certain medley of the members of different animals; or if their imagination is extravagant enough to invent something so novel that nothing similar has ever before been seen, and that then their work represents a thing purely fictitious and absolutely false, it is certain all the same that the colours of which this is composed are necessarily real. And for the same reason, although these general things, to wit, [a body], eyes, a head, hands, and such like, may be imaginary, we are bound at the same time to confess that there are at least some other objects yet more simple and more universal, which are real and true; and of these just in the same way as with certain real colours, all these images of things which dwell in our thoughts, whether true and real or false and fantastic, are formed.

To such a class of things pertains corporeal nature in general, and its extension, the figure of extended things, their quantity or magnitude and number, as also the place in which they are, the time which measures their duration, and so on.

That is possibly why our reasoning is not unjust when we conclude from this that Physics, Astronomy, Medicine, and all other sciences which have as their end the consideration of composite things, are very dubious and uncertain; but with Arithmetic, Geometry, and other sciences of that kind which only treat of things that are very simple and very general, without taking great trouble to ascertain whether they are actually existent or not contain some measure of certainty and an element of the indubitable. For whether I am awake or asleep, two and three together always form five, and the square can never have more than four sides, and it does not seem possible that truths so clear and apparent can be suspected of any falsity [or uncertainty].

Nevertheless I have long had fixed in my mind the belief that an all-powerful God existed by whom I have been created such as I am. But how do I know that He has not brought it to pass that there is no earth, no heaven, no extended body, no magnitude, no place, and that nevertheless [I possess the perceptions of all these things and that] they seem to me to exist just exactly as I now see them? And, besides, as I sometimes imagine that others deceive themselves in the things which they think they know best, how do I know that I am not deceived every time that I add two and three, or count the sides of a square, or judge of things yet simpler, if anything simpler can be imagined? But possibly God has not desired that I should be thus deceived, for He is said to be supremely good. If, however, it is contrary to His goodness to have made me such that I constantly deceive myself, it would also appear to be contrary to His goodness to permit me to be sometimes deceived, and nevertheless I cannot doubt that He does permit this.

I shall then suppose, not that God who is supremely good and the fountain of truth, but some evil genius not less powerful than deceitful, has employed his whole energies in deceiving me; I shall consider that the heavens, the earth, colours, figures, sound, and all other external things are nought but the illusions and dreams of which this genius has availed himself in order to lay traps for my credulity; I shall consider myself as having no hands, no eyes, no flesh, no blood, nor any senses, yet falsely believing myself to possess all these things; I shall remain obstinately attached to this idea, and if by this means it is not in my power to arrive at the knowledge of any truth, I may at least do what is in my power [i.e. suspend my judgment], and with firm purpose avoid giving credence to any false thing, or being imposed upon by this arch deceiver, however powerful and deceptive he may be. . . .

MEDITATION II

The Meditation of yesterday filled my mind with so many doubts that it is no longer in my power to forget them. And yet I do not see in what manner I can resolve them; and, just as if I had all of a sudden fallen into very deep water, I am so disconcerted that I can neither make certain of setting my feet on the bottom, nor can I swim and so support myself on the surface. I shall nevertheless make an effort and follow anew the same path as that on which I yesterday entered, i.e. I shall proceed by setting aside all that in which the least doubt could be supposed to exist, just as if I had discovered that it was absolutely false; and I shall ever follow in this road until I have met with something which is certain, or at least, if I can do nothing else, until I have learned for certain that there is nothing in the world that is certain. Archimedes, in order that he might draw the terrestrial globe out of its place, and transport it elsewhere, demanded only that one point should be fixed and immoveable; in the same way I shall have the right to conceive high hopes if I am happy enough to discover one thing only which is certain and indubitable.

I suppose, then, that all the things that I see are false; I persuade myself that nothing has ever existed of all that my fallacious memory represents to me. I consider that I possess no senses; I imagine that body, figure, exten-sion, movement and place are but the fictions of my mind. What, then, can be esteemed as true? Perhaps nothing at all, unless that there is nothing in the world that is certain.

But how can I know there is not something different from those things that I have just considered, of which one cannot have the slightest doubt? Is there not some God, or some other being by whatever name we call it, who puts these reflections into my mind? That is not necessary, for is it not possible that I am capable of producing them myself? I myself, am I not at least something? But I have already denied that I had senses and body. Yet I hesitate, for what follows from that? Am I so dependent on body and senses that I cannot exist without these? But I was persuaded that there was nothing in all the world, that there was no heaven, no earth, that there were no minds, nor any bodies: was I not then likewise persuaded that I did not exist? Not at all; of a surety I myself did exist since I persuaded myself of something [or merely because I thought of something]. But there is some deceiver or other, very powerful and very cunning, who ever employs his ingenuity in deceiving me. Then without doubt I exist also if he deceives me, and let him deceive me as much as he will, he can never cause me to be nothing so long as I think that I am something. So that after having reflected well and carefully examined all things, we must come to the definite conclusion that this proposition: I am, I exist, is necessarily true each time that I pronounce it, or that I mentally conceive it.

But I do not yet know clearly enough what I am, I who am certain that I am; and hence I must be careful to see that I do not imprudently take some other object in place of myself, and thus that I do not go astray in respect of this knowledge that I hold to be the most certain and most evident of all that I have formerly learned. That is why I shall now consider anew what I believed myself to be before I embarked upon these last reflections; and of my former opinions I shall withdraw all that might even in a small degree be invalidated by the reasons which I have just brought forward, in order that there may be nothing at all left beyond what is absolutely certain and indubitable.

—RENÉ DESCARTES, *Meditations on First Philosophy*

II Rationalism and Empiricism: Two Responses to Cartesian Doubt

When Descartes summarized his proof for his own existence in Latin, he used the phrase **Cogito, ergo sum,** which means "I think, therefore I am." So his proof has come to be known in philosophical shorthand as the Cogito Argument. If you read the selection from the *Meditations* carefully, you will realize that "I think, therefore I am" is not exactly what Descartes says. Instead, he says something slightly but very significantly different, namely, "The proposition, I exist, is necessarily true each time I pronounce it." Pronouncing or asserting the proposition is crucial, because it is the asserting that guarantees its truth. The point is that if the proposition is being *asserted*, then someone must be doing the asserting, and if I am asserting it, then that someone must be me. Needless to say, I cannot use this proof to establish the existence of anyone else. Suppose, for example, that I try to prove my wife's existence by saying, "The proposition, She exists, is necessarily true each time I pronounce it." Well, that just won't work. The fact that I pronounce or assert that she exists in no way guarantees that she does. But it does guarantee that I exist! In fact, my asserting any proposition, true or false, about myself or about anything else, guarantees that *I* exist, because I am the subject, the asserter, the conscious thinker of the proposition. And—this is the key point—propositions or assertions or statements cannot simply hang in midair with no one asserting them. A proposition is an assertion, and therefore it must be asserted *by* someone.

Incidentally, I hope you realize that Descartes' Cogito Argument only proves his existence to him; it doesn't prove his existence to you or to me. "The proposition, Descartes exists, is necessarily true everytime I pronounce it" doesn't hold water at all. Descartes can use his new argument to prove his existence to himself, I can use his argument to prove my existence to myself, and each of you can use his argument to prove your own existence to yourself. But no one can use the argument to prove someone else's existence. This fact about the Cogito Argument has two important consequences for subsequent epistemology. First, it drives each philosopher into the position called **solipsism;** that is, the individual subject knows its own existence prior to, and better than, anything else, and perhaps knows the existence of nothing but itself. Second, it turns the attention of philosophers away from the *objects* of knowledge, the things that we know about, and toward the *subject* of knowledge, the mind that does the knowing. Later in this chapter, we shall see that this pair of implications of the Cogito Argument is used by Kant in his effort to find a way out of the skepticism and solipsism of the Cartesian position.

Descartes got himself, and us, into the skeptical solipsist box in the First Meditation by doubting everything that was not known with certainty. He proceeded, you will recall, by adopting a criterion of certainty so strict that in the end, nothing save the assertion of his own existence could meet its requirements. In surveying the multitude of his beliefs, furthermore, Descartes divided them into two major groups: those which he thought he knew on the basis of the evidence of his own senses and those which he thought he knew on the basis of reasoning with general concepts. In this way, two central problems are raised by the argument in the First Meditation. The first is the problem of *certainty*. What criterion of truth should we adopt as the standard against which to measure

Solipsism Literally, the belief that I am the only person in the universe. Somewhat more generally, solipsism is an extreme form of epistemological skepticism which refuses to acknowledge the existence of anything other than my own mind. Some philosophers have even argued that I cannot be sure of anything but my own mind *right now*, since my memories might also be mistaken.

our various knowledge claims? The second is the problem of the sources of knowledge. Insofar as we know anything, is our knowledge based upon the evidence of the senses, upon abstract reasoning, or upon some combination of the two? The philosophy of the 150 years following the publication of the *Meditations* was very largely a series of variations on these two themes.

Descartes himself offered preliminary answers to the questions of certainty and the sources of knowledge in the latter part of the Second Meditation. Before taking our leave of him, and moving on to survey the attempts of his successors to deal with the problems he raised, perhaps we ought to see what he had to say about them. On the problem of certainty, he offered two criteria, two tests of the certainty of an assertion. Here is what he says:

> ... I am certain that I am a thing which thinks; but do I not then likewise know what is requisite to render me certain of a truth? Certainly in this first knowledge there is nothing that assures me of its truth, excepting the clear and distinct perception of that which I state, which would not indeed suffice to assure me that what I say is true, if it could ever happen that a thing which I conceived so clearly and distinctly could be false; and accordingly it seems to me that already I can establish as a general rule that all things which I perceive very clearly and very distinctly are true.

Clearness and distinctness aren't much as a hedge against the far-reaching skepticism fostered by the method of doubt. How can I be sure that I really perceive a proposition clearly or distinctly? It is no good saying that it really, truly *seems* clear and distinct to me. After all, it really, truly seems to me that I am awake, but as Descartes himself pointed out, I might nonetheless be mistaken. Later on, after using the clearness and distinctness test to prove the existence of God, Descartes turns around and uses the goodness of God as a proof that clearness and distinctness are adequate criteria of certainty. A good God, he argues, would not deceive me! Well, that is about as obvious a case of arguing in a circle as you will find in the writings of great philosophers, and I think we can agree that having posed the problem of certainty, Descartes didn't really have a solution to it.

As for the sources of our knowledge, Descartes came down four-square on the side of reason rather than the senses. That is what you would expect from someone whose dream it was to create a mathematical physics. In place of observation and the collecting of data from sight, smell, hearing, and touch, Descartes wanted a universal system of science derived from logical and mathematical premises and proved by rigorous deduction. In order to persuade his readers of the primacy of reason in our acquiring of knowledge, Descartes uses what is called a "thought experiment." That is, he asks us to imagine with him a situation—in this case, that he is sitting near his fire with a piece of wax in his hand—and then he tries to get us to see, through an analysis of the situation, that our methods of reasoning or of acquiring knowledge must have a certain character. Philosophers frequently argue in this way when they are trying to establish some general proposition rather than to prove a particular fact. The thought experiment isn't supposed to be evidence, in the modern scientific sense. Rather, it is merely a device for exploring the logical or conceptual relationships between different ideas. Here is Descartes' thought experiment to show that our knowledge comes from understanding or reason or the mind, rather than through the senses.

Let us begin by considering the commonest matters, those which we believe to be the most distinctly comprehended, to wit, the bodies which we touch and see; not indeed bodies in general, for these general ideas are usually a little more confused, but let us consider one body in particular. Let us take, for example, this piece of wax: it has been taken quite freshly from the hive, and it has not yet lost the sweetness of the honey which it contains; it still retains somewhat of the odour of the flowers from which it has been culled; its colour, its figure, its size are apparent; it is hard, cold, easily handled, and if you strike it with the finger, it will emit a sound. Finally all the things which are requisite to cause us distinctly to recognize a body, are met with in it. But notice that while I speak and approach the fire what remained of the taste is exhaled, the smell evaporates, the colour alters, the figure is destroyed, the size increases, it becomes liquid, it heats, scarcely can one handle it, and when one strikes it, no sound is emitted. Does the same wax remain after this change? We must confess that it remains; none would judge otherwise. What then did I know so distinctly in this piece of wax? It could certainly be nothing of all that the senses brought to my notice, since all these things which fall under taste, smell, sight, touch, and hearing, are found to be changed, and yet the same wax remains.

Perhaps it was what I now think, viz. that this wax was not that sweetness of honey, nor that agreeable scent of flowers, nor that particular whiteness, nor that figure, nor that sound, but simply a body which a little while before appeared to me as perceptible under these forms, and which is now perceptible under others. But what, precisely, is it that I imagine when I form such conceptions? Let us attentively consider this, and, abstracting from all that does not belong to the wax, let us see what remains. Certainly nothing remains excepting a certain extended thing which is flexible and movable. But what is the meaning of flexible and movable? Is it not that I imagine that this piece of wax being round is capable of becoming square and of passing from a square to a triangular figure? No, certainly it is not that, since I imagine it admits of an infinitude of similar changes, and I nevertheless do not know how to compass the infinitude by my imagination, and consequently this conception which I have of the wax is not brought about by the faculty of imagination. What now is this extension? Is it not also unknown? For it becomes greater when the wax is melted, greater when it is boiled, and greater still when the heat increases, and I should not conceive [clearly] according to truth what wax is, if I did not think that even this piece that we are considering is capable of receiving more variations in extension than I have ever imagined. We must then grant that I could not even understand through the imagination what this piece of wax is, and that it is my mind alone which perceives it. I say this piece of wax in particular, for as to wax in general it is yet clearer. But what is this piece of wax which cannot be understood excepting by the [understanding or] mind? It is certainly the same that I see, touch, imagine, and finally it is the same which I have always believed it to be from the beginning. But what must particularly be observed is that its perception is neither an act of vision, nor of touch, nor of imagination, and has never been such although it may have appeared formerly to be so, but only an intuition of the mind, which may be imperfect and confused as it was formerly, or clear and distinct as it is at present according as my attention is more or less directed to the elements which are found in it, and of which it is composed.

—RENÉ DESCARTES, *Meditations on First Philosophy*

The debate over Descartes' problems soon resolved itself into a conflict between two more or less unified schools of thought, the continental rationalists and the British empiricists. (Since this makes it sound a bit like an international soccer match, let me explain that those are labels we put on the two groups today; they themselves did not go about wearing T-shirts saying "Continental Rationalist" or "British Empiricist.") The rationalists accepted Descartes' demand for certainty, agreed with his view that logic and mathematics were the model for all true knowledge, and sought to discover ways of establishing the principal propositions of science and metaphysics with as much certainty as the truths of the syllogism or geometry possessed. They sought proofs for the existence of God (using some that had been around for quite a while, such as the cosmological and ontological proofs that we have already examined); they offered demonstrations of the fundamental principles of the new physics; and they pursued Descartes' dream of a universal system of knowledge. Like Descartes, they downgraded the senses as a source of knowledge, and instead claimed that all valid knowledge claims must rest upon the operations of reason.

The empiricists also accepted Descartes' demand for certainty, but in progressively more sweeping attacks on the knowledge claims of the rationalists, they argued that nothing could meet that demand. David Hume, the most brilliant and thoroughgoing of the empiricists, produced devastating proofs that neither the theorems of science nor the beliefs of common sense could possibly qualify as knowledge when measured against Descartes' own standard of certainty.

The empiricists also challenged the rationalists' reliance upon reason as the sole source of knowledge. First John Locke, in his *Essay Concerning the Human Understanding,* and then Hume, in the *Treatise of Human Nature,* insisted that all the ideas in the human mind must ultimately be derived from the sights, sounds, smells, feels, and tastes of our sense organs. Reason, they argued, could do no more than rearrange and sort the materials provided to the mind by sensation. This subordination of reason to the senses was one of the most powerful weapons in the empiricists' assault on the systems of science and metaphysics erected by the rationalist philosophers.

If you have managed to follow our discussion of epistemology thus far, it should be obvious to you that there is much more to be discussed in the theory of knowledge than we can hope to touch on in the remainder of this chapter. Rather than mentioning everyone and everything without explaining anything, therefore, I shall limit myself to *three* areas. First, we shall take a brief look at Gottfried Leibniz's attempt to deal with the criteria of certainty, and his very important distinction between what he calls truths of reasoning and truths of fact. Then, we shall examine David Hume's attempt to reduce all the contents of the mind to data of the senses, and his analysis of the criterion of certainty, so that we can understand the full force of his skeptical attack on the claims of science and common sense. And, finally, I will try to explain how Immanuel Kant sought to overcome the division between the rationalists and the empiricists by compromising their dispute over the sources of knowledge and the criteria of certainty. If you can get all that under your belt, then you will have had quite enough philosophy for one chapter!

III *Leibniz and Rationalism*

Descartes' tests of certainty were clearness and distinctness. These essentially psychological criteria tell us very little about the structure of knowledge, about the kinds of knowledge claims that can meet the test of certainty and the kinds that cannot. After all, any belief might, upon inspection, turn out to be conceived clearly and distinctly, or at least it might seem to be. I think I clearly and distinctly apprehend that two things added to two things make a total of four things; but I also think I clearly and distinctly apprehend that I am seated now at a desk in my office, with a typewriter in front of me and a chair under me.

In place of Descartes' psychological tests, Leibniz offered logical criteria of truth and certainty. All truths, he proposed, could be divided into two sorts. The first are truths that can be known merely by application of a fundamental principle of logic called the **law of contradiction.** When we state some truth, we do so by making an assertion. "Two plus two equals four" is an assertion; "Washington, D.C., is the capital of the United States," is an assertion; "$E = mc^2$" is an assertion. Any declarative statement in its ordinary usage makes an assertion. If I have one assertion, I can make another, opposite assertion simply by denying the first. So from "Two plus two equals four" I can make "It is not the case that two plus two equals four." From "Washington, D.C., is the capital of the United States" I can make "It is not the case that Washington, D.C., is the capital of the United States." The denial of an assertion is called its *negation,* and since "It is not the case that" is a little clumsy to keep repeating, philosophers and logicians shorten it to "not." The negation of "Two plus two equals four" would thus be "Not two plus two equals four," and so on.

Law of Contradiction/Law of the Excluded Middle   The two basic laws of formal logic. *The Law of Contradiction* states that a statement and its contradictory cannot both be true. For example, the statement "Fire is hot." may be true, and it may be false. Its contradictory, "It isn't the case that fire is hot." may be true, and it may be false. But it cannot be that *both* the statement *and* its contradictory are true. *The Law of the Excluded Middle* says that for any statement, *either* it is true *or* its contradictory is true. Thus, either fire is hot, or it is not the case that fire is hot.

If you think about it for a moment, you will see that an assertion and its negation cannot both be true. Maybe Washington is our capital—maybe it isn't—but there is just no way that it can both be and not be our capital. Logicians express this in very general form by saying that for any assertion, it cannot be the case that both the assertion and its negation are true. Because two assertions are said to "contradict" one another if they cannot both be true, this general principle about assertions and their negations is called the law of contradiction. There is another law of logic which usually goes along with the law of contradiction, according to which for any assertion, either it is true or else its negation is true. There is no third possibility, no middle ground. This law is called **the law of the excluded middle.** So logic teaches us that no matter what assertion we are thinking about, either it is true or its negation is true, but not both.

According to Leibniz, truths of reasoning are those assertions which we can know to be true merely by using the law of contradiction (and the law of the excluded middle, although he doesn't mention it). For example, suppose a fast-talking door-to-door salesman tries to push a fifteen-volume encyclopedia on you. "This encyclopedia is absolutely free," he says. "You only pay ten dollars per volume." Now you don't have to know anything about encyclopedias to be certain that he isn't telling you the truth. All you have to do is whip out your trusty law of contradiction and perform the following process of reasoning:

Number one, you say this encyclopedia is absolutely free.

Number two, you say I must pay ten dollars per volume for it.

But "free" means "I don't have to pay."

So you are saying that I don't have to pay, and I do have to pay.

Or, as we logicians put it, I do have to pay and not I do have to pay.

And that violates the law of contradiction, so it must be false. What is more, with a quick application of the law of the excluded middle, I can draw the absolutely certain conclusion that

Either I have to pay or I do not have to pay, so stop the fast talk and tell me which it is.

Truths of reasoning are nice, because we can know them to be certain merely by application of these two simple laws, but they leave a good

Valid Arguments

1. *Major Premise*   All dogs are mammals.
   Minor Premise   All poodles are dogs.
   CONCLUSION   All poodles are mammals.

2. *Major Premise*   Some band members are freshmen.
   Minor Premise   No freshmen are frat members.
   CONCLUSION   Some band members are not frat members.

Invalid Arguments

1. *Major Premise*   Some dogs are affectionate.
   Minor Premise   Some affectionate animals are cats.
   CONCLUSION   Some dogs are cats.

2. *Major Premise*   Some preserves are not marmalade.
   Minor Premise   All marmalade is made from oranges.
   CONCLUSION   Some preserves are made from oranges.

The first two arguments are "valid"—that means that the conclusion follows from the premises. Can you figure out *why* they are valid? The second two arguments are not valid. The conclusion does not follow from the premises (even though, in the fourth argument, the conclusion happens to be true). How can we tell whether an argument is valid or invalid?

deal to be desired. Thus, my bit of reasoning doesn't tell me whether I have to pay. It just tells me that either I have to or I don't, but not both. Truths that cannot be certified by appeal to the laws of logic are called **truths of fact** by Leibniz. They include most of what we ordinarily call *knowledge*, and to establish their truth, we must appeal to a quite different principle, which Leibniz labeled the **principle of sufficient reason.** Here is the passage from his short summary work, *The Monadology,* in which he defined and distinguished the two sorts of truths.

Our reasoning is based upon two great principles: first, that of Contradiction, by means of which we decide that to be false which involves contradiction and that to be true which contradicts or is opposed to the false.

And second, the principle of Sufficient Reason, in virtue of which we believe that no fact can be real or existing and no statement true unless it has a sufficient reason why it should be thus and not otherwise. Most frequently, however, these reasons cannot be known by us.

There are also two kinds of Truths: those of Reasoning and those of Fact. The Truths of Reasoning are necessary, and their opposite is impossible. Those of Fact, however, are contingent, and their opposite is possible. When a truth is necessary, the reason can be found by analysis in resolving it into simpler ideas and into simpler truths until we reach those which are primary. . . .

There are finally simple ideas of which no definition can be given. There are also the Axioms and Postulates or, in a word, the primary principles which cannot be proved and, indeed, have no need of proof. These are identical propositions whose opposites involve express contradictions.

But there must also be a sufficient reason for contingent truths or truths of fact; that is to say, for the sequence of the things which extend throughout the universe of created beings, where the analysis into more particular reasons can be continued into greater detail without limit because of the immense variety of the things in nature and because of the infinite division of bodies. There is an infinity of figures and of movements, present and past, which enter into the efficient cause of my present writing, and in its final cause there are an infinity of slight tendencies and dispositions of my soul, present and past.

And as all this detail again involves other and more detailed contingencies, each of which again has need of a similar analysis in order to find its explanation, no real advance has been made. Therefore, the sufficient or ultimate reason must needs be outside of the sequence or series of these details of contingencies, however infinite they may be.

It is thus that the ultimate reason for things must be a necessary substance, in which the detail of the changes shall be present merely potentially, as in the fountainhead, and this substance we call God.

—GOTTRIED LEIBNIZ, *The Monadology*

As you can see, Leibniz thought that when it came to truths of fact, such as the laws of physics or the facts of history, we could only certify them by an indirect appeal to God. The skeptical opponents of the rationalists had very little faith in the proofs for the existence of God, so you can imagine that they were not much impressed by this sort of justification for scientific theories. (Take a look back at Chapter Six for Hume's objections to some of those proofs.)

IV Hume and Empiricism

The first major assault on the continental rationalists was launched by the Englishman John Locke, whose theory of the social contract you have already encountered. Locke hit upon a simple but very powerful strategy for attacking the claims by Descartes and others that reason alone could provide us with knowledge. Instead of examining our knowledge claims directly, Locke suggested, let us instead ask from what source we derive the ideas which we use in stating these knowledge claims. Scientists and metaphysicians had been accustomed to express their theories by statements using terms like "matter," "space," "time," "substance," "cause," "necessary," "possible," "object," and "self." In addition, of course, they used more familiar terms like "red," "hard," "round," and "sweet." If our knowledge claims make any sense at all, Locke argued, then these words must correspond to ideas in our minds. Otherwise, we will simply seem to be saying something, but really we won't be asserting anything at all. (This is what humorists do when they write nonsense verse. Lewis Carroll, the author of *Alice in Wonderland*, wrote a poem that begins, "Twas brillig, and the slithy toves did gyre and gimble in the wabe." That sounds as though it ought to mean something, but it doesn't, because "words" like "brillig" and "toves" don't correspond to any ideas in our minds.)

According to Locke, the mind is a blank when we are born. He compares it to a piece of white paper on which experience writes. Here, from his *Essay Concerning the Human Understanding* (Book II, Chapter 1), is his statement of this famous doctrine:

> Let us then suppose the mind to be, as we say, white paper, void of all characters, without any ideas:—How comes it to be furnished? Whence comes it by that wide store which the busy and boundless fancy of man has painted on it with almost endless variety? Whence has it all the *materials* of reason and knowledge? To this I answer, in one word, EXPERIENCE. In that all our knowledge is founded; and from it ultimately derives itself.

That doesn't sound like such a brilliant philosophical strategy when you first hear it. Indeed, it sounds positively obvious. But in the hands of Locke, of George Berkeley, and especially of David Hume, it turned

Tabula Rasa Literally, blank tablet. The term was used by John Locke to summarize his claim that the mind comes into life blank, or empty, and is written on by experience as though it were a clay or wax tablet waiting to be marked by a writing stylus. Locke was arguing against the widely held view that the mind comes to experience with ideas which are built into it (or "hard-wired," as computer types like to say).

out to be a crusher. To see why this is so, think for a moment about all the assertions that philosophers and theologians have made over the ages about God. Every one of those assertions uses the idea of God somehow. For example, one assertion is that God exists; a second is that God is omnipotent; a third is that God has promised us eternal life if only we will obey His laws; and so forth. If we follow Locke's suggestion, instead of asking directly what evidence there is for these assertions, we will instead ask, Is there an *idea* of God in our minds corresponding to the word "God" which is used in each of the assertions? And following Locke's theory of the blank white paper, we will ask whether the idea of God has come to us through our eyes, our ears, our fingertips, our noses, or our other sense organs. As soon as you put the question that way, it is obvious that we couldn't have derived the idea of God from any sensory sources. God is supposed to be infinite, but we can only see, hear, feel, and taste finite things. God is supposed to be eternal, but we cannot see or hear or feel something that exists outside time, or even something that exists in time forever and ever. God is supposed to be omnipotent, but the most our senses could ever show us is something very powerful, not something infinitely powerful. So it would seem to follow simply and directly from Locke's strategy that *we do not really have an idea of God at all!* We have the word "God," and we make up what we think are meaningful assertions using it, but all that talk about God turns out to have no more meaning than Lewis Carroll's poem about slithy toves. (Incidentally, Locke himself did not draw his antireligious conclusion from his theory of ideas, and he would have been horrified by it.)

Since the last paragraph may have whipped by a bit fast, let's stop a moment and be sure that we understand what the argument is really saying. Lewis Carroll's poem isn't *false*; it is *meaningless*, because it uses "words" which don't correspond to ideas in our minds, and hence have no meaning. An assertion has to mean something before we can ask whether it is true or false. Philosophical books are full of arguments about the truth or falsehood of various theological, metaphysical, and scientific theories. But Locke's attack cuts these arguments off at the knees. Before two philosophers can even begin to argue about the existence of God, they must show that their words have meaning, and according to Locke, that means showing that the words correspond to ideas in our minds which have been derived from the senses. So by his strategy of looking to the sources of our ideas, together with his doctrine of the mind as a blank sheet of paper written on by experience, Locke shifted the whole debate into a new channel.

GEORGE BERKELEY (1685–1753) was an Irish philosopher and cleric who is remembered as the defender of a philosophical position known as "idealism." Berkeley's most important philosophical works, including his *Treatise Concerning the Principles of Human Knowledge* and *Three Dialogues Between Hylas and Philonus*, were all written before his thirtieth birthday. Berkeley defended the view that the only things that could be known to exist are human minds, the ideas in these minds, and God. This doctrine is opposed to the view, defended by Hobbes and others, that physical bodies are the only things that exist ("materialism").

Berkeley spent three years in the New World, seeking to found a college in the Bermudas. Though his plans were never carried out, he did leave his philosophical library to the then recently founded Yale College in New Haven, Connecticut.

Locke's weapon, incidentally, is a double-edged sword. If the theory proves that we do not even have a coherent idea of God, then one possible conclusion is that all our talk about God is nonsense, and all our theories of religion meaningless. But another possible conclusion is that since his theory implies such a ridiculous notion, it must itself be false! It comes down to deciding which is harder to believe. If I do have an idea of God, then it cannot have come through my senses, so I am going to have to explain how the mind can acquire ideas which it does not derive from sense experience; on the other hand, if all my ideas are derived from sense experience, then I cannot have an idea of God, so I am going to have to explain why so many apparently reasonable people firmly believe that they have such an idea, and why people who talk about God think they are making sense and not nonsense.

The empiricist who carried Locke's strategy to its logical conclusion was David Hume. As you will recall from Chapter One, Hume conceived the plan, when still a very young man, of writing a full-scale theory of the human mind along the lines of Isaac Newton's enormously successful theory of the physical universe. In the very opening pages of the *Treatise of Human Nature,* Hume adopts Locke's strategy and stakes out his own version of the "white paper" principle. In the following selection, re-member that Hume uses the word "perception" to mean any content of the mind. He then divides perceptions into those which come directly from our senses and those which we form from our impressions by copy-ing, rearranging, and otherwise altering them.

All the perceptions of the human mind resolve themselves into two distinct kinds, which I shall call IMPRESSIONS and IDEAS. The difference betwixt these consists in the degrees of force and liveliness with which they strike upon the mind, and make their way into our thought or consciousness. Those perceptions, which enter with most force and violence, we may name *impressions*; and under this name I comprehend all our sensations, passions and emotions, as they make their first appearance in the soul. By *ideas* I mean the faint images of these in thinking and reasoning; such as, for in-stance, are all the perceptions excited by the present discourse, excepting only, those which arise from the sight and touch, and excepting the immedi-ate pleasure or uneasiness it may occasion. I believe it will not be very neces-sary to employ many words in explaining this distinction. Every one of him-self will readily perceive the difference betwixt feeling and thinking. The common degrees of these are easily distinguished; tho' it is not impossible but in particular instances they may very nearly approach to each other. Thus in sleep, and in fever, in madness, or in any very violent emotions of soul, our ideas may approach to our impressions: As on the other hand it sometimes happens, that our impressions are so faint and low, that we can-not distinguish them from our ideas. But notwithstanding this near resem-blance in a few instances, they are in general so very different, that no-one can make a scruple to rank them under distinct heads, and assign to each a peculiar name to mark the difference.

There is another division of our perceptions, which it will be convenient to observe, and which extends itself both to our impressions and ideas. This division is into SIMPLE and COMPLEX. Simple perceptions or impressions and ideas are such as admit of no distinction nor separation. The complex are the contrary to these, and may be distinguished into parts. Tho' a partic-ular colour, taste, and smell are qualities all united together in this apple, 'tis easy to perceive they are not the same, but are at least distinguishable from each other.

Having by these divisions given an order and arrangement to our ob-jects, we may now apply ourselves to consider with the more accuracy their qualities and relations. The first circumstance, that strikes my eye, is the great resemblance betwixt our impressions and ideas in every other particu-lar, except their degree of force and vivacity. The one seem to be in a man-ner the reflexion of the other; so that all the perceptions of the mind are double, and appear both as impressions and ideas. When I shut my eyes and think of my chamber, the ideas I form are exact representations of the impressions I felt; nor is there any circumstance of the one, which is not to be found in the other. In running over my other perceptions, I find still the same resemblance and representation. Ideas and impressions appear always to correspond to each other. This circumstance seems to me remarkable, and engages my attention for a moment.

Upon a more accurate survey I find I have been carried away too far by the first appearance, and that I must make use of the distinction of perceptions into *simple and complex*, to limit this general decision, *that all our ideas and impressions are resembling.* I observe, that many of our complex ideas never had impressions, that corresponded to them, and that many of our complex impressions never are exactly copied in ideas. I can imagine to myself such a city as the *New Jerusalem*, whose pavement is gold and walls are rubies, tho' I never saw any such. I have seen *Paris*; but shall I affirm I can form such an idea of that city, as will perfectly represent all its streets and houses in their real and just proportions?

I perceive, therefore, that tho' there is in general a great resemblance betwixt our *complex* impressions and ideas, yet the rule is not universally true, that they are exact copies of each other. We may next consider how the case stands with our *simple* perceptions. After the most accurate examination, of which I am capable, I venture to affirm, that the rule here holds without any exception, and that every simple idea has a simple impression, which resembles it; and every simple impression a correspondent idea. That idea of red, which we form in the dark, and that impression, which strikes our eyes in sun-shine, differ only in degree, not in nature. That the case is the same with all our simple impressions and ideas, 'tis impossible to prove by a particular enumeration of them. Every one may satisfy himself in this point by running over as many as he pleases. But if any one should deny this universal resemblance, I know no way of convincing him, but by desiring him to shew a simple impression that has not a correspondent idea, or a simple idea, that has not a correspondent impression. If he does not answer this challenge, as 'tis certain he cannot, we may from his silence and our own observation establish our conclusion.

Thus we find, that all simple ideas and impressions resemble each other; and as the complex are formed from them, we may affirm in general, that these two species of perception are exactly correspondent. Having discover'd this relation, which requires no farther examination, I am curious to find some other of their qualities. Let us consider how they stand with regard to their existence, and which of the impressions and ideas are causes, and which effects.

The *full* examination of this question is the subject of the present treatise; and therefore we shall here content ourselves with establishing one general proposition. *That all our simple ideas in their first appearance are deriv'd from simple impressions, which are correspondent to them, and which they exactly represent.*

—DAVID HUME, *A Treatise of Human Nature*

Hume's style is not nearly as technical or forbidding as that of Aristotle, Descartes, Leibniz, or Kant, but you mustn't be misled into supposing that his arguments are therefore less powerful. The few simple principles which he lays down in the opening pages of the *Treatise* turn out to be more than enough to destroy some of the most impressive systems built up by his philosophical predecessors. There are three key points to notice in the passage you have just read. The first, of course, is Hume's adoption of the "white paper" theory. The second is what is sometimes called the **copy theory of ideas.** According to Hume, all our ideas are either straight copies of sense impressions or combinations and rearrangements of copies of sense impressions. When we are confronted with some metaphysical assertion, therefore, we need not ask immediately whether it is true or false. Instead, we may simply examine the words in which it is expressed and ask whether they correspond to ideas in our minds. If we do have such ideas, then either they will be copies of sense impressions or they will be constructed out of copies of sense impressions by combinations and rearrangements. We have already seen what a blow this doctrine can be to the claim that we have an idea of God. The third important point is that Hume has an "atomic" theory of the contents of the mind. That is to say, he conceives of the mind as containing little indivisible "atomic" bits of sensation, plus indivisible copies of those bits of sensation, plus what we might call "molecular" combinations of atomic sensations. But unlike chemical molecules, the combinations of atomic sensations don't have any properties that the atomic components lack.

Since all the contents of the mind can be divided into atomic units, it follows that we can always distinguish one unit from another. In addition, Hume says, the mind has the power to "separate" two units of sensation from one another by imagining one away while keeping the other in mind. For example, when I look at a horse, I can distinguish my visual perception of its head from my visual perception of its body. Therefore, I can at least *imagine* the head without the body, or the body without the head. That power of "separating" impressions in imagination, and then recombining the parts in new ways, is of course what we all do when we imagine giants, or unicorns, or little green men, or anything

The mind combines the head and torso of a man (in this case, the French king Louis XIV) with the body of a horse to produce a centaur, which it has never seen. (Left and below: The Bettmann Archive)

else we have not actually seen. Hume summarizes this third point, a bit later on in the *Treatise*, in two principles:

1. Whatever objects are different are distinguishable.
2. Whatever objects are distinguishable are separable by thought and imagination.

By means of these two principles, which follow directly from his copy theory of ideas and his atomic theory of the contents of the mind, Hume constructs an argument which at one blow wipes out all metaphysics, all natural science, and just about all our commonsense beliefs about the world. Here is the entire argument, as it appears in the *Treatise*.

> 'Tis a general maxim in philosophy that *whatever begins to exist, must have a cause of existence*. This is commonly taken for granted in all reasonings, without any proof given or demanded. 'Tis suppos'd to be founded on intu-ition, and to be one of those maxims, which tho' they may be deny'd with the lips, 'tis impossible for men in their hearts really to doubt of. But if we examine this maxim by the idea of knòwledge above-explain'd, we shall discover in it no mark of any such intuitive certainty; but on the contrary shall find, that 'tis of a nature quite foreign to that species of conviction.
>
> All certainty arises from the comparison of ideas, and from the discovery of such relations as are unalterable, so long as the ideas continue the same. These relations are *resemblance, proportions in quantity and number, degrees of any quality, and contrariety*; none of which are imply'd in this proposition. *Whatever has a beginning has also a cause of existence*. That proposition therefore is not intuitively certain. At least any one, who wou'd assert it to be intuitively certain, must deny these to be the only infallible relations, and must find some other relation of that kind to be imply'd in it; which it will then be time enough to examine.
>
> But here is an argument, which proves at once, that the foregoing prop-osition is neither intuitively nor demonstrably certain. We can never demon-strate the necessity of a cause to every new existence, or new modification of existence, without shewing at the same time the impossibility there is, that any thing can ever begin to exist without some productive principle; and where the latter proposition cannot be prov'd, we must despair of ever being able to prove the former. Now that the latter proposition is utterly incapable of a demonstrative proof, we may satisfy ourselves by considering, that as all distinct ideas are separable from each other, and as the ideas of cause and effect are evidently distinct, 'twill be easy for us to conceive any object to be nonexistent this moment, and existent the next, without con-joining to it the distinct idea of a cause or productive principle. The separa-tion, therefore, of the idea of a cause from that of a beginning of existence, is plainly possible for the imagination; and consequently the actual separa-

tion of these objects is so far possible, that it implies no contradiction nor absurdity; and is therefore incapable of being refuted by any reasoning from mere ideas; without which 'tis impossible to demonstrate the necessity of a cause.

Accordingly we shall find upon examination, that every demonstration, which has been produc'd for the necessity of cause, is fallacious and sophistical. All the points of time and place, say some philosophers, in which we can suppose any object to begin to exist, are in themselves equal; and unless there be some cause, which is peculiar to one time and to one place, and which by that means determines and fixes the existence, it must remain in eternal suspence; and the object can never begin to be, for want of something to fix its beginning. But I ask; Is there any more difficulty in supposing the time and place to be fix'd without a cause, than to suppose the existence to be determin'd in that manner? The first question that occurs on this subject is always, *whether* the object shall exist or not: The next, *when* and *where* it shall begin to exist. If the removal of a cause be intuitively absurd in the one case, it must be so in the other: And if that absurdity be not clear without a proof in the one case, it will equally require one on the other. The absurdity, then, of the one supposition can never be a proof of that of the other; since they are both upon the same footing, and must stand or fall by the same reasoning.

The second argument, which I find us'd on this head, labours under an equal difficulty. Every thing, 'tis said, must have a cause; for if any thing wanted a cause, *it* wou'd produce *itself*; that is, exist before it existed; which is impossible. But this reasoning is plainly unconclusive; because it supposes, that in our denial of a cause we still grant what we expressly deny, *viz.* that there must be a cause; which therefore is taken to be the object itself; and *that*, no doubt, is an evident contradiction. But to say that any thing is produc'd, or to express myself more properly, comes into existence, without a cause, is not to affirm, that 'tis itself its own cause; but on the contrary in excluding all external causes, excludes *a fortiori* the thing itself which is created. An object, that exists absolutely without any cause, certainly is not its own cause; and when you assert, that the one follows from the other, you suppose the very point in question, and take it for granted, that 'tis utterly impossible any thing can ever begin to exist without a cause, but that upon the exclusion of one productive principle, we must still have recourse to another.

'Tis exactly the same case with the third argument, which has been employ'd to demonstrate the necessity of a cause. Whatever is produc'd without any cause, is produc'd by *nothing*; or in other words, has nothing for its cause. But nothing can never be a cause, no more than it can be something, or equal to two right angles. By the same intuition, that we perceive nothing not to be equal to two right angles, or not to be something, we perceive, that it can never be a cause; and consequently must perceive, that every object has a real cause of its existence.

I believe it will not be necessary to employ many words in shewing the weakness of this argument, after what I have said of the foregoing. They are all of them founded on the same fallacy, and are deriv'd from the same turn of thought. 'Tis sufficient only to observe, that when we exclude all causes we really do exclude them, and neither suppose nothing nor the object itself to be the causes of the existence; and consequently can draw no argument from the absurdity of these suppositions to prove the absurdity of that exclusion. If every thing must have a cause, it follows, that upon the exclusion of other causes we must accept of the object itself or of nothing as causes. But 'tis the very point in question, whether every thing must have a cause or not; and therefore, according to all just reasoning, it ought never to be taken for granted.

They are still more frivolous, who say, that every effect must have a cause, because 'tis imply'd in the very idea of effect. Every effect necessarily pre-supposes a cause; effect being a relative term, of which cause is the correlative. But this does not prove, that every being must be preceded by a cause; no more than it follows, because every husband must have a wife, and therefore every man must be marry'd. The true state of the question is, whether every object, which begins to exist, must owe its existence to a cause; and this I assert neither to be intuitively nor demonstratively certain, and hope to have prov'd it sufficiently by the foregoing arguments.

—DAVID HUME, *A Treatise of Human Nature*

It doesn't take much imagination to see how deeply Hume's argument cuts. We can hardly get out of bed in the morning without implicitly relying on a host of causal beliefs. I believe that when I swing my legs over the side of the bed, they will naturally fall down toward the floor. (As astronauts have discovered, that is a belief which turns out to be false once we get away from the gravitational pull of the earth.) I believe that when I take a drink of water, it will cause my thirst to be abated. I believe that when I push the light switch, it will cause the lights to go on. The simplest propositions of physics, chemistry and biology either are, or else depend upon, causal judgments. Needless to say, the proofs for the existence of God are invalid if we cannot infer causes from effects or effects from causes.

Hume himself did not believe that it was psychologically possible for human beings to suspend their belief in causal judgments for very long. Although he was absolutely convinced that no adequate justification could ever be found for our beliefs, he also thought that we were naturally so constituted that we believed anyway. In a much quoted passage from the end of the First Book of the *Treatise*, Hume tells how he disperses the clouds of gloom and doubt that settle over him when he follows out the logical conclusions of his powerful arguments.

> Most fortunately it happens, that since reason is incapable of dispelling these clouds, nature herself suffices to that purpose, and cures me of this philosophical melancholy and delirium, either by relaxing this bent of mind, or by some avocation, and lively impression of my senses, which obliterate all these chimeras. I dine, I play a game of back-gammon, I converse, and am merry with my friends; and when after three or four hours' amusement, I wou'd return to these speculations, they appear so cold, and strain'd, and ridiculous, that I cannot find in my heart to enter into them any farther.

V Kant's Resolution of the Rationalism/Empiricism Debate

Immanuel Kant was not content to flee from the skepticism into which Hume had plunged philosophy by his wholesale destruction of causal beliefs. If Hume's arguments were accepted, then I could not even be sure that anything at all existed outside my own mind. Descartes' fanciful notion that his whole life was a mere dream might be true, as far as philosophers could prove. It was, Kant said, a "scandal to philosophy and to human reason in general that the existence of things outside us . . . must be accepted merely on *faith*, and that if anyone thinks good to doubt their existence, we are unable to counter his doubts by any satisfactory proof." So Kant decided to return to Descartes' starting point, the Cogito, or "I think." He wanted to see whether he could derive directly from that fundamental premise an argument that would avoid the skepticism and solipsism that seemed to be implied by the powerful attacks of the British empiricists.

As we have seen, Descartes' philosophical investigations raised two basic problems: the problem of certainty and the problem of the sources of knowledge. But Kant realized that the Cogito argument raised an even more fundamental issue which both the rationalists and the empiricists had tended to ignore. The conclusion of Descartes' argument, you will recall, was the following:

> This proposition: I am, I exist, is necessarily true each time that I pronounce it, or that I mentally conceive it.

On the basis of this conclusion, Descartes went on to argue that he was essentially a "thing that thinks." Descartes' successors concentrated on the criteria to be used in judging the truth of what the mind thinks, and they concentrated on the sources of the ideas with which the mind thinks, but they paid much less attention to the central fact that the mind, in thinking, is *conscious*. Trees are not conscious, rocks are not conscious, even calculating machines (which Descartes and the others did not know about) are not conscious, but the mind is. It occurred to Kant that perhaps a proof of our scientific beliefs in the existence of physical objects and in causal connections between them could be based on the mere fact of consciousness. Such a proof would certainly be very hard to find, for the mere fact of consciousness isn't much to go on in proving anything as large-scale as the truth of science. But if he could find such a proof, Kant would have an answer to anyone who wanted to challenge the claims of reason, even someone prepared to go as far in the direction of skepticism as David Hume.

Descartes had simply accepted consciousness as an indisputable, directly observable, inexplicable fact. I know that I am conscious because I can think about my own thoughts and become aware of myself thinking about them. This self-awareness or self-consciousness is clearly central to the mind's operation; what is more, it is directly self-confirming. Even an evil demon could not trick me into thinking I was conscious when I wasn't, because if I thought anything at all, it would have to be the case that I was conscious. So instead of the premise "I think" as the starting point of all philosophy, Kant instead adopted the slightly different premise "I am conscious." But introspection reveals, and logical analysis confirms, that my consciousness has a certain basic structure or characteristic: it is unified into a *single* consciousness. All the thoughts, impressions, beliefs, expectations, hopes, and doubts that I have are *my* thoughts, etc. They occur in *my* consciousness, and that consciousness is a single consciousness, or—to put it somewhat differently—the consciousness of a single subject, a single center of thought. Kant described this fundamental fact as the **unity of consciousness.** In order to show the connection between what he was doing and what Descartes had done, Kant invoked Descartes' language when he stated his own basic premise. In the central section of the *Critique of Pure Reason*, as he started the argument which he hoped would refute the skeptics and reinstate science as objectively justified, Kant stated his premise in the following way:

It must be possible for the "I think" to accompany all my representations.

Unity of Consciousness   A phrase invented by Immanuel Kant to describe the fact that the thoughts and perceptions of any given mind are bound together in a unity by being all contained in one consciousness. Kant claimed that this fact—the *unity* of individual consciousness—could only be explained by postulating a fundamental mental activity of holding together, or "synthesizing," those thoughts and perceptions.

This was his way of saying that all the contents of my consciousness are bound up in a unity of consciousness.

Kant argued that the *unity* of my thoughts and perceptions could not be a given fact of my experience. The individual thoughts and impressions might just be brute facts of consciousness, but their unity could only be explained by some unifying act of the mind itself. Kant claimed that when my mind unifies its various thoughts and perceptions, when it holds them all together in a single consciousness and thinks of them all as *my* thoughts, it follows a certain set of *rules*. These rules are rules for holding thoughts together in the mind, and he gave them the technical name "categories." The only way in which I can think all of my thoughts as unified in a single consciousness is by following the rules or categories for holding thoughts together. Kant claimed that the categories were innate in the human mind; we are all born with them, he said, and we cannot change them.

What are these rules, or categories? Well, it turns out—if Kant is right—that they are just exactly those crucial concepts which play so large a role in the metaphysics, mathematics, and physics that Hume and the skeptics were attacking. Among the categories are such central concepts as substance, cause and effect, unity, plurality, possibility, necessity, and reality.

It may not look as though Kant moved very far toward an answer to Hume, but stop and reflect for a moment on what he is saying. Descartes claimed I could be conscious of my own thoughts, and even conscious of their unity *as* my thoughts, without knowing whether they were really accurate or truthful thoughts about substances, causation, and a world independent of my mind. In other words, Descartes admitted that my subjective knowledge of my own thoughts was better established than any claims I might make about a world of objects. Locke, Hume, and other critics of the rationalists accepted Descartes' starting point—they agreed that I could know the contents of my own mind—but they threw doubt on all Descartes' attempts to move from that purely subjective knowledge to anything further.

Kant turned the whole argument around by denying Descartes' first premise. I cannot know the contents of my own mind unless I first unify them into a single consciousness, he said. And that means that I must first have applied the categories to them, for those categories are the rules for unifying contents of consciousness. Now the categories are precisely the concepts (substance, cause, etc.) which we use in making objective judgments about the world outside the mind. So Kant concluded that I could not even be subjectively conscious, à la Descartes, unless I had first put my thoughts and perceptions together in ways that would allow me to make objective judgments about them. Descartes' nightmare of life as an endless dream is an epistemological impossibility, Kant argued.

But Kant paid a price for his solution to the problem of skepticism. It might very well be that my objective concepts were guaranteed to apply to my experiences—it might, in short, be a sure thing that I would encounter substances related to one another causally—but such knowledge as I obtained through the use of the categories would not and could not be knowledge of the world as it really is in itself. Rather, my knowledge must be merely of a world of things as they appear to me.

We have already encountered the distinction between appearance and reality in the philosophy of Plato, you will recall. But Plato claimed that we could, by the use of our reason, gain knowledge of true reality. Kant, by contrast, insists that we can only obtain knowledge of appearance, even though such knowledge is real knowledge, and not—as the skeptics claimed—error or unfounded belief.

The dispute between the rationalists and the empiricists was changed by Kant's new theory of the unity of consciousness. Even though many subsequent philosophers rejected his distinction between appearance and reality, they continued to ponder the problem of the nature of consciousness, a problem that Descartes had discovered and that Kant had substantially deepened by his arguments.

The Main Points in Chapter Seven

1. In the seventeenth century, the great French mathematician, scientist, and philosopher, René Descartes changed the course of philoso-

phy by raising a fundamental question about what we can know, and how we know it. Descartes' *method of doubt* called into question every belief that could not be demonstrated with absolute certainty. Descartes was able to show that most of the mathematical, scientific, religious, and everyday beliefs we have really cannot stand up to that kind of examination.

2. Descartes' systematic doubt brought to center stage a question that philosophers had discussed for a very long time: How do we learn about the nature of things, through our physical senses or by reasoning? Philosophers who think sensation is the source of knowledge are called *empiricists*. Philosophers who think reason is the source of knowledge are called *rationalists*. The seventeenth and eighteenth centuries saw a complicated debate between empiricists and rationalists, in which physics, mathematics, theology, and logic were called into play.

3. Descartes himself was a rationalist, as was the German Leibniz. The most original empiricists were a number of British philosophers, including John Locke, George Berkeley, and David Hume. These British Empiricists pushed Descartes' sceptical arguments farther than he had himself, and thereby called into question the validity of the proofs for the existence of God, the basic propositions of physics, and even the theorems of mathematics.

4. The most radical of the empiricists was David Hume, whose *Treatise of Human Nature*, published in 1739 to 1740, raised sceptical doubts about even the unity and existence of the self.

5. By the middle of the eighteenth century, the empiricists and rationalists had fought one another to a draw, philosophically speaking. At this point, the greatest philosopher since Plato and Aristotle, Immanuel Kant, came forward to try to resolve the conflict and get philosophy out of the dead end it was in. Kant's great work, the *Critique of Pure Reason*, published in 1781, transformed philosophy by changing our understanding of knowledge, consciousness, the self, and the relation between what we know and the way things are.

6. Using the old Platonic distinction between *appearance* and *reality*, Kant argued that we in fact never have knowledge of reality, but only of things as they appear to us, and that the mind itself contributes the *form* in which we know appearances. As Kant said in perhaps his most famous statement, "The mind is itself the lawgiver to nature."

The Scientific Status of Extrasensory Perception

Most of us think of ESP—extrasensory perception—as something we find in science fiction movies or television shows, along with teleportation and time travel, but there are in fact large numbers of serious scholars who do scientific research on precognition (foreseeing the future), telekinesis (moving objects with your mind), and telepathy (direct nonphysical communication between two minds). Perhaps I shouldn't say so readily that *most of us* treat these things purely as science fiction. Judging from the number of stories in the *National Enquirer* and other supermarket checkout journals, there probably are tens of millions of believers in the United States.

ESP research poses a number of serious *epistemological* problems for sceptics as well as for believers. What sort of evidence should we demand before we accept the reality of what are generally called "psychic phenomena"? Traditional science placed great store by heaps and heaps of brute facts, and that is exactly what ESP researchers provide. But no sooner have they piled up their data, than the sceptics reply that psychic phenomena *can't* be real, and they charge fraud, either conscious or unconscious.

In order to understand the dispute, as it is set forth in the selections included here, we must keep in mind some elementary facts of what mathematicians call probability theory. Suppose you have a deck of twenty-five cards containing five cards each with one of five different symbols (say, a circle, a star, a square, a half moon, and a triangle). If you try to guess the cards without looking at them, you will almost certainly get some of them right. How many? Well, there is no predicting exactly how many you will guess correctly. You might get lucky, and hit ten or fifteen of them, or you might just miss every single one. But mathematicians tell us that if you try the experiment over and over again, you will tend to get somewhere pretty near to five out of the twenty-five, on average. And the more times you try the test, the more likely you are to average somewhere close to five.

Suppose someone consistently hits eight, nine, ten, or more out of twenty-five. Once or twice could be luck. Strictly speaking, a hundred times COULD be luck, but it is almost certainly not. Instead, as she scores high again and again, we will become more and more convinced that she actually has some way of telling what the cards are.

What might that way be? It could be almost anything. The backs could be marked. Or, the cards could be ever so faintly transparent. It is even possible that there are ultraviolet markings on the backs, and she has eyes that are slightly sensitive to ultraviolet light. But—and this is the key to the entire controversy—even if we have no idea how she is doing it, the sheer unlikelihood of getting so many right answers shows, to a scientist, that some mechanism other than chance is at work. This is, of course, a form of reasoning that is used very widely. The correlation between cigarette smoking and cancer convinced medical researchers that a causal link existed long before any clinical evidence could be found.

In a curious sort of way, the psychic researchers are old-fashioned empiricists, and their critics are like the rationalists. But perhaps it would be better just to take a look at the evidence and see what you think.

The Pearce-Pratt Experiment

C. E. M. HANSEL

Hubert E. Pearce, the divinity student, had been acting as a subject in ESP experiments for more than a year before he took part in the Pearce-Pratt experiment, or Campus Distance Series as it is also known, which was started in August 1933 and completed in March 1934. . . .

It was basically a clairvoyance test, in which Pearce guessed at cards in a pack controlled by Pratt, then a graduate student in the psychology department, while he was situated in another building on the campus.

The two men met in Pratt's room on the top floor of what is now the social sciences building on the west campus of Duke University. . . . Both men synchronized their watches and fixed a time at which the test would start. Pearce then went across the quadrangle to the library, where he sat in a cubicle in the stacks at a distance of about 100 yards from Pratt, who from his window could see Pearce cross the quadrangle and enter the library.

Pratt sat down at a table, took a pack of ESP cards, and, after shuffling and cutting it, placed it face downward on the right side of the table. At the time fixed for the experiment to start, he took the top card and placed it, still face down, on a book in the center of the table. At the end of a minute this card was transferred to the left side of the table, and the second card in the pack was placed on the book. In this manner, each card was placed on the book at its appointed time and then transferred to a pile on the left side of the table. After a run of 25 cards, an interval of five minutes elapsed, and then the same procedure was followed with a second pack. Pratt did not see the faces of the cards until the end of the sitting when he turned them up to record their order. He then made a duplicate of his record, sealed it in an envelope, and later delivered it to Rhine.

In his cubicle in the library, Pearce recorded his guess as to the identity of each card lying on the book. After recording 50 guesses, he made a duplicate copy of his record sheet and sealed it in an envelope that was later delivered to Rhine. The two sealed records usually were delivered personally to Rhine before Pratt and Pearce compared their lists and scored the number of successes.

The above procedure was followed at each of the 37 sittings held between August 1933 and March 1934. The sittings were divided into four subseries: Subseries A consisted of six sittings, carried out under the above conditions; subseries B was composed of 22 sittings at which Pratt carried out his part of the proceedings in a room in the medical building, which would have put him about 250 yards away from Pearce; subseries C consisted of six sittings with the same conditions as subseries A; in subseries D, there were three sittings with the same conditions as subseries A, except that Rhine was with Pratt in the room in the social sciences building.

The. scores at successive sittings obtained in each subseries are shown in Table 1.

Something other than chance obviously was operating in each of the four subseries. The odds against the over-all result arising by chance are greater than 10^{22} to 1, and the result of each subseries is statistically significant.

When discussing the experiment in 1954 in the *Journal of Parapsychology*, Rhine and Pratt stated that the only alternative to an explanation in terms of ESP would involve collusion among all three participants.

It is difficult to see how either Rhine or Pratt, unaided, could have cheated to bring about the result obtained in all four subseries; but, owing to the fact that Pearce was not supervised during the experiment, there are a number of ways in which he could have cheated to attain high scores.

TABLE 1 *Scores in Each Run of the Pratt-Pearce Experiment*[1]

Sitting	Subseries A (100 yards)	Subseries B (250 yards)	Subseries C (100 yards)	Subseries D (100 yards)
1	3	1, 4	9, 8	12, 3
2	8, 5	4, 4	4, 9	10, 11
3	9, 10	7, 6	11, 9	10, 10
4	12, 11	5, 0	5, 4	
5	11, 12	6, 3	9, 11	
6	13, 13, 12	11, 9	2, 7	
7		0, 6		
8		8, 6		
9		9, 4		
10		10, 6		
11		11, 9		
12		5, 12		
13		7, 7		
14		12, 10		
15		6, 3		
16		10, 10		
17		6, 12		
18		2, 6		
19		12, 12		
20		4, 4		
21		3, 0		
22		13, 10		
Total trials	300	1,100	300	150
Total hits	119	295	88	56
Average score per run of 25 trials (hits)	9.9	6.7	7.3	9.3

[1]Rhine, J. B., and J. G. Pratt, "A Review of the Pearce-Pratt Distance Series of ESP Tests," *J. Parapsychol.*, 18 (1954), 165–77.

Pratt saw Pearce disappear into the library; then, some time later, after the sitting was over, he met him and checked his scores. He had no confirmation, other than Pearce's word for it—if he ever asked him—that Pearce had stayed in the library. He could quite easily have walked back to where Pratt was conducting his part of the experiment. In view of this, the possibility that Pearce obtained knowledge of the targets must be carefully considered. . . .

An important point to note is that the experiment was conducted according to a strict timetable. If Pearce had chosen to cheat, he knew to the second—from the time he was supposed to start his recording to the time when he was supposed to make his last guess—what Pratt was doing. He knew that he had 55 minutes during which Pratt would be fully occupied and that at the end of that time Pratt would be busy making first a list of the order of the cards in the two packs and then a duplicate of his record. Provided it was possible to see into Pratt's room, Pearce could have left the library and observed Pratt, gaining sight of the cards when they were turned up for recording at the end of the sitting or, if they could be identified from their backs, he could have inspected them while they were on the book in front of Pratt for a minute. Clearly, it is essential to know something about the two rooms in which Pratt carried out his part of the proceedings and about the way in which he turned up the cards when recording their order. . . .

When I was at Duke University in 1960, Pratt showed me the rooms he used during the experiment. While doing so, he mentioned that since 1934 structural alterations had been made to both rooms. We first visited Pratt's old room, 314, in the social sciences building. Pratt then pointed out that the wall beside the table had been farther back in 1933. After its original position had been located, it was apparent that the room in its original state contained a large clear-glass window that would have permitted anyone in the corridor to see into the room at the time of the experiment. I judged the window to be about two feet square and to be about five feet ten inches from the floor at its bottom edge. Anyone looking through this window from the corridor would have had a clear view of Pratt seated at his desk and of the cards he was handling.

There were similar windows leading into the offices on the other side of the corridor as well as clear-glass windows above the doors of all the rooms. Later, I went into a room on the opposite side of the corridor, 311, and found that the line of vision when looking through the transom above the door was through the window into Pratt's room and down onto his desk. It was impossible to be certain of this point since the wall in its new position hindered my view. However, there was a good possibility that Pearce could have returned to the social sciences building, locked himself in Room 311, and then observed Pratt with comparative safety by standing on a chair or table and looking through the transom above the door. . . .

Later, I asked W. Saleh, a member of the research staff at Duke, to run through a pack of ESP cards while I sat in an office farther down the corridor. He was to record the cards on a sheet of paper at the end of the run using a procedure similar to that used by Pratt during the experiments with Pearce and to keep his door closed and locked. I slipped back to Saleh's room and saw the cards by standing on a chair and looking through the crack at the top of the door. I had a clear view of them and obtained 22 hits in 25 attempts. Saleh's desk was about 16 feet from the door, and he had no suspicion of what I had done until I told him.

In a second test, I asked him to record the cards in a room in which I had left a sheet of blotting paper on the desk to take an impression of what he wrote. I then read off the identities of the cards from the impressions of his writing on the blotting paper. But by this time Saleh was tired of having his leg pulled. He had carefully written out a second list, using the blotting paper for it, so that I was given false information. It was clear, however, from these tests that knowledge of the cards could have been obtained by the use of either method, provided other factors in the situation did not eliminate the possibility.

Now that information has become available about the conditions in which the experiment was carried out, it is clear that it was far from foolproof, and the result could have been brought about in a variety of ways. . . .

A Reply to the Hansel Critique of the Pearce-Pratt Series
J. B. RHINE and J. G. PRATT

In spite of his unconcealed eagerness to give the *coup de grâce* to a piece of ESP research, Mr. Hansel is entitled to our appreciation for bringing our experiment of twenty-seven years ago momentarily back into the limelight. This acknowledgment may be linked with the information that, although Hansel's negative approach to parapsychology was a matter of public knowledge, he was invited and given a travel grant by the Duke Laboratory to make the visit that resulted in his paper. There are still other points of value arising from his critique, but they can best be left to follow our evaluation of his remarks about the experiment. . . .

Were the test conditions adequate? On this issue, there is one very essential point to get straight at the outset, and Hansel has *not* got it straight. Any piece of research under criticism obviously

stands or falls on its strongest, best-controlled section. Anyone confining his attack to any other section is either misled or misleading or both. And that is precisely what Hansel does. He avoids mention of the most advanced section of the experiment, Series D, and confines his attention entirely to the section comprising Series A, B, and C. He is attacking a non-vital organ.

We ourselves, of course, did not stop with Series A, B, and C. If there were any reason to pause and analyze Hansel's remarks about the first three series in terms of the actual situation, it could be shown that, at that time and stage, the procedure represented a definite advance over previous work. The strained alternative hypotheses Hansel suggests are unrealistic to those acquainted with the situation. H.E.P. had no knowledge he was not being trailed, and any spying or collusion on his part would have been most obvious

SOURCE: *Journal of Parapsychology*, 25 (June 1961).

in a department (of psychology) in which there were skeptics ready to suspect him of trickery. The devices proposed by Hansel would have been conspicuous and clumsy in crowded corridors. But for general reasons of precaution, it was recognized at the time that the conditions were such that the validity of the results depended entirely on the experimenter, J.G.P. In order to broaden the base of responsibility and protect both the experimenter and the results from possible charges of fraud, such as those now leveled, the conditions were strengthened in the last subseries of the experiment reported. It is to this improved stage, Section D, that attention must be given for a proper judgment.

We are now ready to look at that series. As a matter of fact, it is not easily overlooked and would be, for most readers, quite obviously the climax series in the paper. First of all, it is in its own right statistically significant, and its scoring average is above that of the paper as a whole. It can well bear the burden of the conclusion by itself. The next question, then, is how Hansel's criticisms apply to it and its conditions.

In this series, J.B.R., who had remained in the background previously, came into the test room with J.G.P. and sat through a series of six runs through the test pack (150 trials) for the purpose of scrutinizing the entire procedure from that point of vantage to ensure that it was faithfully executed. He, like J.G.P., *could see the subject from the window as the latter entered the library* (and, of course, could see him exit as well). He was in the experimental room at the end of each session to receive the independent records from both J.G.P. and H.E.P. immediately on the arrival of the latter at the close of the session. Thus, the subject was obviously allowed no opportunity to enter the room alone and copy the order of the cards or the impressions left on the record pad. H.E.P. had to have his duplicate record in his own handwriting, with one copy sealed in an envelope, ready to hand to J.B.R. on entering the room. J.G.P. had to do the recording of the last run of each session after the test was over and H.E.P. was already on his way to the test room. Yet these final runs of the session were, in themselves, independently significant statistically.

It is clear, then, not only that Hansel's counterhypothesis does not apply to Series D, but also that he did not intend it to do so. One can only wonder why he did not deal with this series and, if he is interested in the case for psi, why he did not follow on up the trail of methodological advances into other researches in parapsychology over the intervening decades. He would have found that the question of honesty which (in this and other papers) preoccupies him with such peculiar personal absorption was practically banished as the research entered the investigation of precognition, in which, of course, the target series is not in existence for some time after the subject has committed his responses to paper. . . .

Study Questions

1. These are strange times, what with *The National Enquirer* regularly featuring stories about people who say they have been kidnapped by aliens, and the actress Shirley MacLaine reporting that in a previous life she was stomped to death by a white elephant. On the other hand, in recent decades we have also seen live television transmissions from the moon and electron microscope photographs of individual atoms. *How* can we tell the difference between truth and fiction? Are the people crazy who refused to believe their own eyes and said that the pictures of men on the moon were faked?

2. Reflect for a bit about all the things you think you know: state capitals, historical events, details of the private lives of rock stars, the difference between reptiles and mammals, how much a Chevy sedan costs, what a Big Mac is really made of. How do you *know* these things? If you were forced to defend any of these beliefs, how would you go about it? Could you produce arguments, evidence, reasons, proof? If not, then is it sensible for you to believe them anyway?

3. The great epistemologists of the seventeenth and eighteenth centuries were, one must admit, a little mad, what with their dreams of settling once and for all, by a philosophical investigation, the limits of human knowledge. Is there *any* way of determining whether there are limits beyond which human knowledge cannot go? Would it help us to know more about the structure and functioning of our sense organs? Would a deeper insight into computers make any difference?

4. Is ESP *in principle* impossible? Why? Why not? If you think the answer is yes, how do you answer the argument that radio waves were as mysterious and unknown only two centuries ago? If you think the answer is no, what kind of evidence would you need to be persuaded that ESP is real?

5. There are three quite different mental powers which are grouped under the heading of ESP, namely thought transference, telekinesis [the ability to move objects with one's thoughts], and precognition [the ability to see the future]. The first two seem to be at least logically possible. After all, an alien might turn up that can communicate directly by something akin to radio waves, let us say. And as for telekinesis, every time I type a letter on my computer, I am making

my fingers move in response to my thoughts. But precognition is something else again. Is there any *logical* obstacle to seeing the future? What? How does seeing the future differ from predicting the future, which all of us do every time we drive a car on a busy street and anticipate what the other drivers will do?

8

METAPHYSICS AND PHILOSOPHY OF MIND

GOTTFRIED LEIBNIZ (1646–1716) was the most original and brilliant rationalist metaphysician of the modern era. Born in Germany, he was very early recognized as an enormously gifted thinker. His efforts to work out a coherent metaphysical foundation for the new science of the seventeenth century led him to the discovery of a form of the differential calculus. This discovery occurred at roughly the same time that Isaac Newton in England was developing a different form of the same branch of mathematics. For years thereafter, a dispute raged between the Leibnizeans and the Newtonians over which thinker deserved credit for having made the discovery first.

Leibniz chose to affiliate himself with the courts of the elector of the Mainz and the Duke of Brunswick, rather than to hold the position of professor which he was offered. His mathematical, scientific, and philosophical theories were set forth in essays, treatises, and letters which to this day have not been adequately edited and collected. Leibniz's theories of space, time, substance, force, motion, and causation were a subtle interweaving of traditional philosophical concepts with radically new scientific and mathematical ideas.

Although he is remembered now for his work in metaphysics, mathematics, and science, Leibniz was also deeply concerned with problems of religious doctrine. In his book on *Theodicy,* he sought to make the absolute goodness of God compatible with the apparent existence in the world of various evils. Leibniz's conclusion, that the actually existing world is, contrary to appearances, the best of all possible worlds, provoked a brilliant satirical attack from the French philosopher Voltaire. In *Candide,* Voltaire painted a hilarious portrait of a Leibnizean pundit whose repeated catchphrase of mindless optimism was, "All is for the best in the best of all possible worlds."

I   What Is Metaphysics?

Some years ago, there appeared a listing in the Yellow Pages of the Manhattan telephone book, between "Metals" and "Meteorologists," for "Metaphysician." A gentleman who shall remain nameless had hung out his shingle in Greenwich Village, and was apparently prepared to offer his metaphysical services for a fee to all comers. The listing has disappeared from subsequent editions of the Yellow Pages, but I continue to wonder just what services he offered, and what his clients imagined they were going to get when they sought him out.

What *is* metaphysics? Or should we ask, What *are* metaphysics? The term itself is a sheer historical accident. As you already know, Aristotle wrote a set of essays on fundamental problems concerning the most basic classifications or categories of being, and the most general concepts by means of which we can think about what is. He called his discussions *First Philosophy,* not because they were about things most easily understood, but because they were about fundamentals. Several centuries after Aristotle's death, when other philosophers commented on Aristotle's arguments, they found that the essays on first philosophy came after the book on physics in the edition or manuscript with which they worked. Because the essays had no name, they were referred to in Greek as "*ta meta ta physika biblia,*" which is to say "the books which come after the physics." Eventually this was shortened to *The Metaphysics,* and the topics dealt with under this title were dubbed "metaphysics." Unfortunately, over the centuries the prefix "meta" has acquired the bogus sense of "super" or "going beyond" or "transcending sense perception." So metaphysics is thought somehow to deal with what transends physics, with what is supernatural, occult, mysterious. Perhaps that is what our Greenwich Village metaphysician's clients expected—a touch of the beyond.

In philosophy, metaphysics is not really a single field or discipline, but rather a catch-all for a number of problems whose scope and significance are so broad that they seem to have implications for virtually every other field of philosophy. Let me mention just a few of the questions that are dealt with by philosophers under the heading of "metaphysics." You will very quickly see why this branch of philosophy is considered truly fundamental.

First, there is the basic question, What sorts of things are there? What are the categories into which whatever is can be sorted? Physical bodies in space? Minds? Properties of things, such as size, shape, color, smell, hardness, and taste? Events, such as the moving of a body from one place to another, or the growth of a tree from a seed, or the change in color of a leaf as it dies and browns? Ideas in a mind, thoughts, feelings, sense perceptions? How many different categories are there? Can some of these sorts of things be reduced to instances of other sorts? Is there one correct set of general categories for classifying things? What shall we say of peculiar things, like the number three, which doesn't seem to *exist,* in any ordinary sense, but on the other hand can hardly be said not to exist? (It would certainly sound odd to say there is no such thing as the number three!)

Then there are more particular questions: What is space, and what is time? Are they dimensions? Containers in which things exist and happen? Relations among things? Forms of our perception of things? Can there be space in which nothing exists—a void, as it is called by philosophers and scientists? Can there be a stretch of time in which absolutely nothing happens? Could there be totally empty time, in which nothing happens and nothing even exists? What sense does it make to speak of "empty" time and "empty" space, as though they were huge boxes waiting to be filled up?

Is there such a thing as a soul? Is it made out of physical matter, and if not, what then is it? Is the soul the same as the mind? Can a soul exist without relation to a body? How? Do souls continue to exist after the body dies? Did they exist before they were associated with, or planted in, bodies? What *is* the relationship of the soul to the body? Is the mind the same as the brain? Is the body just an idea in the mind?

Does the past exist? If not, then does nothing exist save whatever there is right now at this very moment? If the past does exist, then where is it? Is there some other universe of past things? What about future things as well? Is there a whole assortment of possible worlds alongside this actual one that we live in? Does it make any sense at all to say that something has *possible* existence?

Are all my actions absolutely causally determined by what has gone before, or am I free in some sense to choose among a variety of alternative actions available to me? If I am determined to act as I do, then can I also consider myself responsible for what I do? If I am free, what is the nature of my freedom? What sort of thing am I, that I should have this strange capacity to act freely?

Why is there anything at all in the universe? Why is there in general something and not nothing? Is the universe fundamentally absurd, or does it make some sort of rational sense? Was it created? Has it existed from all eternity? Can I even imagine a satisfactory *reason* for the universe? Does the universe stretch infinitely away from me in space? Will it go on existing forever?

And last, but of course hardly least, the question we have already examined: Is there an infinite, omnipotent, omniscient creator of all that is—a God?

Well, no one can accuse metaphysics of wasting its time on trivia! But how are we to get a handle on a field this vast in the confines of a single chapter? Following the practice of previous chapters, we shall begin by focusing on the life and thought of a single great philosopher, Gottfried Leibniz, whose philosophical writings constitute one of the enduring monuments to systematic metaphysical investigation. Our primary concern will be the connections between Leibniz's metaphysical theories of space, time, substance, and God on the one hand, and his interpretation of the new science of the seventeenth century on the other.

In the second part of the chapter, we shall choose a single metaphysical topic, the vexing issue of the relationship between the mind and the body, and examine some of the ways philosophers have attempted to deal with it.

II *Leibniz's Theory of Monads*

Gottfried Wilhelm Leibniz was born in 1646 in the city of Leipzig, in what is now Germany. He was a precocious child, the son of a professor and the grandson, through his mother, of another professor. (In Germany, the title of "professor" is reserved for a very small number of the most distinguished members of a university faculty. Professors in a German university are treated roughly in the way four-star generals are treated in the army.) Very early, Leibniz distinguished himself in his studies, first at the University of Leipzig and then at Altdorf, where he was actually offered a professorship. Rather than taking up the vocation of professor, Leibniz chose instead to affiliate himself with, or enter the service of, a series of rulers in the various principalities, duchies, and electorates of the area now unified as Germany. It was quite common for artists, composers, and men of learning to join the courts of these little independent territories, serving sometimes as performers at court, sometimes as tutors to the royal children, sometimes simply as confidantes or wise men in residence. Until the nineteenth century, much of the financial support for artistic and intellectual work took the form of aristocratic or royal patronage. It is a bit difficult to imagine some man or woman being named "philosopher in residence to the governor of Kansas," but it was not at all odd for Leibniz to serve in effect as resident philosopher to the Duke of Hanover.

Leibniz was a man of the most extraordinarily broad interests. You can get some idea of his brilliance and his breadth if I tell you that he invented a version of the calculus, conceived the idea of a universal encyclopedia of human knowledge, worked out a philosophical explanation for the apparent existence of evil in a world created by an infinitely powerful, infinitely good God, and developed a scheme for sending Jesuits to convert the Chinese!

Today, learned men and women communicate their discoveries to one another by publishing articles in scholarly journals. In Leibniz's day, however, it was much more common for such communication to take the form of long letters. These were not your "Having wonderful time, wish you were here" sorts of things. The writer, after a few courtesies at the beginning, would launch into page after page of technical mathematics, physics, philosophy, or theology. Much of Leibniz's important work was "published" in this form, and it was therefore extremely difficult for several centuries to get a systematic overview of his theories. Only in recent years has anything like a complete edition of the works of Leibniz become available.

Leibniz's metaphysical theory revolves around his conception of the nature of what philosophers call *substance.* This is a technical term that was introduced by Aristotle and has since become one of the key terms in metaphysical disputes. In order to explain what it means, let me do what Aristotle himself did, and take a detour through some facts about language. In English, and many other languages as well, sentences can be put together by combining a subject-term and a predicate-term, using the connector or copula "is." For example, I can make the sentence "Iron is hard" by using "iron" as the subject, "hard" as the predicate, and "is" as the copula or connector. Sometimes, instead of using "is," I just use a verb, as in the sentence "Ice melts." Now, in English and other languages, I can frequently turn a word that has been used as a predicate into a word usable as a subject, simply by adding an ending or altering its form a bit. I can turn the predicate "hard" into a subject by adding -ness to get "hardness." Then I can make the sentence "Hardness is a property of iron." I can also turn the verb "melt" into a subject by adding -ing. Then I can form the sentence, "Melting is what ice does."

It occurred to Aristotle that although many words can be used as both subject and predicate, with appropriate grammatical shifting around, there are some words which can be the subjects of sentences, but cannot also serve as predicates, no matter how they are altered grammatically. For example, I can say, "The earth is round," but there is no way I can change "The earth" into a predicate. Of course, there is the adjective "earthy," but that doesn't do the trick; and there is the rather fancy term "terrestrial," but that means "having to do with, or pertaining to, or existing on, the earth." "Earthness" and "earthing" just don't mean anything.

In short, some terms are ultimate subjects, in the sense that they can be the subjects of predication but cannot themselves be predicated of anything else. The things these terms name or refer to, Aristotle said, are **substances.** The characteristics, states, activities, or features which predicates name or refer to are called **attributes** by Aristotle. So a substance is anything that can have attributes predicated of it, but which itself cannot be predicated as an attribute of any other thing. The most obvious examples of substances, of course, are just ordinary physical objects. A tree is a substance, and the word "tree" is an ultimate grammatical subject. Tallness is an attribute, and so are greenness and leafiness and life. So I can say of a tree that it is green, leafy, and alive. In short,

The famous Cheshire Cat from Lewis Carroll's ALICE IN WONDERLAND, who is said to have faded slowly from sight until nothing was left but the smile. Carroll was actually the Reverend Dodgson, a serious philosopher and logician, and he understood the wackiness of the notion that a smile could remain after the face that was smiling the smile had disappeared.

Illustration by John Tenniel from *Alice's Adventures in Wonderland* published by The Macmillan Company, New York.

I can attribute greenness, leafiness, and life to a tree. But I cannot "attribute" treeness to anything else. So a tree is a bearer of attributes which is not itself an attribute of any other thing, which is to say that it is a *substance*.

Attributes are characteristics of substances, so they cannot exist unless the substance exists. Even though the famous cheshire cat in *Alice in Wonderland* is supposed to have faded slowly away until nothing was left of it but the smile, in real life you cannot have a smile without a face, nor can you have intelligence without a mind, or color without a body. Philosophers express this by saying that attributes must *inhere* in a substance, which is said to "support" them. But substances, Aristotle said, do not inhere in anything, nor do they require the existence of anything other than themselves. A substance can exist without this or that particular property (though it obviously cannot exist without any properties at all), but there are no properties that can exist without being the properties of some substance.

The fundamental idea of Aristotle's theory of "first philosophy"—an idea that persisted into the seventeenth century and beyond, influencing Leibniz and many other philosophers—was that we could get a systematic grasp of the universe by conceiving it in terms of the *substances* that make it up, together with a classification of all the properties or attributes that characterize those substances. Because substances are the sorts of things that can exist without depending on something else, they must be the most real, the most basic things.

What sorts of substances make up the universe? Philosophers have given many answers to this fundamental question of metaphysics, but they have tended to focus on one or more of three candidates. The ancient cosmologists known as "atomists" argued that tiny, indivisible, simple bits of matter called *atoms* are the building blocks of the universe. They pointed out that complex or composite bodies, because they are made up out of atoms, are in a sense dependent upon their component parts. But the component parts are not dependent upon the whole of which they are parts. A piece of rock cannot exist unless its atomic parts exist, but the individual parts can perfectly well exist even though the rock, as a rock, does not (the atoms go on existing after the rock is broken up or worn away). So the atoms must be the substances of the universe, and any larger bodies, or properties of those larger bodies, are merely dependent complexes or attributes.

A number of philosophers, including Descartes, claimed that minds are substances. This raises all sorts of questions, some of which we shall try to explore in the next section. Minds, Descartes held, are not material—they do not occupy space, they do not have shapes, or sizes, or density. They are "immaterial substances," which just means that they are "not matter," and still leaves us trying to figure out what they are. Philosophers have found two important reasons for insisting on the substantiality of minds, even though such a view is hard to explain. First, Christian doctrine teaches that the soul continues to exist after the death and breakup of the material body, so the soul must be a substance. It seems natural to identify the soul with the mind, and to conclude that the mind is a nonmaterial substance. Second (this is Descartes' reason), consciousness is an absolutely undeniable fact, and consciousness is apparently a feature or characteristic or attribute of minds rather than of bodies. Now if consciousness is an attribute, then it must inhere in some substance, and if it doesn't seem to be the sort of attribute that could inhere in bodies, then the mind must be a different sort of substance.

Finally, many philosophers from Aristotle onward have claimed that God is a special, one-of-a-kind substance. Obviously God meets the requirements for "substance-hood." He can exist independently of other things, and attributes can be predicated of Him. But if God is a substance, and if God created the universe of nondivine substances, then it would seem that He is the *only* substance, for everything else depends for its existence on Him. Some philosophers handled this difficulty by distinguishing *created substances from uncreated substance* (God), but at least one philosopher—the seventeenth-century Jewish metaphysician Baruch Spinoza—drew the natural conclusion from the definition of substance and asserted that God is the only substance. Everything else, he said, is merely an attribute of God. Believe it or not, this doctrine led people to accuse Spinoza of being an atheist!

The dispute over the nature and categories of substance has been shaped by different philosophical motivations in different ages. Sometimes, the problems philosophers wanted to deal with by means of a theory of substance were religious or theological; at other times, the problems were mainly logical. But in the seventeenth century, when Leibniz developed his metaphysical theory, the primary motivation was a desire to find an adequate theoretical foundation for the new science, in particular for the physical theories of motion which Galileo, Kepler, Newton, and others were advancing. Three questions at least had to be answered by any philosophical theory adequate to the new science:

First: What is the nature of the substances whose behavior is described by scientific laws of motion?

Second: What is the nature of the interactions between substances? What forces, or causal influences, connect the behavior of one substance with the behavior of another?

Third: What is the relationship, if any, between the universe of spatially located substances governed by the laws of motion, and the God who—at least in the seventeenth century—was agreed on all sides to be the Creator of that universe?

Leibniz's unique and startling theory of **monads** was designed to answer these questions in a manner that permitted the latest scientific discoveries and orthodox Christian doctrine to fit together into a consistent metaphysics.

In 1714, only two years before his death, Leibniz wrote out a short, systematic statement of his metaphysical theory. *The Monadology,* as it is called, remains the best introduction to his philosophy, and in the selection that follows, you will find his answers to the questions we have just articulated. Since this is a summary rather than a full-scale defense, Leibniz's arguments are rather sketchy, but you should be able to form a preliminary notion of his theory from what is presented here.

The Monad, of which we will speak here, is nothing else than a simple substance, which goes to make up composites; by simple, we mean without parts.

There must be simple substances because there are composites; for a composite is nothing else than a collection or *aggregatum* of simple substances.

Now, where there are no constituent parts there is possible neither extension, nor form, nor divisibility. These Monads are the true Atoms of nature, and, in fact, the Elements of things.

Their dissolution, therefore, is not to be feared and there is no way conceivable by which a simple substance can perish through natural means.

For the same reason there is no way conceivable by which a simple substance might, through natural means, come into existence, since it can not be formed by composition.

We may say then, that the existence of Monads can begin or end only all at once, that is to say, the Monad can begin only through creation and end only through annihilation. Composites, however, begin or end gradually.

There is also no way of explaining how a Monad can be altered or changed in its inner being by any other created thing, since there is no possibility of transposition within it, nor can we conceive of any internal movement which can be produced, directed, increased or diminished there within the substance, such as can take place in the case of composites where a change can occur among the parts. The Monads have no windows through which anything may come in or go out. The Attributes are not liable to detach themselves and make an excursion outside the substance, as could *sensible species* of the Schoolmen. In the same way neither substance nor attribute can enter from without into a Monad.

Still, Monads must have some qualities, otherwise they would not even be existences. And if simple substances did not differ at all in their qualities, there would be no means of perceiving any change in things. Whatever is in a composite can come into it only through its simple elements and the Monads, if they were without qualities, since they do not differ at all in quantity, would be indistinguishable one from another. For instance, if we imagine *a plenum* or completely filled space, where each part receives only the equivalent of its own previous motion, one state of things would not be distinguishable from another.

Each Monad, indeed, must be different from every other. For there are never in nature two beings which are exactly alike, and in which it is not possible to find a difference either internal or based on an intrinsic property.

I assume it as admitted that every created being, and consequently the created Monad, is subject to change, and indeed that this change is continuous in each.

It follows from what has just been said, that the natural changes of the Monad come from an internal principle, because an external cause can have no influence upon its inner being.

Now besides this principle of change there must also be in the Monad a manifoldness which changes. This manifoldness constitutes, so to speak, the specific nature and the variety of the simple substances.

This manifoldness must involve a multiplicity in the unity or in that which is simple. For since every natural change takes place by degrees, there must be something which changes and something which remains unchanged, and consequently there must be in the simple substance a plurality of conditions and relations, even though it has no parts.

Let us consider in turn each of our three questions, and see how Leibniz's theory of monads answers them. First of all, the created universe consists of an infinity of simple, nonmaterial spiritual substances, or minds. Each of these minds is conscious, and its attributes or states are the thoughts and perceptions, desires and feelings in its consciousness. Monads, as Leibniz calls his simple substances, are created by God, who has—as we shall see—arranged their inner natures according to a rather complex divine plan.

The monad I am best acquainted with, of course, is myself, my own mind. I am not only conscious; I am also self-conscious, as Descartes pointed out. But Leibniz does not think that self-consciousness is necessarily a characteristic of every monad in the universe. Indeed, there is a sort of hierarchy of monads, rising from those monads whose consciousness is so feeble as barely to occur at all, through clear consciousness not combined with self-consciousness, on through the sort of self-aware or reflexive consciousness human beings have, up to the consciousness of angels (if there are any), and finally to God's consciousness, which we mortals can hardly imagine.

What then is a body? Well, bodies are not substances, for substances are simple and bodies are divisible into parts, hence complex. Substances are conscious and bodies are not. Bodies are, as Leibniz puts it, "colonies" of monads. We can think of a body as a set of monads that bear certain relationships to one another. But if this set of monads is broken up, divided, or redistributed, so that the body as such ceases to exist, the monads go right on existing. Each monad can be thought of as occupying a dimensionless point in space (a point has no length, breadth, or depth; it is merely a location, mathematically speaking). So monads, as nonmaterial substances, have no spatial extension, no size or shape. This sounds odd, of course, but it sounds even odder to suggest that the human mind is triangular, or six feet long, or two inches thick. Minds simply aren't the sorts of things to take up space, and monads are fundamentally minds.

Monads have two sorts of properties, internal and external. The internal properties of a monad are all the contents or states of its own consciousness, all the things that happen inside it. The external properties of a monad are its relationships to other monads. For example, if I see a squirrel run across a branch outside my window, and then feel a twinge of pain where I bumped myself yesterday, that visual perception and that twinge are events in my mind (according to Leibniz); they are internal to me, and as such are part of the life of the monad which is my self or soul. On the other hand, my physical distance from the squirrel is a fact about the relationships between two monads—namely, myself or mind or soul and the self or the mind of the squirrel (assuming, for the moment, that there is some consciousness associated with the body I call a squirrel). That is an external relationship or property both of myself and of the squirrel.

So we have before us now Leibniz's answers to the first question. What is the nature of substances? They are nonmaterial, conscious monads. Let us turn to the second question: What is the nature of the interactions between monads? What forces or causal influences connect the behavior of one substance with the behavior of others?

Leibniz's answer to this central question of science and metaphysics is strange, unexpected, and quite astonishing. Indeed, it ranks as one of the oddest views ever expressed on a major philosophical question by a great philosopher. Leibniz came to the extraordinary conclusion that substances do *not* interact with one another at all, despite what would seem to be overwhelming evidence to the contrary. It was his view that each monad, each simple immaterial substance, was complete and self-sufficient unto itself. None of the inner perceptions or states of consciousness of one monad were actually *caused* by the action of any other monad. As he put it in the selection from the *Monadology* which you

Pre-Established Harmony   Leibniz's claim that God prearranges things in such a way that the ideas in our minds correctly correspond to the objects in the world, even though there is no actual interaction between the world and our minds. Leibniz needed this implausible hypothesis because, according to his metaphysical theories, substances cannot really have an effect on one another.

read earlier, "The Monads have no windows through which anything may come in or go out."

But something is very wrong here! Leibniz is not a skeptic. He does not say that he can have no knowledge of anything save the inner states of his own mind at any given moment. He claims that his thoughts and perceptions accurately represent the world around him, just as they purport to do. Now, if my visual perception of the typewriter in front of me is *caused* by the typewriter, by the light coming from the typewriter into my eyes and affecting the retina, etc., then I can perhaps understand how that perception might accurately represent some aspect of the typewriter. But if nothing outside my mind can affect my mind in any way; if no other substance can cause thoughts or perceptions in my mind; if, in Leibniz's colorful phrase, my mind has no windows; then what conceivable grounds can I possess for supposing that the thoughts in my mind bear any regular relationship at all to the characteristics, events, states, or relations of other substances?

Leibniz's answer provides us at the same time with his reply to the third question, concerning the relationship between God and the universe of created substances. According to Leibniz, there is no *secular* ground for supposing that my thoughts adequately reflect the world beyond the walls of my mind. If there were no God, or if God did not see fit to arrange things in a special way, my internal thoughts would give me no clue at all as to things outside of my own inner consciousness. But God is good, and He is all-powerful, and so, Leibniz claims, He has systematically fitted the internal nature of each monad to the totality of the rest, so that the thoughts in any single monad correspond in some way, more or less perfectly, to the universe they purport to represent. This systematic fitting is described by Leibniz as a **pre-established harmony**. It is *pre*-established because God builds into each monad, when He creates it, the whole succession of thoughts and perceptions which shall pass through that monad's consciousness as time goes on. It is a *harmony* because the subjective thoughts of each monad are, by divine arrangement, fitted to or harmonized with the rest of the monads.

In order to get a notion of what Leibniz means by this odd doctrine, imagine that you have been locked up in a dark room and strapped to a chair facing a wall. Suddenly, a window *seems* to open in the wall, and you see the people, the cars, the trucks on the street outside. But in fact there is no window! Instead, your mysterious captor is using the wall as a screen, and projecting onto it a *movie* of the street beyond the wall.

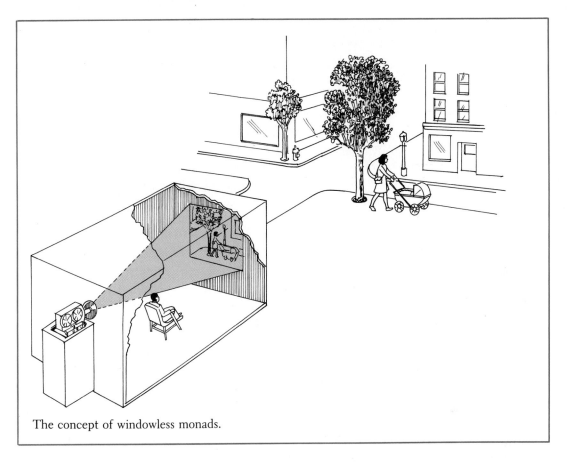

The concept of windowless monads.

Now, this mysterious captor is very rich and rather eccentric, so he hires actors to drive and walk on the street at exactly the moment, and in exactly the way, that perfectly similar characters are walking or driving in the movie he is showing on the wall of your cell. There is no direct causal connection, of course, between the pictures in the movie and the people outside. The movie was made before you were ever thrown into the room, and the "cause" of the pictures on the wall is simply the passing of light through the film in the projector behind you. But thanks to the careful planning of your captor, there is a pre-established harmony between the movie and the events on the street.

Roughly speaking, this peculiar arrangement is what Leibniz claims to be the actual relationship between my perceptions and the rest of the universe. They correspond to one another because of God's infinitely careful plan, but there is no actual causal connection between them. In philosophical language, the correspondence is *virtual* rather than *actual*.

Why would God go to all this trouble? God's ways are traditionally said to be mysterious to men, but this does seem to be carrying mystery a bit far! The truth, I think, is that Leibniz has got himself into a metaphysical box with his theory of simple monads, and he just doesn't know how to get out. The theory of monads is useful for some purposes, but it compels Leibniz to put forward the implausible notion of a pre-established harmony, and to that extent is clearly an inadequate basis for either metaphysics or science.

Lest you think that Leibniz was just being needlessly silly, let me assure you that the problem he was dealing with—namely, the relationship between the subjective contents of the mind and the physical objects they supposedly represent—was a problem as well for virtually all of the metaphysicians of the seventeenth and eighteenth centuries. Indeed, in the next section, we shall see that it continues to stir up philosophical disagreement today.

III *The Relation of Mind to Body: Three Theories*

One of the characteristic symptoms of the mental illness known as schizophrenia is a sense on the part of the patient of being divorced from his own body. The patient's foot, or hand, or torso seems to him to be an alien or independent entity. The patient may say that he doesn't know whether he really has a body; he may wonder whether he can move his hand should he choose to do so; he may speak of his body as not being *his*. Psychiatrists aren't sure just how to treat schizoprenia, but they have no doubt that it *is* a form of mental disorder or disease. We may perhaps be forgiven for wondering, therefore, whether philosophers for the past three and a half centuries have been suffering from some weird intellectual form of schizophrenia, for Descartes, Berkeley, Hume, and others say some pretty strange things about minds and bodies. In this section, in addition to sketching several theories of the relation of mind to body that have been put forward in the literature of modern philosophy, I shall try to suggest what legitimate concerns have led phi-

Mind-Body Problem   The *Mind-Body Problem* is the problem of explaining exactly what the relationship is between our minds and physical bodies in space. There are really *three* problems lumped together under this heading: First, do minds and bodies causally interact with one another, and if so, how? Second, how, if at all, can I [i.e., my mind] gain knowledge about bodies—indeed, can minds really know anything at all about bodies, or do minds only know about themselves? And third, what is the special relationship between *my* mind and *my* body? In the twentieth century, the Mind-Body Problem led philosophers to a related problem, the *Problem of Other Minds*: How, if at all, can I know of the existence and contents of minds other than my own? Is there anyone out there, or am I alone in a world of mere bodies?

losophers to focus so much attention on the so-called **mind-body problem.**

The physical theories developed by Aristotle, and refined by countless philosophers during the many centuries following, placed great emphasis upon the purposive order of nature. Aristotle himself conceived of nature as exhibiting an inherent purpose that need not be traced to the conscious intentions of a divine creator. Later philosophers in the Christian tradition tended to appeal, at some point in their arguments, to such a divine purpose. But whether religiously based or not, physical theories relied heavily upon notions of goal, end, purpose, and rational order usually associated with the operations of conscious agents. As we saw in the last chapter, Descartes focused his attention entirely on the self-conscious self or mind at the outset of his philosophical deliberations. But when he came to develop his theory of the physical universe, he rejected entirely any appeal to properties, concepts, or modes of explanation associated with the mental or the conscious. The material universe, he argued, was characterized by such properties as extension and motion. All explanation in science must be couched in terms of size, shape, density, velocity, and the like.

This exclusion of the mental from the sphere of physical explanation was prompted by the fact that extension and motion could be quantified and treated mathematically whereas purpose, end, goal, intention, or rational order could not be. The tools of arithmetic and analytic geometry

By permission of John Hart and Field Enterprises, Inc.

were inapplicable to the notions that Aristotle and his followers had employed in their physical explanations. So it was the search for a mathematical science which led Descartes to exclude all "mentalistic" characteristics from his physical theories. But having thus shunted aside the
mental, Descartes was forced to ask himself what relationship there was
between the physical realm of extension and motion to which the new
science applied, and the realm of thought, purpose, and reason. For Descartes, the problem was especially pressing because his method of doubt
had focused attention as never before on the sphere of consciousness.

Drawing on metaphysical theories already in circulation, Descartes
put forward a relatively simple but ultimately unworkable theory of the
relationship between the realms of consciousness and physics. He argued
that there are two kinds of created substances, minds and bodies. Minds
are immaterial, unextended, simple conscious substances, and bodies are
material, extended, composite, nonconscious substances. A human being
is thus a combination of a material substance—the body—and a spiritual
substance—the mind.

But in the traditional theory of substance, a substance (or "essence")
of one sort can only interact with or influence another substance of the
same sort. A mind can interact with a mind, a body can interact with a
body. But minds cannot interact with bodies, because there is no way
in which a nonmaterial, unextended substance can be touched, moved,
altered, or affected by a material, extended substance. And there is no
way in which a simple, unextended, conscious substance can touch,
move, alter, or affect an extended, material substance. So having excluded the mind from the arena of mathematical physics, Descartes

found himself with no satisfactory way to reintroduce mind back into the world.

The problem is compounded, of course, by Descartes' search for inner subjective certainty. Beginning as he did with the self's conscious awareness of its own existence, he was forced to ask how such a self-aware self could ever come to know the existence and nature of nonconscious bodies external to it. So for some of Descartes' contemporaries and successors, the "mind-body" problem consisted in finding a place in physical, mathematically describable nature for a nonphysical, nonquantitative mind; while for others, the problem consisted in showing that a mind could acquire well-established knowledge of bodies in space. These two forms of the problem intermingled with one another, as philosophers puzzled over them, so that sometimes the scientific-metaphysical aspect was dominant, and at other times the epistemological aspect took precedence.

There are countless metaphysical solutions to the problem of the nature and relationship of mind and body, some of which are enormously

---

1. **Idealism:** the theory that everything in the universe is either minds, or else ideas in minds (hence, *'idealism'*). Bodies, according to the idealist, are simply particular collections of ideas. Thus, a table is simply the interconnected set of all the ideas—concepts, images, feels, sights, sounds, etc.—that I think of as *ideas of* a table.

2. **Materialism:** the theory that everything in the universe is matter (hence, *'materialist'*) Minds, according to the materialist, are simply collections of very small bodies, or structures and organizations of bodies (such as nerve cells in the brain). Perceptions, to the materialist, are particular sorts of interactions between bodies, and so are thoughts, emotions, and feelings of pleasure and pain.

3. **Psycho-Physical Dualism:** the theory that minds are one kind of substance and bodies are another. The defining characteristic of mind, according to the dualist, is consciousness or thought. The defining characteristic of body is spacial extension (and sometimes also force or impenetrability). For the dualist, the major problem is to explain how mind and matter interact and affect one another.

Three Mind-Body Theories

subtle and suggestive, but in an introductory text of this sort, it would be madness to try to lay them all out for you. Three positions have dominated the history of this debate, and you have actually encountered two of them in this chapter already. The three major theories of the relation of mind to body are the *two-substance theory*, which asserts that minds and bodies are fundamentally different sorts of beings or substances; the *one-substance theory*, which states that everything in the universe is a mind, and that bodies are to be analyzed as collections of, or aspects of, or thoughts in, minds; and the *one-substance theory*, which states that everything in the universe is a body, and minds are to be analyzed as collections of, or aspects of, or configurations of, bodies. The two-substance theory is called *dualism*, the everything-is-a-mind theory is called *idealism*, (not to be confused with a belief in high principles or the flag), and the everything-is-a-body theory is called *materialism* (also not to be confused with an excessive desire for money).

Descartes was a *dualist*, as you know. Leibniz was an *idealist* of a certain sort. He held that there were many minds in the universe, and that bodies were collections or colonies of those minds. Other idealists, such as George Berkeley, developed their theory of mind and body out of epistemological considerations. They argued that bodies could only be collections of perceptions or ideas in the mind of a conscious self, for such perceptions and ideas are the only things that we, as minds, can know anything about. To suggest that there are things outside our minds about which we can know nothing is simply to use words without meaning anything. How, after all, could we even imagine a way of testing such an assertion?

The materialist position is one of the oldest in philosophy, and also one of the most current. The ancient atomists whom you met in the first chapter—Democritus, Epicurus, Lucretius—were materialists. They explicitly stated that the mind is made up of very small, very fine atoms, rather like the atoms which make up air. They saw no problem in explaining the relationship of mind to body, for the mind on their view *is* body, and the interaction of mind-atoms with other atoms was just like the interaction between any atoms at all.

In Descartes' own day, the most famous defenders of the materialist position were the witty French philosopher Pierre Gassendi and the Englishman Thomas Hobbes. You may have encountered Hobbes in other courses, for he is the author of a book called *Leviathan*, which is one of the classics of political philosophy. Hobbes claimed that sense perception, ideas, imagination, deliberation, reasoning, desire, love, hatred, and all the other "mental" events, activities, and traits were really just motions of tiny atomic particles in the sense organs or the nervous system. For him, as for the ancient Greek atomists, there was no difficulty in explaining the interaction of "mind" and "body." Atomic particles strike the sense organs and set up vibrations in our nervous system, which of course also consists of atomic particles. The internal motions of the particles of the nervous system constitute perception, imagination, memory, and deliberation. Desire is merely the tendency of the body to move physically toward some external object, while aversion is the tendency to move away from such an object. When the internal motions in the nervous system build up to such a point that the muscles and bones are moved one way or the other, Hobbes said, then "thought" produces "action," and we say that the mind has caused the body to do something. But actually, of course, all that has happened is that the motion imparted to the particles of the nervous system by bodies striking on them from elsewhere has been transmitted through a chain of internal collisions to other bodies once more external to what we call "the" body—that is, the human body. Here are some selections from the opening chapters of *Leviathan* in which Hobbes lays out some of the basic definitions and theses of his one-substance materialism.

> Concerning the thoughts of man, I will consider them first singly, and afterwards in train, or dependence upon one another. Singly, they are every one a *representation* or *appearance*, of some quality, or other accident of a body without us, which is commonly called an *object*. Which object worketh on the eyes, ears, and other parts of a man's body; and by diversity of working, produceth diversity of appearances.
>
> The original of them all, is that which we call SENSE, for there is no conception in a man's mind, which hath not at first, totally, or by parts, been begotten upon the organs of sense. The rest are derived from that original. . . .
>
> The cause of sense, is the external body, or object, which presseth the organ proper to each sense, either immediately, as in the taste and touch; or mediately, as in seeing, hearing, and smelling; which pressure, by the mediation of the nerves, and other strings and membranes of the body, continued inwards to the brain and heart, causeth there a resistance, or counter-pressure, or endeavour of the heart to deliver itself, which endeavour, because *outward*, seemeth to be some matter without. And this *seeming*, or *fancy*, is that which men call *sense*; and consisteth, as to the eye, in a *light*, or *colour figured*; to the ear, in a *sound*; to the nostril, in an *odour*; to the tongue and palate, in a *savour*; and to the rest of the body, in *heat*, *cold*,

THOMAS HOBBES (1588–1679) is one of the major figures in what has come to be called the "social contract" school of political theory. Deeply moved by the social chaos of the English civil war (1640–1660), and persuaded of the necessity for a strong, authoritative central government as the only defense against man's natural destructive tendencies, Hobbes argued in his most famous book, *Leviathan*, for a state founded upon an agreement among all men to give up their natural liberty and submit to the commands of the sovereign.

Hobbes was a materialist; he believed that physical atoms in motion are the only real things. He combined this metaphysical doctrine with a psychological theory that each human being acts always to satisfy his desires and increase his power. In *Leviathan*, he attempted to deduce his theory of the social contract from these two fundamental propositions. Hobbes was both an acute observer of human behavior and an elegant stylist of English prose. *Leviathan* is the single most impressive piece of political philosophy written in English.

hardness, softness, and such other qualities as we discern by *feeling.* All which qualities, called *sensible,* are in the object, that causeth them, but so many several motions of the matter by which it presseth our organs diversely. Neither in us that are pressed, are they any thing else, but divers motions; for motion produceth nothing but motion. But their appearance to us is fancy, the same waking, that dreaming. And as pressing, rubbing, or striking the eye, makes us fancy a light; and pressing the ear, produceth a din; so do the bodies also we see, or hear, produce the same by their strong, though unobserved action. For if those colours and sounds were in the bodies, or objects that cause them, they could not be severed from them, as by glasses, and in echoes by reflection, we see they are; where we know the thing we see is in one place, the appearance in another. And though at some certain distance, the real and very object seem invested with the fancy it begets in us; yet still the object is one thing, the image or fancy is another. So that sense, in all cases, is nothing else but original fancy, caused, as I have said, by the pressure, that is, by the motion, of external things upon our eyes, ears, and other organs thereunto ordained. . . .

That when a thing lies still, unless somewhat else stir it, it will lie still for ever, is a truth that no man doubts of. But that when a thing is in motion, it will eternally be in motion, unless somewhat else stay it, though the reason be the same, namely, that nothing can change itself, is not so easily assented to. For men measure, not only other men, but all other things, by themselves; and because they find themselves subject after motion to pain, and lassitude, think every thing else grows weary of motion, and seeks repose of its own accord; little considering, whether it be not some other motion, wherein that desire of rest they find in themselves consisteth. From hence it is, that the schools say, heavy bodies fall downwards, out of an appetite to rest, and to conserve their nature in that place which is most proper for them; ascribing appetite, and knowledge of what is good for their conservation, which is more than man has, to things inanimate, absurdly.

When a body is once in motion, it moveth, unless something else hinder it, eternally; and whatsoever hindreth it, cannot in an instant, but in time, and by degrees, quite extinguish it; and as we see in the water, though the wind cease, the waves give not over rolling for a long time after: so also it happeneth in that motion, which is made in the internal parts of a man, then, when he sees, dreams, etc. For after the object is removed, or the eye shut, we still retain an image of the thing seen, though more obscure than when we see it. And this is it, the Latins call *imagination,* from the image made in seeing; and apply the same, though improperly, to all the other senses. But the Greeks call it *fancy;* which signifies *appearance,* and is as proper to one sense, as to another. *Imagination* therefore is nothing but *decaying sense;* and is found in men, and many other living creatures, as well sleeping as waking. . . .

If science fiction writers of an earlier age, like Jules Verne, had been able to imagine the modern personal computer, what fantasies would they have written? The owner of a desktop computer has many times more calculating power at his or her command than the builders of the first electronic computer, which filled an entire large room. (Courtesy of Apple Computer, Inc.)

There be in animals, two sorts of *motions* peculiar to them: one called *vital*; begun in generation, and continued without interruption through their whole life; such as are the *course* of the *blood*, the *pulse*, the *breathing*, the *concoction, nutrition, excretion,* etc., to which motions there needs no help of imagination: the other is *animal motion*, otherwise called *voluntary motion*; as to go, to *speak*, to *move* any of our limbs, in such manner as is first fancied in our minds. That sense is motion in the organs and interior parts of man's body, caused by the action of the things we see, hear, etc.; and that fancy is but the relics of the same motion, remaining after sense, has been already said in the first and second chapters. And because *going, speaking,* and the like voluntary motions, depend always upon a precedent thought of *whither, which way,* and *what*; it is evident, that the imagination is the first internal beginning of all voluntary motion. And although unstudied men do not conceive any motion at all to be there, where the thing moved is invisible; or the space it is moved in is, for the shortness of it, insensible; yet that doth not hinder, but that such motions are. For let a space be never so little, that which is moved over a greater space, whereof that little one is part, must first be moved over that. These small beginnings of motion, within the body of man, before they appear in walking, speaking, striking, and other visible actions, are commonly called ENDEAVOUR.

This endeavour, when it is toward something which causes it, is called APPETITE, or DESIRE; the latter being the general name; and the other oftentimes restrained to signify the desire of food, namely *hunger* and *thirst*. And when the endeavour is fromward something, it is generally called AVERSION. These words, *appetite* and *aversion*, we have from the Latins; and they both of them signify the motions, one of approaching, the other of retiring. . . .

That which men desire, they are also said to LOVE: and to HATE those things for which they have aversion. So that desire and love are the same thing; save that by desire, we always signify the absence of the object; by love, most commonly the presence of the same. So also by aversion, we signify the absence; and by hate, the presence of the object. . . .

And because the constitution of a man's body is in continual mutation, it is impossible that all the same things should always cause in him the same appetites, and aversions: much less can all men consent, in the desire of almost any one and the same object.

But whatsoever is the object of any man's appetite or desire, that is it which he for his part calleth *good*: and the object of his hate and aversion, *evil*; and of his contempt, *vile* and *inconsiderable*. For these words of good, evil, and contemptible, are ever used with relation to the person that useth them: there being nothing simply and absolutely so; nor any common rule of good and evil, to be taken from the nature of the objects themselves. . . .

When in the mind of man, appetites, and aversions, hopes, and fears, concerning one and the same thing, arise alternately; and divers good and evil consequences of the doing, or omitting the thing propounded, come successively into our thoughts; so that sometimes we have an appetite to it; sometimes an aversion from it; sometimes hope to be able to do it; sometimes despair, or fear to attempt it; the whole sum of desires, aversions, hopes and fears continued till the thing be either done, or thought impossible, is that we call DELIBERATION.

Therefore of things past, there is no *deliberation*; because manifestly impossible to be changed: nor of things known to be impossible, or thought so; because men know, or think such deliberation vain. But of things impossible, which we think possible, we may deliberate; not knowing it is in vain. And it is called *deliberation*; because it is a putting an end to the *liberty* we had of doing, or omitting, according to our own appetite, or aversion.

This alternate succession of appetites, aversions, hopes and fears, is no less in other living creatures than in man: and therefore beasts also deliberate.

Every *deliberation* is then said to *end*, when that whereof they deliberate, is either done, or thought impossible; because till then we retain the liberty of doing, or omitting; according to our appetite, or aversion.

Materialism handles the problem of mind-body interaction easily enough, and it also explains quite clearly what place there is for minds in a physical universe of bodies. Minds *are* bodies, so there is no reason why the two should not interact, and as bodies they have a natural place in the physical world. But materialists have a really tough time accounting for the existence and nature of *consciousness*. You remember that

Descartes considered consciousness to be *the* distinctive characteristic of the mind. What is more, self-consciousness served as the logical starting point for his search for certainty. There was no conceivable way, he said, in which a self-conscious mind could doubt its own existence. But if the mind is a collection of atoms, if perception is one movement of those atoms, reasoning another movement of those atoms, and desire, aversion, love, hatred, deliberation, and choice yet other movements, then what becomes of consciousness?

My thoughts may be associated in some way with the motions of the atoms of my body, to be sure. There may be some close causal connection which modern techniques of brain surgery, neurophysiology, and the like can discover. But the most that a brain surgeon can prove, surely, is that when he puts an electrode in my brain and sends a little current through it, then I feel or hear or see or taste something. Does that show that my feeling, hearing, seeing, or tasting *is* the movement of the electricity along my nerve paths?

A number of very shrewd and sophisticated philosophers have argued quite recently that the answer is yes. The arguments are complex, as you might imagine, but you can get some sense of them from the selections with which we shall close this section. The principal selection is a portion of a 1963 article by the Australian philosopher J. J. C. Smart (1920–   ), who has taken the lead in defending the modern version of materialism. The brief criticism that follows is by the well-known American philosopher Norman Malcom (1911–   ), who taught at Cornell University.

> *Smart:* First of all let me try to explain what I mean by "materialism." I shall then go on to try to defend the doctrine. By "materialism" I mean the theory that there is nothing in the world over and above those entities which are postulated by physics (or, of course, those entities which will be postulated by future and more adequate physical theories). Thus I do not hold materialism to be wedded to the billiard-ball physics of the nineteenth century. The less visualizable particles of modern physics count as matter. Note that energy counts as matter for my purposes: indeed in modern physics energy and matter are not sharply distinguishable. Nor do I hold that materialism implies determinism. If physics is indeterministic on the micro-level, so must be the materalist's theory. I regard materialism as compatible with a wide range of conceptions of the nature of matter and energy. For example, if matter and energy consist of regions of special curvature of an absolute space-time, with "worn holes" and what not, this is still compatible with materialism: we can still argue that in the last resort the world is made up

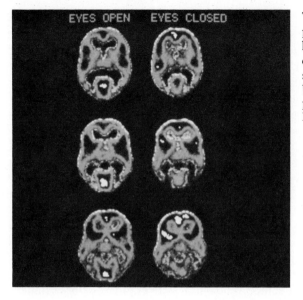

The CAT scan (short for computerized axial tomography) has made it possible for physicians to get a three-dimensional picture of the brain: but not, of course, to get a picture of the mind! (National Institutes of Health)

entirely of the ultimate entities of physics, namely space-time points. . . . [M]y definition will in some respects be narrower than those of some who have called themselves "materialists." I wish to lay down that it is incompatible with materialism that there should be any irreducibly "emergent" laws or properties, say in biology or psychology. According to the view I propose to defend, there are no irreducible laws or properties in biology, any more than there are in electronics. Given the "natural history" of a superheterodyne (its wiring diagram), a physicist is able to explain, using only laws of physics, its mode of behavior and its properties (for example, the property of being able to receive such and such a radio station which broadcasts on 25 megacycles). Just as electronics gives the physical explanation of the workings of superheterodynes, etc., so biology gives (or approximates to giving) physical and chemical explanations of the workings of organisms or parts of organisms. The biologist needs natural history just as the engineer needs wiring diagrams, but neither needs nonphysical laws.

It will now become clear why I define materialism in the way I have done above. I am concerned to deny that in the world there are nonphysical entities and nonphysical laws. In particular I wish to deny the doctrine of psychophysical dualism. (I also want to deny any theory of "emergent properties," since irreducibly nonphysical properties are just about as repugnant to me as are irreducibly nonphysical entities.)

Popular theologians sometimes argue against materialism by saying that "you can't put love in a test tube." Well you can't put a gravitational field in a test tube (except in some rather strained sense of these words), but there is nothing incompatible with materialism, as I have defined it, in the notion of a gravitational field.

Similarly, even though love may elude test tubes, it does not elude materialistic metaphysics, since it can be analyzed as a pattern of bodily behavior or, perhaps better, as the internal state of the human organism that accounts for this behavior. (A dualist who analyzes love as an internal state will perhaps say that it is a soul state, whereas the materialist will say that it is a brain state. It seems to me that much of our ordinary language about the mental is neither dualistic nor materialistic but is neutral between the two. Thus, to say that a locution is not materialistic is not to say that it is immaterialistic.)

But what about consciousness? Can we interpret the having of an after-image or of a painful sensation as something material, namely, a brain state or brain process? We seem to be immediately aware of pains and after-images, and we seem to be immediately aware of them as something different from a neurophysiological state or process. For example, the after-image may be green speckled with red, whereas the neurophysiologist looking into our brains would be unlikely to see something green speckled with red. However, if we object to materialism in this way we are victims of a confusion which U. T. Place has called "the phenomenological fallacy." To say that an image or sense datum is green is not to say that the conscious experience of having the image or sense datum is green. It is to say that it is the sort of experience we have when in normal conditions we look at a green apple, for example. Apples and unripe bananas can be green, but not the experiences of seeing them. An image or a sense datum can be green in a derivative sense, but this need not cause any worry, because, on the view I am defending, images and sense data are not constituents of the world, though the processes of having an image or a sense datum are actual processes in the world. The experience of having a green sense datum is not itself green; it is a process occurring in grey matter. The world contains plumbers, but does not contain the average plumber; it also contains the having of a sense datum, but does not contain the sense datum. . . .

It may be asked why I should demand of a tenable philosophy of mind that it should be compatible with materialism, in the sense in which I have defined it. One reason is as follows. How could a nonphysical property or entity suddenly arise in the course of animal evolution? A change in a gene is a change in a complex molecule which causes a change in the biochemistry of the cell. This may lead to changes in the shape or organization of the developing embryo. But what sort of chemical process could lead to the springing into existence of something nonphysical? No enzyme can catalyze the production of a spook! Perhaps it will be said that the nonphysical comes into existence as a by-product: that whenever there is a certain complex physical structure, then, by an irreducible extraphysical law, there is also a nonphysical entity. Such laws would be quite outside normal scientific conceptions and quite inexplicable: they would be, in Herbert Feigl's phrase, "nomological danglers." To say the very least, we can vastly simplify our cosmological outlook if we can defend a materialistic philosophy of mind. . . .

—J. J. C. SMART, *Materialism*

Malcolm: I wish to go into Smart's theory that there is a contingent identity between mental phenomena and brain phenomena. If such an identity exists, then brain phenomena must have all the properties that mental phenomena have, with the exception of intentional and modal properties. I shall argue that this condition cannot be fulfilled.

a. First, it is not meaningful to assign spatial locations to some kinds of mental phenomena, e.g., thoughts. Brain phenomena have spatial location. Thus, brain phenomena have a property that thoughts do not have. Therefore, thoughts are not identical with any brain phenomena.

b. Second, any thought requires a background of circumstances ("surroundings"), e.g., practices, agreements, assumptions. If a brain event were identical with a thought, it would require the same. The circumstances necessary for a thought cannot be described in terms of the entities and laws of physics. According to Smart's scientific materialism, everything in the world is "explicable in terms of physics." But if the identity theory were true, not even those brain events which are identical with thoughts would be "explicable in terms of physics." Therefore, the identity theory and scientific materialism are incompatible.

c. According to the identity theory, the identity between a thought and a brain event is contingent. If there is a contingent identity between A and B, the identity ought to be empirically verifiable. It does not appear that it would be empirically verifiable that a thought was identical with a brain event. Therefore, if a thought and a brain event are claimed to be identical, it is not plausible to hold that the identity is contingent.

—NORMAN MALCOLM,
Scientific Materialism and the Identity Theory

Let me give a brief explanation of one point that underlies the position Smart is defending. Smart's key claim, of course, is that states of consciousness just identically *are* states of the brain. You might think that you could test a claim like that immediately and conclusively, merely by examining the meanings of the words used in making it. After all, when I say "John Smith identically is John Smith," I can tell that that is true merely from the logical fact that in general anything is identical to itself. By the same token, when I say "Bachelors just identically are unmarried men," I can tell that that is true by examining the words used and realizing that "bachelor" means "unmarried man." So if states of consciousness really are just identically brain states, then I should be able to tell that that is true forthwith. But although this seems natural enough, it turns out not to be true. The reason is that two words or phrases may refer to one and the same thing, even though that fact is not revealed by their meanings. Let me give you a simple example that has become famous in recent philosophy. It is originally from the influential German mathematician and philosopher Gottlob Frege. As some of you may have noticed, it is sometimes possible to see what looks like a very bright star in the heavens just before sunset. From ancient times, that body has been referred to as "the evening star." It is also sometimes possible to see what looks like a very bright star in the heavens just after sunrise. That has long been called "the morning star." The ancients did not know exactly what those two visible bodies were, and because they appeared in different parts of the skies (one in the east, the other in the west), it was assumed that they were different bodies. We now know that both the evening star and the morning star are the planet Venus, which is large enough and close enough to be faintly visible in daylight at certain times in its movements around the sun.

Now think what this means. If a medieval astronomer had said, "The evening star is just identically the morning star," he would have been exactly right, but he would not have been able to prove that he was right without telescopes and other modern astronomical instruments. One of his fellow astronomers might have said, "If they are identical, then you ought to be able to tell that they are just by examining the meanings of the words in your assertion." But plausible though that would have sounded, it would have been wrong. The object named by the phrase "morning star" is identical with the object named by the phrase "evening star," but that fact must be discovered by science; it cannot be deduced merely from the meanings of the words. Philosophers refer to this as a *contingent identity*. J. J. C. Smart claims that the phrase "state of consciousness" names identically the same object or state of affairs as the phrase "brain state," but he says that the identity is a contingent one, and hence must be discovered by science, rather than merely deduced from the meanings of those phrases.

Berke Breathed, *Bloom County: Babylon, Five Years of Basic Naughtiness.* Copyright © 1986 by the Washington Post Company.

The Main Points in Chapter Eight

1. *Metaphysics* is the philosophical study of the fundamental nature of the things that exist. In the seventeenth century, Leibniz put forward the theory that the universe is composed of simple, indivisible things or *substances* which he called *monads.* By means of his theory of monads, Leibniz sought to explain the nature of space, of time, and of the mind.

2. One of the most controversial parts of Leibniz's theory was his claim that there is no actual interaction between our minds and the world around us. Our knowledge of the world, he suggested, really rests on a *pre-established harmony* between what goes on in our minds and what is happening in space and time.

3. Leibniz's metaphysical speculations, and those of Descartes before him, raised the general question of how the mind and body are related. Philosophers have advanced three theories of that relationship:
   a. Idealism: there are only minds. Bodies are really ideas in mind.
   b. Materialism: there are only bodies. Minds are really collections of bodies.
   c. Psycho-physical Dualism: there are two kinds of things—minds and bodies—which relate to one another in various ways.

4. Leibniz was an idealist. Descartes was a psycho-physical dualist. Thomas Hobbes was a materialist.

CONTEMPORARY APPLICATION

Do Computers Think?

According to Aristotle, man is a rational animal. Rationality, he argued, is the distinguishing mark of human beings, the "specific difference" that sets us off from all other animals. In the two thousand years since Aristotle offered his definition, philosophers have called attention to a number of other characteristics that seem to set humans apart: the fact that we play games, that we laugh, that we kill members of our own species, and of course the fact that we speak. Nevertheless, again and again one returns to rationality, for being able to think, to reason, does seem to be what makes us most fully human.

Descartes says, "I am a thing that thinks," thereby making thought his defining characteristic. Animals, he holds, are merely machines, for they have no consciousness, no thought processes. Leibniz echoes this view in his theory of monads. For most philosophers, it is the power of thought that has distinguished us from all other beings, and thought most often means some form of reasoning.

What do I mean when I say that I am rational? Well, one answer is that I can calculate. I can count objects, I can do sums, multiply two numbers together, or divide one by the other, or add or subtract them. The ability to perform computations has always seemed to philosophers to be central to what we mean when we say we are rational.

A second answer, closely associated with the first, is that I can perform logical deductions. Tell me that all men are mortal, and that Socrates is a man, and I can work it out that Socrates is mortal. From the premise that no woman has ever been elected president, and the premise that Zachary Taylor was the twelfth president, I can deduce that Zachary Taylor was not a woman. Many philosophers, impressed by the similarities between this sort of reasoning and arithmetic computations, have tried to find some way to represent logical deductions as a sort of calculation.

A third answer to the question, "What do I mean when I say that I am rational?" is that I learn from experience. I observe, I remember, and I generalize from past experiences so that I am better prepared to face the future. The first time I see fire, I may reach out to touch it, but very quickly I will learn that fire burns, and from then on I will be careful with it. Over time, I and my fellow humans acquire elaborate, complex systems of knowledge based on observation and generalization, with the aid of which we can transform the world around us.

Yet a fourth answer is that I can act in accordance with rules rather than merely behaving instinctively or in response to immediate stimuli. To be rational is to be able to follow a plan, play a game, conform to directions. Or, some philosophers have argued, to be rational is to be able to make up new rules, devise new games, formulate new plans, in the service of some end or goal or purpose.

Finally, to be rational, philosophers like Kant have said, is to be self-aware, self-conscious, capable not only of thinking, but also of thinking that one is thinking.

For two millennia, philosophers have puzzled over the nature of rationality without having to worry very much about whether humans are the only rational creatures in the universe. To be sure, God was assumed to possess reason to the highest degree, and angels, if one included them in one's world, also were rational. But among the things of this world, only human beings could be said to calculate or compute, to make logical deductions, to learn from experience, to make and follow rules, or to be self-conscious.

All this has changed drastically in the past twenty years or so with the invention of the high-speed sophisticated computer. Computers can calculate faster, more accurately, and with greater precision than humans ever could. Computers can also perform logical deductions. Indeed, the basic structure of a computer is modeled on a branch of logic known as Truth Function theory, or the First Order Predicate Calculus (believe it or not, those of you who know how to write simple computer programs, in BASIC or FORTRAN or Pascal, actually know quite a lot of logic without realizing it!). Computers can learn from experience, and they follow rules with great success. Computers are now capable of playing chess as well as a Master, which means better than all but one percent of the serious tournament players in the United States.

Or so it seems! Do computers actually perform arithmetic calculations? Well, they look as though they do. If I punch in "5" and "+" and "7" and hit the appropriate button, the computer prints "12" on the screen. Hasn't it added five and seven to get twelve? What else is there to doing arithmetic calculations?

One answer that springs to mind is consciousness. When I do a sum,

I think to myself, "five plus seven, that's twelve." I am aware of what I am doing. Indeed, I am *self*-aware. That is to say, I am aware that I am aware. And that, as Descartes and Kant agreed, is what distinguishes me from a mere machine.

Can we be sure, then, that a computer is *not* self-aware, not conscious? We could ask it, of course, but what would we do if it assured us that it *was* quite aware of what it was doing? This is the point at which the British mathematician and logician Alan Turing steps into the picture. Turing specialized in thinking up hypothetical situations, "thought experiments" they are called, that help us to reason about questions which puzzle or confuse us.

In this dialogue, written by Douglas Hofstadter, we are introduced to a test Turing thought up to determine whether a computer can think. In the course of the imaginary discussion among three young people, many of the knottiest philosophical issues of rationality, consciousness, and the nature of the self are posed and explored. Because this selection contains within it not one, not even just two, but three sides of the question, I have decided to include it alone. The dialogue ends with a question, not an answer. That is the most appropriate way for an introduction to philosophy to end!

Metamagical Themas
DOUGLAS HOFSTADTER

The participants in the following dialogue are Chris, a physics student, Pat, a biology student, and Sandy, a philosophy student.

Chris: Sandy, I want to thank you for suggesting that I read Alan Turing's article "Computing Machinery and Intelligence." It's a wonderful piece and certainly made me think—and think about my thinking.

Sandy: Glad to hear it. Are you still as much of a skeptic about artificial intelligence as you used to be?

Chris: You've got me wrong. I'm not against artificial intelligence: I think it's wonderful stuff—perhaps a little crazy,

SOURCE: Douglas R. Hofstader, *Metamagical Themas: Questing for the Essence of Mind and Pattern.* © 1985 by Basic Books, Inc. Reprinted by permission of the publisher.

why not? I simply am convinced that you A.I. advocates have far underestimated the human mind, and that there are things a computer will never, ever be able to do. For instance, can you imagine a computer writing a Proust novel? The richness of imagination, the complexity of the characters—

Sandy: Rome wasn't built in a day!

Chris: In the article Turing comes through as an interesting person. Is he still alive?

Sandy: No, he died back in 1954, at just 41. He'd only be 67 this year, although he is now such a legendary figure it seems strange to think that he could still have been living today.

Chris: How did he die?

Sandy: Almost certainly suicide. He was homosexual and was much persecuted for it. In the end it apparently got to be too much and he killed himself.

Chris: Sad.

Sandy: Yes, it certainly is. What saddens me is that he never got to see the amazing progress in computing machinery and computing theory that has taken place.

Pat: Hey, are you going to clue me into what this Turing article is about?

Sandy: It is really about two things. One is the question "Can a machine think?"—or rather "Will a machine ever think?" The way Turing answers the question—he thinks the answer is yes, by the way—is by batting down a series of objections to the idea, one after another. The other point he tries to make is that the question as it stands is not meaningful. It's too full of emotional connota-tions. Many people are upset by the sug-gestion that people are machines, or that machines might think. Turing tries to de-fuse the question by casting it in less emotional terms. For instance, what do you think, Pat, of the idea of thinking ma-chines?

Pat: Frankly, I find the term confus-ing. You know what confuses me? It's those ads in the newspapers and on TV that talk about "products that think" or "intelligent ovens" or whatever. I just don't know how seriously to take them.

Sandy: I know the kind of ads you mean, and they confuse a lot of people. On the one hand we're given the refrain "Computers are really dumb; you have to spell everything out for them in complete detail," and on the other we're bom-barded with advertising hype about "smart products."

Chris: That's certainly true. Do you know that one company has even taken to calling its products "dumb terminals" in order to stand out from the crowd?

Sandy: That's clever, but it just plays along with the trend toward obfuscation. The term electronic brain always comes to my mind when I'm thinking about this. Many people swallow it completely, and others reject it out of hand. It takes patience to sort out the issues and decide how much of it makes sense.

Pat: Does Turing suggest some way of resolving it, some kind of I.Q. test for ma-chines?

Sandy: That would be interesting, but no machine could yet come close to tak-ing an I.Q. test. Instead Turing proposes a test that theoretically could be applied to any machine to determine whether or not it can think.

Pat: Does the test give a clear-cut yes-or-no answer? I'd be skeptical if it claimed to.

Sandy: No, it doesn't claim to. In a way that's one of its advantages. It shows how the borderline is quite fuzzy and how subtle the whole question is.

Pat: And so, as is usual in philosophy, it's all just a question of words.

Sandy: Maybe, but they're emotionally charged words, and so it's important, it seems to me, to explore the issues and try to map out the meanings of the crucial words. The issues are fundamental to our concept of ourselves, so we shouldn't just sweep them under the rug.

Pat: So tell me how Turing's test works.

Sandy: The idea is based on what he calls the imitation game. A man and a woman go into separate rooms and can be interrogated by a third party via some sort of teletype setup. The third party can address questions to either room but has no idea which person is in each room. For the interrogator the idea is to determine which room the woman is in. The woman, by her answers, tries to help the interrogator as much as she can. The man, however, is doing his best to bamboozle the interrogator, by responding as he thinks a woman might. And if he succeeds in fooling the interrogator—

Pat: The interrogator only gets to see written words, eh? And the sex of the author is supposed to shine through? It sounds like a good challenge. I'd certainly like to take part in it someday. Would the interrogator know either the man or the woman before the test began? Would any of them know the others?

Sandy: That would probably be a bad idea. All kinds of subliminal cueing might occur if the interrogator knew one or both of them. It would certainly be best if all three people were totally unknown to one another.

Pat: Could you ask any questions at all, with no holds barred?

Sandy: Absolutely. That's the whole idea.

Pat: Don't you think, then, that pretty quickly it would degenerate into sex-oriented questions? I can imagine the man, overeager to act convincing, giving away the game by answering some very blunt questions that most women would find too personal to answer, even through an anonymous computer connection.

Sandy: It sounds plausible.

Chris: Another possibility would be to explore traditional sex-role differences, such as asking about dress sizes and so on. The psychology of the imitation game could get pretty subtle. I suppose it would make a difference if the interrogator were a woman instead of a man. Don't you think that a woman could spot some telltale differences more quickly than a man?

Pat: If so, maybe *that's* how to tell a man from a woman.

Sandy: H'm. . . . That's a new twist. In any case I don't know if this original version of the imitation game has ever been seriously tried out, in spite of the fact that it would be relatively easy to do with modern computer terminals. I have to admit, though, that I'm not at all sure what it would prove, whichever way it turned out.

Pat: I was wondering about that. What would it prove if the interrogator—say a woman—couldn't tell correctly which person was the woman? It certainly wouldn't prove that the man *was* a woman.

Sandy: Exactly. What I find funny is that although I fundamentally believe in the Turing test, I'm not sure what the point is of the imitation game, on which it is founded.

Chris: I'm not any happier with the Turing test as a test for thinking machines than I am with the imitation game as a test for femininity.

Pat: From what you say I gather the Turing test is a kind of extension of the imitation game, only involving a machine and a person in separate rooms.

Sandy: That's the idea. The machine tries its hardest to convince the interrogator that it is the human being, and the human tries to make it clear that he or she is not the computer.

Pat: Except for your loaded phrase "the machine tries," this sounds very interesting. But how do you know that this test will get at the essence of thinking? Maybe it's testing for the wrong things. Maybe, just to take a random illustration, someone would feel that a machine was able to think only if it could dance so well that you couldn't tell it was a machine. Or someone else could suggest some other characteristic. What's so sacred about being able to fool people by typing at them?

Sandy: I don't see how you can say such a thing. I've heard that objection before, but frankly it baffles me. So what if the machine can't tap dance or drop a rock on your toe? If it can discourse intelligently on any subject you want, then it has shown it can think. It has shown it to me, at least. As I see it, Turing has drawn, in one clean stroke, a clear division between thinking and other aspects of being human.

Pat: Now *you're* the baffling one. If you couldn't conclude anything from a man's ability to win at the imitation game, how could you conclude anything from a machine's ability to win at the Turing game?

Chris: Good question.

Sandy: It seems to me that you could conclude *something* from a man's win at the imitation game. You wouldn't conclude he was a woman, but you could certainly say he had good insights into the feminine mentality (if there is such a thing). Now, if a computer could fool someone into thinking it was a person, I guess you'd have to say something similar about it—that it had good insights into what it's like to be human, into the human condition, whatever that is.

Pat: Maybe, but that isn't necessarily equivalent to thinking, is it? It seems to me that passing the Turing test would merely prove some machine or other could do a very good job of *simulating* thought.

Chris: I couldn't agree more with Pat. We all know that fancy computer programs exist today for simulating all sorts of complex phenomena. In physics, for instance, we simulate the behavior of particles, atoms, solids, liquids, gases, galaxies and so on. But no one confuses any of those simulations with the real thing.

Sandy: In his book *Brainstorms* the philosopher Daniel Dennett makes a similar point about simulated hurricanes.

Chris: That's a nice example too. Obviously what goes on inside a computer when it's simulating a hurricane is not a hurricane. The machine's memory doesn't get torn to bits by 200-mile-an-hour winds, the floor of the machine room doesn't get flooded with rainwater, and so on.

Sandy: Oh, come on—that's not a fair argument. In the first place the programmers don't claim the simulation really *is* a hurricane. It's merely a simulation of certain aspects of a hurricane. But in the second place you're pulling a fast one when you imply that there are no downpours or 200-mile-an-hour winds in a simulated hurricane. To *us* there aren't any, but if the program were incredibly detailed, it could include simulated people on the ground who would experience the wind and the rain just as we do when a hurricane hits. In their minds—or, if you'd rather, in their *simulated* minds— the hurricane would be not a simulation but a genuine phenomenon complete with drenching and devastation.

Chris: Oh, boy—what a science-fiction scenario! Now we're talking about simulating entire populations, not just a single mind.

Sandy: Well, look, I'm simply trying to show you why your argument that a sim-

ulated McCoy isn't the real McCoy is fallacious. It depends on the tacit assumption that any old observer of the simulated phenomenon is equally able to assess what's going on. In fact it may take an observer with a special vantage to recognize what is going on. In this case it takes special "computational glasses" to see the rain and the winds.

Pat: Computational glasses? I don't know what you're talking about.

Sandy: I mean that to see the winds and the wetness of the hurricane you have to be able to look at it in the proper way. You—

Chris: No, no, no! A simulated hurricane isn't wet! No matter how much it might seem wet to simulated people, it won't ever be *genuinely* wet. And no computer will ever get torn apart in the process of simulating winds.

Sandy: Certainly not, but you're confusing levels. The laws of physics don't get torn apart by real hurricanes, either. In the case of the simulated hurricane, if you go peering at the computer's memory expecting to find broken wires and so forth, you'll be disappointed. But look at the proper level. Look into the *structures* that are coded for in the memory. You'll see that some abstract links have been broken, some values of variables radically changed and so on. There's your flood, your devastation. It is real, only a little concealed, a little hard to detect.

Chris: I'm sorry, I just can't buy it. You're insisting that I look for a new kind of devastation, one never before associated with hurricanes. That way you could call *anything* a hurricane as long as its effects, seen through your special glasses, could be called floods and devastation.

Sandy: Right—you've got it! You recognize a hurricane by its *effects*. You have no way of going in and finding some ethereal essence of hurricane, some "hurricane soul" right in the middle of the storm's eye. It's the existence of a certain kind of *pattern*—a spiral storm with an eye and so forth—that makes you say it's a hurricane. Of course, there are a lot of things you'll insist on before you call something a hurricane.

Pat: Well, wouldn't you say that being an *atmospheric* phenomenon is one prerequisite? How can anything inside a computer be a storm? To me a simulation is a simulation is a simulation.

Sandy: Then I suppose you would say that even the *calculations* computers do are simulated, that they are fake calculations. Only people can do genuine calculations, right?

Pat: Well, computers get the right answers, so their calculations are not exactly fake, but they're still just *patterns*. There's no understanding going on in there. Take a cash register. Can you honestly say that you feel it is *calculating* something when its gears turn on one another? A computer is just a fancy cash register, as I understand it.

Sandy: If you mean that a cash register doesn't feel like a schoolkid doing arithmetic problems, I'll agree. But is that what calculation means? Is that an integral part of it? If it is, then contrary to what everybody has thought up to now

we'll have to write a very complicated program to perform *genuine* calculations. Of course, such a program will sometimes get careless and make mistakes and will sometimes scrawl its answers illegibly, and it will occasionally doodle on its paper. It won't be any more reliable than the store clerk who adds up your total by hand. Now, I happen to believe eventually such a program could be written. Then we'd know something about how clerks and schoolkids work.

Pat: I can't believe you would ever be able to do it.

Sandy: Maybe, maybe not, but that's not my point. You say a cash register can't calculate. It reminds me of another favorite passage of mine from Dennett's *Brainstorms*. It goes something like this: "Cash registers can't really calculate; they can only spin their gears. But cash registers can't really spin their gears, either; they can only follow the laws of physics." Dennett said it originally about computers; I modified it to refer to cash registers. And you could use the same line of reasoning in talking about people: "People can't really calculate; all they can do is manipulate mental symbols. But they aren't really manipulating symbols; all they are doing is firing various neurons in various patterns. But they can't really make their neurons fire; they simply have to let the laws of physics make the neurons fire for them." Et cetera. Don't you see how this reductio ad absurdum would lead you to conclude that calculation doesn't exist, hurricanes don't exist, nothing at a level higher than particles and the laws of physics exists? What do you gain by saying a computer only pushes symbols around and doesn't truly calculate?

Pat: The example may be extreme, but it makes my point that there is a vast difference between a real phenomenon and any simulation of it. This is true for hurricanes and even more so for human thought.

Sandy: Look, I don't want to get too tangled up in this line of argument, but let me try one more example. If you were a radio ham listening to another ham broadcasting in Morse code and you were responding in Morse code, would it sound funny to you to refer to "the person at the other end"?

Pat: No, that would sound okay, although the existence of a person at the other end would be an assumption.

Sandy: Yes, but you wouldn't be likely to go and check it out. You're prepared to recognize personhood through those rather unusual channels. You don't have to see a human body or hear a voice. All you need is a rather abstract manifestation—a code. What I'm getting at is this. To "see" the person behind the dits and dahs, you have to be willing to do some *decoding*, some interpretation. It's not direct perception; it's indirect. You have to peel off a layer or two to find the reality hidden in there. You put on your radio ham's glasses to see the person behind the buzzes. It's the same with the simulated hurricane. You don't see it darkening the machine room; you have to decode the machine's memory. You have to put on special memory-decoding glasses. *Then* what you see is a hurricane.

Pat: Oh ho! Talk about fast ones. In the case of the short-wave radio there's a real person out there, somewhere in the Fiji Islands or wherever. My decoding act as I sit by my radio simply reveals that that person exists. It's like seeing a shadow and concluding there's an object out there casting it. One doesn't confuse the shadow with the object, however. With the hurricane there's no real storm behind the scenes, making the computer follow its patterns. No, what you have is just a shadow hurricane without any genuine hurricane. I simply refuse to confuse shadows with reality.

Sandy: All right. I don't want to drive the point into the ground. I even admit it is pretty silly to say that a simulated hurricane *is* a hurricane. I just wanted to point out that it's not as silly as you might think at first blush. And when you turn to simulated thought, you've got a very different matter on your hands from simulated hurricanes.

Pat: I don't see why. You still have to convince me. . . .

Chris: I would want to see if the program could understand jokes. That would be a real test of intelligence.

Sandy: I agree that humor probably is an acid test for a supposedly intelligent program, but equally important to me—perhaps more so—would be to test its emotional responses. So I would ask it about its reactions to certain pieces of music or works of literature—particularly my favorite ones.

Chris: What if it said, "I don't know that piece," or even "I have no interest in music"? What if it avoided all emotional references?

Sandy: That would make me suspicious. Any consistent pattern of avoiding certain issues would raise serious doubts in my mind about whether I was dealing with a thinking being.

Chris: Why do you say that? Why not say you're dealing with a thinking but unemotional being?

Sandy: You've hit on a sensitive point. I simply can't believe emotions and thought can be divorced. To put it another way, I think emotions are an automatic by-product of the ability to think. They are required by the very nature of thought.

Chris: Well, what if you're wrong? What if I produced a machine that could think but not emote? Then its intelligence might go unrecognized because it failed to pass *your* kind of test.

Sandy: I'd like you to point out to me where the boundary line between emotional questions and nonemotional ones lies. You might want to ask about the meaning of a great novel. This requires an understanding of human emotions. Is that thinking or merely cool calculation? You might want to ask about a subtle choice of words. For that you need an understanding of their connotations. Turing uses examples like this in his article. You might want to ask for advice about a complex romantic situation. The machine would need to know a lot about human motivations and their roots. If it failed at

this kind of task, I would not be much inclined to say that it could think. As far as I am concerned, the ability to think, the ability to feel and consciousness are just different facets of one phenomenon, and no one of them can be present without the others. . . .

Chris: I still can't see that intelligence has to involve emotions. Why couldn't you imagine an intelligence that simply calculates and has no feelings?

Sandy: A couple of answers here. Number one, any intelligence has to have motivations. It's simply not the case, whatever many people may believe, that machines could think any more objectively than people do. Machines, when they look at a scene, will have to focus and filter the scene down into some preconceived categories, just as a person does. And that means seeing some things and missing others. It means giving more weight to some things than to others. This happens on every level of processing.

Pat: I'm not sure I'm following you.

Sandy: Take me right now, for instance. You might think I'm just making some intellectual points, and I wouldn't need emotions to do that. But what makes me *care* about these points? Why did I stress the word "care" so heavily? Because I'm emotionally involved in this conversation. People talk to one another out of conviction, not out of hollow, mechanical reflexes. Even the most intellectual conversation is driven by underlying passions. There's an emotional undercurrent to every conversation. It's the fact that the speakers want to be listened to and understood, and respected for what they are saying. . . .

Pat: How can you think of a computer as a conscious being? I apologize if this sounds like a stereotype, but when I think of conscious beings, I just can't connect that thought with machines. To me consciousness is connected with soft, warm bodies, silly though it may sound.

Chris: That *does* sound odd coming from a biologist. Don't you deal with life in terms of chemistry and physics enough for all magic to seem to vanish?

Pat: Not really. Sometimes the chemistry and physics simply increase the feeling that there's something magical going on in there. Anyway, I can't always integrate my scientific knowledge with my gut feelings.

Chris: I guess I share the trait.

Pat: So how do you deal with rigid preconceptions like mine?

Sandy: I'd try to dig down under the surface of your concept of machines and get at the intuitive connotations that lurk there, out of sight but deeply influencing your opinions. I think we all have a holdover image from the Industrial Revolution that sees machines as iron contraptions moving under the power of some chugging engine. Maybe that's even how the computer inventor Charles Babbage saw people. After all, he called his geared computer "the analytical engine."

Pat: Well, I certainly don't think people are just fancy steam shovels or even electric can openers. There's something about people, something that— that—they've got a kind of *flame* inside them, something alive, something that flickers unpredictably, wavering, uncertain—but something *creative.*

Sandy: Great! That's just the sort of thing I wanted to hear. It's very human to think that way. Your flame image makes me think of candles, of fires, of thunderstorms with lightning dancing all over the sky. But do you realize just that kind of thing is visible on a computer's console? The flickering lights form chaotic sparkling patterns. It's such a far cry from heaps of lifeless, clanking metal. It *is* flamelike, by God! Why don't you let the word "machine" conjure up images of dancing patterns of light rather than of giant steam shovels?

Chris: That *is* a powerful image, Sandy. It does change my sense of mechanism from being matter-oriented to being pattern-oriented. It makes me try to visualize the thoughts in my mind— these thoughts right now, even—as a huge spray of tiny pulses flickering in my brain.

Sandy: That's quite a poetic self-portrait for a spray of flickers to have come up with!

Chris: But still I'm not totally convinced that a machine is all I am. I admit my concept of machines probably *does* suffer from anachronistic subconscious flavors, but I'm afraid I can't change such a deeply rooted sense in a flash.

Sandy: At least you do sound open-minded. And to tell the truth part of me does sympathize with the way you and Pat view machines. Part of me balks at calling myself a machine. It *is* a bizarre thought that a feeling being like you or me might emerge from mere circuitry. Do I surprise you?

Chris: You certainly surprise *me*. So tell us—*do* you believe in the idea of an intelligent computer or don't you?

Sandy: It all depends on what you mean. We've all heard the question, "Can computers think?" There are several possible interpretations of this (apart from the many interpretations of the word "think"). They revolve around different meanings of the words "can" and "computer."

Pat: Back to word games again.

Sandy: That's right. First of all, the question might mean, "Does some present-day computer think, right now?" To that I would immediately answer with a loud no. Then it could be taken to mean, "Could some present-day computer, if it was suitably programmed, potentially think?" That would be more like it, but I would still answer, "Probably not." The real difficulty hinges on the word "computer." The way I see it, "computer" calls up an image of just what I described earlier: an air-conditioned room with rectangular metal boxes in it. But I believe progress in computer architecture will eventually make that vision outmoded.

Pat: Don't you think computers as we know them will be around for a while?

Sandy: Sure, there will have to be computers in today's image around for a long time, but advanced computers— maybe no longer called computers—will evolve and become quite different. Probably, as with living organisms, there will be many branchings in the evolutionary tree. There will be computers for business, computers for schoolkids, computers for scientific calculations, computers for systems research, computers for simulation, computers for rockets going into space and so on. Finally, there will be computers for the study of intelligence. It's really only these last that I'm thinking of—the ones with the maximum flexibility, the ones people are deliberately attempting to make smart. I see no reason for these staying fixed in the traditional image. They will probably soon acquire as standard features some rudimentary sensory systems, at first mostly for vision and hearing. They will need to be able to move around, to explore. They will have to be physically flexible. In short, they will have to become more self-reliant, more animal-like.

Chris: It makes me think of the robots R2D2 and C3PO in *Star Wars*.

Sandy: As a matter of fact I don't think of anything like them when I visualize intelligent machines. They are too silly, too much the product of a film designer's imagination. Not that I have a clear vision of my own. But I do think it is necessary, if people are realistically going to try to imagine an artificial intelligence, to go beyond the limited, hard-edged picture of computers that comes from seeing what we have today. The only thing all machines will always have in common is their underlying mechanicalness. That may sound cold and inflexible, but what could be more mechanical—in a wonderful way—than the working of the DNA and enzymes in our cells?

Pat: To me what goes on inside cells

has a wet, slippery feel to it and what goes on inside machines is dry and rigid. It's connected with the fact that computers don't make mistakes, that computers do only what you tell them to do. At least that's my image of computers. . . .

Sandy: I guess I'm a strange sort of advocate for machine intelligence. To some degree I straddle the fence. I think machines won't really be intelligent in a humanlike way until they have something like that biological wetness or slipperiness to them. I don't mean *literally* wet—the slipperiness could be in the software. But biological-seeming or not, intelligent machines will in any case be machines. We shall have designed them, built them— or grown them! We shall understand how they work, at least in some sense. Possibly no one person will really understand them, but collectively we shall know how they work.

Pat: It sounds as if you want to have your cake and eat it too.

Sandy: You're probably right. What I'm getting at is that when artificial intelligence comes, it will be mechanical and yet at the same time organic. It will have the same amazing flexibility that we see in life's mechanisms. And when I say mechanisms, I *mean* mechanisms. DNA and enzymes and so on really *are* mechanical and rigid and reliable. Don't you agree, Pat?

Pat: I have to. But when they work together, a lot of unexpected things happen. There are so many complexities and rich modes of behavior that all the mechanicalness adds up to something very fluid.

Sandy: For me it's an almost unimaginable transition from the mechanical level of molecules to the living level of cells. But it's what convinces me that people are machines. The thought makes me uncomfortable in some ways, but in other ways it is exhilarating.

Chris: If people are machines, how come it's so hard to convince them of the fact? Surely if we are machines, we ought to be able to recognize our own machinehood.

Sandy: You have to allow for emotional factors here. To be told you're a machine is in a way to be told that you're nothing more than your physical parts, and it brings you face to face with your own mortality. That's something no one finds easy to confront. But beyond the emotional objection, to see yourself as a machine you have to jump all the way from the bottom-most mechanical level to the level where the complex lifelike activities take place. If there are many intermediate layers, they act as a shield and the mechanical quality becomes almost invisible. I think when intelligent machines come, that's how they will seem to us—and to themselves!

Pat: I once heard a funny idea about what will happen when we eventually have intelligent machines. When we try to implant that intelligence into devices we'd like to control, their behavior won't be so predictable.

Sandy: They'll have a quirky little "flame" inside, maybe?

Pat: Maybe.

Chris: And what's so funny about that?

Pat: Well, think of military missiles. The more sophisticated their target-tracking computers get, according to this idea, the less predictably they will function. Eventually you'll have missiles that will decide they are pacifists and will turn around and go home and land quietly without blowing up. We could even have smart bullets that turn around in mid-flight because they don't want to commit suicide.

Sandy: A lovely thought.

Chris: I'm very skeptical about all this. Still, Sandy, I'd like to hear your predictions about when intelligent machines will come to be.

Sandy: It probably won't be for a long time that we'll see anything remotely resembling the level of human intelligence. It rests on too awesomely complicated a substrate—the brain—for us to be able to duplicate it in the foreseeable future. That's my opinion, anyway.

Pat: Do you think a program will ever pass the Turing test?

Sandy: That's a pretty hard question. I guess there are various degrees of passing such a test, when you come down to it. It's not black and white. First of all it depends on who the interrogator is. A simple-minded person might be totally taken in by some programs today. But secondly it depends on how deeply you are allowed to probe.

Pat: Then you could have a range of Turing tests—one-minute versions, five-minute versions, hour-long versions. Wouldn't it be interesting if some official organization sponsored a periodic competition, like the annual computer-chess championships, for programs to try to pass the Turing test?

Chris: The program that lasted the longest against some panel of distinguished judges would be the winner. Perhaps there could be a big prize for the first program that can fool a famous judge for, say, 10 minutes.

Pat: What would a program do with a prize?

Chris: Come now, Pat. If a program's good enough to fool the judges, don't you think it's good enough to enjoy the prize?

Pat: Sure—particularly if the prize is an evening out on the town, dancing with the interrogators.

Sandy: I'd certainly like to see something like that established. I think it could be hilarious to watch the first programs flop pathetically.

Pat: You're pretty skeptical, aren't you? Well, do you think any computer program today could pass a five-minute Turing test, given a sophisticated interrogator? . . .

Chris: If you could ask a computer just one question in the Turing test, what would it be?

Sandy: Um—

Pat: I've got one. How about "If you could ask a computer just one question in the Turing test, what would it be?"?

Study Questions

1. What *are* minds? It is easy enough to find objections to the leading philosophical theories, but very hard indeed to come up with an alternative. Does it make any sense to say that my mind is a substance with neither spatial location nor mass? On the other hand, does it make sense to identify my mind with the brain, the heart, the nervous system, or some other anatomical structure?

2. Let us suppose, for the sake of argument, that one or another of the three theories of mind/body relation discussed in the chapter is true. How could we go about deciding which one it was? Would scientific evidence help us? Logical analysis? Inner reflection?

3. Every time we decide that there is some distinctively human capacity that computers cannot imitate, someone invents a way for computers to imitate it! By the time you are my age [fifty-three at this writing], computers may very well be walking, talking, designing houses, writing music, and who knows what else! At what point down the road do we have to start worrying about whether computers should have the vote?

4. Can computers *feel*? Can they love, hate, desire, yearn? Suppose we can build a computer that *imitates* all these human emotional responses, and *looks* rather human besides. Should we be allowed to marry computers? Kill them [that is, turn them off]? Hire them? Ought we to pay them at least minimum wage? Why?

5. Now that you have read all the way to the end of this book, do you have a better idea of what philosophy is? Is it an activity you want to continue to engage in? Why? Why not?

GLOSSARY

Alienation According to Marx, it is the condition of being at war with one's own nature, the products of one's labor, and one's fellow workers. Marx argued that capitalism undermines the human capacity for creative and productive work, making men and women unhappy in their work, dissatisfied in their leisure, and unable to fulfill their human potential. Marx derived the concept of alienation from German philosophers of the early nineteenth century.

Analytic proposition A statement that merely spells out what is already contained in the subject of the statement.

Anarchist One who believes that no state has any right to rule and that governmental authority is illegitimate and undesirable.

Argument from design The attempt to prove the existence of God by demonstrating the high degree of organization and purposive order in the universe, and arguing that such design must be the product of an intelligent, powerful, purposeful creator. The argument is very old, but had a wide popularity in the eighteenth century.

a posteriori As a consequence of experience of objects—an adverb used to modify verbs of cognition, as "to know *a posteriori*" or "to apprehend *a posteriori*." Propositions are said to be knowable *a posteriori* when they are knowable only as a consequence of an experience of the objects they make assertions about.

a priori Prior to, or independently of, experience—an adverb used to modify verbs of cognition, as "to know *a priori*." Propositions are said to be knowable *a priori* when they are knowable prior to, or independently of, any experience of the objects they make assertions about.

Attributes   The characteristics, states, activities, or features which predicates name or refer to.

Bourgeoisie   See Proletariat

Capitalism   An economic system based on concentration of private ownership of the means of production in relatively few hands, a large class of propertyless workers who work for wages, and production for sale and profit rather than for use. The money invested by the property owners for the purpose of making a profit is called *capital*, hence the system is called capitalism.

Categorical imperative   A term invented by Immanuel Kant to refer to a command that orders us to do something unconditionally—that is, regardless of what we want or what our aims and purposes are. According to Kant, we experience the principles of morality as Categorical Imperatives. The term is also used, by Kant and those following him, to refer to one particular moral principle, which Kant calls The Highest Moral Law.

Catharsis   Literally, a cleansing or purging. Aristotle uses the term to describe the effect on us of powerful dramatic performances. By watching a play whose events arouse fear and pity within us, he thought, we are purged of those emotions, so that we leave the theater liberated or cleansed. The opposing view is that such plays (and, by extension, movies and television programs) arouse in us feelings we otherwise wouldn't have, and shouldn't have, such as aggressive and sexual feelings.

Cogito, ergo sum   "I think, therefore I am"—the phrase used by Descartes to prove his own existence.

Copy theory of ideas   The theory that all our ideas are either copies of sense impressions or else combinations and rearrangements of copies of sense impressions.

Cosmological argument   The attempt to prove the existence of God by starting with the mere fact of motion, or change, or the existence of things in the universe, and then arguing that these must have their origin in a being that does not move, or does not change, or does not merely happen to exist. The earliest form of the argument is to be found in the writings of Aristotle.

Cosmology   Literally, the study of the order of the world. Now used to refer to the branch of astronomy that investigates the organization and structure of the entire physical universe, including its origins. In philosophy, cosmology is a part of the subfield called metaphysics, or the study of first principles.

Dialectical method   A technique of probing questions, developed by Socrates, for the purpose of prodding, pushing, and provoking unreflective persons into realizing their lack of rational understanding of their own principles of thought and action, so that they can set out on the path to philosophical wisdom. As used by Socrates, the dialectical method was a powerful weapon for deflating inflated egos.

Dialogue   A process of question and answer between two people.

Empiricism/Rationalism   Empiricism and rationalism are the two leading epistemological theories of the past four centuries. *Empiricism* is the theory that all human knowledge comes from the evidence of our five senses, and therefore that we can never know more, or know with greater certainty, than our senses will allow. *Rationalism* is the theory that at least some human knowledge comes from reason, unaided by the senses, and therefore that we can know about things that the senses do not reveal to us, and can know with greater certainty than the senses alone will allow.

Epistemological skepticism   The doctrine that no adequate justification can be given for any of our beliefs about the world, not even for apparently rock-solid beliefs that there is a physical world, that I have a body, that the sun will rise tomorrow, or that fire causes heat. The aim of epistemological skepticism is to focus our attention on the relationship between our beliefs and their justification, not to get us actually to stop believing.

Epistemological turn   A shift in philosophy from emphasis on metaphysics to emphasis on epistemology.

Epistemology   Literally, the study of knowledge. Epistemology is the study of how we come to know things, what the limits are of our knowledge, and what sort of certainty or uncertainty attaches to our knowledge. Psychology also studies how we come to know, but epistomology is concerned less with the mechanics of knowing than with the possibility of defending, proving, or justifying what we think we know. Since the early seventeenth century, epistemology has been the most important branch of philosophy.

Ethical relativism   The theory that whether an act is right or wrong depends on—is relative to—the society in which one lives. Sometimes ethical relativists merely claim that we must take social contexts and rules into account, but sometimes they assert that one and the same act is right for men and women in one society and wrong for men and women in another. Frequently confused with *Ethical Skepticism,* which doubts that any acts are right or wrong, and *Ethical Nihilism,* which denies that any acts are either right or wrong.

Ethics   In philosophy, the systematic study of how we ought to act, both toward ourselves and to others, and also the study of what things, character traits, or types of persons are good, estimable, admirable, and what kinds are bad, reprehensible, worthy of being condemned. Ethics deals both with general rules or principles, and also with particular cases.

Existentialism   The philosophical doctrine, associated originally with Søren Kierkegaard, according to which our being as subjective individuals (our *existence*) is more important than what we have in common objectively with all other human beings (our essence). Of primary concern for Kierkegaard was his relationship to God. Later existentialists emphasized the individual's creation of himself or herself through free individual choices.

Fascism   The twentieth-century political movement begun in Italy in 1919 by Mussolini, which emphasized the primacy of the nation or people, opposed left-wing political movements, and sought a rebirth of the ancient glory of the Italian people. Subsequently, the term *fascist* has been broadly applied to right-wing popular movements which celebrate military power and use the police power of the state to suppress dissent or opposition. The word derives from the Latin term for a bundle of sticks bound together, a *fasces,* which served as the symbol of Mussolini's party.

Faith   In Christianity, trust that God will keep the promise He made to the Israelites in the Old Testament and renewed to all mankind in the New Testament (hence, "trust in the Lord"). Originally, the promise was to make the Israelites fruitful and populous. In the New Testament, the promise is of life eternal in heaven. According to some Christians, men and women are unable to have and sustain this trust without the miraculous help of God.

The general will   A term invented by Jean-Jacques Rousseau to describe the decision by the citizens of a republic to set aside their private and partisan concerns, and instead collectively aim at the general good. According to Rousseau, to say that a society "has a general will" is to say that all the members of the society are public-spiritedly aiming at the general good in their political actions and deliberations. Rousseau was very pessimistic about the possibility of ever achieving a general will.

Historical materialism The Marxist theory that ideas and social institutions develop only as a reflection of a material economic base.

Idealism The Mind-Body theory that everything in the universe is either minds, or else ideas in minds (hence, *idealism*). Bodies, according to the idealist, are simply particular collections of ideas. Thus, a table is simply the interconnected set of all the ideas—concepts, images, feels, sights, sounds, etc.—that I think of as ideas *of* a table.

Identity crisis A term invented by the psychoanalyst Erik Erikson to refer to the period of instability, uncertainty, and personality formation through which teen-agers pass in societies like ours. Erikson intended to suggest, by the term, that the period is one of genuine flux and indeterminacy, with the outcome—a healthy, coherent adult personality—hanging in the balance.

Intrinsic value/Instrumental value To say that something has *intrinsic value* is to say that it is valuable, good, worthwhile, purely for itself alone, regardless of what it may produce or lead to. Some people say that pleasure has intrinsic value, others that beauty does, still others that moral goodness does. *Instrumental value* is the value something has as a means, or instrument, for producing or getting something else. A tool or instrument that is useful for some purpose is said to be instrumentally valuable.

Irony A mode of discourse by which the speaker communicates, to the real audience, a meaning opposite from that conveyed to the superficial, or apparent audience.

Laissez-faire Literally, to allow to do. Laissez-faire is the system of free market exchanges, with an absolute minimum of government control, which nineteenth-century liberals believed would result in the most efficient use of resources, and the greatest material well-being for a society. Laissez-faire capitalism refers to the early stage in the development of capitalism, when firms were small, owner-run, and controlled both in their purchases and in their sales by market pressures.

Law of contradiction/Law of the excluded middle The two basic laws of formal logic. *The Law of Contradiction* states that a statement and its contradictory cannot both be true. For example, the statement "Fire is hot," may be true, and it may be false. Its contradictory, "It isn't the case that fire is hot" may be true, and it may be false. But it cannot be that *both* the statement *and* its contradictory are true. *The Law of the Excluded Middle* says that for any statement, *either* it is true *or* its contradictory is true. Thus, either fire is hot, or it is not the case that fire is hot.

Legitimate authority The right to give commands that others have a moral obligation to obey. States claim legitimate authority when they say that they have a right to pass laws which citizens or subjects *ought* to obey, regardless of whether they are in danger of being caught for not obeying. Democratic states base their claim to legitimate authority on the fact that they are elected by the people whom they rule, and therefore speak with the voice of the people.

Logic The discipline that investigates the correct principles of formal reasoning—sometimes characterized as the science of the laws of thought.

Marxism   The economic, political, and philosophical doctrines first set forth by Karl Marx, and then developed by his disciples and followers. Although Marx himself considered his theories scientific, his followers have often treated them as a form of secular religion. The principal doctrines are: first, that capitalism is internally unstable and prone to fall into economic crises; second, that the profits of capitalist enterprises derive from the exploitation of the workers, who receive in wages less than they produce; third, that as capitalism develops, workers will tend to become more self-aware of their situation, and hence more likely to overthrow capitalism by force; and finally, that the society that comes into existence after capitalism is destroyed will be socialist and democratic in its economic and political organization.

Materialism   The Mind-Body theory that everything in the universe is matter (hence, "materialist"). Minds, according to the materialist, are simply collections of very small bodies, or structures and organizations of bodies (such as nerve cells in the brain). Perceptions, to the materialist, are particular sorts of interactions between bodies, and so are thoughts, emotions, and feelings of pleasure and pain.

Metaphysics   In modern philosophy, the study of the most fundamental principles of the nature of things. The term derives from an early description of the set of essays by Aristotle, called by him "First Philosophy," which came after the Physics in an edition of Aristotle's works, (*ta meta ta physica* or "after the Physics.")

Method of doubt   The suspension of judgment in regard to knowledge claims until they have been demonstrated to be either true or false.

Mind-body problem   The *Mind-Body Problem* is the problem of explaining exactly what the relationship is between our minds and physical bodies in space. There are really *three* problems lumped together under this heading: First, do minds and bodies causally interact with one another, and if so, how? Second, how, if at all, can I (i.e., my mind) gain knowledge about bodies—indeed, can minds really know anything at all about bodies, or do minds only know about themselves? And third, what is the special relationship between *my* mind and *my* body? In the twentieth century, the Mind-Body Problem led philosophers to a related problem, the *Problem of Other Minds*: How, if at all, can I know of the existence and contents of minds other than my own? Is there anyone out there, or am I alone in a world of mere bodies?

Monad   A simple substance without parts—the fundamental element in the metaphysical theories of Leibniz.

Natural law   A rational principle of order or a norm in accordance with which the universe has been created or organized. Both the physical universe and the moral order of human society are thought, by one major philosophical tradition, to be guided by natural law.

Neo-classicism   The philosophy of art that exalts order, proportion, and reason, and subordinates artistic creativity to objective principles of aesthetic taste.

Ontological argument   The attempt to prove the existence of God by starting with nothing more than the mere concept of the most perfect being. The argument is extremely controversial, and has been rejected as invalid by many religious philosophers, including the leading medieval proponent of the Cosmological Argument, St. Thomas Aquinas.

Philosophy   Literally, love of wisdom. Philosophy is the systematic, critical examination of the way in which we judge, evaluate, and act, with the aim of making ourselves wiser, more self-reflective, and better men and women.

Popular sovereignty   The doctrine that ultimate political authority (sovereignty) belongs to the people who are governed.

Pre-established harmony   Leibniz's claim that God prearranges things in such a way that the ideas in our minds correctly correspond to the objects in the world, even though there is no actual interaction between the world and our minds. Leibniz needed this implausible hypothesis because, according to his metaphysical theories, substances cannot really have an effect on one another.

Principle of sufficient reason   A principle, stated by Leibniz, according to which no fact can be real and no statement true unless it has a sufficient reason why it should be thus.

Proletariat/Bourgeoisie   In Marx's writings, the *proletariat* is the urban population of wage-earning workers. The *bourgeoisie* is the middle class consisting of factory owners, shop-keepers, bankers, financiers, and their associates. The term proletariat comes from the old Latin word for the lowest class of people in Rome. Bourgeoisie comes from the medieval term *bourg*, meaning walled city. Burghers, or bourgeois, were the inhabitants of a walled city—by extension, the merchants and master craftsmen who formed the economic elite of the city, as opposed to the aristocracy, whose wealth and power was based on landholdings.

Psycho-physical dualism   The Mind-Body theory that minds are one kind of substance and bodies are another. The defining characteristic of mind, according to the dualist, is consciousness or thought. The defining characteristic of body is spatial extension (and

sometimes also force or impenetrability). For the dualist, the major problem is to explain how mind and matter interact and affect one another.

Rationalism   See Empiricism

Repression/Sublimation   Two terms from the psychological theories of Sigmund Freud referring to the primitive operations of the human mind. *Repression* is the forcible pushing out of consciousness of desires, wishes, thoughts, or feelings that the mind considers bad, dangerous, or otherwise unacceptable. According to Freud, what is repressed does not go away, but remains, with all its emotional power, in the unconscious portion of the mind. *Sublimation* is the redirecting of sexual or aggressive energies into socially or morally acceptable channels—for example, aggressive energies directed away from physical violence and into philosophical arguments, or sexual energies diverted from immediate sexual activity into flirting.

Romanticism   The late eighteenth-century and nineteenth-century movement in art and literature that stressed the powerful expression of feeling and the free play of imagination over the observation of formal limits on artistic creativity. The term comes originally from the late medieval term *romance*, meaning a poem, play, or story written in the local popular language, such as French, rather than in Latin.

Social contract   A voluntary, unanimous agreement among all the people of a society to form themselves into a united political community, and to obey the laws laid down by the government they collectively select. In seventeenth- and eighteenth-century political theory, the legitimacy claims of the state are said to rest on an actual or hypothetical social contract.

Social relationships of production   The system of relationships into which people enter by virtue of the role they play in the material production of goods and services in society.

Socialism   An economic and social system based on collective social ownership of the means of production, rational planning of economic investment and growth, roughly equal distribution of goods and services, and production for the satisfaction of human need rather than for private profit. Modern socialism dates from the teachings of the French socialists of the early nineteenth century, but the leading socialist philosopher is the German, Karl Marx.

Solipsism   Literally, the belief that I am the only person in the universe. Somewhat more generally, solipsism is an extreme form of epistemological skepticism which refuses to acknowledge the existence of anything other than my own mind. Some philosophers have even argued that I cannot be sure of anything but my own mind *right now,* since my memories might also be mistaken.

Sublimation   See Repression

Sovereignty   Supreme political authority. A right to rule that takes precedence over all else.

State, the   The group of people who rule, give orders, run things, and enforce the rules of social groups within defined territorial limits or borders.

Stoics   Ancient Greek philosophers who believed that the natural world exhibits an order that can be understood through rational inquiry.

Substance   Anything that can have attributes predicated of it, but which itself cannot be predicated as an attribute of any other thing.

Synthetic proposition   A statement that adds something to what is contained in the idea of the subject of the proposition.

Tabula rasa   Literally, blank tablet. The term was used by John Locke to summarize his claim that the mind comes into life blank, or empty, and is written on by experience as though it were a clay or wax tablet waiting to be marked by a writing stylus. Locke was arguing against the widely-held view that the mind comes to experience with ideas which are built into it (or "hard-wired," as computer types like to say).

Tautology   A proposition that can be known to be true merely on the basis of the meanings of the words used in it.

Teleology   A study of the purposes, or ends, of natural things—also, the belief that nature has a purpose or goal toward which it tends.

Transcendence   A going beyond the given natural or social reality—in Marcuse, the imaginative leap beyond the given social world, with its repressions, oppressions, and its reality-oriented sacrifices, to the conception of possible future social orders in which some of the repressed libidinal energy has been liberated.

Truth of fact   Truths that can be certified only by appeal to empirical evidence.

Unity of consciousness   A phrase invented by Immanuel Kant to describe the fact that the thoughts and perceptions of any given mind are bound together in a unity by being all contained in one consciousness. Kant claimed that this fact—the *unity* of individual consciousness—could only be explained by postulating a fundamental mental activity of holding together, or "synthesizing," those thoughts and perceptions.

Utilitarianism   The moral theory that holds that everyone—private individuals or law-making governments—should always seek to produce the greatest happiness for the greatest number of people. *Act Utilitarianism* asserts that each of us should use this rule in choosing every single act that we perform, regardless of whether we are private citizens or legislators making general laws for a whole society. *Rule Utilitarianism* says that governments should use this rule in choosing the general laws they enact, but then should simply treat individuals fairly according to the existing rules, with like cases handled in a like manner.

SUGGESTIONS FOR FURTHER READING

Chapter 1: What Is Philosophy?

JOHN AUSTIN, *Sense and Sensibilia*

ALFRED J. AYER, *Language, Truth, and Logic*

RENÉ DESCARTES, *Discourse on Method*

ERNEST GELLNER, *Words and Things*

G. W. F. HEGEL, Introduction to *The Philosophy of History*

MARTIN HEIDEGGER, *What Is Metaphysics?*

DAVID HUME, "The Epicurean," "The Stoic," "The Platonist," and "The Sceptic" in *Collected Essays*

RICHARD RORTY, *Philosophy and the Mirror of Nature*

JEAN-PAUL SARTRE, *Existentialism as a Humanism*

WILFRED SELLARS, "Philosophy and the Scientific Image of Man," in *Frontiers of Science and Philosophy*, ed. R. Colodny

Chapter 2: Ethics

KURT BAIER, *The Moral Point of View*

MICHAEL D. BAYLES, ed., *Contemporary Utilitarianism*

JOHN DEWEY, *Human Nature and Conduct*

ERIK H. ERIKSON, *Childhood and Society*

W. K. FRANKENA, *Ethics*

IMMANUEL KANT, *Groundwork of the Metaphysic of Morals*

——, "On a Supposed Right to Lie from Altruistic Motives"

C. I. LEWIS, *Values and Imperatives*

JOHN STUART MILL, *Utilitarianism*

G. E. MOORE, *Principia Ethica*

W. D. ROSS, *The Right and the Good*

BERTRAND RUSSELL, "What I Believe," in *Why I Am Not a Christian and Other Essays*

M. G. SINGER, *Generalization in Ethics*

S. F. TOULMIN, *The Place of Reason in Ethics*

EDWARD WESTERMARCK, *Ethical Relativity*

Chapter 3: Social Philosophy

MILTON FRIEDMAN, *Capitalism and Freedom*

JOHN KENNETH GALBRAITH, *Economics and the Public Purpose*

FRIEDRICH VON HAYEK, *The Road to Serfdom*

WALTER LIPPMAN, *The Public Philosophy*

HERBERT MARCUSE, *An Essay on Liberation*

——, *Eros and Civilization*

KARL MARX, *Capital*, Volume I

—— and FRIEDRICH ENGELS, *The Communist Manifesto*

JOHN STUART MILL, *On Liberty*

——, *Utilitarianism*

KENNETH MINOGUE, *The Liberal Mind*

ROBERT NOZICK, *Anarchy, State, and Utopia*

MICHAEL OAKESHOTT, *Rationalism in Politics*

JOHN RAWLS, *A Theory of Justice*

GEORGE BERNARD SHAW, *The Intelligent Woman's Guide to Socialism and Capitalism*

Chapter 4: Political Philosophy

CARL COHEN, ed., *Communism, Fascism, and Democracy*

G. W. F. HEGEL, *The Philosophy of Right*

THOMAS HOBBES, *Leviathan*

L. T. HOBHOUSE, *The Metaphysical Theory of the State*

V. I. LENIN, *State and Revolution*

C. B. MCPHERSON, *The Political Theory of Possessive Individualism*

KARL MARX, *A Contribution to the Critique of Hegel's Philosophy of Right*

JOHN STUART MILL, *On Representative Government*

RICHARD E. NEUSTADT, *Presidential Power*

ROBERT NOZICK, *Anarchy, State, and Utopia*

J. ROLAND PENNOCK and JOHN CHAPMAN, eds., *Anarchism* (NOMOS, Vol. XIX)

PLATO, *Crito*

GEORGE F. REEDY, *The Twilight of the Presidency*

EUGENE V. ROSTOW, ed., *Is Law Dead?*

HENRY DAVID THOREAU, *On Civil Disobedience*

ROBERT PAUL WOLFF, *In Defense of Anarchism*

Chapter 5: Philosophy of Art

MONROE BEARDSLEY, *Aesthetics*

CLIVE BELL, *Art*

HARRY M. CLOR, *Obscenity and Public Morality*

R. G. COLLINGWOOD, *The Principles of Art*

PATRICK DEVLIN, *The Enforcement of Morals*

JOHN DEWEY, *Art as Experience*

G. W. F. HEGEL, Introduction to *Philosophy of Fine Art*

JOHN HOSPERS, *Meaning and Truth in the Arts*

IMMANUEL KANT, *Critique of Judgment*

SUSANNE LANGER, *Philosophy in a New Key*

KARL MARX, *Economic-Philosophic Manuscripts of 1844*

PLATO, *Symposium*

G. PLEKHANOV, *Art and Social Life*

I. A. RICHARDS, *The Principles of Literary Criticism*

MORRIS WEITZ, *Philosophy of the Arts*

RICHARD WOLLHEIM, *Art and Its Objects*

Chapter 6: Philosophy of Religion

A. J. AYER, *Language, Truth, and Logic*, Chapter VI

J. BAILLIE, *The Sense of the Presence of God*

LUDWIG FEUERBACH, *The Essence of Christianity*

H. M. GARELICK, *The Anti-Christianity of Kierkegaard*

CHARLES HARTSHORNE, *The Logic of Perfection*

J. HICK, ed., *The Existence of God*

WILLIAM JAMES, *The Will to Believe*

A. KENNY, *Aquinas: A Collection of Critical Essays*

SØREN KIERKEGAARD, *Fear and Trembling*

A. C. MACINTYRE, *Difficulties in Christian Belief*

ASHLEY MONTAGU, ed., *Science and Creationism*

A. PLANTINGA, ed., *The Ontologial Argument*

———, *God and Other Minds*

BERTRAND RUSSELL, *Why I Am Not a Christian and Other Essays*

Chapter 7: Theory of Knowledge

J. L. AUSTIN, *Sense and Sensibilia*

A. J. AYER, *The Foundations of Empirical Knowledge*

GEORGE BERKELEY, *Three Dialogues Between Hylas and Philonus*

V. C. CHAPPELL, ed., *Hume: A Collection of Critical Essays*

R. M. CHISHOLM, *Perceiving—A Philosophical Study*

DANIEL DENNETT, *Brainstorms*

H. G. FRANKFURT, *Demons, Dreamers, and Madmen*

C. A. FRITZ, *Bertrand Russell's Construction of the External World*

DOUGLAS HOSTADTER, *Gödel, Escher, Bach*

A. KENNY, *Descartes: A Study of His Philosophy*

C. I. LEWIS, *An Analysis of Knowledge and Valuation*

G. E. MOORE, "The Refutation of Idealism," in A. C. Ewing, ed., *The Idealist Tradition from Berkeley to Blanshard*

H. H. PRICE, *Perception*

BERTRAND RUSSELL, *Human Knowledge*

PETER STRAWSON, *The Bounds of Sense*

R. J. SWARTZ, ed., *Perceiving, Sensing, and Knowing*

ROBERT PAUL WOLFF, *Kant's Theory of Mental Activity*

Chapter 8: Metaphysics and Philosophy of Mind

BRUCE AUNE, *Metaphysics: The Elements*

LYNN RUDER BAKER, *Saving Belief*

THOMAS HOBBES, *Leviathan*

C. I. LEWIS, *Mind and the World Order*

SIDNEY SHOEMAKER, *Self-Knowledge and Self-Identity*

PETER STRAWSON, *Individuals*

INDEX

Saleh, W., 367
Salvation, promise of, 267-68
Schizophrenia, 386
Schwarz, Roy, 201
Science
  cosmology and, 23
  ethics and, 49-51
Scopes, John, 311
Second Treatise of Government (Locke), 173-75
Secularization of Western society, 304
Sentience, abortion and, 93-98
Sentimentalism, 154, 155
Shakespeare, 261
Shame, importance of, 260-62
Sin, original, 317
Skepticism
  epistemological, 332
  ethical, 57
Slavery, Aristotle on, 188
Smart, J.J.C., 396-400
Smith, Adam, 105, 106-7
Social contract, 155-75
  Burke's attack on, 176-78
  criticisms of, 171-75
  decision-making and, 168-69
  defined, 163
  freedom and, 167-70
Social contract school of political theory, 392
Socialism, 190
  defined, 133
  Marx and, 127-34, 141
Socialist attack on capitalism, 126-37
Social philosophy, 100-153
  capitalism
    conservative attack on, 117-26
    socialist attack on, 126-37
  classical laissez-faire liberalism, 101-17
  welfare state, 139-52
    defense of, 148-52
    Rand on, 142-47
Social relationships of production, 185-87
Social responsibility, 148-52
Society
  analogy between soul and, 83-86
  traditions of, 179
  Western, secularization of, 304
Socrates, 4-18, 37, 83, 204
  criminal charges against, 2, 5-6
  on healthy personality, 81-86
  Plato's relationship to, 5
  theory about examination of life, 7-8
Solid geometry, 23
Solipsism, defined, 339
Soul
  analogy between society and, 83-86
  functional parts of, Plato on, 81-83
Souleles, David, 195, 196
Sovereignty, 163
  popular, 164-65
Soviet Union, 192
Spinoza, Baruch, 380
State, the. *See also* Political philosophy
  characteristics of, 159-62
  defined, 158, 162
  future after proletarian revolution, 190-91
  Marx's theory of, 183-92
  organic, 176-83
  purposes of, 158-59

welfare state, 139-52
  defense of, 148-52
  defined, 140
  ethical defense of, 148-52
  Rand on, 142-47
  utilitarianism and, 140-41
Steady-state (continuous creation) theory, 25-26
Stipulating, 331-32
Stoics, 27-31
Subjectivity of truth, 273-74
Sublimation, 241
  defined, 240
Substances, 377
  created vs. uncreated, 380
  nature of, 381-83
Sufficient reason, principle of, 346
Summa Theologica (Aquinas), 291
Superficial audience, 9-11, 14
Superstition, utilitarianism and, 104-5
Superstructure, Marxist concept of, 187
Surplus repression, 242-45
Synthetic proposition, 301

Tabula rasa, defined, 348
Tacit contract, 175
Talk, philosophy as, 40-43
Tautologies, 300
Taxonomy, 23
Taylor, Harriet, 100
Technique, knowledge of, 121
Teleology, defined, 159
Tertullian, 310
Thales, 19-20, 21, 37
Theism, 283
Theodicy (Leibniz), 373
Theory, defined, 313
Third audience, 12, 14
Thomism, 291
Thought experiment, 341
Thrasymachus, 13-15, 18
Tocqueville, Alexis de, 124-26, 179
Tolstoy, Leo, 232-38
Tradition, 179
  defense of, 122
  legitimacy of, 118
Tragedy, Aristotle on, 260-61
Transcendence, Marcuse's sense of, 245-47
Treatise of Human Nature, A (Hume), 32, 33-36, 343, 350-53, 355-57, 358
Tropic of Cancer, The (Miller), 259
Truth(s)
  of fact, 346-47
  inwardness (subjectivity) of, 273-74
  of reasoning, 344-46
Truth Function theory, 403
Turing, Alan, 404
Tyranny, shame and, 260-61

Ulysses (Joyce), 249-54, 259
Unconscious, content and structure of, 241
Unity of consciousness, 359
  defined, 360
Universe, 18-27
  human nature and, 27-37

435

436